In Search of Research Excellence

To Cynthia and Melanie who inspire excellence in us;
and to all those in search of research excellence.

In Search of Research Excellence

Exemplars in Entrepreneurship

Ronald K. Mitchell

Texas Tech University, USA

and

Richard N. Dino

University of Connecticut, USA

LIBRARY OF
CONGRESS

SURPLUS
DUPLICATE

Edward Elgar

Cheltenham, UK • Northampton, MA, USA

© Ronald K. Mitchell and Richard N. Dino 2011

Published by
Edward Elgar Publishing Limited
The Lypiatts
15 Lansdown Road
Cheltenham
Glos GL50 2JA
UK

Edward Elgar Publishing, Inc.
William Pratt House
9 Dewey Court
Northampton
Massachusetts 01060
USA

A catalogue record for this book
is available from the British Library

Library of Congress Control Number: 2010934049

MIX
Paper from
responsible sources
FSC
www.fsc.org   FSC® C018575

ISBN 978 1 84980 762 3 (cased)

Typeset by Servis Filmsetting Ltd, Stockport, Cheshire
Printed and bound by MPG Books Group, UK

Contents

EDITOR/AUTHOR SESSION CONTRIBUTORS

APPENDICES: CONFERENCE CONTEXT

EXHIBITS: BACKGROUND INFORMATION

Preface

This is a best-practices book with a difference.

Yes, we do focus on product exemplars: works of entrepreneurship research excellence that can be examined and emulated. But the difference is that we also focus on people-exemplars: on making the 'how-to' skills used by top-tier entrepreneurship researchers explicit.

We have been able to accomplish the task of uncovering the 'tacit and implicit' understandings of top-tier researchers, and making these 'concrete and explicit,' through the generosity and support of an entire research community. As a result, the Excellence in Entrepreneurship Research Exemplars Initiative has been recognized by the Academy of Management Board of Governors at the 2009 Annual Meeting as an Academy-wide best practice. Thank you to all who have assisted.

Within these pages, and on the companion website (www.research exemplars.org), you can read and hear the narratives from many contributors, who explain how top-tier research capabilities can be acquired. You can also obtain descriptions of the 'how-to' process for publishing work in ten top journals. Why is enabling your access to this previously hard-to-get-at information important to us?

Throughout our careers, we have worked under the assumption, perhaps even the world-view, that there is captive value inherent in human relationships that we can help to release. Our interest in entrepreneurship as a field of research flows from our belief that – in very real ways – entrepreneurs identify and remove the obstacles to the emergence of this inherent value in an economic sense. Moreover, we consider entrepreneurship research itself to be crucial to identifying and removing these obstacles within our society; and we see it as our entrepreneurial role (in the scholarly sense) to help our colleagues remove the obstacles to their capability to produce more top-tier research in our field. This is, therefore, a book about the acquisition and retention of top-tier research capabilities.

These capabilities may productively be conceptualized as the '[best practices] whose purpose is to improve the productivity of the other resources' (Makadok, 2001: 389), or the 'capacity to deploy *Resources* . . . to effect a desired end' (Amit and Schoemaker, 1993: 35, emphasis in original). In this sense, top-tier research capabilities are a 'stock' of best-practice behaviors that are enriched by the 'inflow' of new and effective practices, and are further enriched by the 'outflow' of unproductive assumptions and practices (see Dierickx and Cool, 1989). And since inflows, outflows and capabilities-stock accumulation occur within the scholarly environment, we also see our task as one of helping colleagues to engage this environment constructively. Additionally, then, this is a book about person–environment (P-E) fit.

We therefore begin (Chapter 1) with a broad-brush application of P-E fit concepts to offer a high-level 'flyby' of the narratives that have been produced for your use. These narratives are organized in three sections: (1) seven keynote addresses (Chapters 2–8) from leaders in the top-tier entrepreneurship research community; (2) ten editor/author sessions (Chapters 9–18) – where Ron Mitchell, with the help of several co-moderators, engages editors or associate editors from ten top journals which publish entrepreneurship research (see also Exhibit I) and authors who have recently published their work within those journals, to elicit the specific 'how-to' process of successfully publishing entrepreneurship research therein; and (3) four appendices (Appendices A–D) which provide access to the context: A: setting the stage, B: building your publishing career, C: worldwide reach, and D: where to from here?

We note that the narratives have been edited for clarity and flow; and so we ask your indulgence where small departures from the spoken narrative have been made to aid the written one. We also note that for ease of access, both the keynotes and the editor/author sessions have been arranged alphabetically (keynotes by contributor's last name, and editor/author sessions by journal name) instead of in their order of appearance at the Exemplars Conference (Exhibit II).

This book may be experienced in a variety of ways, depending upon web accessibility and time constraints. You may use it as a workbook to assist with note-taking and idea-generation as you experience both video/spoken (via the web: www.researchexemplars.org) and written works in tandem. You may use it as a reference guide, simply to look up what might assist you as you prepare to submit your research: either in trying to decide which journal to target, or – if targeted – how to position your work most effectively for a given journal. Or, you may use this book in a more general way: to gain insight into the top-tier research publishing craft by seeing it through the eyes of those who are presently engaged therein. And there may be other, even more productive ways which you will discover in applying the information we present here. We invite you to explore each of these possibilities as you examine with us exemplars in entrepreneurship research: in search of research excellence.

Ron Mitchell
Texas Tech University

Rich Dino
University of Connecticut

March, 2011

REFERENCES

Amit, R. and P.J.H. Schoemaker (1993). Strategic assets and organizational rent. *Strategic Management Journal,* **14** (1), 33–46.
Dierickx, I. and K. Cool (1989). Asset stock accumulation and sustainability of competitive advantage. *Management Science*, **35** (12), 1504–11.
Makadok, R. (2001). Toward a synthesis of the resource-based and dynamic-capability views of rent creation. *Strategic Management Journal,* **22** (5), 387–40.

Acknowledgements

One of the most difficult tasks in a project of this magnitude is to find the appropriate language that rises to the level of our respect and gratitude to all who have contributed to this undertaking. Coming in a close second is making certain that no individual is omitted.

In our attempt to satisfy the latter, who might we include?

- Certainly those who helped us to identify and evaluate the 'market need' to enlist the entrepreneurship research community in an engaged effort to increase both the quality and quantity of scholarship in this domain;
- Certainly those who helped us to develop a solution to satisfying that market need, through the unselfish giving of their time, efforts, and talent;
- Certainly those who provided us with keen and creative insights that led to the development of both the strategy and tactics required to obtain our common desired outcome;
- Certainly those who helped us to operationalize said strategy and tactics;
- Certainly those who stepped forward unselfishly without hesitation and provided us with unfettered access to their hard earned reputational capital and broad and diverse networks to engage the entrepreneurship research community – the exemplars, journal editors, and innumerable scholars;
- Certainly those who participated in the 2009 and 2010 Exemplars Conferences – the 125 on-site contributors and the more than 650 web participants from nearly 250 institutions in 35 countries representing every continent except Antarctica;
- Certainly those individuals who lent us their sharp sets of eyes that found every place we had fallen short in our effort to transform words into tacit knowledge and communicate that knowledge to you, the reader; and
- Certainly our families who provided us the time and support to devote to this project and many of our colleagues who provided their insights that sharpened our focus.

In our attempt to find the words, we have concluded that oftentimes the most polished and complete communiqués rely on their simplicity. We trust that this is one of those times. With this in mind: if you helped, supported, or contributed to this project in any way, you have our sincerest recognition, thanks and appreciation.

Ron and Rich

Introduction

1. In search of entrepreneurship research excellence: a person–environment fit approach

Ronald K. Mitchell, Keith H. Brigham, H. Jackson Walker, Richard N. Dino

As a second-year PhD student, my feeling is simply 'the sun has shined.' I would call my experience with this conference 'completely transformative'; the conference extraordinarily succeeded in transferring tacit knowledge about excellent scholarship, which helped [in] clearing up the myth associated with top journal publications.

Sondos Abdelgawad, PhD candidate ESADE Business School Barcelona, Spain

For many new scholars, the craft of top-tier journal publication seems to be shrouded in myth. But, as noted in the opening quote to this chapter, when knowledge is revealed from behind this veil of myth, it can be transformative!

Transformation is the purpose of this book. Our aim is to make the transformative ideas evoked during the first Entrepreneurship Research Exemplars Conference more accessible to new and emerging scholars and to those who advise them. This Conference was an invited best-practices conference for advancing research excellence in entrepreneurship, which was held May 28–30, 2009 at the University of Connecticut School of Business, with one purpose in mind: learning from example. Within the pages of this book you will find transcripts of candid and enlightening editor/author interactions with respect to publishing high-quality entrepreneurship research in ten top journals,[1] as well as the keynote addresses of leaders in top-tier entrepreneurship research[2] who shared their insights about the 'process' of producing outstanding works within the entrepreneurship research craft.

While these insights are specifically focused on crafting top-tier 'entrepreneurship' research, the material presented in this book applies even more broadly to many other areas of research within the social sciences. We think it appropriate to conceptualize social science research as a unique but broadly encompassing craft similar to that of the specialty guilds that have been skill-repositories for many centuries; thus, we use the term 'research craft' deliberately for the following three reasons. First, in the research craft as in most guilds, skill and quality are adjudicated by peer review. Second, progression within the guild hierarchy depends upon the quality and quantity of specialized 'works' and the extent to which these 'works' influence succeeding work (e.g., in the research case, the extent to which they produce citations). And, third, the titles awarded within its membership – such as apprentice, journeyperson and master craftsperson – signify status which, as paralleled in academe, translate into corresponding ranks – specifically, PhD students (apprentices), assistant and associate professors (journeypersons) and full professors (masters) (NRC, 2000).

In this book we present the process of guild-like progression toward top-tier achievement as seen through the eyes of successful scholars. And accordingly, in this introductory chapter, we offer the reader a means to frame the narratives of the Exemplars Conference in such a way that their meaning can be further clarified and the dialogues that have been transcribed and appear in subsequent chapters can be helpfully interpreted. We offer a 'bird's-eye view' of the underlying structure of the expert discussions as seen from a vantage point that is intended to enhance usability for you, the reader.

UNDERLYING STRUCTURE: A PERSON–ENVIRONMENT FIT MODEL

As is the case with many phenomena in the social sciences, finding the underlying structure within a set of social interactions (such as the keynotes and dialogues that comprise the narratives contained within this book) can be aided by outlining a theoretical framework that identifies key elements and their relationships. Merton (1968) suggests that it is the role of the social scientist to abstract the latent structure that explains the unseen connections among the many phenomena that are 'manifest' in an observer's field of view. He suggests that middle-range theories, which explain the generic features of specific social phenomena, can be quite useful in assisting with this theory-advancing task. In the case of this book, we reason that our use of mid-range-theorizing might therefore help us to identify common themes more effectively and to articulate more clearly their import across editor-author-exemplar communities.

In this spirit of mid-range theory development for the purpose of aiding in the sense-making task, we have analysed the Conference narratives in light of various theoretical frameworks and have identified within the dialogues the elements that distinguish the process of building a top-tier research career – specifically, a guild-type social structure, required works of skill, criteria for evaluation, sequential career progression, status conferral mechanisms, etc. In so doing, we have sought to identify overarching frameworks that provide a direct line of conceptual continuity and encompass the differing spheres of social behavior and structure represented by these narrative elements. Our intention is that the resulting model will be able, as suggested in our reference to Merton (1968), to transcend both the sheer descriptions and explicit empirical generalizations that are found within any given narrative. Through discussion and examination, we found ourselves gravitating toward a mid-range theoretical representation which seeks to explain, through the use of person–environment fit (P-E fit) theory (e.g. Schneider, 2001), the road to top-tier research excellence.

Management scholars have long recognized the interaction effects of persons and environment on important outcomes such as performance, stress and withdrawal (e.g., see meta-analysis findings from Kristof-Brown, Zimmerman, and Johnson, 2005). P-E fit is broadly defined as the match between individuals and work environment characteristics with more specific assessments – including the domains of person–group, person–supervisor, person–job and person–organization fit. In this chapter, we employ a commonly used model of person–organization fit (P-O fit) to offer the reader some possible ways to bring order to the phenomena in these narratives and to aid in their interpretation. We believe the P-O model structure is especially representative of P-E fit in general and addresses social structure, the demand and supply attributes that flow from the characteristics of both person and environments, and the notions of supplementary and complementary fit (such as evaluation, career progression and status conferral) between person and environment. Based upon our analysis, we are then enabled to frame the Conference narrative in a helpful way and offer instances where some of the phenomena that emerge in the Exemplars Conference narratives can be illustratively arranged for informed interpretation according to a fit model, similar to the one shown in Figure 1 (Kristof, 1996: 4).

As specified by P-E fit theory and represented in the P-O model illustrated in Figure 1, the relationships among constructs suggest that fit may be defined to be: 'the compatibility between people and organizations that occurs when: (a) at least one entity provides what the other needs, or (b) they share similar fundamental characteristics, or (c) both' (1996: 4–5). For reference, connections among the elements of the model (beginning

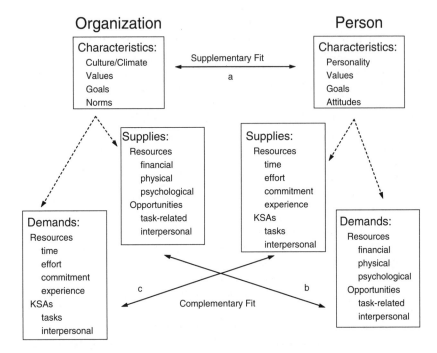

Source: Kristof 1996: 4.

Figure 1   A P-O fit model

with 'fit' and working backwards to include the elements and their relationships) are (as described by Kristof, 1996: 3–4):

> In this model, supplementary fit (arrow 'a') is represented as the relationship
> between the fundamental characteristics of an organization and a person. For
> the organization these characteristics traditionally include the culture, climate,
> values, goals, and norms. On the person side of the model, the characteristics
> most often studied are values, goals, personality and attitudes. When there is
> similarity between an organization and a person on these characteristics, 'sup-
> plementary fit' is said to exist.
>   In addition to these underlying characteristics, organizations and individuals
> can also be described by what they supply and demand in employment agree-
> ments. These demands and supplies are likely to be influenced by the underlying
> characteristics of both entities (Hogan, 1991; Schein, 1992), as is indicated by
> the dotted arrows in Figure 1; however, they represent distinct dimensions on
> which fit or misfit may occur. More specifically, organizations supply financial,
> physical and psychological resources as well as the task-related, interpersonal,
> and growth opportunities that are demanded by employees. When these organi-
> zational supplies meet employees' demands, needs – supplies fit is achieved

(arrow 'b' in Figure 1). Similarly, organizations demand contributions from their employees in terms of time, effort, commitment, knowledge, skills and abilities. Demands–abilities fit is achieved when these employee supplies meet organizational demands (arrow 'c' in Figure 1). Both of these demand–supply relationships can be described by expanding Muchinsky and Monahan's (1987) definition of 'complementary' fit. (Emphasis added)

Under the learning-from-example logic of the Exemplars Conference, the nature of P-E fit helps us to situate the information generated in the Conference sessions in career-development terms. What can we learn from examining the latent structure of the Exemplars Conference narratives in light of this fit model? To answer this question, we analysed the keynote speeches and editor/author sessions for representative excerpts. We sought those excerpts that could illuminate, and could in turn be illuminated by a fit-type conceptualization of the top-tier research skill development process; and in doing so provide to the reader some outlines of the 'preliminary knowledge scaffold' that is the foundation of accelerated expertise acquisition (Glaser, 1984). Therefore, the excerpts that we have identified, we now present as a way to contextualize, frame and introduce, and to at least partially explain and interpret, the narratives that follow. Using these excerpts from the narratives themselves, we first seek to illustrate (as shown in Figure 1) the characteristics, supplies and demands of the guild-like structure of the academic environment, within which we as scholars learn to function and to flourish. Then, under the assumption that the purpose of the learning-from-example logic is for persons to attain compatibility with the top-tier research guild environment, we also present selected quotations from authors to demonstrate a few of the means whereby person–environment compatibility/fit can be achieved.

THE TOP-TIER RESEARCH GUILD ENVIRONMENT

We contend that three elements of the top-tier research guild – (1) who we are (characteristics); (2) what we offer (supplies); and (3) what we need (demands) – define the compatibility/fit space. In the following paragraphs, we present selected excerpts from Conference participants: keynotes, editors, authors, panelists and other contributors, who provide definition and texture to each 'element' of our top-tier research guild, and the process of progression within it. Note that we reference Kristof's (1996) P-O fit model throughout this chapter because, as noted previously, it provides a clear representation of P-E fit in general and addresses the same requisite dimensions of fit (i.e., supplementary, complementary needs–supplies and complementary demands–abilities).

Characteristics

Kristof (1996) suggests that characteristics of an organization tradition-ally include its culture, climate, values, goals and norms. In our analysis of the narratives, this structure applies well to the case of the entrepre-neurship research guild environment. For example, within numerous dialogues, we have identified both a culture and climate of 'inclusiveness,' values and goals centered on 'making a difference,' and norms that focus on producing 'interesting' research, as important characteristics of the top-tier research guild. These characteristics are related to supplementary fit and allow for an assessment of similarity between individuals and the top-tier research environment.

Culture and climate of inclusiveness

What do we mean when we say that top-tier entrepreneurship research-ers foster a culture and climate of inclusiveness? Patricia McDougall, a Conference Keynote and former Chair of the Entrepreneurship Division of the Academy of Management (AOM) – who herself has been a career-long champion of entrepreneurship-research-community inclusiveness – says:

> . . . A distinctiveness that the Entrepreneurship Division of the Academy
> of Management has always had has been our inclusiveness; but I think this
> Conference takes our culture of inclusiveness to an entirely new level . . . We
> have tried to keep our entry barriers low, and that has been one of the things
> I most value about our culture. I would not want us to change this culture . . .
> (Patricia P. McDougall, Keynote: Chapter 6)

This assertion is supported by the AOM's Entrepreneurship Division history. Beginning with the formation of the Entrepreneurship Interest Group in 1972 (led by Karl Vesper and held in Arnie Cooper's basement) and as highlighted by McDougall's term as Division Chair (1996–7), inclusiveness has been an explicit part of the culture and climate of the Entrepreneurship Division of the Academy of Management. For example, the relatively recent 2006 Entrepreneurship social event at the AOM Annual Meeting had as its theme 'crossing bridges,' and dozens of scholars from sister divisions of the Academy attended. Certainly the Exemplars Conference itself is an inclusiveness-emphasizing initiative, and has been recognized by the AOM Board of Governors as an Academy-wide best practice. So, as you read (or 'listen to' via the web: www.researchexemplars.org) the dialogue that unfolded during the Conference, we suggest that attention to the inclusiveness dimension within the narra-tive will be one of the key themes that readers/listeners can use to make less mysterious (alluding again to the opening quotation) some of the mythical aspects of the top-tier entrepreneurship research culture.

Values and goals: making a difference
If the purpose of research in general is to discover new knowledge, then a key responsibility encompassed within the values and goals of our specific research community (as observed by one who has the comprehensive vantage point of a top-tier journal editor) might have bearing upon these values. In his keynote address, Duane Ireland, the editor of the *Academy of Management Journal* (*AMJ*), had this to say:

> As knowledge producers – as people involved in knowledge – it is important that we seek to make a difference with our work. And if we accept the responsibility to try to make a difference with our scholarship, then the question becomes 'How do we go about making a difference as entrepreneurship scholars with our work?' (R. Duane Ireland, Keynote: Chapter 5)

This emphasis on making a difference was also presented in a thought-provoking manner by a scholar well-known for such outcomes. In his keynote address, Jay Barney offered the following challenge about making a difference:

> My goal today, especially for the senior scholars, is literally to inspire some of you to change your research agendas . . . Don Hambrick (1994) issued a challenge to the Academy of Management in his presidential speech that was later published in the *Academy of Management Review*. The title of his article was 'What if the Academy actually mattered?' . . . The article goes on to suggest that the Academy could matter in at least two ways: first, it might matter for practicing managers (that is, the work we do might actually make a difference for people in practice); second, he also suggests that it could matter for discussions of broader social and economic policy . . . That's my challenge for my senior colleagues and for the junior people. This is why we do the work. This is what we have to aspire to. We need to aspire to change our goals from producing just another publication in *AMR* or *AMJ* to changing lives. (Jay B. Barney, Keynote: Chapter 3)

Of course, as indicated by the words spoken by these two highly respected keynoters, 'making a difference' will have unique meaning to each observer. Some might even consider such vision statements to be more idealistic than practical. But we suggest that the task of assessing the similarity of values and goals in the environment within which we seek to work and flourish requires that such perspectives be articulated: perhaps to serve as helpful anchor points, as points of departure, or as the source of thought-provoking challenge.

Norms: producing 'interesting' work

If there is one norm that might be considered to be standard in the production of top-tier research, it would be that those who produce it view the production of 'interesting' work to be their benchmark. This insight is not intuitive. In fact, *Journal of Business Venturing* editor Sankaran (Venkat) Venkataraman explained how he came to this realization:

> Like any new doctoral student, I labored under the belief that a theory or a theorist is considered great because his or her theories are true – but I discovered that was really not true. That's false. A theory or a theorist is considered great not because his/her theories are true, but because they're interesting. Murray Davis goes on to develop about a dozen criteria for why a theory is interesting. It will take me too much time to go through all of those points, but the gist of Davis's point is that interesting ideas are those that point out that things are not really what they appear or you think they appear to be. (Sankaran Venkataraman, Keynote: Chapter 7)

This thought is echoed by Duane Ireland, who offers:

> . . . I believe an appropriate view to take is that in order to make a difference, our scholarship has to be interesting. Quoting from Murray Davis (1971), a reason for this is 'The first criterion by which people judge anything they encounter, even before deciding whether it is true or false, is whether it is interesting or boring.' Now, one might argue that interesting scholarship has quite a few characteristics, including the following: counter-intuitive arguments, multi-level designs, use of qualitative and quantitative data in the same study, innovative and robust datasets, and innovative integrations of theories. The important point is that as we think about trying to make a difference, what we want to do is to think about designing and completing interesting scholarship. (R. Duane Ireland, Keynote: Chapter 5)

And then University of Connecticut, panelist, Mike Lubatkin, after a particularly poignant session[3] summed up the top-tier research guild norm of 'producing interesting work' to the assembled conferees, as follows:

> . . . Jim is reflecting on it and he's tearing up a little bit. That's what we are about. We are putting our heart and soul into our ideas. We embody the concept of entrepreneurship by the very virtue of the fact that we are willing to fight and die for what we believe is interesting. (Michael Lubatkin, Panelist: Chapter 15)

In terms of P-E fit, norms are at the core of characteristics that define the top-tier research-centered environment because they tend to sum up the associated expectations in this guild. In turn, these characteristics define both the supplies provided and the demands they require, where an inclusive community is committed to making a difference through the production of interesting research. In the next two sections we first explore Conference participants' impressions of the supplies offered by, and second, the demands made by the top-tier research guild. These are important considerations and can be used to assess complementary fit in terms of whether or not individual and organizational characteristics 'fill gaps' for each other.

Supplies

As suggested by P-E fit and represented in the P-O fit model structure (Figure 1), an important complementary fit consideration is the financial, physical and psychological resources, as well as the task-related, interpersonal and growth opportunities supplied. Within the top-tier research guild, these resources and opportunities may be characterized along three dimensions: (1) critical feedback resources (the scarcest resource in any guild due to time and attention constraints); (2) task-related opportunities for monetary and psychological rewards/satisfaction; and (3) interpersonal opportunities for interaction and learning. In our analysis, we note several comments in the narratives that support this interpretation.

Resources: critical feedback

It is not intuitive to the novice in any guild-type structure that the review process whereby critical feedback is generated and passed back to the producers of the work is, in fact, the most positive and helpful resource that the skill community can provide. Consequently, for those who are new (and sometimes not so new) to the research craft, the production of works and their submission for review to peers within the guild is often viewed negatively. However, as narratives from the Exemplars Conference suggest, there is a helpful perspective that can be adopted. As suggested by Ron Mitchell, for example, in recounting a conversation with *AMJ* author/panelist, Tom Elfring:

> One of the things Tom and I were talking about over breakfast was this idea that when you first see a diamond, it doesn't look all cut and sparkly. It needs to be cut and then it needs to be put into a setting. So in a sense, what happens is [that] as the effort is added to these papers, we ought not to always think that necessarily because we were rejected at the top journal, the paper is in fact a poor paper. Rather, what you get, which is from the scarcest resource in our business, is a critical review from thoughtful colleagues. Once you get that, it is like cutting a diamond. You can actually use it to increase the sparkle. (Ronald K. Mitchell, Moderator: Chapter 9)

However, it is one thing to understand rationally the process of improving 'diamonds in the rough,' but quite another to deal with the emotional realities that accompany constructive criticism. Consider the natural tendency for each one of us, as recipients of critical feedback, to project the weaknesses of our work back upon the reviewers who, in giving scarce time resources to the developmental task, raise sensitive and often troublesome points concerning the work – not the authors. Helpfully, Talya Bauer, editor of the *Journal of Management* offers the following commentary, referring to the manner in which three authors in their editor/author panel session responded to the feedback they received on their paper:

> . . . I think these three did a great job with this: being really responsive, going above and beyond, being diligent, being timely and writing well. Being nice only goes so far. I would say that the biggest thing is not having an argumentative attitude, but rather asking, 'How can I make this paper better?' My mantra is, 'Feedback is a gift.' So many people are threatened by feedback, but when someone gives you that tough love feedback, that is the best thing they can do. We would be doing a disservice if we published the first drafts that people sent in. (Talya N. Bauer, Editor: Chapter 14)

As supplies go (at least within the top-tier research guild), critical feedback is the primary resource. But, of course, it is not the only one. There is also a kind of coaching; a type of considered-judgment direction that sometimes also surfaces, as suggested by *Organization Science* senior editor, Pam Tolbert:

> In the first couple of rounds, I think the main contribution was actually just trying to point a path, because the reviews really did say, 'Do this and do this and do this;' so the main job was to say, 'You could do this, but I think this might be a good strategy,' which is something that people should pay attention to when senior editors do this stuff. Because on one hand they're trying to not alienate reviewers; obviously there's a lot of labor involved there, but sometimes you don't always think they're going in the right direction. What you do in writing a decision letter is try and point to a path among the differing options. (Pamela S. Tolbert, Editor: Chapter 16)

Then there are the less-tangible resources, such as the task-related opportunities that the guild provides for rewards and satisfaction, which we discuss next.

Task-related opportunities: rewards and satisfaction
What kind of work should an aspiring member of the top-tier research guild seek to produce? Because the rewards and levels of satisfaction vary based on how one may answer this question, it is helpful to view this decision in terms of approach to opportunity: specifically to the opportunities supplied by the top-tier research guild. Howard Aldrich, senior scholar

and 2009 Foundational Research IDEA Award winner suggested the following:

> Perhaps the most important dilemma facing junior scholars and graduate students is what Donald Campbell (Campbell, 1969) talks about as the 'real' goal of science. Don Campbell, a great scholar and wonderful man, contributed to general systems theory, anthropology, philosophy, psychology and sociology. Also he was very pragmatic and instrumental. He described science essentially as 'the struggle for citations.' How do you achieve your place in the citation world?
>
> There are two central strategies. I like the analogy of somebody out looking for gold in the old West. What are the choices? One we could call the 'mining choice.' It's going out into the mountains, finding a hole already dug, seeing people streaming in and out of it, realizing, 'Yes, there's probably gold here. The seam has been opened and now I can just follow those people. It could be the case that I will find large pieces of ore, but also it is quite likely that because people have been there before me, my incremental contribution is probably going to be fairly small.' What's the alternative? The alternative is the 'prospecting strategy.' Think about Humphrey Bogart in *The Treasure of the Sierra Madre*, if you remember that movie (that's the very famous movie with the 'badges' joke that Mel Brooks followed up in *Blazing Saddles*). You can imagine being on the frontier; there's no map, you just set off and try to find gold. The chances are quite good that what you'll encounter are dry holes; although it could also be the case that you are the first to stumble onto something never before seen (in which case the returns to you are substantial, but you're also taking a substantial risk).
>
> . . . What I want to talk about today is not that you should choose either of these paths. I want to talk about, in a mindful way, trying to manage the tension between the 'mining' that is inevitable in our profession and the 'prospecting' that I think returns the largest rewards to people. (Howard E. Aldrich, Keynote: Chapter 2)

And in addition to the more pecuniary rewards that come from one's citation-stature 'treasure,' as supplied by the profession (promotion, tenure, endowed professorships or chairs, awards and honors, etc.), there are also the intangibles, as succinctly stated by Duane Ireland:

> . . . what could be more exciting . . . than to have the answers that we derive from our studies have the potential to positively affect individuals, firms, and for societies? (R. Duane Ireland, Keynote: Chapter 5)

Many of us, if asked, could name jobs that, in our view, would be entirely lacking in satisfaction – we'd 'hate' them. Yet here we are in a profession that supplies task-related rewards and satisfaction that – where a fit can be engineered – are truly remarkable for all parties involved. But in addition there are human interaction-type opportunities that are supplied by the top-tier research guild, and in the next section we encounter several observations that outline these possibilities as well.

Interpersonal opportunities: interaction and learning

Primarily, an intellectually driven craft can offer/supply a variety of interpersonal opportunities – specifically those for productive interaction with like-minded colleagues and learning about what interests us. Several Conference participants offered observations about these types of opportunities as supplied through participation in the top-tier research guild:

> I enjoy the opportunity to interact with such a great group of colleagues, and it is also an excellent opportunity to interact with people from all over the world (even though the interaction is a little less personalized). So please accept my not only congratulations on an outstanding conference, but also my 'thank you' for inviting me to this conference and the opportunity. (Michael A. Hitt, Keynote: Chapter 4)

Here the profession is seen to provide the opportunity for interaction at the more general collegial level. Of course, interaction around specific topics also occurs, as noted by *Entrepreneurship Theory & Practice* (*ET&P*) editor, Candy Brush:

> . . . there is a community around family business – and there is also a community around women's entrepreneurship (of which I am a part), and around international or transitioned economies. So you have these different communities and it is an opportunity, I think, to collaborate and to develop theories more deeply in these perhaps niche areas. (Candida Brush, Editor: Chapter 11)

And in the following quote the opportunity for interaction is seen also to prompt learning.

> . . . when you get a group of masters together and you throw them into unanticipated and new situations, sometimes just the newness of the situation, the emergent dialogue itself, creates the opportunity for understandings to surface, to be articulated, to become concrete and to become usable by all of those who desire to do work in the craft at the top tier. (Ronald K. Mitchell: Appendix B)

Mike Lubatkin, as a co-moderator in the *Journal of Management Studies* editor/author session, expanded this view, suggesting that the profession also supplies the opportunity for growth:

> There's an evolution to us as scholars in our careers. We start off very much in a skill-building mode as doctoral students and as junior faculty members. I liken that to developing skills as a musician; at some point we need to make the transition from musician to composer. (Michael Lubatkin, Moderator: Chapter 15)

This thought is echoed and, furthermore, cast in a resources-supplied perspective by senior scholar and panelist in the *Strategic Entrepreneurship Journal* editor/author session, Elaine Mosakowski, who says:

You know, Jay Barney talks obviously all the time about resources; bringing these resources to bear to creating this critical mass to get the institution snowballing and our expectations rising, I think, is – as you say – the objective . . . (Elaine Mosakowski, Moderator: Chapter 17)

So, as we use a P-E fit perspective to amplify meaning from the variety of perspectives offered by Conference participants, we can readily begin to see how the characteristics of the top-tier research guild translate into the 'supplies' it offers its organizational members. But under the 'matching' logic that is endemic to a fit-type model, 'supply without demand' is in many ways inert. The supplies produced are therefore enlivened and made relevant by the existence of the demands and expectations held (in our case by the top-tier research guild) of its members.

Demands

The demands of the top-tier research guild have their own forms of complexity, and a big part of the complexity in this case emanates from the demands that are placed upon its members. Top-tier entrepreneurship research is especially complex in this respect because of the many disciplines contributing to it, each of which has some degree of uniqueness that accompanies its demands. As described by Conference Co-Chair, Rich Dino as he introduced the first session of the Conference:

> . . . I was trying to figure out how to convey what I see. I was talking with a colleague today and we concluded that it was a busy intersection; and then we asked, 'What is the busiest intersection in the world?' And most people will say 'Well it must be Grand Central Station.' Well actually it's not. It is a place in Tokyo, Japan, called the Shibuya Station. It is interesting because there is a confluence and an intersection of six roadways, six pedestrian walkways, and one of the busiest train stations in the world. You could actually go out on the Internet and watch this intersection – and it is something else. I was trying to think of how to characterize the world of entrepreneurship, and it pretty much is one of the busiest intersections in the research world. Instead of having six roadways or 12 roadways (including the pedestrian walkways together), there are many, many more. Just thinking about it, if you think about the disciplines that make up entrepreneurship (economics, sociology, organizations, institutions, strategy, psychology, finance, micro, macro, go on and on); it's a very busy intersection. (Richard N. Dino: Appendix A)

So as we examine the narratives to ascertain the demands of the top-tier research guild, we once again turn to P-E fit for help in outlining the latent structure of the dialogue. This framework suggests that both task-specific and people-specific elements are part of the demands placed upon its members. Of course in the case of academe, the task-specific demands are research-production focused. The people-specific (interpersonal) demands have more to do with the way that time, effort, commitment and experience are provided in the service of requirements, where patience/ perseverance is expected, and uniquely personal demands, skills and imagination figure prominently. In our analysis, we noted several observations by Conference participants that aptly represent each of these points.

Task-specific demands: research-production focus

The top-tier research guild is very clear about the specific tasks expected of its members: the constant production of top-quality work in reasonable-to-high volume over time. However, stating the demands/expectations for producing a series of successful papers is much easier than is enacting them. For example, Venkat states:

> From my own experiences reviewing as well as editing, the observations I can make are: successful papers are more than likely to have something novel to say rather than just a repetition of well-trodden areas – and that novelty is either in the theory, the approach, the data, the methods, the empirical context or in the conclusions. (Sankaran Venkataraman, Keynote: Chapter 7)

Yet calling for novelty, and locating the pathway to find it are again distinct actions with differing complexities. In the following exchange between Tom Lumpkin (serving as the 'real-time editor' of questions and comments coming into the Conference from around the world through the magic of technology) and Howard Aldrich (video conferencing his keynote session), the articulation of this challenge and some counsel on how to help emerge:

> *Lumpkin, Tom*: Howard, this is Tom Lumpkin. I have some questions from the web. First, when teaching junior scholars, how do you help them to identify the initial research area to specialize in? Too often it seems that just pursuing questions can leave students stranded – especially as their questions change.

> *Aldrich, Howard*: So the question is, how to help them find their own voice?

> *Lumpkin, Tom*: And the kind of research to specialize in.

> *Aldrich, Howard*: Again, I can certainly see what happens to people who approach that choice in a mindless way. One of the classic things we see students doing is coming to graduate school with some work experience. Especially PhDs in our field, typically people have been out five, six, ten years who come to graduate school with a very powerful image of an experience they had as a manager or maybe as an entrepreneur. What they spend their first

couple of years trying to do is to figure out how to understand that experience. That is a very bad way to choose a research project. The first thing I would do in working with students is to help them have a cathartic moment: 'Why are you here? What do you think about entrepreneurship? What are the emotional associations you have?' I try to get them to think about the powerful passions that they may have and the powerful feelings they may have. Get that on the table.

The second thing I would suggest to them is that their personal experience might be the basis for building a program; but it's not going to be a very good basis. I say this because I have seen it over and over again – not only for the people I teach personally, but also at the doctoral consortia, I've seen the same thing. When people are asked about what they are interested in, inevitably they take us back to some personal experience they had, either as a worker, a manager or an entrepreneur. I think they have a very serious problem if they don't get past that. (Howard E. Aldrich, Keynote: Chapter 2)

During the last 35–40 years, the field of entrepreneurship emerged from obscurity to today's present level of legitimacy. During this process, numerous demands of the top-tier research guild had to be addressed and satisfied. Patricia McDougall described a few of those, as follows:

Admittedly, we did have some problems in the early research; no doubt about it. I would describe that research as not very cumulative. It didn't lead to many new insights or knowledge gains. We had an absence of quality databases. Many of the articles lacked a theoretical foundation or methodological rigor. There was a real bias toward descriptive research. And the big one for me was that there was not a very clear understanding of what was unique about entrepreneurship research. (Patricia P. McDougall, Keynote: Chapter 6)

So we can conclude from the foregoing insights that the research-production focused, task-specific demands of the top-tier entrepreneurship research guild are becoming quite clear, and, in fact, are somewhat inflexible. As a result, flexibility is demanded and must come from top-tier research guild members.

Interpersonal demands: patience/perseverance
Inflexibility is rarely pleasant to encounter. But often (as appears to be the case with the top-tier research guild) the demands have temporal dynamics that are discipline-based, and therefore are likely to be highly stable (Lawrence, Winn, and Jennings, 2001: 634), and thereby 'less than flexible.' Accordingly, the interpersonal demands of patience and perseverance are placed upon/demanded from members. As Mike Hitt observes:

. . . you should leave no stone unturned in order to do quality research. Have patience and persevere. You also must be goal-directed and highly motivated to do quality research. . . . you need to listen to your colleagues and you are going to have to be honest with yourself. Yet, I continue to believe that sometimes you also have to persevere. So you should not let it go too soon. (Michael A. Hitt, Keynote: Chapter 4)

However, this does not necessarily mean drudgery. Yes, commitment and perseverance do have to come from within each of us, but there's an 'up' side to the attitude/stance that we can adopt, as Rich Dino suggests:

I opened the conference by talking about lyrics of songs. I like lyrics of songs. There was a song years ago by a group called, believe it or not, Chumbawamba. I don't know if you remember the lyrics, but the lyrics are the following: 'I get knocked down, I get up again. Nobody's going to keep me down.' That's what research is about, isn't it? Continually getting knocked down and having the tenacity to get up, believing in what you are doing and (Jim, back to you again) believing in what you're doing and getting it done. (Richard N. Dino: Appendix D)

In short, the top-tier research guild, in demanding highly specific and excellent research products from its members, also (of necessity) demands interpersonal staying-power. And, as we shall see, this kind of staying power is enabled – at least in part – by skill and imagination.

Personal demands: skill and imagination
Yes, our capability to meet demands compatibly, i.e., to enact a P-E fit, comes down to adjusting to the demands placed upon us as members. And this requires an imaginative approach to theory and methods, as illustrated in an exchange among Maw-Der Foo (author), Ron Mitchell (session moderator), and Jing Zhou (*Journal of Applied Psychology* associate editor):

Foo, Maw-Der: . . . What we thought was interesting and counterintuitive was that positive affect actually increased the amount of effort that entrepreneurs put into their ventures, primarily through a future temporal focus.

Mitchell, Ron: So, one of the things that was cool about the method was that you emphasized the word 'experience.' And was this experience-sampling methodology where you had the entrepreneurs who were participating respondents actually call in (was it twice a day?) on their cell phones? How was that received at *JAP*?

Zhou, Jing: It was cool. It was very nice. It is a method that actually the 'affect' people (the people who do research in social psychology and affect) started to use. So in some ways there are several interesting things about this paper that I really like. First of all is the theory: the mood, as information theory, is relatively new in our field – in the applied field; and they used that correctly and in a very counterintuitive way, if you will, of looking at the immediate versus future, and both the negative and positive mood each have as a functional impact on people's effort. It's just different temporal dimensions. Also, the way social psychologists collect data really is new and appropriate; so those are very nice features. (Maw-Der Foo, Author; Ronald K. Mitchell, Moderator; Jing Zhou, Editor: Chapter 12)

Some of the counsel offered by Howard Aldrich applies well to such settings because it suggests that the way to meet the demands of the top-tier research guild is to invoke a personal strategy that combines both skill and imagination. He states:

> There actually are ways to get the brain out of the miasma that it is in and train it to be better at dealing with challenging environmental stimuli. So, with regard to the question about skill and imagination, I would say skill is a matter of experience. It is a matter of attaching yourself to good mentors and learning how to read mindfully. Imagination may require you to spend a little money on technology. Find people, coaches and trainers. There are ways to put yourself in situations beyond your comfort zone. That is possible. I would say both of those tracks can be pursued. The imagination track is going to be harder; it is going to be more painful, but it is possible. (Howard E. Aldrich, Keynote: Chapter 2)

Summary

So, as we can see, P-E fit theory and the representative P-O fit model enhance the interpretability of the narratives and provide additional meaning from the variety of perspectives offered by Conference participants. Through this lens, we are able to observe how the characteristics of the top-tier research guild as described in the narrative, translate both into the 'supplies' it offers its members, and into the 'demands' it makes upon them. Under the matching logic of P-E fit, we can see how the supplies produced by the top-tier research guild are enlivened and made relevant by the unique demands and expectations it places upon its people. In the next section, we seek to illustrate from a 'people's perspective' (that is, from the authors who participated in the editor/author dialogues) how this 'fitting' of the person to the top-tier research environment has been accomplished. Additionally we outline possible pathways to satisfy the premise of this Exemplars Conference: transformative learning from example.

FITTING IN: AN EDITOR/AUTHOR PERSPECTIVE

The P-E fit perspective also articulates the characteristics, supplies and demands of the 'person' in the environmental dyad. While in this introductory chapter we felt it necessary to demonstrate the usefulness of fit with representative narratives, it appeared to us to be somewhat trivial to extract from the Conference narratives person-specific evidence of various individualized attributes (on the 'person' side of the dyad – Figure 1). We reasoned that each reader would bring their own characteristics (personality, values, goals, attitudes), supplies (time, effort, commitment and experience resources) and demands (financial, physical and psychological expectations) to their experience with the narratives presented in this book.

However, what is truly non-trivial (and the focus of this book) is the process whereby the individuals in the editor/author panel sessions actually have shaped their professional responses to the characteristics, supplies and demands of the top-tier research guild and succeeded beyond publishing their research in one of ten top journals in their field to create a sense of 'belonging' to the guild. As may be readily ascertained, each of the editor/author sessions was constructed with the task of 'making what had been tacit, explicit.' And this construction has produced dialogues that are representative of how, in real situations, these colleagues have been enabled to connect with similar others who value similar things. In some sense, these are proxy individuals for each of us as authors. Put differently, colleagues who have experience with the process can provide insights about finding acceptance, support and reinforcement for the things that they value – and from which the rest of us can benefit.

Therefore, in the following paragraphs, we offer a few (hopefully salient) excerpts from the dialogues of these sessions, with the hope that they can be 'priming' in nature. Our intention is to give enough 'compatibility/fit' examples that readers who peruse the remainder of this book will gain great benefit from likening the experiences of these exemplars to their own experiences. To the extent this does occur, our 'priming of the fit pump' will be a success. As suggested by P-E fit and as illustrated in the P-O fit model diagram (Figure 1) there are two types of fit: supplementary and complementary. We now define each in turn, again quoting from the Conference narrative to illustrate.

Supplementary Fit

What does one look for to begin the matching process of the person to the top-tier research social environment, where a person's flexibility must exceed that of the top-tier research guild? This matching process can first be characterized by the term 'supplementary fit,' where a person 'supplements, embellishes or possesses characteristics which are similar to other individuals in an environment' (Muchinsky and Monahan, 1987: 271).

Supplementary fit involves an interpersonal component in that matching on characteristics (e.g., values and goals) is often achieved and reinforced through personal interactions with 'similar others' who share the same characteristics. This type of fit is represented by arrow 'a' in Figure 1 (Kristof, 1996: 3). Supplementary fit (as we interpret it for application to persons trying to succeed within the top-tier research guild) can occur as persons find acceptance and support from like-minded individuals within the guild's social environment.

In the case of the top-tier research guild, supplementary fit might occur, for example, when a lead author assembles a research team, thereby enabling fit among like-minded authors within that team. In the *Organization Science* session, author Wesley Sine offered the following illustration:

> I had experience working with both of these co-authors; they didn't have experience working together, and we were at one point all students at Cornell. We knew each other, and I knew their strengths and knew their weaknesses. I brought them in for their strengths. As first author, I selected both of them for various strengths that they brought to the process. (Wesley D. Sine, Author: Chapter 16)

Or supplementary fit might occur as individuals find that their values and goals match those of other guild members: some in the author role, and others in the editor role – thereby promoting an environment conducive to productive exchange between author(s) and editor(s). For example, Yasemin Kor in the *Strategic Entrepreneurship Journal* (*SEJ*) editor/ author session explained this supplementation process in dialogue with editor Mike Hitt, as follows:

> *Kor, Yasemin*: I think our experience with the *SEJ* is that we have gotten very strong, very high-quality feedback. Mike has been a truly exceptional editor in terms of providing us with this magic map; like an ancient treasure map, really, in terms of how we would . . .
>
> *Hitt, Mike*: She doesn't mean ancient.
>
> *Kor, Yasemin*: No. That's meant in a good sense. Actually, telling us all the steps, but also guiding us (because we were going into multiple research streams), also providing us some potential relevant articles, every one of which we read. All the insights come together. It was like magic as things fell together. That was very positive. But I also wanted to bring up the point that there was very strong guidance. It was very illuminating . . . (Yasemin Y. Kor, Author; Michael A. Hitt, Editor: Chapter 17)

Here we can see the 'embellishment' process in action: feedback leads to guidance (potential readings, etc.), which in turn leads to insights that 'come together.' While working toward the shared goal of publication, we see evidence of the support and reinforcement offered by the editor and reviewers to the author.

In the context of top-tier research, supplementary fit may also be important in determining appropriate submission outlets. As illustrated in the *Journal of Business Venturing* (*JBV*) editor/author session, author Dimo Dimov notes the value of commonality, when he states (after being asked by co-moderator John Mathieu):

> *Mathieu, John*: How does your paper fit into the universe of entrepreneurship?
>
> *Dimov, Dimo*: In our case, what's interesting is that as the paper was developing we thought of *JBV* as the natural home. It was clear and the reason for that is there's been a longstanding conversation in the journal about venture capital – and when you have a context like this, it comes with a lot of dirty laundry. There are problems with working with venture capital data, and when you have reviewers that are in that area, they are aware of these issues so you can safely navigate these waters because everyone knows that these are problems. So with that said, this was a natural home. (Dimo Dimov, Author; John E. Mathieu, Moderator: Chapter 13)

In this exchange, we are able to observe the 'similar characteristics' aspect of supplementary fit: in this case, a data set to journal-expertise/focus. Furthermore, the author succeeded in finding an outlet that not only valued his area of research, but also had a history of carrying on a 'conversation' regarding his interest: venture capital. It appears that interacting with similar others who value similar things (i.e., editors and reviewers) allowed the author to find a natural home for his research, thus achieving supplementary fit.

But while supplementary fit is perhaps the more intuitive or more likely interpretation of fit, it is not the whole story. As illustrated in Figure 1, there are also 'complementary' ways where demands/supplies of individuals complete or 'make whole' the demands/supplies of the environment – and vice versa.

Complementary Fit

Complementary fit is distinct from supplementary fit. Whereas supplementary fit emphasizes compatibility through 'congruence' (e.g., personal isomorphism with the environment), complementary fit emphasizes compatibility through 'completion,' which is 'when a person's characteristics 'make whole' the environment or add to it what is missing' (Muchinsky and Monahan, 1987: 271, as cited in Kristof, 1996: 3). We find two sets of instances where Conference participants articulate complementary fit-type situations, and we highlight several of these comments in the quotes that follow. We expect that in engaging the narratives, however, you (the reader) will identify even more such instances. These two typical complementary matches take the following form:

1. A person demands what environmental characteristics supply, or vice versa (arrow 'b,' in Figure 1), or
2. Person-based characteristics supply what the environment demands, or vice versa (arrow 'c,' in Figure 1).

Persons demand what environmental characteristics supply. As a representation of P-E fit, the P-O fit model suggests that 'organizations supply financial, physical and psychological resources as well as the task-related, interpersonal and growth opportunities that are demanded by employees. When these organizational supplies meet employees' demands, "needs-supplies" (complementary) fit is achieved' (Kristof, 1996: 4, emphasis added). As we have previously noted, we have identified within the Conference narrative at least three zones of compatibility – areas where the top-tier research guild supplies: (1) critical feedback resources in the form of reviews; (2) task-related opportunities for monetary and psychological rewards/satisfaction; and (3) interpersonal opportunities for personal interaction and learning. In the narrative, we find several examples of this kind of complementary fit described by editors and authors during their discourse. For example, during the *Academy of Management Review* (*AMR*) editor/author session, we suggested that Mason Carpenter, associate editor representing *AMR*, described in detail the manner in which the needs–supplies process is enacted in the reviewer–author interchange:

> I think one rule of thumb that I like to use is that, as an editor, I am not a vote-counter. So I don't get a tally and just say, 'This is a number, this is what you got and so "thank you" or "no thank you".' It is really gaining some traction with the particular article. If there's energy – if there is passion in a reviewer, they could say, 'I hate everything about this paper but this,'. . . We want to see our work published. . . . The reviewers want to see that too, but they want it to meet the criteria – to meet that hurdle of what quality is. And they get frustrated; but when reviewers find something, they go, 'There is a diamond in the rough here.' So the task is to coach that out of the paper in cooperation with the authors.
>
>   The authors have that same perspective. Is that something they want to see come out of the paper? Because one of the things that you see in the review process and in the revision process is that, just in the writing, a lot of choices are made. It is making those choices that resonates with a sort of coherent story in the paper, but also with the spirit of what the author is wanting to do. Because if you beat that spirit out, it usually comes out in a poor paper, but if the spirit is there, it is those papers that you read and go, 'That's really unique. It helps

me understand a part of the world that I would not even have known to ask that question before.' (Mason A. Carpenter, Editor: Chapter 10)

Here we can see how the top-tier journal guild supplies the critical feedback which at the same time is needed by the authors to improve their work. This needs–supplies exchange 'makes whole' the scholarship environment – and by providing critical feedback yields satisfaction-based psychic rewards for authors. We see this value exchange described in the following comment by Keith Hmieleski, one of the authors in the *AMJ* editor/author session, who says: ' . . . the more effort you put into it up front before the submission, the much more enjoyable the whole review process is that follows from there' (Keith M. Hmieleski, Author: Chapter 9).

Of course, a clearly important outcome of the needs/supplies-based complementary process within the scholarly setting is the interaction and learning that occurs. This result is especially important for new colleagues as the scholarly journey is just beginning. Helpfully, Joe Mahoney, as an associate editor representing *Strategic Management Journal* (*SMJ*) described the reflexivity that is core to the needs–supplies exchange: the 'individual attention' that is provided, as those who are experienced in the top-tier research guild begin to engage each new colleague. Here is how he described the process from his vantage point, in response to an audience question from Yasemin Kor during the *SMJ* editor/author session:

Kor, Yasemin: I have a general question. If you have a burning desire to do research on a topic that is very new and not very well known, and there is not much research on it (or the opposite being that it is researched to death, the area is declining or is very mature), is that a high-risk proposition? And if you still want to do it, what are some ways to go about it?

Mahoney, Joe: . . . for every single student, I think the right approach depends on the student. . . . If I have a student that has had ten years' work experience, then we start from the experience and we work to the theory. If I have someone coming right out from undergraduate, we start from reading the theory and then we move to experience. My final message is that Vygotsky had a 'Theory of Learning' and (to summarize), the theory noted that you need to start from where the person is. I would say there is not a cookie-cutter answer to your question. For each person, you have to start from where you are. (Yasemin Y. Kor, Author/Audience; Joseph T. Mahoney, Editor: Chapter 18)

So in short, the complementary process, as 'wholeness-creating,' can be seen to be much more of a two-way exchange in this first type of situation, where the top-tier research guild supplies what new members need in a give-and-take manner. In a similar way, this completion logic can operate in service of the top-tier research environment as well.

In the next part of this section, where the top-tier research guild demands are the point of focus, we shall examine further evidence from the narratives, which describes situations where once again, the wholeness or completeness logic of complementary fit permeates the person–environment interface.

Persons supply what the environment demands. P-E fit theory further suggests that environments demand contributions from individuals in terms of time, effort, commitment, knowledge, skills and abilities. In terms of P-O fit, 'demands–abilities' fit is achieved when employee supplies meet organizational demands (arrow 'c' in Figure 1) (Kristof: 1996: 4). The demands of the top-tier research guild (as characterized by the participants quoted earlier in this chapter) revolve around: (1) research-production-focused task-specific demands; (2) patience/perseverance-centered interpersonally specific demands; and (3) skill and imagination-based personal demands.

As the story of Tom Elfring, one of the authors in the *AMJ* editor/author session, unfolded, Conference participants learned how a group of European authors stepped up to the challenge of submitting to an American top-tier outlet. As Tom describes it:

> To us it was really a positive surprise that we got an R&R [revise and resubmit]. We were kind of new. None of us had published before in any of the top American journals (coming from the European context) because it was not so much necessary. We didn't even intend to submit it to *AMJ*. We were thinking of *JBV* [*Journal of Business Venturing*]; but one of the American people in our department, hired for one day a week to coach and help us to get published in the American journals (which is kind of the target), had said, 'Well, you have very interesting data. Why not submit it to *AMJ*?' We said, 'Well, that's too difficult.' But we did it anyway. Then we got this letter (which I was kind of shaking when we opened the mail), and it was very encouraging. It was a tough job, but it was very encouraging . . . (Tom Elfring, Author: Chapter 9)

The foregoing quote provides a clear example of how individual persons (authors) supplied the effort demanded by the top-tier research guild (as represented by both the American colleague [unnamed], and by *AMJ* itself). The result: a demands–abilities-based complementary fit.

Then there is the situation described by Venkat as a new author (Chapter 7) trying to meet the expectations of the top-tier research guild. He recounts the following as it relates to the second demand that we identified in the narratives – perseverance:

> I would assert here today that top journals look for papers that are interesting, provocative, useful to either practice or to researchers by raising new and fruitful research questions, are empirically tractable and have a clear answer to the

'so what' questions. That, I figured out, is really what journals are looking for. That's really their stock-in-trade. Journals are not really after truth. Journals are not really after a kind of statement about a phenomenon, which everybody agrees as a consensus that 'This is what it's all about.' They are really in the business of attracting attention – spreading their own genes, in some sense. So they look for the provocative. They look for the interesting. They do it in a very sophisticated way, but that's a large part of the story.

A third event for me was the first publishable paper out of my dissertation, and where I should send it. Taking Andy's [Andy Van de Ven, dissertation advisor] dictum to me seriously, I decided I should aim for *ASQ* [*Administrative Science Quarterly*], and start at the top and see where the equilibrium point might eventually be. After some while, I got the reviews back. It was a substantial revision, so at least I had survived the rejection process (which was personally very satisfying for me), but it was very high risk. It had nearly 13 pages of single-spaced comments from three reviewers and one associate editor. When I read it, it was frankly beyond me at that stage. I could not handle it by myself, but I learned several lessons from that experience. First, publishing in top journals requires tremendous perseverance, great stamina, a lot of help and a good dose of luck. Subsequently, I could never get all three reviewers to agree on that particular paper. Convincing three reviewers is a really tough business – no question about that. (Sankaran Venkataraman, Keynote: Chapter 7)

In a similar vein, Mike Hitt – as a mid-career author – also recounts a tale of perseverance and patience, as follows:

A few years ago I had a project that I was working on in which we had the idea, developed it, collected data, analysed it, wrote a draft and presented a paper at the Academy of Management conference. We then obtained additional feedback on the research and paper from colleagues. Then, the next natural step was to go to a journal. But, I still had concerns that we needed to do more to enhance the quality of the work before submitting it to a top journal. I really liked this research and felt it had potential to make a contribution. My colleagues wanted to submit the manuscript; they were younger and they had reasons for desiring submission (such as the evaluation time clock). But if you send a paper in before it is ready, it is unlikely to be accepted for publication. Thus, I recommended that we not submit the paper. I then presented the paper at several research seminars at other universities. That is not something I normally do, but I received some excellent feedback from two different places – one on the theory and one on the methods. Based on the feedback, we collected more data and worked on the theory. Both actions improved the paper. We then submitted it to the journal and received a high-risk R&R. Now, if we had not taken the additional actions, we would not have received the high-risk R&R – it likely would have been rejected. Fortunately, we were able to develop it and eventually the paper was accepted and published in *AMJ*. So that's one story where we had to have a little patience and perseverance. (Michael A. Hitt, Keynote: Chapter 4)

Perseverance is demanded by the top-tier research guild, and as a result the complementary fit that is possible is uncertain – even for the (now) research 'superstars.' What we find to be interesting about the recounting of these experiences, is that it helps us, as observers of the process, to understand more thoroughly why the complementary matching process is one that involves 'completion' of a whole. Those who engage in this type of complementary demands–abilities matching (willingly stepping up to environmental demands) chart a path that is less limited from a practical standpoint, and can be (as we see from these narratives) highly effective.

And, yes, the third 'demands' theme we identified – skill and imagination – are also highly valued and expected by the top-tier research guild. We presented several passages in the earlier section of this chapter that illustrated the importance of skills and imagination. But what we did not do in that section was illustrate how the complementary demands–abilities process might work in the journal–author dialogue. Fortunately, a comment by Yasemin Kor in the *SEJ* session sums up this 'co-creative' element invoked as a part of the complementary fit:

> I really view the publication process as a co-creative act, so to speak, just like in entrepreneurship teams. I really think that, yes, the authors are the original creators, I guess; but I think it is a very important role the reviewers and especially the editors play. For us, what worked was to engage in a positive dialogue, to be receptive, listen to the comments and really consider their feedback, but it also really helped to have an editor and the reviewers really understand and appreciate our points of view. It is coming together both ways as a co-creative team act. (Yasemin Y. Kor, Author: Chapter 17)

So here we can see that skill and imagination – as a demand of the top-tier research guild – reaches completeness through a positive-loop dialogue where editors and authors each contribute to the crafting of fit.

ONWARD

It seems slightly odd to us to produce an 'introductory' chapter with a conclusion. Rather, we hope our closing comments will be those of encouragement. In this chapter, we have endeavored to provide a structure to the narrative that will now unfold as you navigate the Exemplars Conference dialogue. We encourage you to visit the website (www.researchexemplars.org) where these narrative sessions are available for downloading and viewing electronically, and to utilize this book as the means whereby you can make the ideas herein your own. As members of the social science research guild, we are also continually in search of research excellence despite those parts of the process that are shrouded in myth. We offer 'exemplars in entrepreneurship' as another step toward fulfilling that aspiration.

NOTES

1. The editor-author participants represented the following journals: Academy of Management Journal; Academy of Management Review; Entrepreneurship, Theory & Practice; Journal of Applied Psychology; Journal of Business Venturing; Journal of Management; Journal of Management Studies; Organization Science; Strategic Entrepreneurship Journal; and Strategic Management Journal.
2. The keynote addresses were given by: Howard Aldrich, University of North Carolina – Chapel Hill; Jay Barney, The Ohio State University; Michael Hitt, Texas A&M University; Duane Ireland, Texas A&M University; Patricia P. McDougall, Indiana University; and S. 'Venkat' Venkataraman, University of Virginia.
3. In the Journal of Management Studies editor/author session, James O. Fiet, as an author explaining how he had 'finally' been able to get research which he believed to be deeply important published in a top journal, 'shed a tear' when asked to explain its importance to him personally.

REFERENCES

Campbell, D.T. (1969). Variation and selective retention in socio-cultural evolution. *General Systems*, **14**, 69–85.

Davis, M.S. (1971). That's interesting! Towards a phenomenology of sociology and a sociology of phenomenology. *Philosophy of the Social Sciences*, **1**, 309–44.

Glaser, R. (1984). Education and thinking. *American Psychologist*, **39**, 93–104.

Hambrick, D. (1994). What if the Academy actually mattered? *Academy of Management Review*, **19** (1), 11–16.

Hogan, R.T. (1991). Personality and personality measurement. In M.D. Dunnette and L.M. Hough (eds), *Handbook of Industrial and Organizational Psychology*. Palo Alto, CA: Consulting Psychologists' Press, Vol. 2, pp. 873–919.

Kristof, A.L. (1996). Person–organization fit: an integrative review of its conceptualizations, measurement, and implications. *Personnel Psychology*, **49** (1), 1–49.

Kristof-Brown, A.L., R.D. Zimmerman and E.C. Johnson (2005). Consequences of individuals' fit at work: a meta-analysis of person–job, person–organization, person–group, and person–supervisor fit. *Personnel Psychology*, **58**, 281–342.

Lawrence, T.B., M.I. Winn and P.D. Jennings (2001). The temporal dynamics of institutionalization. *Academy of Management Review*, **26** (4), 624–44.

Merton, R.K. (1968). *Social Theory and Social Structure*. New York: The Free Press.

Muchinsky, P.M. and C.J. Monahan (1987). What is person–environment congruence? Supplementary versus complementary models of fit. *Journal of Vocational Behavior*, **31**, 268–77.

NRC (National Research Council, Chemical Sciences Roundtable Board on Chemical Sciences and Technology) (2000). *Graduate Education in the Chemical Sciences: Issues for the 21st Century: Report of a Workshop*. Retrieved: March 16, 2010: http://www.nap.edu/catalog/9898.html.

Schein, E. (1992). *Organizational Culture and Leadership*. San Francisco: Jossey-Bass.

Schneider, B. (2001). Fits about fit. *Applied Psychology: An International Review*, **50**, 141–52.

Keynote contributors

2. Mindful scholarship

Howard E. Aldrich

Dino, Rich: Please join me in welcoming research exemplar, Howard Aldrich.

Aldrich, Howard: Welcome to the ACC, Big East Basketball Challenge. Tipoff's going to be starting very soon.

Haggard, Rory [off camera]: Hey, wait a minute; that's over and done with!

Aldrich, Howard: Oh never mind. I'm very happy to be able to join you by this long-distance route today. When I was asked to be a speaker, one of the things that occurred to me was that you'll be hearing a great deal about some of the general principles of doing entrepreneurship research. What I will do is talk more about 'best practices' and in particular, as you saw from the title slide, what I want to talk about in the time available is mindful scholarship.

When I was asked to do this, it occurred to me that I was probably asked because I am seen as an 'expert.' Now, what's an expert? According to neuroscience or cognitive science researchers, about 10,000 hours of experience typically gives you the possibility of insights into a phenomenon. But it is more than experience. It's more than the fact of having 10,000 hours. Being an expert means noticing distinctions. It means being aware of differences, being attentive to things that novices and amateurs don't pay attention to. Much of what I'm going to talk about actually comes from some books that I have found helpful in thinking about mindful activities in general: the Zanders' *The Art of Possibility* (Zander and Zander, 2000), Ellen Langer's work on mindfulness (Langer, 1989), *Counterclockwise* (Langer, 2009) and Robert Boice's work (Boice, 2000).

You can find all of these books mentioned on my website. In Google, just type my name in the search bar, and on my webpage you'll be able to find this information and more. Or type in the URL: http://www.unc.edu/~healdric/.

Now I'm going to be mindful myself in talking to you about these ideas. That means I'm not telling you the way to do something. As Ellen Langer might say, 'Here are some possibilities.' This is simply one way to do it. It's my way; it's not the only way. And as a mindful scholar, the first thing to be aware of is that you have options, and you have to make choices.

Perhaps the most important dilemma facing junior scholars and graduate students is what Donald Campbell (Campbell, 1969) talks about as the 'real' goal of science. Don Campbell, a great scholar and wonderful man, contributed to general systems theory, anthropology, philosophy, psychology and sociology. Also he was very pragmatic and instrumental. He described science essentially as 'the struggle for citations.' How do you achieve your place in the citation world?

There are two central strategies. I like the analogy of somebody out looking for gold in the old West. What are the choices? One we could call the 'mining choice.' It's going out into the mountains, finding a hole already dug, seeing people streaming in and out of it, realizing, 'Yes, there's probably gold here. The seam has been opened and now I can just follow those people. It could be the case that I will find large pieces of ore, but also it is quite likely that because people have been there before me, my incremental contribution is probably going to be fairly small.' What's the alternative? The alternative is the 'prospecting strategy.' Think about Humphrey Bogart in *The Treasure of the Sierra Madre*, if you remember that movie (that's the very famous movie with the 'badges' joke that Mel Brooks followed up in *Blazing Saddles*). You can imagine being on the frontier; there's no map, you just set off and try to find gold. The chances are quite good that what you'll encounter are dry holes; although it could also be the case that you are the first to stumble onto something never before seen (in which case the returns to you are substantial, but you're also taking a substantial risk).

So what I want to talk about today is not that you should choose either of these paths. I want to talk about, in a mindful way, trying to manage the tension between the 'mining' that is inevitable in our profession and the 'prospecting' that I think returns the largest rewards to people. I have on the board the five points that I will be making in my talk today. These are five advisories, suggestions and guidelines – not rules. These are offered in a mindful spirit, meaning I am making suggestions that one might follow to create a mindful scholarly career. You have heard some of these things already in other sessions.

I am proposing that you consider a portfolio model for your scholarly career. Clearly, some combination of a mining strategy with a prospecting strategy (if one can find the right balance) is the way to go. That is pretty self-evident. However, how do you lessen the risks you are taking on, particularly when you go into the prospecting part of your portfolio? Here's where I'm going to talk about some practices that have served me very well over the last 40 years.

My first point: collaboration. In his keynote address, Venkat [Sankaran Venkataraman: Chapter 7] described his dean telling him about some data he had seen regarding multiple authorships. I think the dean's point was that there was an increase over time in papers with more than one author. I think he probably took that from the work of my friend Brian Uzzi (Guimerà et al, 2005), published recently. Brian and his colleagues looked at all the sciences: the natural sciences, the social sciences and also the humanities, looking at the pattern over the last decades – many decades – of solo versus co-authored articles. The trend was clear. The natural sciences were the first, followed by the social sciences, and now increasingly in the humanities: multiple authored papers are dominant. That is, fewer and fewer papers every year are appearing with a single author. Two authors, three authors – in the natural sciences, four, five and six authors are routine. Now why do people do that?

Well, the other piece of the puzzle that Venkat didn't mention is that this study also shows, in terms of the struggle for citations, that it's the multiple-authored papers that are getting disproportionate numbers of citations. So it's clear it is not simply a fad having to do with people feeling more sociable about their research. It is also clearly something that people see as beneficial to their careers. Co-authorships increase the likelihood that what people are doing will be noticed and cited by others.

In 40-plus years of working in this field, I have had occasion to work with many collaborators, and I can tell you that it is possible (believe it or not) to make a mistake. You can pick somebody to work with who maybe isn't such a compatible person. So let me offer a couple of suggestions. One of the things I have discovered is that it is extremely important to make certain that your objectives and your co-authors' objectives are aligned. Do you intend to submit papers only to top-tier journals (and if they don't succeed, file them in a drawer)? Or are you the kind of person who starts, as Venkat and also Duane [R. Duane Ireland: Chapter 5] mentioned in their keynote addresses, at the top tier, then goes down to A-, B+, B, B-, C, and just keeps going down until you find a home? Get that clear with your co-author.

A second issue that you need to also get straight with your collaborators is 'time orientation.' I mention this because I have some students who are very aware of my working style. They pretty much expect me 24/7. I have other people I work with on a nine-to-five schedule. Weekends they don't check their computer. My European friends, God bless them, think that July and August are months for spending time away from the office. So when we talk about planning ahead, those two months are just blocked out on the calendar. My point is simply that when you are going to choose a collaborator and try increasing your citation count, be certain it is somebody who you really and truly are going to want to work with.

A third principle: create constructive critics. You like that? Did you get the alliteration there? 'Create constructive critics.' Who might these critics be? When I talk to students about this point, the first people they think of are their mentors and their peers. In talking to junior faculty, I find they sometimes mention graduate students and maybe also their peers. I'm going to add 'senior scholars' into the mix in a moment, but let's just talk about the most obvious people you could choose. Why would we do this? Why would we need to create constructive critics? Well, what is the alternative? I am sure in the audience there is somebody who sent off to a big-time journal a paper that they had not shown to anyone else – and subsequently received blind reviews telling them they might want to seek another line of work and not to give up their day job. Am I right? The worst possible time to find out there is a hole in your theory and that your research design is fundamentally flawed is when the editor sends back the rejection notice saying 'Our reviewers decided not to give you another chance.' That is the worst possible thing that could happen. So my goal in mentoring my students is not to get their papers accepted; my goal is to make certain that the first submission gets an R&R [revise & resubmit]. I think that is what some of the journal editors were saying to you earlier today.

How do you do that? How do you find these people? I'm a sociologist, so where do I look for the principles of recruiting collaborators? I look to the principles concerning norms of reciprocity and norms of obligation. You need first to volunteer to help other people, believe it or not. You are not going to get very good advice from other people until you have not only worked for them, but also worked with them to show them what you want.

How many of you have had the experience of taking a paper down the hallway or emailing it to somebody, waiting two, three, four weeks and then receiving a comment like, 'Really nice work. You're doing a great job. Keep it up.'? Or they bring the paper back (they printed it out) and you notice in the margins they have penciled in notes on the order of 'misspelled word, comma splice, dependent clause without a conjunction.' That's not going to help. You want your constructive critics to attack your paper with the same ferocity as the anonymous reviewers at *SMJ* [*Strategic Management Journal*] That means showing the people who are going to be helping you what you want.

So what do you do? You ask a colleague, 'Can I see something you're working on that I might be able to help you with? Great. Send it to me in electronic form.' Go through the paper, not using 'track changes.' 'Track changes' is for co-authors. Write this down: '"Track changes" is for co-authors. "Insert comment" is for critics.' You go through the paper, mark the text off to the side where you have as much space as you need, write your comments – something like, 'You've neglected this literature. This concept is ill-defined. There's a logical flaw in this paragraph. You need to get more sleep. Your topic sentence introduces other materials that aren't in the paragraph,' and so forth. Show people that higher-order feedback is what you want, not the lower-order stuff. In turn, they take on a fairly serious obligation to you. It's a rare individual (although actually I think I have one down the hallway in my department) who can resist the appeal to make similar responses to the stuff you send.

A final point about this. It turns out that at major conferences you will meet people – senior scholars – who you can approach. I am talking now to the graduate students in the audience and some of the junior faculty. The senior faculty in the room or watching on the web may want to plug their ears. You will meet people who actually need help. They may not realize it, but they do need help. You can approach them and ask, 'Can I have a paper of yours? Are you working on something?' Help them out. Email them your comments. The same principle applies: once you get them hooked, you can expect help.

Let me go on to the fourth point: reading mindfully. To illustrate the problem here, let's turn to an anonymous student (I pointed to my graduate student, Tiantian, seated in front of the camera). When you sit down to write a paper, are you like Tiantian here (surrounded by your books and papers)? That's a very bad sign. If you sit down to write surrounded by your books and papers, it means that essentially you are not ready to write. I often talk to graduate students and they ask, 'Well, how am I going to find out what I'm going to say about somebody's work? I need the originals in front of me.' To them I say, 'It's too late. The time to do that is when you're reading the stuff, not when you're sitting down to "write" your own paper.'

What's the better strategy? The better strategy is to sit down with a conceptual outline and your interpretive notes and draft your paper. Now what does that mean? Again I often look at my student's notes. What I see in those notes are summaries, abstracts, descriptions and the voice of the author captured very well. What I don't see in those notes on what they have read is the voice of the person who is going to write the paper. What you need to do in reading the literature mindfully is to interpret what you read for yourself, taking what you have read, making notes not to describe what is in the article, but instead to say what it means to you. What is this article saying to me about this subject? That is mindful reading. It's about what you say – not about what the author says. Anybody can faithfully reproduce the author's words. If I want to read what Herbert Simon said about something or James March or Karl Weick, I will go read them in the original. If I want to read what you have said, I need to hear your voice; and the way to do that is to have your notes reflect your interpretation at the time you read the paper or book.

[*Aldrich holds up a sheaf of paper*] This is a sample of some of the notes I prepared when I was working on that paper that was in *SEJ* last year, on social networks (Aldrich and Kim, 2007). Do you see this? These are not summaries. What did I do? I read papers I thought would be relevant. As I read them, I wrote down what I thought they meant for the topic; and that is what is in my file – not summaries.

The final point: create a conceptual outline. This is CCO (can anybody help me out? I couldn't get another 'C' here). So when I sit down to write I have – oh, let me stop. Look at the warning sign. Tiantian, will you help us out here? Hold that up. What do you see there? What is that – can somebody in the audience tell me? What is she holding up? [*Answer*: A blank page] The worst possible situation is to sit down to write and be facing a blank page. That's terrifying. That's terrifying. Instead, when you sit down to draft a paper, you should have a conceptual outline. You should have your interpretive notes and what you should be doing is taking the outline and translating it into prose. If you sit down to a blank piece of paper without a conceptual outline, you are actually at a pre-writing stage. You are at a writing stage that Peter Elbow described in his book, *Writing with Power* (Elbow, 1998) as 'free writing.' You can free write on blank paper or free write on a blank computer screen. However, 'writing a paper' requires a conceptual outline.

Maybe an analogy will help you think about this. The terrifying thing to many of our students is that they think about writing a paper as 'writing a paper,' and it's a gigantic project. They see an enormous boulder on the top of a hill rolling down at them and they need to grasp it all at once and push it back up the hill. I say, 'Well, don't think about it that way. Your job is to read the literature, write interpretive notes and build your outline section by section, pebble by pebble, stone by stone, rock by rock. Eventually what you will have will be a boulder. But if you set out with a blank piece of paper as your starting point and say to yourself, "This must be turned into a paper," it's not going to work. You will be crushed.'

So think 'mindful scholarship, mindful scholarship.' When you set out to work on your project, find a collaborator who is compatible, cultivate critics with norms of reciprocity, create the outline that you need for your writing through mindful reading, be mindful in taking notes and then, finally, do the writing from a conceptual outline as opposed to thinking about it as writing from scratch. This concludes the formal part of my talk. I'll take questions.

Dino, Rich: Okay, questions from Storrs and questions worldwide, please. Anyone? Jay Barney has a question for you, Howard.

Barney, Jay: Hey, Howard. How are you?

Aldrich, Howard: Hey, Jay. How you doing?

Barney, Jay: I'm good. It's good to see you. I want to go back to point number one about portfolio. Could you comment on the following? You were talking about the fact that you thought it was self-evident that there should be some 'mining' and some 'prospecting.' Could you talk about the different skills that are involved in those two different kinds of activities?

Aldrich, Howard: Well, I think that prospecting is probably going to work better for people who have an expert's eye; and thus early in one's career I suspect that prospecting will be mostly random generation and random variation. One of the differences between you as a senior scholar and your graduate students is that a graduate student can bring you an idea (thinking that it is at the frontier) and you say, 'Oh no, back in 1978 Bill Ouchi had the same idea. He published it in *ASQ* [*Administrative Science Quarterly*]. You obviously just started reading *ASQ* when you entered graduate school, so you aren't aware of this.' That's a joke. And so it's quite likely that the difference between the two to some extent is a function of how mindful you have become as a scholar. So I say early on, it probably is the case that the constraints are such that it would be very difficult for a junior scholar to do a lot of successful prospecting. It's going to be probably more like semi-random variation than it would be in the hands of somebody like you with the ability to remember and to put together ideas and make connections that just won't be there for the junior scholar.

Barney, Jay: So that portfolio you have in mind is a temporal portfolio more than a simultaneous portfolio?

Aldrich, Howard: Yes. Let's say somebody works with Jay Barney. They like the idea of what he does so much that they set out to be the next Jay Barney or the next Karl Weick or the next Jim March. The alternative is to say to them, 'All this stuff is really wonderful, but it needs to be replicated and needs to be extended. We need to find new domains in which it can be applied.' But junior scholars also need to think about the possibilities of putting their own names on their work – and their own citation counts, so to speak. So early on, prospecting would be more of an aspiration than a reality.

Barney, Jay: How about one last comment? What about the transition from mining to prospecting, given the temporal nature of this, as you're suggesting. When does that occur and how does that occur?

Aldrich, Howard: That's back to the 10,000 hours. One of the experiences that sticks in my mind comes from my mentor back in my days at Michigan, Albert J. Reiss, Jr. I remember him getting a book prospectus from somebody who had been out of graduate school maybe six years or seven years, and the prospectus was about a book that was to review criminology or something like that. Al just said, 'This person hasn't lived long enough to do this. It's not possible. It will be workman-like, but it's not going to make any difference to the field.' When I was preparing my 1979 book (Aldrich, 1979), [*Aldrich holds up a book and points to the image of Milwaukee on the cover*] I had been out of graduate school a little more than eight years. I couldn't have written this book before then. It wasn't possible. I just didn't know enough. I wasn't savvy enough. I didn't have the vision that eventually came to me. So what I would say now is that I think it is a matter of mindful maturation. For more information on the context in which I wrote that book, see the new edition (Aldrich, 2008).

At the time I didn't know the word 'mindful,' but now I would say it is a matter of mindful maturation, and these books are also wonderful books about entrepreneurship. The Zanders' book, *The Art of Possibility* (Zander and Zander, 2000), is probably the single best book about an entrepreneurial mindset I have ever read. The latest book by Langer (Langer, 2009) comes very close to being a classic in that sense – very much about noticing differences, being attentive to differences and being receptive to the noticing of differences. Langer has lots of experimental evidence in this book, showing how being attentive makes a difference. You can actually teach people to recognize differences that they couldn't see before (Fiet, 2002). So I'm hopeful, back to your point about transitions, that with mindful reading, junior scholars can get to the point where that transition is possible.

Barney, Jay: Thanks, Howard.

Lumpkin, Tom: Howard, this is Tom Lumpkin. I have some questions from the web. First, when teaching junior scholars, how do you help them to identify the initial research area to specialize in? Too often it seems that just pursuing questions can leave students stranded – especially as their questions change.

Aldrich, Howard: So the question is, how to help them find their own voice?

Lumpkin, Tom: And the kind of research to specialize in.

Aldrich, Howard: Again, I can certainly see what happens to people who approach that choice in a mindless way. One of the classic things we see students doing is coming to graduate school with some work experience. Especially PhDs in our field, typically people have been out five, six, ten years who come to graduate school with a very powerful image of an experience they had as a manager or maybe as an entrepreneur. What they spend their first couple of years trying to do is to figure out how to understand that experience. That is a very bad way to choose a research project. The first thing I would do in working with students is to help them have a cathartic moment: 'Why are you here? What do you think about entrepreneurship? What are the emotional associations you have?' I try to get them to think about the powerful passions that they may have and the powerful feelings they may have. Get that on the table.

The second thing I would suggest to them is that their personal experience might be the basis for building a program; but it's not going to be a very good basis. I say this because I have seen it over and over again – not only for the people I teach personally, but also at the doctoral consortia, I've seen the same thing. When people are asked about what they are interested in, inevitably they take us back to some personal experience they had, either as a worker, a manager or an entrepreneur. I think they have a very serious problem if they don't get past that.

Cardon, Melissa: Hey, Howard, it's Melissa Cardon. I want to go back to the prospecting versus mining issue. We have been talking a lot here for the last day about targeting top-tier journals. Is there room in top-tier journals for mining as well as prospecting? Because I would suspect that most of these editors will tell us they want the brand-new novel creative stuff – not the mining where other people have panned before. Is there room there in the top-tier journals?

Aldrich, Howard: Here's where I think there is an interesting social psychological dilemma facing editors and reviewers. I'm an evolutionary theorist and, so by definition, the next big thing is completely opaque to us right now. There is no possible way that you can tell me what in two or three years will be the hottest thing going. It is impossible. There's no way to do that. Why is that? Well, because we are totally creatures of our experience. Our cognitive frames are set in ways that make it very difficult for us to evaluate stuff that really is radically different. So, no matter what the editors say, and no matter what the reviewers say, they are still using a criterion of 'How does this fit into what I already know?'

I'm going through that experience right now. Two top-tier journals have asked for R&Rs of papers I'm working on. Both of these are team-based papers. We look at their reviews sent to us after the first round of reviewing and the reviewers are mentioning authors we didn't cite and that we should cite. They're citing received concepts and principles. They're not talking about stuff that doesn't yet exist; they're talking about stuff that already exists. What I'm saying is that it is very difficult to get away from this practice, and you have to be an incredibly courageous editor to pick the one of the three reviews that's positive and go with the paper. Here's a question for you. Melissa, you might ask the editors who are still in Storrs, 'Would you accept a paper if only one of the three reviewers said this is great? Would you do that? How could you do that? Could you look your reviewers in the eye after you've done that and say, "Thanks for the good job you did?"' It's a very dangerous thing for an editor to do, but that's what they would have to do to really privilege the prospecting part to this. It's a very difficult issue.

Lumpkin, Tom: Howard, again from the web. This is going to also have to be the last question. Last night Dean (Chris) Earley made a comment about the importance of both skill and imagination; lacking one or the other might result in sub-par work was the point. In terms of mindfulness, which is more important? And if the answer is both, how much of each do you need, and how do they work together?

Aldrich, Howard: Well, I think the first thing you will recognize is that neither skill nor imagination is totally genetically determined, right? That's the beauty of reading Langer's stuff, for example, or Zander's stuff. There is a lot of work in cognitive neuroscience, again, that shows you can actually teach people to be more imaginative. If I could put a plug in for my oldest son's company, Posit Science (www.positscience.com), there are computer programs that can actually help you improve your mental acuity. There actually are ways to get the brain out of the miasma that it is in and train it to be better at dealing with challenging environmental stimuli. So, with regard to the question about skill and imagination, I would say skill is a matter of experience. It is a matter of attaching yourself to good mentors and learning how to read mindfully. Imagination may require you to spend a little money on technology. Find people, coaches and trainers. There are ways to put yourself in situations beyond your comfort zone. That is possible. I would say both of those tracks can be pursued. The imagination track is going to be harder; it is going to be more painful, but it is possible.

Dino, Rich: Howard, it's Rich Dino. On behalf of all of us here with the organizing committee and if I may speak for the Academy Entrepreneurship Division, we greatly, greatly appreciate your participation. For everyone, when I called Howard to invite him to the Conference he said, 'I really, really want to be there.' [*Aldrich picks up basketball*] Put that ball down. He knows my back . . .

Aldrich, Howard: Tell Gino Auriemma (UConn women's basketball coach) that Sylvia Hatchell (UNC women's basketball coach) is laying in wait for him next year.

Dino, Rich: Yeah, yeah, yeah. You know, it's about outcomes, not about talking. [*Authors' note*: On their way to another National Championship, their seventh – and their second consecutive perfect season – the University of Connecticut women's basketball team beat North Carolina, 88–47.] That was a good one, wasn't it? Yes, men's basketball is another story.

Anyway, he said, 'I really, really want to be there, but, Rich,' he said, 'I've tried everything and I just can't get in and out of Hartford given where else I have to be that week.' He said, 'Let's see if we can work it out,' – and we did. Howard, again, thank you so much for your contributions, and your willingness to participate. It was a wonderful session and we wish you a good day.

Aldrich, Howard: Thank you.

Dino, Rich: Thank you.

REFERENCES

Aldrich, H.E. (1979). *Organizations and Environments*. Englewood Cliffs, NJ: Prentice-Hall.
Aldrich, H.E. (2008). *Organizations and Environments*, new edition. Stanford, CA: Stanford Business Classics of Stanford University Press.

Aldrich, H.E. and P.H. Kim (2007). Small worlds, infinite possibilities. *Strategic Entrepreneurship Journal*, **1** (1), 147–65.

Boice, R. (2000). *Advice for New Faculty Members: Nihil Nimus*. Boston: Allyn and Bacon.

Campbell, D.T. (1969). Variation and selective retention in socio-cultural evolution. *General Systems*, **14**, 69–85.

Elbow, P. (1998). *Writing with Power*. New York: Oxford University Press.

Fiet, J.O. (2002). *The Systematic Search for Entrepreneurial Discoveries*. Westport, CT: Quorum Books.

Guimerà, R., B. Uzzi, J. Spiro and L.A.N. Amaral (2005). Team assembly mechanisms determine collaboration network structure and team performance. *Science*, **308** (29 April), 697–702.

Langer, E. (1989). *Mindfullness*. Reading, MA: Addison-Wesley.

Langer, E. (2009). *Counterclockwise: Mindful Health and the Power of Possibility*. New York: Ballantine Books.

Zander, R.S. and B. Zander (2000). *The Art of Possibility*. Boston: Harvard Business School Press.

3.   The missing conversation

Jay B. Barney

Barney, Jay: Now for something entirely different. Much of the conversation last night (and especially this morning) seems to have been aimed primarily at our junior scholars. I suppose my conversation today is aimed primarily at senior scholars, both in entrepreneurship and in the field of management more generally. I want to talk about what I'm going to call 'the missing conversation.' My goal today, especially for the senior scholars, is literally to inspire some of you to change your research agendas. I use the word 'inspire' carefully.

Don Hambrick (1994) issued a challenge to the Academy of Management in his presidential speech that was later published in the *Academy of Management Review* (*AMR*). The title of his article was 'What if the Academy actually mattered?' In this article Professor Hambrick hypothesizes the existence of an alternative to the Academy of Management that he calls 'the Society for Administrative Science,' or SAS. Not the best acronym in the world; but nevertheless, it would be an alternative professional organization that has as its mission to promote research and teaching that will enhance the administrative effectiveness and overall functioning of organizational enterprises. In this hypothetical world that Professor Hambrick generates, he notes, the SAS has been: instrumental in creating a Nobel Prize in administrative science; instrumental in writing a code of managerial ethics that is widely accepted by many firms; instrumental in creating a President's Council of administrative advisors; and helpful in advising the Polish government on transforming its economy. Note this paper was originally written in the 1970s.

The article goes on to suggest that the Academy could matter in at least two ways: first, it might matter for practicing managers (that is, the work we do might actually make a difference for people in practice); second, he also suggests that it could matter for discussions of broader social and economic policy. I want to talk briefly about both of these areas where the Academy could actually matter. I'm going to propose that while we spend a fair amount of time with respect to the first point, we do not dismiss the second. Indeed, the second way we could matter is what I am labeling as 'the missing conversation.'

Of course, there is a fair amount of controversy with respect to the implications of our research in the Academy of Management for practice. For example, several articles (Ghoshal, 2005; Pfeffer and Fong, 2002) suggest that our research has either been irrelevant or, even worse, bad for practice.

I have a slightly different view on this than these articles. My view is that if you examine the cumulative impact of our research in the Academy of Management, that it has actually been rather fundamental and very large. Consider just a few examples.

I think organizational behavior has had a very strong impact on the growth of a more participatory approach to management. I'm old enough now to remember my first consulting project in 1980 with a Fortune 500 company. All we did in that project was to argue with senior management about the importance of adopting a more consultative and participative approach to decision-making. This is now taken for granted. OB [organizational behavior] and OT [organization theory] scholars have been deeply involved in teaching and diffusing this perspective.

Thinking more broadly about business schools, I think the field of finance has fundamentally altered the way that we think about capital markets and the way they operate (sometimes for the good and sometimes for the bad). In my home field of strategy there is no doubt that there are certain strategy models and frameworks that have become de facto standards in practice. These are just some examples of our cumulative impact. The problem we have (with many criticisms of our research and its impact on practice) is the assumption that every paper we write has to have some practical implications. My view is that the unit of analysis for evaluating practical impact is not the paper. Papers are usually designed to push a particular research agenda forward, not to inform practice.

However, the cumulative impact of numerous papers can have a fundamental impact on practice conversations. Just because a research paper published in a journal on cancer research does not have direct practical implications, it does not mean that this research has not had an impact on cancer treatments. So, too, not every research paper in management has direct implications for practice; but that does not mean that research *collectively* has not had an impact on practice. Most active management scholars, and not just management scholars, do research that is designed to be read only by other research scholars and our mothers. Some of this work has implications for management, but I call this a 'happy accident.' It turns out that some of the research questions we ask are inherently interesting to managers; and so that's a good thing, and as a 'happy accident,' some of those things can actually have a nice impact. As I tell my assistant professors and my associate professors, 'If you write an article for which the purpose is to try and help managers, you are not writing an article for any journal. What you're doing is consulting.' Consulting is fine, but do not confuse the two – consulting and scholarship. We write articles to solve theoretically interesting questions, whether they have practical implications or not. Now it turns out that it is sometimes the case that they do have practical implications, and that's the 'happy accident.' As you get more senior and more experienced, you can start looking in other directions. And I think another 20 percent of our research-active management scholars actually do work for practicing managers directly – trying to affect that conversation – and that's where a lot of the translation work comes from. My sense is that there's a market out there for these ideas, and there are a lot of people who are influenced by them. While I respect my colleagues who sort of decry the lack of connection between our research and practice, I think they miss the point because they've used the wrong unit of analysis, which is the paper rather than the cumulative impact.

So, while we can all agree that more needs to be done, we need not conclude that nothing has been done with regard to practice. But that's the conversation we've had and need to continue to have.

I want to talk about the 'missing conversation.' The missing conversation is: What are the implications of management research (whether it's strategy, entrepreneurship, organizational behavior, human resources and so forth) for the economic policy and broader societal issues we face? I want to present to you a series of what I'll call 'missed opportunities' – opportunities where the theories that we use as scholars in our scholarly work could have had a fundamental impact on changing the conversation around certain social and economic policy issues; and that if we had been involved in that conversation, things would have been better.

The first example is from the S&L [savings and loan] crisis in the 1980s. There was massive deregulation in the savings and loan industry in the 1980s. The federal government allowed savings and loan companies, who had historically only loaned money for small homes and mobile homes, to start making loans on large complicated commercial real estate projects overnight. Now, what does our theory tell us about what the implications of that move are going to be?

Traditional economics adopts the assumption that the skills and capabilities needed to make those different kinds of loans are very mobile; therefore firms will learn quickly how to make them profitable. However, our theories say that those kinds of resources and skills are in fact not mobile; they are very sticky and take a long time to learn and develop. And if you let S&Ls (overnight) try to diversify in ways that do not build on some core competencies and skills, they will fail. They failed.

If we had been part of that conversation, I'm not sure that the deregulation would've gone the same way. I'm not arguing against deregulation in this context; I'm arguing against the failure to consider the underlying resource-based challenges associated with it.

Sarbanes-Oxley is another conversation. It strikes me that much of the conversation about Sarbanes-Oxley was led by accountants in an attempt to try to create something they might call 'full transparency.' Our theory says that some of the most critical sources of sustained competitive advantages are intangible assets that are never likely to ever be transparent. That conversation was never included in this debate; therefore, the debate about Sarbanes-Oxley has suffered and the costs of Sarbanes-Oxley activities continue to rise (without getting to the core issues inside the company in terms of the control).

Consider anti-trust policy. This is not a partisan comment. However, it strikes me as strange that our current and historical anti-trust policies represent some sort of weird combination of structure, conduct and performance logic, and economics and political expediency, instead of having conversations of social and economic policy that are based in theory that we actually know. Some of the theories we know, for example, offer that one reason firms can dominate a market is not because they're engaging in anti-competitive behavior, but because they actually meet customer needs more effectively. This was an idea originally proposed by Harold Demsetz (1973) and central to findings in strategy and entrepreneurship – but it's not in the conversation about anti-trust. We're not part of that conversation.

Consider international development. There is something in economics called 'endogenous growth theory' that takes a very macro approach to understanding international development. It doesn't recognize that international development typically (as entrepreneurship has told us) really comes at a much more micro level, as individual entrepreneurs create new companies. Endogenous growth theory turns out not to work that well, although we have spent trillions of dollars over three decades trying to eradicate poverty around the world and have made remarkably little progress. During that same period of time, there has been economic development in Taiwan and South Korea, but it has been driven largely by entrepreneurial activities and not by the macro-economic approach that has dominated most policy discussions. Again, we're not part of that conversation.

Consider also the impact of tax policy on entrepreneurial behavior. There are conversations about capital gains taxes, about the death tax and tax on estates. There was research that was done a few years ago that showed that one of the reasons entrepreneurs engage in certain activities is so that they can leave a legacy for their children and grandchildren. What is the impact of the estate tax changes that are being proposed on the level of entrepreneurial activity in our economy? I don't know the answer to that question. It's a question the people in this group who are listening to this and are involved in this conversation should be addressing. It strikes me, but we're not at the policy table.

Consider the current financial crisis. There are lots of things we can talk about here. My personal favorite is the Fiat/Chrysler merger. Again, this is a non-partisan comment. However, we already know that realizing synergies across mergers is a very low probability event. It is likely to be an even lower probability in a shotgun wedding between Fiat and Chrysler. Fiat is going to teach Chrysler how to make small cars to sell to the United States? The business part of that conversation is not taking place; it's dominated by other more political parts of the conversation.

Consider the relationship between compensation and risk-taking. Some of these conversations are also something that we (as management scholars) should be able to participate in, but we haven't. We've ceded these incredibly important conversations to the economists and policy researchers, or worse, to the accountants and lawyers (even though the models that we all know actually have really important implications for these discussions). Indeed, I think I can say that we have failed part of our fiduciary responsibility as scholars because we have not systemically engaged in these conversations.

Now I'm going to share with you my own personal journey about how I came to these conclusions. It began when I was invited to attend an initial reading of the new FTC [Federal Trade Commission] and Department of Justice regulations for regulating high-velocity, high-technology environments. The purpose of these regulations was to prevent the next Microsoft from occurring. The proposed regulations imagined (ironically) a 12-step process for regulating these high-velocity environments. The first step was to 'identify all relevant technologies.'

Well that's the problem, isn't it? Because that's the thing you can't do in these high-velocity environments. We have a regulatory regime that assumes away the reality we know exists in these environments. How are you going to be able to identify every technology in every garage in Silicon Valley or in Boston or in Connecticut?

That was an interesting experience.

I then started trying to apply some basic management principles through a relationship I had with the Columbus Public School District. If you think about a school (like a high school), it's actually a medium-sized business in terms of total assets, the number of employees, the total revenues that come into the school from taxes and things like that. It's actually like running a medium-sized business, and in Columbus public schools (and this is actually very typical) the principal in these schools, who should act or could act something like a plant manager in a diversified corporation, will typically have $10,000–$15,000 discretionary budget. In Columbus, half of that money has to be used to buy toilet paper and other supplies.

In other words, this school district is massively centralized in decision-making authority. Teachers are given teaching plans, independent of the specific needs, wants or desires of the kids in their classes. In general, management theory suggests that it is best to push decision-making down as close as possible to the customer. If the customer is the student in this context, that decision-making authority doesn't seem to be happening.

So we had conversations trying to make this happen by empowering principals. After two years, I decided that the only way I could make significant progress in this area is if I abandoned every other thing I was doing and focused exclusively on making schools better. It's a very tough change process.

So, that led to a third activity. This is a course that Professor Sharon Alvarez and I teach on International Development and Micro Enterprise at Ohio State University. We teach the course and then we take a group of students to rural Bolivia, in what is known as the Alto Plano. The Alto Plano is at 12,500 to 13,500 feet; so a bunch of 'flatlanders' go there and we all have a hard time breathing and eating and sleeping, and bathrooms are holes in the ground – and it's an interesting experience. What we do there is we take our MBA students and work with villages to try to create entrepreneurial businesses.

So let me tell you a story about applying resource-based theory to economic development in a village called Muruamaya. Muruamaya is a village of 200 people scattered over a 30-square-mile area. I have some pictures. These are some of the kids that were in our village.

We were trying to find an entrepreneurial opportunity in this village. We were meeting with the students while we were in this village and asking: what is this village's source of competitive advantage? What makes them distinctive?

All the villages have weavers. They use very, very archaic hand-weaving looms. But all the villages in the area weave the same products and they're of marginal quality. The women gather together a few times a week, do the weaving, and then they take all the stuff once a month or so out to La Paz, sit on the sidewalk and (along with another thousand villagers) they all sell about the same thing.

This is obviously not a very high-margin business model. So our question was, how can we take their weaving skills and generate a competitive advantage for them?

So we started thinking about products; but we know products are not likely to be a source of sustained competitive advantage. So we started thinking, 'What makes this village distinctive?' And the answer was their relationship with Ohio State (because we only went to that village). That distinguishes them from every other village.

So how do you take advantage of that relationship and leverage these weaving capabilities? You have them make Ohio State scarves. So this is an officially licensed Ohio State scarf (100 percent alpaca), that is made by women on the Alta Plano and other parts of Bolivia. We imported 200 last year and they're $49.99.

The student group who was with us formed a not-for-profit organization to import them and manage that process. We've ordered 2,000 for this year.

Two thousand scarves. If we get 2,000 scarves and we sell them at that price and we get the margin back to the individuals in the village, what that does is take the average income of the women that are associated with this weaving effort from $2 a day to $12 a day. And that is big enough so that they can let their children stay in school, so they can graduate and go to high school, and (sometimes) go to college.

Now, this business is also scalable. We're already in conversations with the University of Michigan to make officially licensed Michigan scarves – and we'd like to spread this out through the Big 10. If we do all of the Big 10 (and each Big 10 school does 2,000 scarves), then we have 600 women in the Alta Plano of Bolivia whose income goes from $2 a day to $12 a day; and we now have made a difference – a huge difference. We're already making a difference in a few lives and there's opportunity for more.

Now, that is the practice of entrepreneurship. That is the application of research-based theory in as practical a way as you can – to address a social policy need. These photos are some of the kids that will benefit from this process. This is the school that we visited. And here is one of the weavers; you can see the high technology that's in the background.

What do we do next? If we take this challenge seriously, what do we do next? Assistant professors, associate professors – you do exactly what you've always done and I don't think you change. I think what you do is you write papers for other professors and hope to get them published, and try to get them published in the top journals. I'm not asking for heroes here.

Professor Pfeffer (2007), in one of his papers, calls for changes to become more socially conscious in our activities. To do that, he proposes that we change the promotion and tenure decision and change the decision-making system with the journals. That is not going to happen, so let's not even pretend that that's going to happen. If we have to wait until the university changes in order to do these things, then they're not going to happen. So let's not pretend.

So, assistant and associate professors: do your thing and get published. My own experience is that any strategy that requires heroes for its implementation is guaranteed to fail. Maybe you can broaden your samples. Maybe you can discuss some social policy implications in your papers.

Point two: I don't think we should ever abandon the first point that was made by Professor Hambrick (1994), which is that we need to continue to figure out how our work has an impact on practice. If you really want to do just social psychology, or just economics, you should be in a social psychology or economics department and get paid that wage. If you want to do research that has implications for business, then you need to be in the business school, and there is a differential compensation for that.

But my real message is to my senior colleagues, and I chose this topic because I knew that there would be a lot of senior people (that's code for old) here. We need to develop a forum for discussing the implications of strategy and other kinds of research on economic and social policy.

Editors, there are several of you here (including me). We have to create room in our top journals for these kinds of papers. Can we do it? And, really (for my senior colleagues), isn't it time for us to change our personal objective function from just another publication to actually making a difference on a much broader stage, whether that stage is in Washington DC, in Hartford or Bolivia – or any place else in the world?

I gave a version of this talk for the first time at a conference recently held at Emory University, and I was really struck by a Roberto Goizueta quote (the former CEO of Coca-Cola and the individual who endowed the Emory Business School). Referring to the founding of this school, Roberto Goizueta asked, 'Will we have the courage and wisdom . . . to aspire to build a school completely distinctive in its ability to add value to our society?' I think this is a challenge to us as scholars in management. Do we have the courage – and it does take courage – to change the objective you've been very good at for 30 years? Do we have the courage, and then do we have the wisdom to be able to organize it efficiently? That's my challenge for my senior colleagues and for the junior people. This is why we do the work. This is what we have to aspire to. We need to aspire to change our goals from producing just another publication in *AMR* [*Academy of Management Review*] or *AMJ* [*Academy of Management Journal*] to changing lives. Thank you.

Mitchell, Ron: Okay, we're open for Q&A.

Phan, Phil: Jay, that was very good.

Barney, Jay: Thank you.

Phan, Phil: I really appreciate it. But, given your history and the impact that you've had on the Academy, your point about management scholars and entrepreneurship scholars making a difference in the public realm (I think) also deserves a conversation around 'how.' Who are the talking heads? You know, you don't see too many . . .

Barney, Jay: We're not there.

Phan, Phil: We're not there; and somehow finding a way to break into this very (in my opinion) closed space, and be willing to be controversial [is important]. Because [non-rigorous thought] often shows up in these [public forums] and, frankly tends to drive a lot of what I would consider maybe even misguided policies.

Barney, Jay: Yeah. That's right.

Phan, Phil: And that's important. Your encouragement to senior scholars to step out and get into the public forum is very important; but I think to do that, in our day and age, you do have to be controversial and be willing to take a stand.

Barney, Jay: Yeah. I think you're absolutely right and it seems to me that step one is to, in an evangelical way, try to encourage my colleagues to think broadly about this – but then also to get together with a group of smart people and figure out how to organize this. I don't have the answers to those questions, but I know that we can answer them because it's possible to do it. I do know, with respect to the press, that once you get in the loop, you're in the loop; and so it's just a matter of getting into the entry point, and with the right partnerships. Or if you're thinking about partnering with some other business organizations that bring scholarship to bear on the questions of the day, I think there could be a lot of potential. I'm thinking of some sort of blogging kind of thing. So we are making progress here, but it's early days. You're exactly right.

McKinley-Floyd, Lydia: Thank you so much. To your comments I can only say 'amen.'

Barney, Jay: Thank you.

McKinley-Floyd, Lydia: I think about my own experiences. Now being one of the old heads (my hair is dyed, so you can't see all the gray), and sitting in the B-School at the University of Chicago and asking questions about social responsibility and having the professor say 'there's no social responsibility in business,' and thinking about all of these issues that you raised – I think they're very much on point. But my question is: how realistic is it that journal editors (not deans necessarily, but that journal editors) will indeed embrace your ideas and make a portion of, if not a significant effort, to include this kind of a scholarship?

Barney, Jay: Frankly, in the short to medium term, zero chance. I mean, the system is in place. I am not criticizing the system; it functions very well for what it does. I'm asking it to do something differently. And so that's why I don't look to people who still have the 'publish or perish' criteria they have to meet to help make these changes. I look to my colleagues for whom the next *AMR* or *AMJ* or *SMJ* [*Strategic Management Journal*] (or whatever it is), is not going to change their life very much. And I want to be absolutely clear. I am not in any way suggesting that this effort should take the place of ongoing research. I will always personally be engaged in numerous research activities to continue to sharpen the saw, as they say, and to continue to learn and do those things. So, I don't see this as one or the other. We have to do, to some extent, both. That said, I and others like me are in a position where we have more flexibility. Many of us have chosen not to take that flexibility in this direction. For those who are still research active, this is something that I think that we need to think about. So in the short to medium term, I'm not optimistic at all. I will say this: you know how economists dominate these conversations we see on TV? That was not always the case. The field of economics – at one of their annual meetings, a group of very senior economists, most of whom had won Nobel prizes or would win Nobel Prizes – said, 'We need to get economic theory more into public space. How are we going to do that?' And they actually had meetings in the 1960s and built up a strategy for making that happen. Well, they have a huge first-mover advantage. There are huge barriers to entry. But, you know what? We have better ideas. I won't get into that, but we just have better ideas that are more in tune to what's actually happening in organizations. So, I think that's where an opportunity still lies.

McKinley-Floyd, Lydia: So are you suggesting this kind of research should not be published?

Barney, Jay: No, no, no, no, no, no. I would love for it to be published, and really good work in this area will get published. So there's emerging work in social entrepreneurship and there's some interesting work in corporate responsibility. So there are some things on the margin. The problem is, even *that* work (as good as it is), is still not part of the public debate around the policies of the day. So, even when there is good work, we still haven't met that last link – and that's the challenge. That's what the field appropriately points out.

Mosakowski, Elaine: Yeah, hi. I want to ask you two questions. Or maybe the first is more of a comment. The second is a question.

Barney, Jay: Sure.

Mosakowski, Elaine: The comment is, I worry a little bit that you are too pessimistic in your predictions . . . From my own personal experience, pushing through more of a programmatic venture, as well as venturing into the research area with social values and whatnot – I'm not sure it's as bleak a picture as you paint. And in that regard (I happen to be married to a dean of a business school) I think deans of business schools, both coming from academic backgrounds or business backgrounds, are definitely starting to get it.

Barney, Jay: Oh, yeah. I agree with that.

Mosakowski, Elaine: And part of the reason they're getting it is because donors, who are their number one constituents show that that is what they're really, really interested in—

Barney, Jay: Donors want to support this.

Mosakowski, Elaine: Yeah. Exactly.

Barney, Jay: Absolutely.

Mosakowski, Elaine: They want to support that. So, maybe we're a little bit where . . .

Barney, Jay: I don't think deans are the problem. I don't think donors are the problem.

Mosakowski, Elaine: It's us.

Barney, Jay: I think we are the problem.

Mosakowski, Elaine: That's what my point was going to be; exactly that it's us. This is almost like (not that I've ever been) an AA [Alcoholics

Anonymous] meeting, but coming forward and instead of saying, 'Hi, I'm Elaine and I'm an alcoholic,' saying, 'Hi, I'm Elaine and I'm interested in social entrepreneurship and innovation.' It's a little bit like these dark secrets that we carry around, and I think . . .

Barney, Jay: Well, I revealed mine.

Mosakowski, Elaine: Exactly. Yeah. Because I think the perception that interest in social entrepreneurship and innovation maybe made us less serious academics or whatnot. Okay. My question is that, obviously you are one of the major founders of the resource-based view of strategy, and you talk about bringing our theories both to practice, as well as having social impact; but the major tenet of the resource-based view of strategy is really based on notions of scarcity and competition – and I wonder if those are the appropriate ideas in a social context. And, if not, might you consider writing a resource-based view for social organizations?

Barney, Jay: Okay. We obviously won't have time in this context to have that debate, but the point is that that's the debate we should have. Okay? The answer is (by the way), no. But, setting that aside, I mean it really is a conversation asking, 'Is social entrepreneurship fundamentally different from entrepreneurship?' That's a question that we actually debated at a recent conference. I thought it was a fascinating conversation, and that's one that we have to take forward and continue. So, good questions.

Mitchell, Ron: Is there one more question, please?

Langlois, Richard: Jay, I don't mean this comment entirely seriously.

Barney, Jay: Okay.

Langlois, Richard: You criticized the deregulation of the savings and loans . . .

Barney, Jay: Sure.

Langlois, Richard: . . . and said that all of a sudden, the savings and loans were extending their capabilities illegitimately to areas that they didn't know anything about.

Barney, Jay: No. It was legitimate because it was legal, but it was not clear that it was wise.

Langlois, Richard: Wise. But now, of course, you're suggesting the same thing for management scholars; that they should extend their capabilities to things that they had before talked about. I don't know that I mean that entirely seriously; but, as you know, I'm a capabilities person.

Barney, Jay: Sure.

Langlois, Richard: But, I still have some allegiance to economics . . .

Barney, Jay: Sure.

Langlois, Richard: . . . and I feel I should defend economics a little bit. Economists would wonder whether the problem with the savings and loan was 'capabilities' or whether it was 'incentives' – that the insurance that was being offered to depositors in savings and loans wasn't actuarially fair, and so loan officers had an incentive to do the wrong thing, and it was external institutions, not so much . . .

Barney, Jay: And I don't mean to imply that there's only one explanation going on here. And both explanations are relevant and could be subject to great conversation and debate using a more managerial approach to things. So we do have theories about incentives. We do have theories about institutions and those kinds of things. And also, we have theories about capabilities. It did strike me, however, that conversations around policy that recognize that capabilities, resources, and knowledge are sticky and not completely mobile, do allow us to have a slightly different conversation on more of these issues than what most economists would have. Thanks.

REFERENCES

Demsetz, H. (1973). Industry structure, market rivalry, and public policy. *Journal of Law and Economics*, **16** (1), 1–9.

Ghoshal, S. (2005). Bad management theories are destroying good management practices. *Academy of Management Learning & Education*, **4** (1), 75–91.

Hambrick, D. (1994). What if the Academy actually mattered? *Academy of Management Review*, **19** (1), 11–16.

Pfeffer, J. (2007). Financial incentives can create bad employee behavior. *Journal of Economic Perspectives*, **21** (4), 115–34.

Pfeffer, J. and C.T. Fong (2002). The end of business schools? Less success than meets the eye. *Academy of Management Learning & Education*, **1**, 78–96.

4. Entrepreneurship research and the maturation of the field

Michael A. Hitt

Dino, Rich: Ladies and gentlemen, it is my absolute privilege to introduce research exemplar, Professor Michael Hitt.

Hitt, Michael: It's a real pleasure to be here. I enjoy the opportunity to interact with such a great group of colleagues, and it is also an excellent opportunity to interact with people from all over the world (even though the interaction is a little less personalized). So please accept my not only congratulations on an outstanding Conference, but also my 'thank you' for inviting me to this Conference and the opportunity.

I don't want to say the same thing as everybody else, and I speculated on what others would talk about and then I tried to add something different (and hopefully of value). So, I focus on entrepreneurship and maturation of the field. Not that I have better information than others on these topics, but they are worthy of our consideration. I will first focus on the field, and then (specifically because of this Conference), on research.

So let's take a trip back to 1988 – a little over 20 years ago. Porter and McKibbin (1988), two business school deans at the time, authored a report for the Association to Advance Collegiate Schools of Business (AACSB) on the future of business education. Lyman Porter (Dean at the University of California at Irvine at the time – not Michael Porter), was a very well-known and respected scholar in organizational behavior, and played a prominent role in the development of the study on which the report was based. The report explored the expected foci for business schools as they moved into the 21st century. There are multiple topics of importance in that report. It represents a partial follow-up to the earlier report that prompted the significant development of research in business schools, and thereby the growth and popularity of business schools (the changes and development of business schools began in earnest in the 1960s). Porter and McKibbin noted five fields that they thought would be very prominent in the development of business schools for the 21st century. I will not discuss all five, but 'international' was one of them (e.g., globalization).

Importantly, entrepreneurship was one of those five that they felt was critical for business schools to develop and (involving major curriculum and research programs) to be at the forefront in the 21st century. Being included in this report emphasizes the importance of this field, and the perceived importance even 20 years ago. We all know entrepreneurship was important at that time, but having this emphasis from prominent business school deans looking to the future suggests the critical nature of the entrepreneurship field.

In support of the report's conclusion regarding entrepreneurship, Katz (2006) examined the development of the field – especially the education dimensions. He stated that the entrepreneurship field was mature, but that it lacked legitimacy. By maturity, he meant that the content of the field as taught in courses was well known and accepted. He noted that 1,400 universities had courses in entrepreneurship (not necessarily complete programs). He projected that just in a few years about 1,600 universities worldwide would be teaching courses in entrepreneurship. One of the ways which he judged agreement on the content was a survey of basic entrepreneurship textbooks. In addition, in a recent five-year period, there was a 58.4 percent increase in the number of entrepreneurship chairs funded (Katz, 2004). This is an important issue worth highlighting. While I do not have comparative data, I would guess that rivals funding for endowed positions for any other discipline within business (or frankly throughout the university) for education and research.

Katz (2006) suggested that entrepreneurship lacked normative and cognitive legitimacy. Green (2009) concluded that entrepreneurship education was going to become increasingly multidisciplinary – and include disciplines external to business. I think the field already is multidisciplinary and has been to some degree for some time; yet, they concluded that it will become even more interdisciplinary, and that entrepreneurship will not be (and should not be assumed to be) the sole domain of business schools. And again, I think that has some relevance for our discussion of entrepreneurship research; it is and will become more interdisciplinary in future years.

Legitimacy is a topic worth further examination. I think legitimacy is important for the field of entrepreneurship. Some likely believe that it is already legitimate, and frankly, if you are doing research in this area, you want to believe that entrepreneurship has achieved legitimacy in some areas. I also think legitimacy is in the eyes of the beholder. And, to determine legitimacy, we must identify the important stakeholders with whom you want to believe entrepreneurship to be legitimate. Legitimacy from a research standpoint refers to acceptance primarily from our colleagues in business disciplines. This form of legitimacy is important particularly for the younger scholars because reward systems are critical for promotion, tenure and so on. Thus, what is valued in order to receive rewards is very important; your field and the work you do must to be viewed as legitimate by your colleagues. I believe that the primary concern of legitimacy is in the realm of research. What and how we teach are unimportant, but even the content of what we teach should be based on the research – the theories and results of our research.

Speaking to the legitimacy of research in entrepreneurship, Candy Brush chaired a committee for the Entrepreneurship Division of the Academy of Management that primarily focused doctoral education in entrepreneurship (Brush et al, 2003). The committee took multiple actions, but a portion of effort involved developing and conducting a survey of business school deans. The survey was a complex paper based on the results, published in the *Journal of Management* (Brush et al, 2003). I encourage you to examine the article if you are interested in more detail. While the results are about six years old (and we must acknowledge that entrepreneurship is a dynamic field), some conclusions are worth noting. For example, business school deans were strongly supportive of entre-preneurship education. Unfortunately, their evaluation of research in the field differed from education. The kindest way to put it is that their evalu-ation of research in the field was lower. In short, they felt entrepreneur-ship research was not nearly as high quality as the academic programs, the curriculum and related programs. That is bothersome because deans are critical in the reward process. Most of the entrepreneurship doctoral programs identified were in management and in some subdiscipline within; however, a few of them were more interdisciplinary. The most common subdiscipline which housed it was strategic management. The deans rated the doctoral programs in entrepreneurship relatively low as well (about the same as they rated the research). Of course, research and PhD programs are complementary. However, in the last six years there have been a lot of changes; development of the field is occurring at a rapid pace.

There's no doubt that there is a high quantity of research on entrepre-neurship. It is a very popular area in scholarly work, education and prac-tice worldwide. The number of journals specializing in entrepreneurship is more than 40 and continuing to grow. That is a lot of journals to publish research in entrepreneurship. While I do not have comparable data, I would guess that there is no other discipline within business that has that many specialty journals. And entrepreneurship is commonly considered a subdiscipline of management (not a discipline). The problem is that only a few of those journals are very well respected – and they are represented in this room. Now this doesn't count the general management journals that also publish management research (e.g., *Academy of Management*

Journal (*AMJ*), *Journal of Management* (*JOM*) and *Administrative Science Quarterly* (*ASQ*)). So, perhaps two or three of the specialized entrepreneurship journals have respect from deans and your colleagues.

A few years before Duane Ireland became the editor of *AMJ* (he was associate editor at *AMJ*), he analysed the number of articles published in mainline journals – primarily in *AMJ*. The number of entrepreneurship articles in these journals has been increasing, although the total number of them still remains low. The same is occurring with more entrepreneurship articles being published in general business journals, such as *Journal of Financial Economics* and *Journal of Marketing*. So why is that important? It is important because scholars in other fields (outside of the limited but not unimportant group of entrepreneurship scholars) are suggesting this is quality research. It is published along with the work being done in that journal's field. So that adds legitimacy to the work done in entrepreneurship. It is important that entrepreneurship research be published in those journals along with the key journals that specialize in entrepreneurship.

I believe that now (2009), deans in general have a greater understanding of and respect for the field of entrepreneurship. This respect extends to entrepreneurship research to some extent, but there remain some lingering concerns. And the concerns extend beyond deans to colleagues on promotion and tenure committees. Thus, colleagues in other business disciplines are important for legitimacy. The quality research that you do is important. Where you publish your research is important. However, I believe that the legitimacy of entrepreneurship research is starting to increase. Its acceptance is gaining and I am optimistic about the future. Using Duane's comments [R. Duane Ireland: Chapter 5], 'the glass is half full.' In fact I think it's more than half full. We have more well-trained scholars. Look around this room; it is primarily younger scholars who have entered the field of entrepreneurship. They are better trained, overall. And I'm not trying to denigrate any of you who have gray hair – I'm in the same boat. And I believe that the current entrepreneurship research done by a lot of people (the young people in this room and others who are gravitating to this field from other related disciplines) are meeting high standards – and their research is being published in respected journals (as noted earlier). So as we have more people in the field doing quality research, and we also have more people who can do a better job of reviewing. These are mutually reinforcing to improve the quality of entrepreneurship research that is published. Of course, quality editorial direction is important as well.

Lastly, the research opportunities in entrepreneurship are substantial. I think we have only barely tipped the iceberg in this field. The opportunities are incredibly rich, and that means that the future is very bright. Thus full legitimacy is coming soon, where people won't question it anymore.

The deans are charged with recruiting money to support the educational mission and other important activities of the colleges of business. They can raise money about as easily in entrepreneurship as they can in any other field (even compared to accounting and finance). That is one of the reasons deans find the entrepreneurship field to be attractive – partly because donors often are attracted to it. And frequently, donors like to see education programs, thus providing impetus to their development. In my opinion (but I'm not an expert), many of the entrepreneurship educational programs are quite good – and some are excellent. I think they are very creative. Many things we do in entrepreneurship education could be transferred and be used in the other disciplines in business, for example. Entrepreneurship programs are often very creative in the teaching and opportunities for learning. Such opportunities for students aren't necessarily available in some of the other business disciplines, including management.

Yet, although there is much that can be learned from entrepreneurship programs (and the donors gravitate to it), we also need to be championing the entrepreneurship research that is done. At least a few donors also like to see entrepreneurship research. Frankly, effective teaching and research produce the most effective entrepreneurship programs overall.

So let's talk about doing quality research. We have already had several presentations yesterday and the night before that discussed quality research. These presentations highlighted some key points.

Yesterday, Sharon Alvarez [Chapter 15] talked about what it takes to be a good researcher. An article currently in press at *SEJ* [*Strategic Entrepreneurship Journal*] by Baron and Henry (2010) explains expert performance. They build on some of Henry's prior work and the work of others in psychology (especially Ericsson and colleagues, e.g., Ericsson, Krampe and Tesch-Romer, 1993; Ericsson and Charness, 1994; Charness, Krampe and Mayer, 1996) who have done a lot on expert performance. They emphasize that innate talent really doesn't explain the outstanding performance by people in any field or endeavor (e.g., music, science, art, etc.). Many believe it takes innate talent to be a special artist. While a person may need to have innate talent, it alone does not explain exceptional performance. Sharon said 'Everybody in here is smart,' but more is required. Intellect is not the primary differentiator in our field. It is a necessary but insufficient condition to do quality research and to be exceptional at doing it.

Consider your PhD students – the ones you have now and the other ones you have had in the past. What has made the difference in the ones who are truly successful? Highly motivated, committed, goal-directed and learning-oriented actions make the difference. First, to do quality research, you must be highly motivated to do it: you have to be motivated to get the PhD, you have to be motivated to be in this profession, but you also have to be motivated to do high-quality research and to stay with it when you encounter challenges. So perseverance and commitment to do high-quality work are very important. I'll quickly review a couple of my own recent experiences with papers and research projects.

A few years ago I had a project that I was working on in which we had the idea, developed it, collected data, analysed it, wrote a draft and presented a paper at the Academy of Management conference. We then obtained additional feedback on the research and paper from colleagues. Then, the next natural step was to go to a journal. But, I still had concerns that we needed to do more to enhance the quality of the work before submitting it to a top journal. I really liked this research and felt it had potential to make a contribution. My colleagues wanted to submit the manuscript; they were younger and they had reasons for desiring submission (such as the evaluation time clock). But if you send a paper in before it is ready, it is unlikely to be accepted for publication. Thus, I recommended that we not submit the paper. I then presented the paper at several research seminars at other universities. That is not something I normally do, but I received some excellent feedback from two different places – one on the theory and one on the methods. Based on the feedback, we collected more data and worked on the theory. Both actions improved the paper. We then submitted it to the journal and received a high-risk R&R [revise and resubmit]. Now, if we had not taken the additional actions, we would not have received the high-risk R&R – it likely would have been rejected. Fortunately, we were able to develop it and eventually the paper was accepted and published in *AMJ*. So that's one story where we had to have a little patience and perseverance.

The second story relates to a major project that actually started several years ago with two of my PhD students. The topic required a significant amount of data which, although available, was not easy to obtain or format. It required intensive work to build the dataset. First, we worked on the data, analysed it and took a short version (abstract) to a resource-based review (RBV) workshop. One of my young co-authors discussed our research and paper ideas at the workshop and received a healthy critique. He came away from the workshop with concerns about the efficacy of the research. Then, our team had a question of, 'Should we invest more time on this, especially if the idea may not be attractive to scholars in the field?' But after discussing it, we decided to keep moving forward. So we developed it further, completed a paper and sent it to an academic conference. We got it accepted and we presented it, but the feedback we received from the reviewers and from the audience in the presentation was 'lukewarm.'

The feedback was helpful, but not strongly positive. My two colleagues then asked the question, 'Should we be investing more time?' They had work (manuscripts) of their own that they were moving along, so they were trying to decide where to invest their time. However, I still believed this project had potential; thus, we continued working on it. We developed the paper further (theory and analyses) based on the feedback received, and then we sent it out for collegial reviews. One of those colleagues is in this room, and I'm going to recognize him because his feedback was very important and helpful. Joe Mahoney (who gave us feedback on this paper) understood well the context of the data, which was professional baseball. Some of our colleagues have used professional sports samples without success. They sometimes received feedback that the sports organization did not match well the context of business organizations. So, we really worked hard to justify the use of the sample for the question the research addressed. After receiving feedback from several scholars, we developed it further and then finally submitted it to a major journal. We concluded the process with an acceptance and publication in a major journal (*AMJ*). Although very pleased with the outcome, it required commitment and perseverance in the face of weak or negative feedback early on.

Therefore, you have to be committed to a learning orientation. Learn from the feedback you get and use it. In each of the stages mentioned above, the feedback was critical to improving the quality of the papers – increasing the potential for a positive decision on the first round at good journals. And then we received a lot of feedback from the journal that helped us develop the manuscripts further. They were much better papers because of the feedback from reviewers and editorial direction.

So, if you want to do quality research, you have to be patient and you should view the research as part of a journey in a long career and not only a short-term goal. Certainly as a young professor, tenure is very important and most of us were, or are, short-term oriented at that time. But in retrospect, the best work I have done was when I used a long-term lens, in which I invested effort and even ignored some negative feedback. However, it was also very difficult to do.

I had a dean once tell me that I did good research but I was never going to make it in the field because I worked in too many disparate areas (which I did and I still do to some degree). But I decided that I'm going to do what I want to do. I want to follow research questions in which I am interested because that is one of the reasons I came into this profession. But I also believe that you leave no stone unturned in doing research. Invest your best effort into each project and paper. Do not send a manuscript out until it's ready; but also don't wait too long before submitting it to a journal. You have to balance the opposing forces of continuing to improve the manuscript but not waiting too long. There's no perfect manuscript – even those published. The field is dynamic and thus is constantly changing. The field may change in ways to devalue the content of your research if you wait too long.

I have one other point to make related to changes in the field. When I was editor of *AMJ*, we gave an R&R to a young scholar along with feedback on some things he had to do in order to improve the work and increase its probability of publication. He called me and said, 'I just wanted to make sure that a specific point was very important, because it's going to be difficult to do.' I said, 'Okay, what is it?' He said, 'By the way – I checked the article you had in *AMJ* 10 years ago and you didn't do it.' I said, 'No, it met the standards of the field at that time; if I were trying to publish that same work today, I would have to do it or it would not be published. And you have to do it.'

In summary, you should leave no stone unturned in order to do quality research. Have patience and persevere. You also must be goal-directed and highly motivated to do quality research. Lastly, I believe that entrepreneurship research is increasing in quantity and quality. In fact, it is one of the reasons that we established the *Strategic Entrepreneurship Journal*. We identified an opportunity where the field is growing in quantity and in also quality. As such, there is a need for high-quality journal space that values and publishes quality research. There is greater depth and breadth in entrepreneurship research.

I enjoyed the discussion of the articles that are published in the journals. It displays the quality research being done in the field, making me believe that the future is bright. But the future is most bright in research for the motivated, for the committed, for the goal-directed and the learning-oriented scholars.

Dino, Rich: We will open the session for Q&A.

Veiga, Jack: It seems to me we have seen similar patterns in fields – at least I have in my career. I recall at one time when strategy research was viewed as a bunch of idiots doing case studies.

Hitt, Michael: That's true.

Veiga, Jack: And that's all that people published were case studies. I remember starting out in organizational behavior and colleagues asking, 'You teach touchy feely stuff; what could you possibly teach them?' If you think back, a lot of what we did was based on what people told us worked. We didn't have quality research to really build our lectures on or our learning on, and I think the same thing is probably true now of entre-preneurship. I think back to the early days when we had entrepreneur-ship classes here in Connecticut and the faculty members were generally non-research faculty. They filled their classes largely with entrepreneurs themselves, and the perception became fairly loud and clear. 'They can't teach that stuff.' In fact, if you go talk to someone in the public and say, 'I teach entrepreneurship,' nine out of ten will say, 'You can teach that?' So I think the field has come a long way, as you've said, and I think part of the legitimacy question probably still deals with that issue of 'Can you teach it?' I think when the day comes when you say, 'We absolutely can teach it,' the field will have arrived. What do you think?

Hitt, Michael: Actually, I agree with you. That's why I said earlier, even though Jerry Katz had said the field was mature (largely based on the content), I don't believe that it is yet mature. I believe that there's a con-nection between the research and the teaching. In fact, I believe strongly that the content of what we teach in the classes should be based on the theory and the research. Thus, even though maybe we have agreement on the content (in the textbooks) right now, that doesn't mean that is where we want to be.

The content in the field is dynamic, similar to strategic management. So, I believe that the entrepreneurship field is developing and it will continue to change. There is a lag effect with reputations. There is a lag effect as the field improves. It takes a while before others acknowledge that the field has improved. I don't think the field has reached its potential yet but it is improving in quality and quantity, and that is important. It's headed in the direction it should be. Of course, there is a lag effect when a field declines as well, but we don't want to be on that side.

Lumpkin, Tom: I have an entrepreneurship education question to follow up with. What are the implications, advantages and disadvantages (if any) of entrepreneurship education being multidisciplinary?

Hitt, Michael: There are advantages to that. I think one is that it will involve more people – more people from across the university – and the more people involved should produce higher commitment to it overall. For example, those people will also serve on promotion and tenure com-mittees. So, I think that interdisciplinary involvement should heighten the legitimacy and the acceptance.

I think the field will benefit from more inputs. In other business disci-plines and certainly in management, we draw on the other social sciences in particular. But entrepreneurship, probably as much or more than any other discipline, draws on the different disciplines, even in engineering and technology. So, interdisciplinary thinking and involvement should actually enhance both entrepreneurship education and research.

There are also some potential problems – especially with regard to how to manage interdisciplinary involvement. Because of the way universities are structured, multidisciplinary efforts are difficult to manage. We have colleges and departments generally focused around disciplines, and then the rewards, the budgets and the resources tend to flow through that system. A multidisciplinary effort is difficult to overlay onto that system. Higher administration can facilitate these efforts if they desire. They have to ensure that there are resources and that people are rewarded for what they do in those efforts.

Phan, Phil: Mike, I've been reflecting on what you said about the connection between research and the teaching of entrepreneurship being perhaps one of the conditions for its 'eventual arrival' legitimacy-wise. I think certainly one of the things that journals can do, and at the *Journal of Business Venturing* (*JBV*) we've been trying to do (although I would argue not always successfully) is to move authors towards thinking more about the implications of what they find – not only for theory, but also for practice and really also for instruction (for teaching). At *JBV* we have this thing called the 'executive summary' and the point of that really is to have authors think about what the implications are for the person that is supposed to be using that knowledge – both in the entrepreneurial venture as well as in the classroom. I think if editors and authors thought more carefully about that, then perhaps consciously we could move those two dimensions of the field together and achieve what you are talking about.

Hitt, Michael: That's a very good point. What you do in the executive summary is unique relative to most other journals of which I'm aware; so accolades to you for doing that. When authors present managerial implications, they can be useful for the classroom (e.g., in MBA courses that I teach). So I do find that to be helpful to me and thus your point resonates.

I have another point. When I was editor of *AMJ* (even though it was a long time ago), I was often asked to participate in forums. The dean would ask me to talk to business executives or I would be speaking in other settings in which there were executives in the audience. At that time there was an emphasis on questions about academic research and irrelevance. I was the editor of an academic journal and I found myself frequently defending academic research. So I actually started reading articles, and particularly ones we published, to identify practical implications – and I found much of our research did have practical implications. I agree with Jay Barney's point from yesterday [Chapter 3]: that we are not writing the articles for practitioners – most of them are targeted for the scholarly audience. But I actually think that many times implications can be drawn from them.

Fiet, Jim: One of the challenges that I have when I teach a doctoral seminar is that of the evolution of standards. Inevitably what happens is I'll be talking to students about the particular way they ought to handle a research problem, and then they'll read one of my papers from 10 years ago where I didn't do it and then I find myself in the same position you are (as an editor) saying, 'But you have to do it because the field is different now.' I wonder: can you give us any guidance on how you make a decision, as an editor, about when it's time to move on into the next level of sophistication?

Hitt, Michael: That's actually a good question. I don't know that I have an appropriate answer. You rely to some degree on your reviewers because they can play a big role in this to help us identify changes and new trends. As an editor, I am not (and cannot be) a specialist in all areas – even in a specialized field such as entrepreneurship. I certainly could not be for a more general journal such as *AMJ*. I use the reviewers' input, read the manuscript and develop judgments about such issues as, 'Can they develop it?' and 'Can they effectively handle the problems identified?' I think that is where editorial judgment can and should be applied. In some cases, I may go to an extra reviewer to help me make a decision, even where there is good feedback but not enough to provide guidance to the author.

Fiet, Jim: The reason why I asked that question is because when we, as authors, are trying to anticipate this, we would like to make sure that we're not submitting to the review process too early. It would be nice to know: 'Do I really have to deal with endogeneity while inevitably . . .'

Hitt, Michael: The answer is yes.

Fiet, Jim: Well, with that one, that one's answered so I don't have to worry about that. But then there are some other questions. One of the problems that I've had my entire career is: how do I know when my measures are good enough? I've never been able to face that problem.

Hitt, Michael: I will try to answer it as best I can. I think one way to make judgments is to read the most current work in that journal and in other sister journals publishing work similar to what yours is. You don't know if it's right at the precipice and getting ready to move. For example, Shaver's work on endogeneity was published in 1998 (Shaver, 1998). While relevant before that, few in the field gave this potential problem much consideration. And it took a few years for it to reach the mainstream mindset of researchers. In fact, I had a paper published in 1998 (Kochhar & Hitt, 1998) in which a reviewer forced us to control for the reverse causal effect of our dependent variable on the independent variable. It was highly relevant to our study.

Dino, Rich: The unfortunate consequence of a time schedule is that it forces us to leave some things on the table; and I suspect we can probably go on with this session all morning. So if we can have one more question, please.

Mathieu, John: Okay, this one I'm going to toss to you, Mike, but I'd also like other people to speak to it as well. In brief, I worry about the availability heuristic that we've had for the last day here. What we've been featuring are the survivors and the winners, and I worry that may be giving off the 'Disney impression' that the dogs always come home and the underdog always wins. I wonder if you could speak to the signals of when a study should be buried ('We either shouldn't do this or let it go and let's spend our time on other kinds of things') because I think that's as critical a skill for the junior scholar to learn when to persist and when to move on.

Hitt, Michael: Actually, your question is a good one but I am not certain that I have a good answer. I think there are two things you might do. First, I recommend obtaining collegial feedback (in other sessions at this Conference the kind of feedback needed was noted). You really need people that will be critical, objective and truthful with you. However, care should be taken because, as I noted earlier, we received feedback on our baseball study that was lukewarm. It was partly because we hadn't developed it well, and I realized that from the feedback received. We were very fortunate that we continued to listen, learn and develop it; and were able to develop it into a publishable paper – research of which we could be proud. What you have got to do is listen to that feedback and ask yourself: 'Can I do it? Can it really be done if they're asking for certain things?' If for some reason they are recommending changes that cannot be done, maybe you should let it go.

Second, you should be honest with yourself in answering the question, 'When should I let it go?' It is difficult to do because our ego is involved in our research. In many cases I have personally persevered (not anything like Jim Fiet explained in another session [Chapter 15] about his study). I was highly impressed with what Jim did. I once had a paper about which my wife gave me a hard time; she's my worst critic. There was this one paper that I had trouble getting published. It got rejected from several journals; I kept getting the same reviewer, and I wasn't going to get it past this person. I had to find a journal that would not send it to him/her. But, I finally got it published (my wife told me that it was not very good and I should quit trying). To this day, every time I get another cite on that article I tell my wife. I was determined to get it published, but perhaps I should have let it go.

Mathieu, John: Yes, but you're still doing 'Disney.' Tell me about one of the ones that you let go.

Hitt, Michael: Because the paper to which I referred previously perhaps should have been let go, it hasn't had the impact I thought it should. Part of it is where I had to publish it, and I attribute that largely to the reviewer. Maybe I shouldn't have stuck with that as long as I did (I probably did so partly because my wife told me I couldn't). So, I expended some energy on it that might have been more productively invested in other projects.

In summary, you need to listen to your colleagues and you are going to have to be honest with yourself. Yet, I continue to believe that sometimes you also have to persevere. So you should not let it go too soon. If my two young colleagues had been able to make the decision alone, we would have let it go and lost an eventual *AMJ* article. It is a judgment call.

Dino, Rich: Ladies and gentlemen, Professor Michael Hitt. Thank you.

REFERENCES

Baron, R.A. and R.A. Henry (2010). How entrepreneurs acquire the capacity to excel: insights from research on expert performance. *Strategic Entrepreneurship Journal*, **4** (1), 49–65.

Brush, C.G., I.M. Duhaine, W.B. Gartner, A. Stewart et al. (2003). Doctoral education in the field of entrepreneurship. *Journal of Management*, **29**, 309–31.

Charness, N., R. Krampe and U. Mayer (1996). The role of practice and coaching in entrepreneurial skill domains: an international comparison of life-span chess skill acquisition. In K.A. Ericsson (ed.), *The Road to Excellence: The Acquisition of Expert Performance in the Arts and Sciences, Sports, and Games*. Mahwah, NJ: Lawrence Erlbaum Associates, pp. 51–80.

Ericsson, K.A. and N. Charness (1994). Expert performance: its structure and acquisition. *American Psychologist*, **49** (8), 725–47.

Ericsson, K.A., R.T. Krampe and C. Tesch-Romer (1993). The role of deliberate practice in the acquisition of expert performance. *Psychological Review*, **100** (3), 363–406.

Green, W.S. (2009). Entrepreneurship in American higher education. In *Kauffman Thoughtbook 2009*. Kansas City: Ewing Marion Kauffman Foundation.

Katz, J.A. (2004). *2004 Survey of Endowed Positions in Entrepreneurship and Related Fields in the United States*. Kansas City: Ewing Marion Kauffman Foundation.

Katz, J.A. (2006). And another thing. (The 2006 Coleman Foundation White Paper on Entrepreneurship.) Presented at the Annual Meeting of the US Association for Small Business and Entrepreneurship (USASBE). Tucson, AZ: January 13.

Kochhar, R. and M.A. Hitt (1998). Linking corporate strategy to capital structure: diversification strategy, type and source of financing. *Strategic Management Journal*, **19**, 601–10.

Porter, L.W. and L.E. McKibbin (1988). *Management Education and Development: Drift or Thrust into the 21st Century?* New York: McGraw-Hill.

Shaver, J.M. (1998). Accounting for endogeneity when assessing strategy performance: does entry mode choice affect FDI survival? *Management Science*, **44**, 571–85.

5. Challenges we face as entrepreneurship scholars publishing in top journals

R. Duane Ireland

Ireland, Duane: Good morning and thank you very much for the opportunity to be here – it is certainly a significant honor for me. As Rich Dino and Ron Mitchell have said, this room is filled with incredible scholars. I have learned so much from all of these scholars and certainly the scholars who are with us internationally and domestically via the Internet as well. So, thank you for the opportunity to be here and thank all of you for the scholarship that you have produced over the years. It is your scholarship that is the foundation for what we have today – and what we will build on to produce tomorrow's scholarship. Thanks to all of you for your contributions and for the intellectual stimuli you provide to each of us as we continue to think about significant entrepreneurship research questions.

This is an outline as to the topics that I will address in our time together. I'll discuss my journey with entrepreneurship research. I will try to provide a little bit of perspective about entrepreneurship research from my viewpoint. And, this will be somewhat consistent (I hope) with what Venkat talked partly about in another session with respect to interesting research [Sankaran Venkataraman: Chapter 7]. We actually did not talk to each other before this, so this is truly a coincidence that we both chose to speak about interesting scholarship/interesting research. I then will draw from some inputs from journal editors to speak to identifying challenges that we face as entrepreneurship scholars publishing in top journals, as well as some potentially interesting research questions that we may want to pursue. And then of course, hopefully we'll have time for a couple of closing observations.

With respect to my journey with entrepreneurship research, I should note that I was actually trained initially as a strategy person. In that respect, I had interests in mergers and acquisitions as part of diversification strategies, and I also had an interest in strategic alliances early on. Collectively, these initial interests blended into a desire to learn more about innovation

(I'll have more to say about this interest in a few moments). But, if I could mention something here that has been incredibly significant to my journey as a scholar, I would like to do so. What I want to mention here concerns the tremendous importance of collaborations.

I was very, very fortunate to begin my career at Oklahoma State University. The reason my initial academic appointment was so significant is that at that time, Oklahoma State had an incredible cadre of scholars – including Dennis Middlemist, Bob Greer, Kirk Downey and of course (my great friend and long time collaborator) Michael Hitt. I could not have been more blessed and more fortunate than I was to work with these individuals, and these collaborations between Michael Hitt and I have lasted now over 30 years. Given my experience with collaborations, I think it is appropriate to emphasize the importance of long-term collaborations with productive scholars. Productive collaborations can indeed be the foundation for multiple contributions by scholars sharing their insights and skills.

These initial scholarly interests fed into an interest in innovation, which essentially caused me to begin to examine questions related to innovation within the context of entrepreneurial settings. There were other things happening at this time that influenced my interest in innovation, and certainly in entrepreneurship, including emerging dynamism in the field. This was also the time period when entrepreneurship was beginning to emerge in a more formalized sense within the Academy of Management (although this was certainly before the establishment of the Entrepreneurship Division within the Academy). Nonetheless, this was a time period during which entrepreneurship was becoming more widely recognized in the Academy of Management as a legitimate and interesting domain of management research.

There were some other aspects of my interest in entrepreneurship that were essentially structural in nature. Research evidence indicates that strategy and structure have a relationship; and for me, certainly structure influenced (to a degree), my emerging interest in entrepreneurship. The structural issues that I have in mind here include some of the time that I spent at Baylor University. More specifically, I am thinking about my work as the director of the Entrepreneurship Center at Baylor and my good fortune to be appointed to an entrepreneurship chair at Baylor. These structural realities also supported my emerging interest in entrepreneurship and innovation.

I am highlighting this background information because it provides the foundation for my interest in understanding why some large firms seem to be able to innovate somewhat successfully across time, while some other large firms are not able to do so. I don't know that the firms that I will mention here are the best exemplars in consistent innovation over time;

but some believe that 3M, P&G and privately-held W.L. Gore are large firms that are able to do so. In contrast, we know that other large firms are not able to continuously innovate with the degree of success that has been achieved by the three firms I just mentioned. Some might say that General Motors is an example of a firm that has not innovated effectively across time. Although much more is involved with the firm's current standing than its ability to innovate, the firm's current situation is potentially very interesting to organizational scholars. The firm's stock price is certainly intriguing at this time. I checked this morning and discovered that General Motors stock closed at $1.12 a share yesterday. Who among us would have thought even in the recent past that you could take a five-dollar bill, buy four shares of GM stock, and have money left over? I mean, it's just incredible. It really is. And, of course, Polaroid Corporation essentially no longer exists. It has been sold again. In actuality, the firm's name is about the only remaining asset.

In turn, this interest in the ability of some large firms to successfully and effectively innovate led to a subsequent, yet related, interest in the corporate entrepreneurship research domain. To meaningfully inform this interest, I studied the scholarship produced by scholars such as Robert Burgleman and Danny Miller. Additionally, I began engaging in conversations with scholars who were also working in the corporate entrepreneurship space: Jeff Covin (Indiana University), Don Kuratko (Indiana University) and Shaker Zahra (University of Minnesota) are three scholars whose work I thoroughly enjoyed reading. Moreover, I thoroughly enjoyed visiting with these scholars during academic meetings to discuss various questions associated with the corporate entrepreneurship domain. Over the years, I have been involved with a number of publications concerned with corporate entrepreneurship. And a fair amount of these publications found me working with Jeff Covin, Don Kuratko and Shaker Zahra to examine what we believe are interesting research questions.

There were several other entrepreneurship-related questions in which I had an interest over the years, such as international expansion by new ventures. A paper published in 2000 in an *Academy of Management Journal (AMJ)* Special Research Forum was a primary outcome of this interest (Zahra, Ireland and Hitt, 2000). I am proud to say that Patricia McDougall and Ben Oviatt served as the guest co-editors of this Special Research Forum. The interest in this domain resulted from a desire to understand how new ventures expand internationally – and do so innovatively and successfully. Privatization and entrepreneurial transformation was another interest I had in the entrepreneurship domain. I worked with Michael Hitt, Shaker Zahra and Isabelle Gutierrez to explore this interest. A special issue of the *Academy of Management Review (AMR)* was the primary outcome of this interest. Zahra, Gutierrez, Hitt and I (Zahra, Ireland, Gutierrez and Hitt, 2000) wrote a paper to introduce this special issue. Essentially, our core interest was to work with scholars exploring how entrepreneurship could facilitate privatization of various firms as well as their development as productive enterprises in emerging economies.

Integrating entrepreneurship research with research in other disciplines is an interest I have developed in the last couple of years with Justin Webb, one of our recent graduates from our PhD program at Texas A&M University. Webb is now a member of the entrepreneurship faculty at Oklahoma State University. This interest led to a publication in the *Journal of Management* (*JOM*) that Webb and I co-authored (Ireland & Webb, 2007). Our primary purpose with this publication was to argue that there are emerging themes in other disciplines with the potential to influence entrepreneurship work. Anthropology, sociology, economics, political science, etc. are examples of research domains that we believe can meaningfully inform entrepreneurship research. The fact that entrepreneurship scholarship is interdisciplinary in nature continues to interest me; as such, this is a topic that I hope to continue exploring. I find the opportunity for us (as entrepreneurship scholars) to draw from the theories and methods featured in other disciplines as a means of informing our work to be quite fascinating.

Strategic entrepreneurship is another entrepreneurship-related domain in which I still have a very keen interest. Along with colleagues Mike Hitt, Michael Camp (The Ohio State University) and Don Sexton (now retired, formerly of Ohio State University), I have been involved with two special issues that examine strategic entrepreneurship. Both of these special issues appeared in 2001. One of these issues (Hitt, Ireland, Camp, and Sexton, 2001) was published in the *Strategic Management Journal* (*SMJ*), while the other (Ireland, Hitt, Camp, and Sexton, 2001) appeared in an issue of the *Academy of Management Executive* (*AME*). We wrote introductory articles for each of these special issues. We believe the papers published in these two special issues provided some of the foundation for what is still the rapidly emerging concept called 'strategic entrepreneurship.' A keen interest we had in developing these special issues was to publish the work that outstanding scholars were completing as initial entries in the dialogues about how to effectively integrate entrepreneurship and strategic management in order to better understand organizational actions and success.

A paper Mike Hitt, David Sirmon and I (Ireland, Hitt and Sirmon, 2003) published in the *Journal of Management* (*JOM*) extends the earlier work in strategic entrepreneurship (including the work published in the two special issues we were honored to guest edit) in that we developed a robust model to capture strategic entrepreneurship's domain. We continue to have a strong interest in this domain and seek to be a part of the dialogue occurring about strategic entrepreneurship. We believe that additional scholarly inquiries will result in important contributions to our overall ability to identify interesting entrepreneurship-related questions that warrant additional exploration and attention.

'Entrepreneurial opportunities' is another entrepreneurship topic in which I have an interest. Venkat spoke eloquently about entrepreneurial opportunities and their importance to the field in another session [Chapter 7]. Recently, Jeremy Short (Texas Tech University), Dave Ketchen (Auburn University), Chris Shook (Auburn University) and I (2010) had a paper dealing with entrepreneurial opportunities accepted for publication in *JOM*. In essence, this paper speaks to entrepreneurial opportunities (what we know, what is in the literature about entrepreneurial opportunities) and suggests research directions that scholars interested in this domain may want to pursue. We are excited about the array of intriguing research questions associated with entrepreneurial opportunities – and whether and how they are created or discovered.

Lastly, for me, is an interest in entrepreneurship in informal economies. Justin Webb (Oklahoma State University), David Sirmon and Laszlo Tihanyi (both of Texas A&M University) are my collaborators in this area of research. We recently published a paper in *AMR* that deals with entrepreneurship in informal economies (Webb, Tihanyi, Ireland and Sirmon, 2009). We are really excited by this work and the possibilities for future scholarly endeavors that we believe flow from completing this particular theoretical analysis. Basically, we use theories in this work to explain how entrepreneurship evolves and can flourish within informal economies.

Entrepreneurship theory, collective identity theory and institutional theory are the theories we used to explore this interesting phenomenon. The foundation for this work was our conviction that theory should allow us to understand successful entrepreneurship in informal economies just as theories allow us to understand successful entrepreneurship in formal economies (where entrepreneurial activities are both legal and legitimate). But, we know that entrepreneurial activities also surface in the informal economy, and at least for a period of time, may operate quite successfully even though the activities may be legal but illegitimate or illegal yet legitimate in the eyes of a large group of people. Again, our primary interest with our initial work in this space was to say: if theory can help us to explicate the emergence of entrepreneurship in the formal economy, it likewise should be able to explicate the emergence of entrepreneurship in informal economies. While this is an interest that is new for me, it is one to which I am fully committed. As a result, I am currently in the process of working with others to design additional studies to examine questions about entrepreneurship in the informal economy.

So, that's a little bit about my journey with entrepreneurship and why I have become so interested in this domain and find it to be filled with such a fascinating set of issues for us to examine.

Well, what about a bit of a perspective regarding entrepreneurship research? To begin, I guess we should recognize that, according to some, entrepreneurship scholars are still sort of the 'new kids on the block.' I don't know that that's really quite as true today as it has been, but certainly we have heard this for a number of years. We know that entrepreneurship PhD programs are still relatively new. However, the number of universities offering PhD programs in the entrepreneurship domain is increasing. And we know that the entrepreneurship paradigm is drawing increasing scholarly attention, and of course, that's certainly a key reason that all of us are gathered together at this Exemplars Conference. There is no doubt in my mind that the quality of entrepreneurship scholarship continues to increase. I think there is a significant, rapidly increasing quality of entrepreneurship scholarship, which is very exciting.

Another perspective of entrepreneurship research is that new journals continue to emerge, including the *Strategic Entrepreneurship Journal* (*SEJ*) that Michael Hitt is representing during this Conference. We also know that entrepreneurship scholars are now being considered for appointments as associate editors and as editors for many other journals. This, too, is an important milestone; considering entrepreneurship scholars for these prestigious appointments denotes the increasing flow of entrepreneurship work in some of our fields' most important and significant journals. In addition, study of the members of journals' editorial review boards (even for general management journals) shows that a larger number of entrepreneurship scholars are now serving as members. So in my mind, entrepreneurship is now a common 'sort' to consider when editorial review boards are being formed and associate editors and editors are being chosen. I believe these developments are very important and that they serve as a strong indication of the increasing value that entrepreneurship scholars bring to editorial work.

Continuing with that perspective, we know that there are a number of dialogues that have taken place and/or continue to take place about entrepreneurship research, including: what is the domain of entrepreneurship, and do we need a theory of entrepreneurship? We have all engaged in this discussion about 4,247 times, right? We will probably keep talking about it. Questions we may consider tonight, tomorrow and beyond may include ones such as 'How do we define entrepreneurship and entrepreneurs?' and 'When does the firm exist?' A number of people in this room have explored these questions. And of course, the age old question, 'Are we legitimate as a field of inquiry and (if we aren't), what do we do about it? Do we care about it?' I think all of us in this room, as well as all of those listening to our discussion in various locations around the world would certainly agree that we are legitimate, and that it is no longer an issue worthy of significant debate.

Now, let me mention something here that I'm going to go through rather quickly. In my view, all of us as scholars (certainly as entrepreneurship scholars) need to be meaningfully involved with knowledge. Producing knowledge, integrating knowledge and disseminating knowledge – these are the essential tasks we complete as scholars. We are knowledge producers. We are knowledge consumers. Ernest Boyer (1990) and his colleagues speak to four types of scholarship: discovery, integration, application and teaching. The important point is not necessarily the precise definition for our discussion of these types of scholarship. I think the important point is that there are journals that speak to, or deal with each type of scholarship.

For example, if we think about the Academy of Management, we might argue that the Academy publishes journals that deal with different types of scholarship. In this regard, if we consider knowledge 'discovery' as defined here (which is basically the commitment to developing knowledge for its own sake, to freedom of inquiry, etc.), we can conclude that *AMJ* publishes this type of scholarship. If we think about the scholarship of 'integration,' as defined here, this is essentially the purview of the domain of *Academy of Management Review*. If we think about the scholarship of 'application,' that certainly was the purview of *Academy of Management Executive* (*AME*). I might note that we have a former editor of *AME* with us in the room. And of course, the scholarship of 'teaching' is the domain of the *Academy of Management Learning and Education* (*AMLE*). So, the point for our consideration here is that there are journals that have each type of knowledge production as part of their legitimate domain – as part of their editorial mission – and I'll come back to that point in just a moment.

As knowledge producers – as people involved in knowledge – it is important that we seek to make a difference with our work. And if we accept the responsibility to try to make a difference with our scholarship, then the question becomes 'How do we go about making a difference as entrepreneurship scholars with our work?' This is a point of consistency with Venkat's comments from another session [Chapter 7]. I believe an appropriate view to take is that in order to make a difference, our scholarship has to be interesting. Quoting from Murray Davis (1971), a reason for this is 'The first criterion by which people judge anything they encounter, even before deciding whether it is true or false, is whether it is interesting or boring.' Now, one might argue that interesting scholarship has quite a few characteristics, including the following: counterintuitive arguments, multi-level designs, use of qualitative and quantitative data in the same study, innovative and robust datasets, and innovative integrations of theories. The important point is that as we think about trying to make a difference, what we want to do is to think about designing and completing interesting scholarship.

Let's do this. About six months ago, I contacted journals and asked the editors to provide answers to us (to me) for these questions: what challenges do we face as entrepreneurship scholars to publish our research in the top-tier journals, and what are some interesting entrepreneurship questions that we as scholars may want to study in order to go through the process that hopefully would yield a publication in top-tier journals? Editors and associate editors of journals (listed alphabetically) who responded to these questions are *Entrepreneurship Theory & Practice* (*ET&P*), *AMJ*, *Academy of Management Perspectives* (*AMP*), *AMR*, and the *Journal of Business Venturing* (*JBV*). Obviously, we are very appreciative of the opportunity to benefit from the insights of those representing these journals who provided inputs to us.

Here is the first question for which our respondents provided inputs: what are the three key challenges entrepreneurship scholars face in their efforts to publish their research in top-tier journals? In all fairness I should say that I have integrated the commentaries from the editors. If I have misrepresented something as a result of doing so, that's my responsibility. However, I have tried to be very careful to the spirit and to the details of the input we received.

With these parameters as background to what we will consider, let me highlight some of the feedback we received from the editors and associate editors. With respect to the challenges we entrepreneurship scholars face as we seek to publish in top-tier journals, here are some of the items that were mentioned: being able to conceptualize or articulate a significant research question, being able to clearly articulate the work's contribution (and that the contribution is truly important and capable of advancing the field), gathering appropriate and interesting data to examine the research question, and so forth.

Let's turn attention to the second challenge. Here we see that the challenge for us, as scholars, is the ability to sell a theoretical story that is familiar to reviewers, but represents a contribution beyond extending known stories to another context. I think this is really interesting and again, is consistent, I believe, with commentary from Venkat when he said [Chapter 7] that what we want to be able to do is to sell (and that word choice, 'sell,' was provided by the respondent) the theoretical story that we have to tell in a different, new, novel and interesting context. There are other challenges and ideas as well.

Finally, the third of our three questions deals with the challenges the respondents identified. Here we see a challenge of choosing a dependent variable that is relevant both to the study and to the journal – and dealing with the inherent messiness and difficulty associated with obtaining entrepreneurial data. We have all wrestled with this potential challenge. In the final analysis, I am not certain that we would agree with all of these challenges. We might say that we have satisfactorily dealt with two or more of those challenges, or we might say, 'Here are some others that we've not identified.' If we were to do this, we would be able to add to the list. Nonetheless, at any given time these are some challenges that current editors and associate editors of journals publishing significant entrepreneurship research identified as issues that we as scholars may want to address.

What conclusions can we draw from this input? Well, I think one thing is that we want to know the journal to which we are submitting our work. In other words, I think, as entrepreneurship scholars, we want to challenge ourselves to be familiar with the dialogues and the conversations that are taking place in the journal to which we want to submit our work. So if I want to submit my work to *JBV, ET&P, SEJ, AMJ, AMR,* or some other journal, I should challenge myself (it seems to me the editors are saying) to be familiar with the dialogue – with the conversation in that journal about entrepreneurship. The reason this is so important, in my judgment, is that we need to understand the journal's mission (and we know that each journal has a unique editorial mission). We also know that the reviewers for journals and certainly the editors and the associate editors (who after all are the decision makers), are using the editorial mission as a guide to determine the value of a work with respect to that particular journal. So, I think it is really important that we challenge ourselves to know the mission – the editorial mission of the journal to which we are submitting our work – and the conversations and the dialogues taking place in each journal with respect to the topic of entrepreneurship.

Now, for the answers to the next question. What are the three or four of the most significant entrepreneurship-related questions that you (as editors) believe we (as scholars) perhaps should or could examine today? Let's mention some of the entrepreneurship-related questions our respondents offered to us.

First, what constitutes success and failure, and what are the characteristics, the downside if any, to failure? 'Look at the last question/issue; international entrepreneurship. Where, how and when?' – this is an exact quote from one of the respondents. I think it is really interesting to focus on the construct of international entrepreneurship. A couple of additional questions the editors identified are also significant: how do entrepreneurial opportunities come into being? Much of our discussion in other sessions dealt with this topic. What are the boundaries between entrepreneurship and corporate venturing? What are the parameters? When do we leave one space and enter the second space? What are the effects of factors such as geography, country, government policy, etc. on entrepreneurial practices? What influences the choice of organizational form in the governance of entrepreneurial ventures? What accounts for performance differentials among entrepreneurial ventures? What is the meaning of opportunity in a social entrepreneurship context? This last question seems to ask us to take the whole phenomenon of entrepreneurial opportunities and ask what it means in the context of social entrepreneurship.

And why – and why not – does entrepreneurial action arise from organizational failure? So if we see failure (perhaps if General Motors files for bankruptcy, which seemingly is imminent), what does that mean? What kind of an entrepreneurial context might surface from that – and what context surfaces from other failures?

Last, we see questions such as the following: Why are some individuals and organizations able to thrive in resource-scarce environments while others cannot or do not? What allows some to survive but not others? What is the contextual set of factors that favor some but does not favor others? And then, the final two points here.

So, let's ask ourselves this question: so what? What might we potentially take away from the time that we have spent together? Well, I think we have to, as scholars, be at the 'top of the hill with everything we have.' And to me, that means basically that what we need to do is to continuously seek to achieve excellence. If we wish to publish in the top-tier journals, we have to challenge ourselves to do this. We have to learn from the best and consider modeling the best behavior. We have to remain confident, but always hungry to learn and grow as scholars. We have to 'learn to live with what we can't rise above' as well. This means we are going to receive some negative feedback from time to time. We all have been rejected. We all have a stack of rejection letters. It's just part of our life. We know this, but we have to accept each of those seemingly less than positive experiences in a positive way and grow and develop from them and learn as scholars.

Certainly sometimes we may feel that we are taking two steps forward while taking three steps backward; and I think that's a challenge for us. We have to focus continuously and energetically on moving forward and viewing the glass as half full – not half empty. It is really important to accept the position that high-quality, interesting scholarship is always (has always been and will always be) enthusiastically received by top-tier journals. Quality work is clearly sought. All of our journals, we know, want to publish quality work. There is no question about it. None of us will ever know an editor who says, 'Gee, I really hope I publish nothing.' It's just not the way the process works. So, we all want to publish high-quality work. But there are some realities here. It's challenging; but all of us have an opportunity to positively influence the paradigm development that continues to evolve and take shape in the entrepreneurship domain. And, we all have opportunities to publish interesting scholarship!

And finally, it's truly the 'Glory Days' for those of us wanting to engage in high-quality entrepreneurship research. In this sense, I believe that our careers as entrepreneurship scholars can be enriched by these very, very exciting times and the questions we have a chance to explore. In my opinion, this is a truly exciting and invigorating time for entrepreneurship scholars. The questions available for us to consider are rich and important. And, what could be more exciting than carefully and meaningfully examining intellectually rich and challenging questions regarding entrepreneurship and entrepreneurial ventures? As we know, the answers we derive from our studies have the potential to positively affect individuals, firms and societies. What could be more exciting than having opportunities to positively influence multiple levels through the results of our scholarship?

So let me stop here and thank you for your time and see if there may be questions or issues for us to explore.

Veiga, Jack: I hear the word 'interesting' a lot. Karl Weick used the word 'interesting.' A lot of people have used it. I also am aware that in many cases, the word 'interesting' is a way of describing something that we don't know is going to happen, i.e., 'Gee, that's going to be interesting, I hope.'

There are [various] ways that word is often used. Interesting [to me] is, the person receiving it says it's interesting. So my question is: I know you gave examples of what could be objectively interesting kinds of structures of papers that would provide interest and so forth – but, deep down, who or what defines interesting? I'm thinking of the young scholar out there now that's trying to start. You know, how do they know what they have is interesting?

Ireland, Duane: Yes. It's a great question. And certainly, this phenomenon of 'interesting,' or 'interestingness' continues to be talked about and evaluated. Basically, what we have to do is to say, 'Look, we know this, but how might I tease this out differently? How might I parse this in a way that we really have not examined?' For example, to me, that one question of entrepreneurial opportunities in a social context is really interesting. It's something that we've not (in my judgment, at least) thought about in great detail; and it has possibilities of surfacing some fascinating issues to examine. So to me, trying to find a way to parse what we know and saying, 'Let's take this in a different direction, theoretically, perhaps even methodologically as well,' would be the way to engage in interesting research.

Lumpkin, Tom: Question from the web. We have had a rigorous debate about the future of entrepreneurship as a field of study. Do you think entrepreneurship can survive as a field in itself, or will it get absorbed into any of the sister disciplines, such as strategic management or marketing?

Ireland, Duane: Yes and, boy, we've all had this discussion many times as well. If we are going to be absorbed, let's go with strategic management rather than marketing. I mean, at least it is closer to many of our backgrounds, right? At least there's some proximity there that feels more like home. Seriously, though, this is a great question and I think in a broader context, this discussion is actually, I believe, beyond entrepreneurship and strategic management. I think that the question even applies at a business school level where we continue receiving inputs from scholars saying we all need to collaborate more. Those of us engaged in strategic management questions, we are told, need to collaborate perhaps more with finance scholars, economists and accountants. And so I think the question we are considering is certainly germane for entrepreneurship and strategy (perhaps marketing and other fields), but I think it's a broader discussion point with respect to how do all of our disciplines within business collaboratively examine questions. So, I think the fields of entrepreneurship and strategic management will remain rather unique as domains, but I think there will be additional collaborations taking place between these disciplines – and I don't know that either will lose its domain status. In my view, though, the intersection is going to yield more interesting work in the short run, and may become yet a third field. Who knows . . . And it seems pretty bizarre to even suggest, but maybe there's yet another field out there.

Gras, David: You said that when submitting articles to the major journals, we need to understand the mission of that journal and cater to that mission, and make sure our papers match up with that mission. As an editor, I have one or two things. Number one, when you take on the job as an editor, do you feel like you need to remove your personal missions that you've been going through your whole life (you've published on certain things, you think certain things are interesting . . .)? Do you feel that you need to remove those and submit to the mission of the journal? And if not, should we learn the missions of the editor in particular at the time and cater to those as well?

Ireland, Duane: It's an interesting question, and clearly, in my view as an editor, one must comply with the mission that has been established for the journal. In the instance of the four academy journals, the missions are established essentially by the Board of Governors, through the journal's committee – and this is a very collaborative process. There's a lot of input from all of us as members of the Academy of Management. And by the way, of course as members of the Academy of Management, we essentially own those four journals. They are part of the Academy of which we are members, and so that is a very collaborative effort. But I think that we are charged, as agents, to follow the guidelines – the dictates of the editorial mission that has been established by the principles that we represent. I believe that most (if not all) editors would agree with this position.

Lumpkin, Tom: To what extent is entrepreneurship research concerned with unique phenomena versus merely unique context?

Ireland, Duane: Another question that I know Jay Barney, Michael Hitt and Patricia McDougall will want to answer as well. But I can say that we are often told that context is the only difference between issues examined by entrepreneurship scholars and issues examined by scholars working in other domains. In my opinion, entrepreneurship scholars want to be concerned with unique theories and questions, rather than worrying about the context. We know our context, but I think one of our key challenges is to ask, 'What is the unique theory that can be used here to help me explain the entrepreneurship phenomenon that interests me, and what are some unique methods I might use in order to address what is an interesting question?'

Okay. Well, thank you very much. I appreciate the opportunity to be here and I wish everybody the best with their work. We look forward to receiving your high-quality entrepreneurial scholarship at *AMJ* and to learning from the insights associated with your entrepreneurship research. I truly wish each and every one of you nothing other than the very best with your scholarly endeavors.

REFERENCES

Boyer, E.L. (1990). *Scholarship Reconsidered: Priorities of the Professoriate.* Princeton, NJ: Carnegie Foundation for the Advancement of Teaching.

Davis, M. (1971). That's interesting! Towards a phenomenology of sociology and a sociology of phenomenology. *Philosophy of the Social Sciences*, **1**, 309–44.

Hitt, M.A., R.D. Ireland, S.M. Camp and D.L. Sexton (2001). Strategic entrepreneurship: entrepreneurial strategies for wealth creation. *Strategic Management Journal*, **2**, 479–91.

Ireland, R.D., M.A. Hitt, S.M. Camp and D. Sexton (2001). Integrating entrepreneurship and strategic management action to create firm wealth. *Academy of Management Executive*, **15** (1), 49–63.

Ireland, R.D., M.A. Hitt and D.G. Sirmon (2003). A model of strategic entrepreneurship: The construct and its dimensions. *Journal of Management*, **29**, 963–89.

Ireland, R.D. and J.W. Webb (2007). A cross-disciplinary exploration of entrepreneurship research. *Journal of Management*, **33**, 891–927.

Short, J.C., D.J. Ketchen, C.L. Shook and R.D. Ireland (2010). The concept of 'opportunity' in entrepreneurship research: past accomplishments and future challenges. *Journal of Management*, **36** (1), 40–65.

Webb, J.W., L. Tihanyi, R.D. Ireland and D.G. Sirmon (2009). You say illegal, I say legitimate: entrepreneuring in the informal economy. *Academy of Management Review*, **34**, 492–510.

Zahra, S.A., R.D. Ireland, I. Gutierrez and M.A. Hitt (2000). Privatization and entrepreneurial transformation: emerging issues and a future research agenda. *Academy of Management Review*, **25**, 509–24.

Zahra, S.A., R.D Ireland and M.A. Hitt (2000). International expansion by new venture firms: international diversity, mode of market entry, technological learning and performance. *Academy of Management Journal*, **43**, 925–50.

6. Entrepreneurship research: past, present and future

Patricia P. McDougall

McDougall, Patricia: Welcome colleagues. I'm very honored and actually quite humbled to be a keynote at what (I think) will prove to be a very historic conference.

A distinctiveness that the Entrepreneurship Division of the Academy of Management has always had has been our inclusiveness; but I think this Conference takes our culture of inclusiveness to an entirely new level, and I want to commend those who had the vision for this Conference and also to commend those who so successfully executed this Conference.

Given my spot as the last keynote (in the ordering of the Conference), I thought it might be appropriate if I used this opportunity to look back a bit at the field and how we have evolved, where we are in entrepreneurship research today and the opportunities for us in the future. There has never been a time in my career when I have felt more excited or more positive about the field of entrepreneurship – and specifically about entrepreneurship research. When I entered the field slightly more than 25 years ago, I never would have predicted the absolutely stimulating and amazing ride that entrepreneurship has been. I could never have predicted that entrepreneurship would be in such an esteemed position that it enjoys today.

For those of us who have been around a while, it has been a journey. And it has been a journey from a lack of legitimacy to a point where entrepreneurship is a bright beacon of scholarly opportunity that expands well beyond the bounds of just the traditional entrepreneurship scholar. It reaches out into many other disciplines.

For our discussion today, I would like for us to take a very brief look back at the early days in the field when there was a lack of legitimacy. I do not want to spend a lot of time on this because I totally agree with Duane Ireland's point [R. Duane Ireland: Chapter 5] that we are legitimate today, and a lack of legitimacy is not a topic that is worthy of our discussion; but let us look at this in a historical context to better understand where we are today. Let us take a quick little journey through some of the milestones toward achieving legitimacy, examine the current state of entrepreneurship research and ask some questions. Are there some downsides that we are experiencing because of this tremendous success that we have had? I will conclude by focusing on the beacon of scholarly opportunity that we have today.

Everybody talks about the early days. Well, when were the early days? One could begin back in the early 1900s with some of the research, but I think when we really started to come together as a discipline and as a field was in the 1940s when Harvard offered the first course in entrepreneurship. Then in 1957, the International Council for Small Business was formed, and then a journal (the *Journal of Small Business Management* in 1963). The Kauffman Foundation was established in 1966 and the first entrepreneurship research conference occurred in 1970 at Purdue University. We were international very early in our roots. There was an international conference on entrepreneurship research held in Toronto in 1973. In 1974, Karl Vesper convened a group of scholars within the Business Policy and Planning Division of the Academy of Management. Out of that meeting, the Entrepreneurship Interest Group was formed within the Academy. Another journal was launched in 1975 – that was the *American Journal of Small Business* – and the first Babson Research Conference was in 1981.

In the early days, entrepreneurship was primarily in business schools, and it absolutely did lack legitimacy. I recall my first Academy of Management Conference (which would have been in the mid 1980s) that virtually every meeting discussion would break down into a 'we don't have legitimacy' discussion, and those discussions occurred frequently into the 1990s.

In the early days, entrepreneurship was definitely marginalized. I can remember my friend and colleague, Don Sexton (who held a chair in entrepreneurship at Ohio State) saying that on the occasions when he would receive a phone call from one of his fellow entrepreneurship scholars from somewhere else in the world, he would often close his door, sit back and enjoy the conversation. Don Sexton expressed that it was so great to talk with someone who valued and appreciated entrepreneurship research. And look at how different it is today. At Ohio State, we have Jay Barney, Sharon Alvarez and other great entrepreneurship scholars.

It was difficult to earn tenure with an entrepreneurship research record if one was at a top research school. When I went up for tenure in the very early 1990s (I think it must have been about 1991 or so), I was at Georgia Tech and I was fortunate to have a great set of external reviewers. They were really supportive and they wanted me to earn tenure. My research record was almost entirely entrepreneurship research. Several of the external reviewers sent me copies of the letters that they had written. Over the years as I have learned more about the tenure process, I have come to better recognize and appreciate the tremendous task that those reviewers had before them. They wrote beautiful letters. In their letters they not only discussed my scholarly contributions, they sold the field of entrepreneurship. I contrast their letters with the set of letters written when I moved to Indiana University 10 years ago. Some of those external reviewers are in this room today (and I thank them again because they wrote wonderful letters); but their letters were really different from the letters in the early 1990s. These more recent letters focused only on contributions to entrepreneurship and did not need to mention the value or legitimacy of entrepreneurship research.

Back in the early days when one was submitting a paper to a journal that was other than a journal devoted specifically to entrepreneurship, one actually debated on whether or not to use the 'E' word in the paper: did you include the 'entrepreneurship' word or did you avoid using the term? And there was good reason for considering this issue as there were few, if any, entrepreneurship scholars on editorial boards. It is very different today. Duane made a comment that when editors do their sorts for editorial board members, entrepreneurship is in that sort; but it absolutely was not like that in the past. Today, I think the question of whether or not to use the 'E' word is almost reversed as I believe authors sometimes look for a way to put the 'entrepreneurship' word in their papers.

Admittedly, we did have some problems in the early research; no doubt about it. I would describe that research as not very cumulative. It didn't lead to many new insights or knowledge gains. We had an absence of quality databases. Many of the articles lacked a theoretical foundation or methodological rigor. There was a real bias toward descriptive research. And the big one for me was that there was not a very clear understanding of what was unique about entrepreneurship research. What was core for us?

It has been a journey and it's been a great journey. I want to apologize ahead of time that I have only listed a few milestones and highlights on these slides and am leaving out many important events, and perhaps things that may have happened at your school, or things that you may have done. But my attempt here is to recall some of the things that I took particular notice of as I progressed on my entrepreneurship journey.

The David Birch (1987) studies: I am not sure that Birch's findings were necessarily that new, but he did a great job of publicizing that entrepreneurship was an engine of growth in our economy. At that time, I think the widespread belief was that jobs were created by corporations – and Birch's findings really generated some public excitement about entrepreneurship. Then we had management guru Peter Drucker (1985) publish his book and put 'entrepreneurship' in its title. So, one did not have to debate about using the 'E' word anymore.

The Entrepreneurship Interest Group achieved division status at the Academy in 1987. In that same year, the *Journal of Management* included an article from Max Wortman (1987) that was a review of entrepreneurship research. So entrepreneurship research was beginning to be a little more in the mainstream about this time. In the early 1990s doctoral programs began emerging; and I sincerely believe that doctoral education, whereby we are educating great scholars, is the key for the future of our research. We must invest in our doctoral students.

Next, the Entrepreneurship Division of the Academy of Management created the Task Force of Doctoral Education, which you have heard referenced many times here in the last few days. The National Consortium of Entrepreneurship Centers was created in 1998. The Academy of International Business provided some validation to entrepreneurship research in 2004 with their recognition of an article (Oviatt and McDougall, 2005) that my co-author (Ben Oviatt) and I had published in the *Journal of International Business Studies*, their major journal. Their Decade Award is given for the article that has had the most significant impact on the field of international business in the last 10 years. This was significant for us in entrepreneurship in that it was a highly respected scholarly organization that recognized entrepreneurship as having something to offer the international business (IB) field. Entrepreneurship research helped changed the IB conversation from an exclusive focus on large, well-established multinational firms to a conversation that also included young, entrepreneurial firms.

The journals that were being created and developed added to the legitimacy of entrepreneurship research. To note a few of those key journals and their launch dates:

- *American Journal of Small Business* in 1975. It was renamed under Ray Bagby's leadership in 1988 as *Entrepreneurship Theory & Practice*.
- in 1985, Ian McMillan launched the *Journal of Business Venturing*.
- in 1989, Zoltan Acs and my colleague at Indiana University, David Audretsch, launched *Small Business Economics*.
- in 2007, *Strategic Entrepreneurship Journal* (*SEJ*) was launched. We are so thankful for the leadership that Mike Hitt is putting into *SEJ* such that it can fulfill its incredible potential.

There were a number of special issues related to entrepreneurship in top journals. I will only highlight two, but there were several others. The *Strategic Management Journal* (*SMJ*) (1990) did a special issue on corporate entrepreneurship and then the *Academy of Management Journal*

(*AMJ*) (2000) did a special research forum on international entrepreneurship. Something that's really special about the *AMJ* Special Research Forum (and the reason I wanted to highlight it) is that an article in that special research forum by Zahra, Ireland and Hitt (2000) received the *AMJ* Best Paper of the Year recognition. I am unaware of any other entrepreneurship paper up until this time that had received a best paper award in a top journal.

So where is the state of entrepreneurship research today? I do not think that we can fully understand where we are today unless we think a little more broadly and think about entrepreneurship as an academic discipline. If we think about entrepreneurship in general, I think a word that describes it well is 'excitement.' There is so much excitement about entrepreneurship. It is well established in business schools. It is making important inroads throughout universities. It is embraced by donors, alumni and by governments all over the world. We are permeating the academic market. Over 600 US universities offer entrepreneurship majors. A fact that Mike Hitt presented earlier [Michael A. Hitt: Chapter 4] is that over 1,600 universities worldwide offer at least one entrepreneurship course. There are a huge number of entrepreneurship endowed chairs and professorships, and the number is growing. We have over 40 refereed journals and over 350 entrepreneurship centers.

There is strong evidence that entrepreneurship has achieved legitimacy within the mainstream of academe. It is increasingly accepted, sometimes grudgingly, but increasingly accepted by later-stage academics. Entrepreneurship is attracting investment from public and private sectors. The real litmus test for us is that entrepreneurship scholars are being tenured at top research schools; that is no longer a rare event. The ideal situation will be when junior scholars do not even recognize the challenges of the past; and I would bet that there are some scholars out there in our worldwide audience who are listening and are unaware of the past challenges. That is marvelous if it is the case; and if not, I believe we are close to a time when those challenges are regarded as ancient history.

Today, we are in what I term the 'Golden Age of Entrepreneurship.' Duane Ireland referred to these as the 'Glory Days,' and I like Duane's term a little better and may start using it [R. Duane Ireland: Chapter 5]. I am having a tremendous amount of fun – I hope you are. I hope you are enjoying what we have. It has been a long journey of several decades and a lot of people have toiled to get us to this point, but we are now in a very special time – a wonderful time – and we need to enjoy it.

How did we get there? I think the number one reason, quite frankly, is money. A lot of the money was gifted from donors and foundations, and this came at a time when US public schools had an increased reliance on soft money. It was not just this past year that states cut funding. If you look at the percentage of state funding for universities, it has been a steady downward slope. Until last year, it was a gradual slope. Funding is going to become even more important to public universities as state funding is projected to continue to decrease. The drop in the value of endowments impacts both publics and privates. The interest in entrepreneurship was also fueled by the 'dotcom' era. While I believe that was a very destructive time in many ways for our entrepreneurship courses, it certainly did generate a lot of demand for our courses – and many schools added entrepreneurship course offerings.

In addition, there has been a convergence of globalization and technological advancement such that we have this excitement in the general public that anyone, at any place in the world, can be an entrepreneur. Grant agencies have helped us. The National Science Foundation (NSF) and National Institute of Health (NIH) often require proposals to include a commercialization plan. I receive a fair number of calls from medical school faculty and from scientists who call the business school and they ask, 'Hey, we're writing a grant. Do you have someone in the business school who might want to be part of that grant, because we need to have a business plan in it?'

Universities are incorporating economic development as part of their mission. I believe this is important and is going to have a big impact on us in the future. This may not be of the magnitude of the change that US universities experienced shortly after World War II when they embraced research as part of their mission, but, in the last few years, many universities have expanded their mission and are seeking to play a significant role in their state's economic development. This is positive for entrepreneurship as we are right at the core of that conversation.

How and when did entrepreneurship research cross the chasm into legitimacy? I believe it occurred in the mid-to-late 1900s. This was a hard sell, and I imagine there are probably a few schools that may continue to not view entrepreneurship as legitimate; but in general, I think it has occurred. Legitimacy was a hard sell to that core academic community, and what we had to have were visionaries who helped the pragmatists appreciate the unique domain and distinct value of the proposition that entrepreneurship offered. Looking back, there were several key individuals who played a role in helping us cross the chasm. The one who was the most significant for me was S. Venkataraman (1997) when he wrote his thought-leadership piece about entrepreneurship's distinct domain. I was fascinated on the opening night of this Conference when Venkataraman was describing his personal feelings about the 1997 paper, and contrasting those feelings with how he felt about the subsequent paper (Shane and Venkataraman, 2000) he co-authored a few years later with Scott Shane (which was published in the *Academy of Management Review*).

I think I understand why the 1997 piece, in Venkataraman's words, 'means more' to him. Those of us who were in entrepreneurship – when we saw that 1997 piece, every one of us knew immediately that this was an important paper. I remember when I read the article that my thoughts were that this article needed to be written, and we embraced it. But it took publishing in a top journal for the article to have significant impact. Venkataraman's 1997 piece just did not have an outlet that gave it a wide audience as he was speaking to entrepreneurship scholars only in that outlet. It took publishing it in a top journal, with its wide audience for his original thoughts, to have the impact that they ultimately did. His was a real 'crossing-the-chasm' piece for us.

We also benefited from scholars who were rooted in other disciplines but who were interested in entrepreneurship. Duane Ireland was one of those. Duane was an early person in entrepreneurship, but he was more recognized for his work in strategy. Duane was a very established scholar in strategy, and his work in entrepreneurship helped us cross the chasm.

Howard Aldrich (a respected scholar in sociology), David Audrestch on economics in public policy, Jerry Hills in marketing, and Robert Baron in organizational behavior all helped. We have had several finance scholars who helped us cross the chasm. When I talk with my finance colleagues, a name that stands out for them as giving more legitimacy to entrepreneurship research is Josh Lerner. One could go on and on listing key people, and I apologize to all who I did not include in this short listing, but the point I want to make is there were a lot of people who were in other fields and other disciplines that helped us. One final scholar who I would like to note as a 'crossing-the-chasm-person' is Mike Hitt. Mike, because of his leadership position in the Academy and the respect that he holds, made a difference as to how entrepreneurship was perceived when he chose to become involved.

Today we are in our glory days, but are there potentially some downsides? I put these next two slides up at risk because I expect some of the points will be controversial and perhaps offensive to some, but I am going to put the elephant on the table. There is what I call the 'cashing-in phenomenon.' In some of the papers that I review it seems as though researchers are trying to call everything entrepreneurship, because entrepreneurship is hot.

A second potential downside is what some people would term 'insincere career changes.' Let us face it; we have a lot of endowed positions. I do believe that the vast majority of scholars from other disciplines who have accepted entrepreneurship chairs have simply seen the light and they have transitioned their careers to an interesting area; but there are probably a few scholars who have just seen it as an opportunity and really do not have the commitment or belief in entrepreneurship. But I think that that number is exaggerated greatly. My message to you today would be, 'Do not worry about this.' Doing so is analogous to worrying about the neighbor having a better house or a better car. Worrying about this is no more than a distraction, and if you worry about it, you are letting something take from the enjoyment that you should be having every day for where we are. The potential downside that is really getting the conversation these days is domain grabs. Are other disciplines saying, 'Hey, we do not think entrepreneurship scholars can do that research as well as we can, so we are going to show them how to do it,' or is this the ultimate compliment? Is this the ultimate form of flattery?

I hope that the Dale Meyer (2009) prediction (which is in an *Entrepreneurship Theory & Practice* article that came out in 2009) that the concerns regarding a strategic management takeover of entrepreneurship will turn out to be overstated and perhaps downright silly, is correct. I am absolutely with Dale on this one, and I just hope we get there fast. I hope we do not spend the energy worrying about domain grabs that we spent discussing legitimacy. Frankly, I was struck with Mike Hitt's comment when he said [Michael A. Hitt: Chapter 4], 'Well, no one ever talks about entrepreneurship taking over strategy,' and that may be a better discussion in some ways. Again, and I do not want to be misunderstood here, but suppose if I were to look up in our studio audience and ask Jay Barney, 'Jay, based on your research, tell me what's really distinct about entrepreneurship,' I think one of the things that Jay might respond with is, 'The name. You have the name. You have the brand.'

The excitement out there in the world is entrepreneurship. That is what everyone is relating to and clamoring to. And it is not just strategy that wants a piece of entrepreneurship. They are not the only discipline that has recognized that we have really interesting questions. There are many other disciplines in which their scholars are seeking to be involved in entrepreneurship as well, so I believe that these fears of absorption by strategic management are far overrated and overstated. We worked hard to bring scholars from other fields into our disciplines. We should relish their interest. We should cherish it. There was an earlier web question and it asked, 'Do you fear absorption?' I genuinely do not think we should. I think that this is something that we need to embrace. And we also need to follow a point that Duane made in response to that web question when Duane said we need to collaborate more [R. Duane Ireland: Chapter 5]. I am amazed at how multidisciplinary in collaborating across disciplines our junior scholars are. As an associate dean of faculty and research, I interview every faculty member that the Kelley School of Business hires – and if they are a tenure track candidate, I read their job paper. I interviewed a candidate a year or two ago, and I had not seen the person's vitae. Had I just picked up the paper and read it first, I would not have known if they were a candidate for a job in operations management, marketing or business economics. Some of today's junior scholars could fit in multiple disciplines. Entrepreneurship is well positioned for a multidisciplinary approach.

The potential downside that I hesitated most on listing was the bullet point: 'Welcoming, low entry barriers and accepting – is this all positive? Does it devalue what we do?' We have really prided ourselves and worked hard to be welcoming and accepting. We have tried to keep our entry barriers low, and that has been one of the things I most value about our culture. I would not want us to change this culture, but I think that it is worth considering that sometimes there are people who may misperceive the message of our being so welcoming and misinterpret it as we do not value entrepreneurship as much as we do. As an example, one of our colleagues at a recent conference overheard some prestigious scholars from fields outside of entrepreneurship who were sitting together and talking; and they were kind of puzzling over why they had been invited to this entrepreneurship conference. I think you and I know why we invited them. We have worked to bring other disciplines into entrepreneurship. We have had a 'big tent' approach. The scholars in the example I just gave felt instead that they had been invited to help legitimize the conference – they totally misperceived the invitation. I do not believe we should change our culture of inclusiveness, but I think we do need to be mindful and be careful that the message that we are trying to send is not misperceived.

The last point (and this next point), are the potential downsides that I worry about most. If entrepreneurship becomes everything, then it is nothing. We have always struggled somewhat with a boundary issue. We have fortunately made good progress on identifying our distinctive domain, but we still have fuzzy boundaries. It may be even more difficult today to define our boundaries as scholars who are seeking to include topics within the entrepreneurship domain that were once considered outside of the domain. I believe that we, as a research group, are going to have to struggle with this over the next decade.

Today entrepreneurship is this bright beacon of scholarly opportunity. One of the major opportunities I see is that we have creation as our central focus. I do not know of another discipline that has creation as its central focus, and this is something we need to leverage. We need to leverage this distinctiveness. There is a good reason why scholars are flocking to entrepreneurship, and that is because entrepreneurship is a perspective that makes sense. It generates useful insights and it is valuable for multiple units of analyses. You can study the individual, the firm, government or society, so we have the ability to attract many people.

A lesson that I would suggest for junior scholars is that if you have a senior faculty member at your school and that senior faculty member is warning you about the problems of engaging in entrepreneurship research, I think you need to step back and see that person as a fairly lonely voice. You need to consider his or her generation and their possible biases. The numbers of these people are dwindling. They are dwindling dramatically, and if you have one at your school, you can probably take heart that they are going to retire very soon. Do not worry about the downsides. That would be a major point I want to convey. I know it is very difficult for some senior entrepreneurship scholars who feel they are witnessing what they may perceive as an invasion of their domain. We have a lot of people who have toiled in the salt mines for years. They have advocated entrepreneurship their entire lives, and I think that some of them perceive that there is not the proper deference being made to their contributions and that others are coming in and seeking to redefine the domain. I wish that this great acceptance of entrepreneurship could instead be viewed as a long-awaited validation. It is not a threat to us. It is a validation. It is what we have always wanted. Let us enjoy it.

Entrepreneurship is not a fad. It is not going away because the substance is there. We have the substance. Early entrepreneurship scholars had the message correct – they absolutely had it correct. Entrepreneurship research is worthy of scholarly consideration. What early entrepreneurship scholars lacked was the critical audience to be heard. We have that critical audience now. Maybe we need to think about what Jay Barney said in his keynote address at this Conference, and we need to be heard on a broader scale than we are currently being heard on. But we are clearly being heard within the academic community. So I hope that you all are enjoying the glory days – I certainly am. I will take any questions that you may have at this point, or at least try.

Mosakowski, Elaine: I realize you know that I like to stir things up, so I want to stir things up a little.

McDougall, Patricia: Well, that was what my presentation intended on doing.

Mosakowski, Elaine: Good, it actually did – and in my own mind I thought it was very interesting. I guess if what you're saying is correct, why are we having this conference? Why has Sharon [Alvarez], over the past five to seven years or whatever, been organizing conferences for junior scholars to learn about processes of publishing in top-tier journals, working on processes to help junior scholars and doctoral students create high-quality research? I don't see activities like this in what I would consider to be established . . .

McDougall, Patricia: Well, I think it's because we're innovative, for start-ers. You see it here. Perhaps I should defer to the Conference organizers on this, but my perception of why we're having this Conference is not really so much for the people that are in this room; my perception is this is a part of our being able to leverage technology for great inclusiveness into the Academy. I think that there are many scholars in various parts of the world who may not be so fortunate to have a key entrepreneurship researcher at his or her school, and this is an opportunity for them to interact with them. Travel budgets have really been cut significantly, and this is an opportunity for viewers. It also is creating some product for the Division. We do not do a very effective job in our conferences of codify-ing knowledge and distributing it. Normally it's only the people who are attending the conference that are helped. Attendees advance their thinking on a paper and then it is published later in a journal. I think this is a way that the Division has very creatively created some products that people from all over the world (who might not be in entrepreneurship, but have an interest in it) can download. So I think it's the audience that you're thinking of for the conference, and I see the audience as much broader than the people in this room. There were a bunch of slides in my presen-tation whereby, had I been creating a presentation only for the people in this room, those slides are not what I would have created. I tried to create something for our distance audience.

Alvarez, Sharon: I just kind of wanted to follow up on that a little bit because we have held the Society for Entrepreneurship Scholars (SES), and many of my colleagues – when you hold SES at the school you're at, you rope everybody in. So many of my colleagues, whether they're OB [organizational behavior] or international or anthropology, have been roped in, and they've tried to steal the concept for their fields – the organizational behavior people in particular (which I found interesting because they thought it was such a wonderful mentoring for young people) and, kind of with what Tricia said, they found it to be innovative. Even though they're in a more-established field, they were like, 'Gosh, we don't mentor our young people the way you guys do,' and I've found that to be a wonderful compliment.

McDougall, Patricia: We always need to invest in the future and I would emphasize it again that we have to invest in our doctoral students and in our junior scholars. That is where we are going to get the biggest return on our investment.

Lumpkin, Tom: Is there a risk that entrepreneurship will fall from favor in universities if the money dries up? In terms of research, is it more likely that reliance on private money will cause our research to be compromised, or by contrast, raise the standards and the importance of entrepreneurship research?

McDougall, Patricia: All right, that's a couple of questions, and I've actually thought about the first one. I see money flowing into central universities for entrepreneurship, and I think that that money is tenuous money. I do have some concerns about entrepreneurship programs that are central administration driven because I think that some of these programs have been driven primarily as a response to the money. Business schools are different. I really believe that entrepreneurship would continue to have a place in business schools if funding decreased. I support cross-campus initiatives (and we have created many of these at Indiana University), but I believe the business school needs to be the axis of these programs. Entrepreneurship programs need to come out of the business school because it's the business school that's going to have the long-term commitment to entrepreneurship. This is the natural fit for it. Entrepreneurship has been in business schools since 1947. Undoubtedly, we can deliver better programs if we have money. So money matters, but I don't expect that entrepreneurship would dry up if the money fell off. I don't see that happening any time in the near future.

Now the second part of the question is, in terms of research, is it more likely that reliance on private money will raise our standards or compromise our research? I don't worry much about private funding compromising our research. I think you have to worry about that kind of thing much more in fields like medical research (for example, tobacco studies). Universities have conflict-of-interest regulations. I'm on the university's Conflict of Interest Committee and I help review all of the conflict-of-interest cases (such as when one has more than a certain percentage of ownership in a company, or more than $10,000 a year in certain income and various situations). Faculty are always required to report all of these potential conflicts. You know, there's just never a major problem out of the business school. Research conflicts related to entrepreneurship research would be rare. Those are not issues that I worry are going to have serious conflicts of interest that might compromise our work. Thank you.

REFERENCES

(1990). *Strategic Management Journal,* Special Issue: Corporate Entrepreneurship, **11**.

(2000). *Academy of Management Journal,* Special Issue: Entrepreneurship, **43** (5).

Birch, D. (1987). *Job Creation in America: How our Smallest Companies put the Most People to Work*. New York: The Free Press.

Drucker, P. (1985). *Innovation and Entrepreneurship: Practice and Principles.* Oxford: Elsevier.

Meyer, G.D. (2009). Commentary: on the integration of strategic management and entrepreneurship: views of a contrarian. *Entrepreneurship Theory and Practice*, **33** (1), 341–51.

Oviatt, B.M. and P. McDougall (2005). Toward a theory of international new ventures. *Journal of International Business Studies*, **36**, 29–41.

Shane, S. and S. Venkataraman (2000). The promise of entrepreneurship as a field of research. *Academy of Management Review*, **25** (1), 217–26.

Venkataraman, S. (1997). The distinctive domain of entrepreneurship research. In J. Katz (ed.), *Advances in Entrepreneurship Firm Emergence and Growth*. Greenwich, CT: JAI Press, vol. 3, pp. 119–38.

Wortman, M. (1987). Entrepreneurship: an evaluation of empirical research in the field. *Journal of Management*, **13** (2), 259–79.

Zahra, S.A., R.D. Ireland and M.A. Hitt (2000). International expansion by new venture firms: international diversity, mode of market entry, technological learning, and performance. *Academy of Management Journal*, **43** (5), 925–50.

7. Entrepreneurship and entrepreneurial opportunity: made as well as found

Sankaran (Venkat) Venkataraman

Dino, Rich: Ladies and gentlemen, our first keynote of the 2009 Entrepreneurship Exemplars Research Conference and recipient of the 2008 Foundational Paper IDEA Award, Professor Venkat Venkataraman.

Venkataraman, Venkat: Thank you. I'm very happy to be here. It's a great honor, first of all, to receive the Inaugural Award. It's also a great privilege to be chosen to be a speaker at the Exemplars Conference, and for that I am grateful. But I'll also say this: I'm honestly very nervous because as I look around the room I find so many distinguished people that, frankly, I feel somewhat inadequate.

I would like to thank Rich Dino for the invitation to come here and present to you folks. I'd like to thank Ron Mitchell for the initiative that he has started on behalf of the Academy of Management, and Dean Earley for providing the funding and the actual political license to pull this off. I'm sure you folks had a lot of people in the background helping you to eventually let me come here, stand here in front of you and start the process. For that, I'm grateful to you all.

Rich Dino gave me two suggestions in terms of what I should cover in this talk. The first topic, he said, was 'Just tell us how you got here in terms of how you got some of those papers into the top journals of the field. Just tell your story.' The second charter he gave me was to touch upon some interesting emerging research themes in my own work. So I'll try and spend about 10 minutes on the former and about 20 minutes on the latter.

Talking about how I got here and how I cracked the top journals of the field, if you will, I can't help but start with my first experience of sending a paper to a journal. I was a second-year doctoral student at the University of Minnesota. I had just completed my first paper (Venkataraman, Van de Ven, Polley, and Garud, 1989) with my advisor, Professor Andy Van de Ven. Andy suggested that this was an excellent paper and that I should send it to *Administrative Science Quarterly* (*ASQ*). By then I had been in the field long enough to know that *ASQ* was the top of the heap and a very tough nut to crack; so I pointed out to Andy that perhaps he should rethink his aspirations. But Andy said, 'No, no. You should always start at the top. This paper is good enough for *ASQ*. Send it out.' So, like a good doctoral student, I packaged it, gave it to Andy (Andy being the senior author perhaps would get a better hearing from the journal) and he sent it off in his name to *ASQ*. About four, five, six months later (I forget), the packet of reviews came back. It went to Andy because he was the corresponding author, and he looked at the stuff, rearranged the materials, and put them in my mailbox. So, that afternoon, I go to my mailbox with shaking hands and pick the stuff out from my inbox. Andy has rearranged the materials so that one of the reviews is on top, and it's a very brief review. It's about three or four lines. I think it consisted of three sentences. The middle sentence said, 'In one of the paragraphs the author states, ". . . in a nutshell. . . . " In my opinion, that's the appropriate container for the ideas in this paper.' That was my welcome to the field of publications. I didn't know what to do or what to say, but I think there were three or four things that stood out from that experience – not all of which sank in at that point in time.

The first thing that sank in for me was Andy's reaction to the whole thing. He didn't blink an eye. He just said, 'Let's look at the reviews and see what needs to be fixed. Let's fix it and send it on to the next journal.' The second thing that struck me was that I had to develop a thick skin. It was not personal. It was not about me. The ideas were probably not good enough. You just had to work harder. The third thing was this idea that you start at the top and work your way down. Most papers will find their home at that equilibrium spot. They'll settle where they ought to settle. There's a lot of luck in the process and there are things that will happen, but there is an equilibrating process here. I think those three lessons sort of happened to me in the course of the two or three years that I was at Minnesota.

The next big event that happened in my life was also in the second year of my doctoral program. In one of the doctoral courses we were asked to read the Murray Davis (1971) paper 'That's interesting!' That paper left a deep impression on me as well. I would highly recommend it to everyone. I'm sure most of the people here would've read the paper; but if you have not, that's a paper worth getting and reading.

Like any new doctoral student, I labored under the belief that a theory or a theorist is considered great because his or her theories are true – but I discovered that was really not true. That's false. A theory or a theorist is considered great not because his/her theories are true, but because they're interesting. Murray Davis goes on to develop about a dozen criteria for why a theory is interesting. It will take me too much time to go through all of those points, but the gist of Davis's point is that interesting ideas are those that point out that things are not really what they appear or you think they appear to be. That was the sum and substance of what he argued. Now, although I have never been able to practice successfully the various suggestions he provided, I was able to abandon this notion of truth as a criteria for judging what's publishable and what's readable. I had to replace it with other attributes of what makes papers imminently publishable and readable. In addition to the notion of 'interesting,' later in my career I was introduced to the philosophy of the American pragmatists (such as James Dewey and more recently Richard Rorty) and then I added 'usefulness' as another criterion for judging the value and ideas of papers.

I would assert here today that top journals look for papers that are interesting, provocative, useful to either practice or to researchers by raising new and fruitful research questions, are empirically tractable and have a clear answer to the 'so what' questions. That, I figured out, is really what journals are looking for. That's really their stock-in-trade. Journals are not really after truth. Journals are not really after a kind of statement about a phenomenon, which everybody agrees as a consensus that 'This is what it's all about.' They are really in the business of attracting attention – spreading their own genes, in some sense. So they look for the provocative. They look for the interesting. They do it in a very sophisticated way, but that's a large part of the story.

A third event for me was the first publishable paper out of my dissertation, and where I should send it. Taking Andy's dictum to me seriously, I decided I should aim for *ASQ*, and start at the top and see where the equilibrium point might eventually be. After some while, I got the reviews back. It was a substantial revision, so at least I had survived the rejection process (which was personally very satisfying for me), but it was very high risk. It had nearly 13 pages of single-spaced comments from three reviewers and one associate editor. When I read it, it was frankly beyond me at that stage. I could not handle it by myself, but I learned several lessons from that experience. First, publishing in top journals requires tremendous perseverance, great stamina, a lot of help and a good dose of luck. Subsequently, I could never get all three reviewers to agree on that particular paper. Convincing three reviewers is a really tough business – no question about that.

I also discovered that top journals require contributions at the frontiers of the field – and the frontiers can be pushing boundaries theoretically; or it could be a new data source; or it could be a methodological breakthrough; or it could be a phenomenological breakthrough, empirical breakthrough or empirical context. There should be some novel element: something interesting and something that pushes the boundaries of the field. If you don't have that, the chances that the paper will get in are going to be highly limited.

Around that time and a little before that, I also discovered that I had another problem. My papers were going out with entrepreneurship in the foreground and the mainstream disciplines in the background. Journals wanted exactly the opposite. They wanted the mainstream disciplinary theories and received wisdom in the foreground and entrepreneurship in the background. I was trained and skilled in putting entrepreneurship in the foreground and the supporting cast was all the other stuff in the background, and so I couldn't communicate with the reviewers. The problem was such that if you wanted to talk to the mainstream, then you had to talk the mainstream language. That took me a couple of years to fully grasp. It is at that point that an inspirational breakthrough happened for me. I read the Aldrich and Auster (1986) paper 'Even dwarfs started small.' I read the paper for the first time in 1986, but I didn't fully grasp the significance of it. I read the paper and understood what it was about, but I didn't understand why it was important. It was only around 1987 that I understood the importance – because in that paper Aldrich and Auster talked in a balanced way, both to the mainstream sociologists and the social psychologists, as well as to the entrepreneurship folks, equally. It is that kind of balance that I had to get right if I wanted to be successful in the mainstream journals. That penny didn't drop for quite some time.

So, the challenge in those days was for an entrepreneurship scholar to be able to communicate with the other fields, the sister fields in the discipline; but I figured it out only slowly. Aldrich and Auster's paper was not published in a journal. It was a book chapter. It was a wonderful book chapter. Beautifully written. It was a great inspiration to me, and at the same time, Singh, House and Tucker (1986) published two papers in *ASQ* where they showed beautifully how the received wisdom from sociology could be put in the foreground, but you could have a very compelling entrepreneurship story in the background. At that time, I thought these were great papers. When I read them now I realize they're really not very great papers. They used voluntary social service organizations as their empirical context. It was not at all compelling. It was not at all persuasive. But the contributions they made were two-fold: they took a sociological theory, which was in the mainstream at that point in time – specifically, Stinchcombe and Hannan and Freeman's ideas – and juxtaposed these with March's ideas on change and put them together in two papers, which introduced the hazard rate model to the management field. In fact, they actually used the Gompertz distribution, which was subsequently disputed by others, but the paper got into *ASQ* – the top of the heap.

So for me the 'Dwarfs started small' paper and these two papers sort of showed the way. In fact, as a young scholar coming out in the field of entrepreneurship, they gave me the recipe, if you will, to be able to break into these journals. So to cut a long story short, from that point on I made it into the *Journal of Business Venturing (JBV)*, which was not a top journal at that point in time; but it gave me the break, and then I got into the *Journal of Management*. Then I worked my way up into *Management Science* and got into the *Strategic Management Journal (SMJ)*. But in the process, I've been rejected by *Administrative Science Quarterly (ASQ)*, *Academy of Management Review (AMR)*, *Academy of Management Journal (AMJ)*, *Management Science (MS)*, *Organization Science (OS)*, *Strategic Management Journal (SMJ)* and *Journal of Business Venturing (JBV)*. So I've had the privilege of being rejected by all of them, which led me to the next lesson for me, which is rejection is part of the process. Failure is in the path to success, so you have to be willing to accept it. Develop a thick skin. Just get on with the process and take the best suggestions of the previous reviewers. Make the changes to the paper, put it in an envelope and ship it out to the next journal. If you have a hierarchy, that's great.

The other thing I also learned is that you have to collaborate. You can't do everything yourself. If you want to crack the top journals, then you have to publish at the frontier; and it's not easy publishing at the frontier. My dean recently told me that he had done some analysis, and that roughly 50 to 60 percent of the papers published in the 1970s were published with co-authors. In the 1980s it had crossed two-thirds. In the 1990s it had crossed 85 percent, and today apparently, fully 93 percent of the papers are published with co-authors (and most of them are three authors or more). So that was another thing I learned: you don't have to do it by yourself. You can do it with co-authors, etc.

I think the problem today for entrepreneurship scholars is different. I think the mainstream challenge has vanished. It has gone away. As we heard just a little while ago from both Chris Earley as well as from Rich Dino, that entrepreneurship is part of the mainstream. The challenge today is not so much worrying about mainstream and background stories, etc.; the challenge today is just designing good research and executing it well. That's the challenge. It is an easy challenge, but it's easier to say than to accomplish. For me there are just six or seven attributes of what good research needs in order to make it into the top journals, and successful papers usually demonstrate that. These are commonsensical things, but they bear repeating because we often forget them. From my own experiences reviewing as well as editing, the observations I can make are: successful papers are more than likely to have something novel to say rather than just a repetition of well-trodden areas – and that novelty is either in the theory, the approach, the data, the methods, the empirical context or in the conclusions. Successful papers provide a precise description of the research problem, and the literature to which they will contribute. Surprisingly, a lot of papers are not very clear on this. Authors are not very clear about exactly who they want to contribute to (their audience), or clear about the scholars in their community (their intellectual mentors). This type of clarity may be achieved, not only by citing others' work, but also by synthesizing their ideas into that mainstream to which they are intending to contribute.

Next, the literature review must be up-to-date and include papers from the journal to which they are addressed (often we get papers where the authors don't cite other papers in the journal). Why would the editor or the reviewers be interested in that?

Next, the core arguments are supported with sound logic, contemporary theory and are persuasive from a communications perspective. It took me a long while to figure out that communicating your research is very different from doing your research. A lot of younger scholars write the papers as if they are doing the research (what they did and how they did it). I think the two are very separate things, so pay attention to the communications perspective. Paying attention to communication was important for me.

Next, both the data and the data sources are of superior quality and are robust. The methods are state of the art and very apropos. They have interesting, non-obvious and non-trivial results. The results are checked and rechecked from a variety of standpoints – including reliability, validity and robustness, or their equivalents (in the case of qualitative research).

Finally, they conclude clear, persuasive and satisfying implications for theory, methods, future research and, occasionally, practice. This is just basic stuff that we teach in introductory doctoral courses. We hear it every day, but somehow when it comes to practice we don't do it that well; and for that reason it is good to take on co-authors. For that reason, it is good to do papers with others who have been there and done that.

Lastly, I would say that it is good to present papers in colloquiums and forums, which allow you to sharpen your arguments and get the paper ready for primetime.

Having said all of that, I will lastly say that successful papers have intangible qualities that are difficult to reduce to a formula. It's useful to ask, 'What's the interesting angle here that an editor and three reviewers will take a chance with this paper out of every 10 to 15 papers that they could potentially publish?' While it is one thing to get published in a leading journal, it's an entirely different matter to be taken seriously, cited often and form the basis or foundation of other people's work. For that, you not only need a good paper and a good narrative, but great timing and a lot of luck. I will not dwell on what makes for an influential paper – that's a topic for another day. But I think one of the reasons that the 'distinctive domain' paper and the *AMR* 2000 paper (Shane and Venkataraman, 2000) with Scott Shane became successful is because people found the notion of entrepreneurial opportunity interesting and intriguing (although there were many other ideas in these papers). Personally, I didn't think the entrepreneurial opportunity idea was interesting at all, but that was the one that was picked up by the field. There is no way I could've predicted that, so, accordingly, in the rest of my talk I will attempt to extend, develop and enrich this notion of entrepreneurial opportunity, and fulfill the promise I made to Rich Dino that I will try and develop a theme or two in this talk.

Although I'm the one who's presenting on this topic, this could well have been presented by Saras Sarasvathy or Nicholas Dew, two of my collaborators and co-authors on this particular topic and effort. I'm going to call it 'Entrepreneurship and entrepreneurial opportunity: Made as well as found,' concerning the theme of entrepreneurial opportunity being conceptualized both as 'made' and as well as 'found.'[1]

[*Authors' note:* At this point in the speech Professor Venkataraman summarized portions from a forthcoming book with Dew and Sarasvathy, which he has since further condensed for inclusion herein as follows.]

Venkataraman, Venkat [*continuing*]: Let me begin with an example from our book. While working as a management consultant in Washington DC, Jennifer Lovitt Riggs developed a blister while walking across a Pentagon parking lot (in her beautiful high-heeled shoes) to a meeting with a top-ranking defense official. Riggs started Nota Bene Shoe, a line of women's dress shoes that combines smart design, high style, quality construction and superior materials to create a distinctive shoe (one that is not only beautiful, but also feels good enough to walk in all day). Riggs claims that she never wanted to be an entrepreneur; she just wanted beautiful shoes that were really comfortable. She could not find them on the market so she decided to make them. In making the shoes of her dreams she also remade herself into an entrepreneur.

This simple story contains several themes of particular interest to the entrepreneurship researcher. These themes can be examined using either of two lenses –specifically, 'made' and 'found.' If you presume opportunities, products and markets exist *in potentio* in a universe of all possible ventures, we would be led to organize the themes in a different way than if we approach new ventures as made *de novo* through the actions of entrepreneurs and their stakeholders. A large portion of current research assumes the former; although there are many cases where the created worldview is coming into the literature. The overall approach is based on the assumptions in the two worldviews embodied in research questions such as the following:

'Made' questions:
- What experiences, actions and reactions lead to the formation of new opportunities, ventures and markets?
- How does one act entrepreneurially?
- What are the antecedents and consequences of acting entrepreneurially?
- How do entrepreneurial actions create new markets?

'Found' questions:
- How do entrepreneurs recognize opportunities?
- What traits and abilities distinguish effective opportunity recognition or successful entrepreneurs?
- What necessary conditions lead to the discovery and successful exploitation of opportunities?
- What actions and reactions lead to the development of opportunities?
- How does one act entrepreneurially?
- What are the antecedents and consequences of such actions?
- How does entrepreneurial action create new markets?

Now, in the rest of the talk I will highlight four concepts; four concepts among many others that may be valuable in the development of the 'made' view of entrepreneurship. For each of these concepts, in keeping with the objectives of this Exemplars Conference, I shall introduce an exemplar paper or a book that could form the foundation for that concept. And in keeping with my earlier theme that entrepreneurship scholars should embed their work in the larger history of science and sciences (and that entrepreneurship should inform the sciences), I am going to take four exemplar papers from fields completely unrelated to entrepreneurship and even to, perhaps, management. Those four concepts (which I refer to as 'the building blocks of "made"') are: (1) studying entrepreneurship and entrepreneurial opportunity as a science of the artificial: artifactual science; (2) adding notions of inter-subjectivity to the usual notions of subjective and objective ideas in entrepreneurship; (3) studying entrepreneurial opportunity as a creative process in addition to a discovery process; and (4) studying entrepreneurial opportunity as a transformative process other than just a recombination process.

[*Authors' note:* These four concepts were subsequently condensed for inclusion in this volume as follows:]

THE BUILDING BLOCKS OF 'MADE'

1. Study entrepreneurship as a science of the artificial (Simon, 1988): include the language and logic of design and fabrication given the constraints of the natural world.
2. Include subjective, objective and inter-subjective knowledge (Davidson's three varieties of knowledge, 2001: 205–20) in our theories and facts about entrepreneurship.
3. Treat entrepreneurship as a creative process (Buchanan & Vanberg, 1991) rather than just a discovery process; and
4. Use language of a transformation process rather than just a recombination process (Goodman, 1978: 1–32).

Entrepreneurship as a Science of the Artificial

A science of the artificial studies objects and phenomena in which human purpose as well as natural laws are embodied. So bringing in the human purpose is very important. Therefore, an airplane would be a legitimate object of interest to a science of the artificial, while a bird may not (unless the bird serves a specific human purpose such as that of pigeons bred for carrying messages). Note here that the interest, then, is in human artifacts; and the key elements of this concept may be defined and developed as follows:

*   Artifact: meeting point (interface) between the inner and the outer environments.
*   New venture creation can be studied as a process of design and fabrication.
*   Natural, economic, psychological and sociological laws become constraints in the design and fabrication process.

Throughout *The Sciences of the Artificial*, Simon repeatedly emphasized that natural laws constrain, but do not dictate, the fabrication of artifacts. That is, it is possible to design artifacts. So we get this important idea of design. This suggests that a phenomenon, like new venture creation, can be studied on its own beyond the sciences that govern the inner and outer environment for which it forms the interface. In other words, if you factor the founding of a firm into the motivation and psychological characteristics of its founders on the one hand and the institutional cultural characteristics of the society they live in on the other, we need not be limited to psychology, sociology or economics to study it. We can study new venture creation as a process of design that matches up psychology with sociology or economics – and even transform the relevant elements in each of these sciences.

This is a very different way of thinking about the field. It is possible, particularly in business schools, to construe entrepreneurship very narrowly. I hope you will change that to think about entrepreneurship as studying and building artificial things using natural and other social scientific laws as constraints.

Three Varieties of Knowledge

Let me now turn to the second concept, the subjective, objective and inter-subjective ideas that are together important for the 'made' worldview.

The concept of 'opportunity' in entrepreneurship research provides fertile ground for the application of Davidson's thesis about the inextricable tripod of subjective, inter-subjective and objective knowledge that constitutes all of epistemology. Opportunity has become a central construct of interest to entrepreneurship researchers. Recently there have been numerous arguments in the literature about the nature of the entrepreneurial opportunities: what they are, how to define them theoretically, how to operationalize and measure them empirically, and so on. In particular, there are debates about whether they exist out there in the objective sense or whether they are mere perceptions, subjective phenomena, that are unobservable *ex ante*. There are also controversies about whether opportunities can be created *de novo* or can only be discovered or selected from the universe of all possible opportunities. For me, an opportunity is an epistemological construct: a kind of knowledge about the world. Its ontological status is irrelevant. For taking Davidson (2001) seriously requires taking the existence of the world as given. I therefore summarize my application of these three varieties of knowledge as follows:

- Subjective: I know (mostly) what I think, want and intend and what my sensations are.
- Objective: I know a lot about the world around me.

- Inter-subjective: I know something about what goes on in other people's minds.
- The three varieties of knowledge do not exist in isolation from each other and are intertwined.
- The nexus of the entrepreneur and the opportunity are intertwined with the three varieties of knowledge.

So, even if you choose to conceptualize all opportunities as a means–end framework for the achievement of given human purposes, and entrepreneurial opportunities as new means–ends frameworks (as Shane in 2003, and Shane and Venkataraman in 2000 do), the artifactual nature of the entrepreneurial economy (along with the subjective, inter-subjective, and objective tripod of epistemology, and the inherent creativity of market processes) argue for an open-endedness. In other words, [*gesticulating in circling motion*] the 'found-made, found-made, found-made' circle just keeps repeating itself.

A strong case for the last of these three claims is made by Buchanan and Vanberg (1991). They located this open-endedness directly in entrepreneurial action, to which I turn next.

Entrepreneurship as a Creative Process

The third conceptual idea is that market is a creative process; and I use the paper by Buchanan and Vanberg, 1991 as my exemplar. Buchanan and Vanberg's worldview of entrepreneurship as a creative process is particularly relevant for developing a 'made' view of entrepreneurship because it not only explicates a creative view of the market, but offers an important critique of the discovery view of Kirzner (cf. Kirzner, 1973, 1979, 1985) that informs so much of the current theorizing in entrepreneurship research. Much of our recent conversation about entrepreneurial opportunities is based on Kirzner's ideas, which are inherently teleological. Buchanan and Vanberg's criticism of Kirzner is anchored in the inherent unknowableness of the future that in turn is rooted in a non-teleological perspective on understanding the world. Their argument builds on Lachmann's thesis (1977) that time and knowledge belong together; and that time cannot pass without modifying knowledge. Accordingly, I suggest two comparisons between conceptualizations of discovery and of creation (From Discovery to Creation I and From Discovery to Creation II).

[*Authors' note:* The following are summaries of the actual text which is forthcoming as previously noted.]

From Discovery to Creation I

Discovery	*Creation*
● Emphasizes analytical rationality	● Considers ecological rationality
● Emphasizes more informed analysis	● Includes fast and frugal heuristics
● Searches for domain-independent success factors	● Includes contingent factors
● Looks for and finds biases and errors	● Emphasizes judgment under uncertainty

From Discovery to Creation II

Discovery	*Creation*
● Preferences are given, well-ordered and stable	● Preferences are constructed 'on the go'
● Preferences are clear and widely shared	● Preferences are ambiguous and 'inchoate'
● Rent/profit is the 'best' dependent variable	● Rent/profit is a constraint in creating and distributing distinctive value

So the 'found' view, that is the teleological conception of the market economy, suggests opportunities of markets and potential, and the job of the entrepreneur is to find them. Entrepreneurship in this view is akin to an Easter-egg hunt. The 'made' view argues instead that when entrepreneurs make do with what is found in the world – how they combine those raw materials with their own abilities, aspirations and experiences – it creates opportunities that (when attested to, brought into and co-shaped by others) can (under certain conditions of sufficiency) converge, coalesce and come of age into markets. Entrepreneurship in this view is akin to making a communal sculpture or painting a mural by a sufficiently large group of stakeholders. How this making can and does and should happen, who makes it happen, and the consequences of such happening ought to form (in our opinion) the content of entrepreneurship research. In effect, we could understand entrepreneurship as 'new worldmaking.'

Language of Transformation Process

I will now elaborate on the final theme. That is using the language of transformation rather than just the language of Schumpeterian recombination to understand worldmaking. For my fourth concept and final concept, I will use Nelson Goodman's (1978) idea of worldmaking as an exemplar. In his book, *Ways of Worldmaking*, Nelson Goodman elaborates on the transformative process for making new worlds that are more immediately applicable to entrepreneurship research. Goodman's main argument is very simple. I quote him: 'The many stuffs that worlds are made of are made along with the worlds, but made of what? Not from nothing after all, but from other worlds. Worldmaking, as we know it, always starts from the world already on hand. The making is a remaking' (1978: 6).

What we need to think about is this process of transforming existing worlds into new ones. A combination is defined as follows: given as the set of all possible unique limits, a combination is a subset of the element of 'S'. This definition implies a search-and-selection process that picks out the relevant elements and combines them into new sets; but the new set is always a subset of the larger set 'S' that we began with. If transformation and contrast is any variety of different operations, and it relies more on geometry, transformation can increase the dimensionality of the original space. Interaction and space are essential elements of transformation. That is why the notion of transformative process might better capture the application of Goodman's ideas to entrepreneurship than Schumpeter's ideas of combinations. Moreover, transformation allows us to go from the realm of physical space and time into social space and history. Goodman outlines five candidacies for worldmaking processes. This list is not meant to be exhaustive or mutually exclusive, it is just meant to illustrate the many different kinds of transformational operations that can help make worlds. Let me briefly articulate these five possibilities for going beyond new combinations to the language of transformations:

1. Composition and decomposition: Take the example of Starbucks. Starbucks is not simply a collection of coffee shops. Composing the venture of Starbucks consisted of a variety of transformative operations on people's taste and habits, on sourcing coffee beans, on creating a unique identity and so on. This included decomposing the Italian ambiance into its constitute parts, and distorting habits of beverage consumption into a social aesthetic that could be woven into the urban landscape in ways that have recomposed entire neighborhoods. Worldmaking spotlights a richness and complexity of transformative as contrasted with clearer and simpler lines of combinatorial processes.

2. Weighting: The Atkins diet, for example, transformed the diet market and even markets for regular food products – even on supermarket shelves by overweighting proteins against carbohydrates.

3. Ordering: In this example, The Body Shop essentially reordered (or reprioritized) by emphasizing that 'no animal testing was undertaken in the development of their products.' It had nothing to do with beauty. It had nothing to do with any of those other things that might lift your spirits. By simply reordering the attribute of 'no animal testing,' they were able to create a whole new kind of market.

4. Deletion and supplementation: Henry Ford weeded out everything that was not essential in order to come up with a cheap design of automobiles, the Model T. The literature on the subject, however, only emphasizes its creative recombination of technologies to create the production line; but nobody talks about what he eliminated in any systematic way.

5. Deformation: One could easily argue that the Hummer is a deformed tank or a Jeep gone wild or that Taco Bell is deformed Mexican food (not to mention the deletion of all flavor from its composition: I like Mexican food, so I know what I'm talking about).

An important assumption underlying these and other 'yet to be discovered processes of worldmaking' is the freedom to choose one's end as well as one's courses of action. This freedom, however, is not arbitrary or unconstrained. There are self-imposed constraints, as well as those imposed by physical and other social scientific laws, aspirations and endowment of others; yet these constraints themselves are not deterministic. At any given point in time, they provide stable boundaries within which human designs work to make new worlds.

I will stop at this point and conclude with one final idea. What I've presented today are broad outlines of suggestive ideas and how the notion of entrepreneurial opportunity could be developed, extended and enriched; but I'll emphasize that these ideas are very suggestive. In this regard, I would like to close with another nugget I learned in the process of trying to crack the top journals in our fields. I discovered the hard way that it's very difficult to publish suggestive papers in leading journals – however interesting or provocative they may be. Journals like specific papers with ideas where the authors make specific commitments to arguments and points of view that are empirically tractable. Further, these arguments have to be internally consistent. It is ironic that the Foundational Research Award was given to my 'Distinctive domain' paper (Venkataraman, 1997), which I personally like very much; but it is a very general and suggestive paper that does not take a definite position on the various issues that it raises. There is no way the 'Distinctive domain' paper could have been published in its original form in a leading peer-reviewed journal. However, its derivative paper (Shane and Venkataraman, 2000) with Scott Shane, 'The promise of entrepreneurship research' was indeed published in 2000 in the *Academy of Management Review*. But to do that, Scott and I had to sacrifice suggestiveness and pluralism for narrow arguments, with which I was very uncomfortable but clearly did suit Scott very well. In other words, I had to sacrifice richness and generality to gain specificity and tractability in order to get published in a top journal. In the end, we should not forget that publishing in top journals is necessary to be an accepted scholar of standing, but the purpose of scholarship is not necessarily to publish in top journals. Publishing in top journals is merely one means to achieve broader and richer aim of scholarship. If I had to choose between the 'Distinctive domain' paper and the *AMR* paper, I would always choose the 'Distinctive domain' paper as the more interesting one. Thank you very much.

Dino, Rich: Thank you, Venkat. Venkat will entertain questions.

Venkataraman, Venkat: I realize that I took more than my fair share of my time, so I probably exceeded your patience; but I will take a few questions if you have any.

Lumpkin, Tom: Please say more about your idea about combinations and recombinations for the fertile field of research.

Venkataraman, Venkat: What I meant by that was we talk about combinations and recombinations. In Schumpeter's original idea he talks about five different ways in which new ideas can come to market and how creative destruction can happen, and the resource-based view of the firm brings forth this idea about combining resources (knowledge being recombinations of ideas, etc.). But we usually do not pay attention to the different ways in which we can categorize combination. What is the language of talking about combinations? We take combinations and recombination as givens, and then go on to make other statements about outcomes of that – about the antecedents of that – but we do not stop to specify exactly the content of these combinations. So I'm asking for a vocabulary. I'm asking for a dictionary and I'm asking for relationships between different ways we can talk about combinations. In other words: treating combinations as a focus of research. If I could think immediately, I could give you an example; but it's not falling into my mind right now, which I think is very valuable for entrepreneurship research especially (and I dare say) for folks who are also interested in the resource-based view of the firm. There may not be such research, to the best of my knowledge; I just want you to always acknowledge that. It's not a fertile area as yet.

Fiet, Jim: Yes, I was going to ask if there is a combination of time and space and market action as a way of looking at this idea of combinations.

Venkataraman, Venkat: That's not the way in which I was thinking about combination. You could use time, space and market as a combination; but I want to know, what are the different ways that you can talk about combinations of those three elements? In other words, what's the action of that combination? Can that combination be spoken of in a variety of different ways, and do those different varieties have different implications for how time, space and market action combine in order to produce certain kinds of outcomes? Do you see what I mean?

Bauer, Talya: I think, maybe to the uninitiated, someone might get the impression that you have a negative view of publishing in top journals. Can you highlight a few of what you think are the positive features of papers that go through that process?

Venkataraman, Venkat: I'm curious. Did I come across as being negative at publication?

Bauer, Talya: Sometimes, yeah; but I think if you're published, as we all are . . .

Venkataraman, Venkat: Let me put it this way. Obviously the listener's perception matters. If I gave the impression that there is a negative side, if I appear to have a negative view of publishing in top journals (far from it), it's because there's more to complete the story. That's an impression that I do want to convey. Publishing in top journals is required and is a responsibility of a good scholar. Having said that, what I would say is (in my own case), the 'Distinctive domain' paper would not have gotten as much publicity and notoriety if not for the *AMR* paper. What a top journal does is it gives the idea public view – a public airing. It increases the scale of reach. I think those are all the positive aspects of top journals. Submitting to a top journal is a very disciplined rigorous process. It forces you to work on your idea, to relate it to other ideas that have gone before, and to connect and talk to a group of people with continuity. It's there in the archives of the knowledge base; and for all of those reasons, I would highly encourage everyone to attempt to publish in the top journals. Even if you don't get in, just the process of trying to publish in the top journals is a very, very worthwhile one. So please, do not get the idea that I'm against publishing in the top journals.

Barney, Jay: If you take the discovery and creation implication and push that forward, how would that affect how we teach entrepreneurship?

Venkataraman, Venkat: If you take the discovery and creation perspective and push that forward, what are the implications and how would we teach entrepreneurship in our classrooms? I think it matters a great deal. It matters fundamentally to how we teach entrepreneurship. I think in the discovery view, we teach entrepreneurship more as an intelligent search-and-selection process; whereas in the created view and the made view we would teach it as a worldmaking process. We would teach it as a design process. You design your entrepreneurial opportunities, you design firms, and you design and fabricate markets. We will use a different set of subject matters. We would access different knowledge sources. We would provide different kinds of exercises, experiments and classroom activities. In fact, I think we would teach very, very differently. It would be a course designed around teaching design – and teaching design is very different from teaching search and selection. It would emphasize creativity, it would emphasize experimentation, it would emphasize failure, it would emphasize learning from failure and a whole host of other things which I think matter a great deal. That's a very astute question and I think it has a lot of possibilities. My personal view is that we are already there and we should evolve to that next step. We have done the search-and-selection bit. I think that body of work is well fleshed-out. We understand that very well. So the next frontier for entrepreneurship research and the next level for entrepreneurship research is (harking back to Ron Mitchell's plea) to think about entrepreneurship as a design process.

The second thing I would say is the scientific method is a method for designing a lot of things and solving a lot of problems in society. Entrepreneurship is also a method for society to create new things and solve a lot of problems. So the other thing that I would say in addition to thinking about entrepreneurship as design is entrepreneurship as a method for solving social problems, and realizing the promise of a lot of things as well. So, teaching entrepreneurship as a method is also another way in which we could extend the frontier of the field.

Lumpkin, Tom: A great deal of entrepreneurship research is from the supply side: resources, aspirations and knowledge. What role does the demand side play in entrepreneurship research?

Venkataraman, Venkat: My short answer to the question would be that much of the entrepreneurship research is from the supply side – resources, aspirations, etc. Is there any role for the demand side in entrepreneurship research that is from a need or from the market or problem perspective? My answer to that would be the same for either the demand or supply side. We can study it. We can teach it as 'found' or 'made.' There are implications for accessing it or studying it from a 'found' perspective, and there are also implications for accessing it and studying it and/or teaching about it or prescribing from a 'made' perspective. I think we understand a lot from the 'found' perspective. I think it's time that we moved a little more towards the 'made' perspective. Let's study design. Let's study need from a design and from a method perspective. Thank you very much.

NOTE

1. Please note that these ideas appear in a book to be published by Yale University Press in 2011.

REFERENCES

Aldrich, H.E. and E. Auster (1986). Even dwarfs started small: liabilities of age and size and their strategic implications. *Research in Organizational Behavior*, **8**, 165–98.

Buchanan, J.M. and V.J. Vanberg (1991). The market as a creative process. *Economics and Philosophy*, **7**, 167–86.

Davidson, D. (2001). *Three Varieties of Knowledge: Subjective, Intersubjective, Objective*. New York: Oxford University Press.

Davis, M. (1971). That's interesting! Towards a phenomenology of sociology and a sociology of phenomenology. *Philosophy of the Social Sciences*, **1**, 309–44.

Goodman, N. (1978). *Ways of Worldmaking*. Indianapolis: Hackett Publishing.

Kirzner, I.M. (1973). *Competition and Entrepreneurship*. Chicago: University of Chicago Press.

Kirzner, I.M. (1979). *Perception, Opportunity and Profit*. Chicago: University of Chicago Press.

Kirzner, I.M. (1985). *Discovery and the Capitalist Process*. Chicago: University of Chicago Press.

Lachmann, Ludwig M. (1977). *Capital, Expectations, and Market Process*. Kansas City: Sheed, Andrews and McMeel.

Shane, S. (2003). *A General Theory of Entrepreneurship: The Individual-Opportunity Nexus*. Cheltenham, UK and Northampton, MA, USA: Edward Elgar.

Shane, S. and S. Venkataraman (2000). The promise of entrepreneurship as a field of research. *Academy of Management Review*, **25** (1), 217–26.

Simon, H.A. (1988). *The Sciences of the Artificial*. Cambridge, MA: MIT Press.

Singh, J.V., R.J. House and D.J. Tucker (1986). Organizational change and organizational mortality. *Administrative Science Quarterly*, **31** (4), 587–611.

Singh, J.V., D.J. Tucker and R.J. House (1986). Organizational legitimacy and the liability of newness. *Administrative Science Quarterly*, **31** (2), 171–93.

Venkataraman, S. (1997). The distinctive domain of entrepreneurship research. In J. Katz (ed.), *Advances in Entrepreneurship, Firm Emergence, and Growth.* Greenwich, CT: JAI Press, vol. 3, pp. 119–38.

Venkataraman, S., A.H. Van de Ven, D. Polley and R. Garud (1989). Process of new business creations in different organizational settings. In A.H. Van de Ven, H. Angle and M. Scott-Poole (eds), *Research on the Management of Innovation.* New York: Harper and Row, pp. 221–97.

8. Emerging themes in entrepreneurship research: Editors' Keynote 2010

Keynote editors: *Candida (Candy) Brush, Michael A. Hitt, R. Duane Ireland, Dean A. Shepherd, Mike Wright**
Moderator: *Ronald K. Mitchell*
Comments editor: *G. Thomas Lumpkin*

[*Author's note:* Emerging themes were discussed at the 2010 Entrepreneurship Exemplars Conference held at the University of Connecticut School of Business, May 20–22, 2010]

Dino, Rich: We are moving now into our second roundtable discussion around emerging themes and this is with a number of folks from various journals, in their role as editor or past journal editor. So I'll turn it over to my colleague, Ron Mitchell.

Mitchell, Ron: Thank you very much, Rich. It's been a very helpful time for us to move from 'enduring' through 'enabling' to 'engaging' themes, and now we're in this zone of considering 'emergence.'[1]

In some sense, we are in the classic skill-creation model: learn, look, do. So in the emerging themes sessions, we set the stage to move from learning and looking to 'the doing.' In the next two sessions, we will do this from two vantage points: the first we could say is more macro, the second more micro. This is the emerging theme [keynote] roundtable with journal editors. We have Mike Wright representing the *Journal of Management Studies* (*JMS*); Duane Ireland, *Academy of Management Journal* (*AMJ*); Candy Brush, *Entrepreneurship Theory & Practice* (*ET&P*); Mike Hitt,

---

* Candida Brush, *Entrepreneurship Theory & Practice*; Michael A. Hitt, *Strategic Entrepreneurship Journal*; R. Duane Ireland, *Academy of Management Journal*; Dean A. Shepherd, *Journal of Business Venturing*; Mike Wright, *Journal of Management Studies*.

Strategic Entrepreneurship Journal (*SEJ*); and Dean Shepherd, *Journal of Business Venturing* (*JBV*). Thank you very much for your willingness to join us on this panel.

The idea here is that, based upon the vantage point that comes from those who see manuscript flow, you can get a sense for how a field is developing. I know those of us who have, on occasion, served as program chair for a conference see all the papers that are submitted. There is an ebb and a flow of topics; but over the years you see more ebb in one thing or more flow in another. And that would be the basis of the first question that I would like to open with today. From your perspective as an editor, what themes have ebbed and flowed over the years? Mike, if I could just throw the ball to you first. You have seen this now from multiple vantage points – I'm not going to go into the . . .

Hitt, Mike: Does this have to do with age?

Shepherd, Dean: This is the elderly panel.

Hitt, Mike: This is the epic.

Mitchell, Ron: I almost walked into the same trap that somebody walked into last year, but I'm hoping I didn't go that far. Anyway, I'd like to throw the ball to you and ask, from your perspective, please give us a sense for the research in entrepreneurship – the themes that have ebbed and flowed.

Hitt, Mike: Well there are a number of different ones that you could probably talk about. I will start with one. If you look at some of the early work in entrepreneurship, at least what I read, there is a lot of work initially or early on about the characteristics of entrepreneurs. What does it take to be an entrepreneur? What does it take to be successful? Again, characteristics of an entrepreneur. And in fact, there was quite a bit of research on this, but I think when we got to the end of it, it didn't produce a lot (from talking to my colleagues in entrepreneurship and from what I have read).

Now let me take it another way, though. I think today that questions have evolved into a lot more effective and richer research in probably a variety of ways; but I'll just mention one without trying to go into great depth. Today, I see a lot of research on using theoretical domains and, actually, other kinds of methodologies, using knowledge from other fields in psychology, organizational behavior, etc. This is not researchers from other fields doing work in our area, but we're using it. I'm talking about entrepreneurship researchers doing work in entrepreneurial cognition. And in other areas, you can see this moving in other ways. I think (for example) self-efficacy of entrepreneurs; and I think that this is richer in helping us better understand entrepreneurs, and who they are, and what they do or what helps them do things better (that lead to successful outcomes). So I again use that as one example.

Mitchell, Ron: So would it be fair to characterize this observation – we are using a particular case, the characteristics case – that for a while there was a flow and then there was an ebb; but when it comes back, the flow that we are seeing now is richer because the science, the capability, and the training of the people who are engaged has actually been able to pick up the flow that petered out and add new energy to it, etc? Am I overstating that?

Hitt, Mike: No, actually I think that you probably captured it fairly well in terms of what has happened. It's probably true in a lot of other fields. You can see it in other fields when they're younger in their development (some of the early research that is being done) and then you see it come on. The people that are doing it today are better trained and/or broader in terms of bringing in the richness that we see in methodologies, as well as theoretical domains. That doesn't mean it's not being developed also within the field of entrepreneurship. So I'm not trying to suggest that it is all being imported, although some is and some is being developed internally as well. In fact I think it is being exported out as well.

Mitchell, Ron: I remember the Academy session that I was in, and it has been a few years, when this re-emergence of the 'characteristics' look at the field came about in the session for many of us who had considered that the ebbing was pretty much permanent. This re-emergence of the 'characteristics' views came about. I watched everybody sit up and bristle for a few minutes because we get invested in the way that we framed the research in our field; and so one bigger idea that's coming out of this last little exchange is that emerging themes don't have to be brand new. They can be added to and improved upon, based upon the skill sets, the perspectives, the importing and the exporting that goes on. Dean, let me throw this ebb-and-flow question to you next, if you would.

Shepherd, Dean: I think it's an interesting point. I agree with everything that Mike said, but I also see it from a slightly different perspective in what I think – or as discussed in Venkat's 1997 foundational paper [on 'The distinctive domain of entrepreneurship research'] – I think he said it very eloquently when he said 'There's a lot of water that's gone under the relative performance bridge.' And I think what we might have done is started on entrepreneurship; we started with the traits and the characteristics, and that was the story that Mike told. But I think we also started with a lot of strategy researchers and we were just looking at relative performance. And while we still look at relative performance, and while relative performance is still an important dependent variable, I think people have been very clever in thinking about new dependent variables (more proximal dependent variables); dependent variables that are more interesting or more related to the entrepreneurship questions that are important to the field. So I think that's been an ebb and a flow there as well.

Mitchell, Ron: If I could just follow up? I realize it is kind of putting you on the spot, but new dependent variables such as . . .?

Shepherd, Dean: I think the work that Duane has been doing. Strategic entrepreneurship is a classic case there. I think we were looking at relative performance. In some ways we were doing strategy-related research, but we have been able to do work in the area of strategic entrepreneurship, which is important. Jeff Covin's work, of course, all of his history of work in corporate venturing, corporate entrepreneurship, those particular areas. I think you're looking at product innovations and their creations, specifically, ventures. Mike [Wright]'s work on spinouts – all of these areas have importance, rather than just having a default position of relative performance; we are talking about these other more interesting (or I think are most interesting) variables depending on the questions that are being asked.

Mitchell, Ron: Thanks. That has helped me to clarify that. Now I'll turn next to Candy. Ebb, flow – in your experience?

Brush, Candy: I actually went back and looked at the last three years of submissions to *ET&P* because I was curious to see what that looked like. Now, *ET&P* is a little different because we have several special issues and so the special issues have focused on family cognition, international aspects, women, entrepreneurial cognition, governance and several topics. So, leaving those special issues aside and looking at the refereed journal issues, I have developed a couple of observations. I agree with what Mike and Dean just said in terms of the re-emergence of looking at individuals differently. But one of my observations is what the unit of analysis tends to be. We've moved from looking at just individuals to now really taking a careful look at the firm. I'd say about 50 percent of the studies that we receive use the firm as the unit of analysis. Now I am not saying that is a bad thing, but it's an interesting difference in our focus from the early 1990s when we really were focused on the individual. The idea of other kinds of units of analysis is intriguing.

Now to answer your question more specifically, things like franchising; we used to see lots of research on franchising and we aren't seeing as much of that. I think of it as seedlings, saplings and evergreens because there are certain themes that are continuous that we often see (like corporate venturing, for example). We continue to see good work on corporate venturing, or corporate innovation, new venture start-up; some of those topics. And then the saplings might be the growing areas and areas that are merging, and then the new areas would be the seedlings. And I didn't fully answer all of those because I would like my colleagues to be able to jump in.

Mitchell, Ron: Perhaps a little bit of structure when we talk about emerging. You know, emergence does (as we started to say) come from older growth. And it comes from new growth. And maybe we are in a growth metaphor – we will see. Now you probably noticed this (looking at the panelists sitting here), that we have representation from three specialty journals – the *JBV*, *SEJ*, and *ET&P* – but we also have representation from the more general management journals: the *Academy of Management Journal* and the *Journal of Management Studies*. So as we look at the ebbing and flowing of entrepreneurship research, we are going to see it through the lenses of those who have watched it in the more general context. Duane, if we could ask for your thoughts on that next . . .

Ireland, Duane: Yes, and certainly as Ron has said, as we know, *AMJ* is a journal that many would call a big-tent journal. It has a very broad domain, so entrepreneurship is one of many domains in which the journal has an interest to publish research. But as I've thought of this, I think consistent with what Dean (and really Candy and Mike, too) have said, I think *AMJ* historically received a great deal of what I would view as content-oriented entrepreneurship research. That would be basically the strategy-related dependent variable work that Dean spoke to quite eloquently.

I think now we are receiving more process-oriented entrepreneurship research. I recall a paper that came to us that dealt with passion and the effect of passion on entrepreneurial processes. We have a paper that was published in (I believe it's in either the April or the June 2009 issue of) *AMJ*; its qualitative work but it basically deals with the issue of trust as it is played out in entrepreneurial ventures that are acquiring other firms. So again, a process-oriented set of issues instead of strict relative performance kinds of issues. So I think for *AMJ* we are seeing more process-oriented work in the entrepreneurship domain rather than strictly outcome dependent-variable oriented work.

Mitchell, Ron: I recall (it's probably a year or three ago) that you did a bit of a summary about the proportion of entrepreneurship research in *AMJ*. I don't remember, Duane, if it was manuscript flow or if it was actual published papers.

Ireland, Duane: It was publications.

Mitchell, Ron: Publications. Just for the audience, what . . .?

Ireland, Duane: What Ron is addressing is a 'From the editors' column that was in *AMJ* in 2007; and basically what we did was to very simply count the number of publications that *AMJ* has published that have been in the entrepreneurship space. That is increasing. That is on the rise. I cannot give you exact numbers, but I did notice a couple of days ago (earlier this week I was looking through a couple of issues of *AMJ*) and in the April 2009 issue we published one entrepreneurship paper. In the June 2009, we published three – excuse me, two. So a total of three entrepreneurship papers in those two issues – and those were consecutive issues for us. So clearly *AMJ* is very interested in entrepreneurship research and I believe it is being very well received.

And as a big-tent journal, and Mike may speak to this as well, this issue surfaces; every domain thinks it should have an equivalent percentage of the publications in the journal (and there are about 25 interest groups and divisions in the Academy of Management). And so there are 25 product champions who basically feel that there is 1/25th of the space that they should receive. I don't mean that critically at all. It is just that it is a very broad domain that we call management, and every part of the domain has a very legitimate interest in being represented in terms of scholarly publications. I think, clearly within the last couple of years, if not the last ten years or so, the number of papers published in *AMJ* on entrepreneurship continues to increase.

Mitchell, Ron: There is an underlying driver that editors, it seems to me, have to deal with – and that is you really can't publish what's not submitted. And so it is like, 1/25th isn't real estate that's divided by a legislative or executive mandate. It really has to do with an ebb and flow that happens from the community at large. If the flow increases in a particular area, then the editorial group simply responds to that. Obviously there are journal standards, and if the flow is below par, then, of course, it is not going to have an impact in terms of what is published. But assuming (as we were alluding to) that the capability sets that have been coming into entrepreneurship and the questions and the approaches have been richer, then you can see that the consequence might be actually in the publication. So I was asking about proportion, not in terms of equity theory, but in terms of . . . really I was hoping to get to manuscript flow. So I realize you didn't actually count that up. Do you have anything anecdotal from which you could give us a feel for manuscript flow?

Ireland, Duane: Sure. And very well stated, Ron. Excellent points. I don't have the exact numbers. We receive a large number of papers in total. My sense clearly is that the number of entrepreneurship manuscripts we receive is increasing. There is no question about that. I think very definitely that the quality of the papers we receive from entrepreneurship scholars is clearly increasing as well. I think importantly that entrepreneurship is a 'sort' that is very carefully evaluated when a team chooses associate editors for *AMJ* – and certainly for choosing board members. There is a very specific discussion that is held that we are receiving a great deal of entrepreneurship research or an increasing amount and increasing quality in entrepreneurship; and therefore, we need to have the capability to evaluate that fairly and appropriately.

Shepherd, Dean: Can I just make a point about your question? I just want to try and . . . I have had a change in mindset, and I think you would probably reflect on this as well. Rather than call us specialty entrepreneurship journals and call them general management journals, maybe it should be the other way around. Maybe we should be general entrepreneurship journals and, they, specialty management journals. Because, given what you have done with these Exemplar Conferences, and we're saying that we are going to sociology, we are going to IS (information systems), we're going to other departments within business schools, we are going to other schools that aren't even in the business school. Isn't entrepreneurship broader than that? So in some ways – I mean, I think we started off as these niche journals; but I would like to try and think of us as more than a specialty entrepreneurship journal.

Mitchell, Ron: Two points: one – standing corrected is good TV, and thank you. The second thing is that we need to follow up. So Mike [Wright] – apologies. I'm going to come back to this point about manuscript flow after we develop Dean's point for just a second because I've written down a question about the tent – this 'big-tent' idea – and I was actually going to ask you what we're doing to expand the tent within entrepreneurship, given the new juxtapositions of big-tent entrepreneurship journals.

Shepherd, Dean: I think we've been thinking about saying this for a long time, but we use multi-disciplinary, multi-contextual, multi-functional aspects of entrepreneurship to study entrepreneurial phenomena. I think we have always said that, but we've always seen ourselves as a subset of management, for example. Primarily focused there or maybe a subset of economics. But really, as this Exemplar Conference has shown over the last two years, we can branch out. We can bridge to sociology, to psychology, to marketing, to finance to accounting and to information systems, as we've seen earlier. So if we think about what we're interested in studying regarding the entrepreneurial phenomena, we can do it from different theoretical perspectives, different disciplines (such as the international context, the social context or the sustainable context). We've become a general entrepreneurship journal. So we've just become broader and broader. The unifying theme obviously is that we study entrepreneurship.

Mitchell, Ron: So when I throw the ball to you, Mike [Wright], I'm going to change the nature of the question just because the discussion is moving along. Dean just re-characterized, for the benefit of all, 'specialty versus general.' How does that hit you?

Wright, Mike: From *JMS*'s point of view, I think we would see ourselves as a general management journal, and I think the specialty issue comes as to how big the big tent is perceived. Partly, that has to do with some of the editorial signals that are sent out. I think until I took over (it's one of the reasons I was asked to be editor of *JMS* – was to bring back lots more of the entrepreneurship work), it had been perceived that we were less welcoming to entrepreneurship work because there had been certain directions over the previous five to ten years. Whereas if you go back to the early 1970s, even with *JMS*, there was quite a lot of entrepreneurship-type work, and some members of this panel have published, and Jeff Covin in the audience have published, that kind of work in *JMS*. So I think part of our remake was actually to bring back, or make the tent bigger: to make us more general and not just focusing on a particular subset of general management that happened to reflect a certain set of editors.

Mitchell, Ron: Now you raise a point that's sort of buried in the general, which is 'editorial direction has an influence on the ebb and the flow.' To what extent do you think it's a strong influence or a weaker influence?

Hitt, Mike: I guess I'll jump into that. I think it has some impact on it, yes, because these are the outlets where you publish your work. And if you are encouraged to do this, if you invite and you are encouraging, you are more likely to receive manuscript flow than you are without such an invitation. And it's likely to encourage younger scholars, I suspect, to move in certain directions – one or the other. On the other hand, where you are at any given time, whatever we're working on, we're going to then look for outlets. I think that's what we are going to do. So in some ways it will maybe encourage research over time, but it also will mean that those of us that have streams of research – all of us have – that we're working on, then we are going to look for outlets where we think our work will be the best placed. Certainly visible, but also be receptive to the work we're doing. So I see both; it encourages and invites, but it may be where people place it. But the other side, I think it has at least indirect (if not sometimes direct) influence on the directions of certain research streams.

Mitchell, Ron: I'm hearing agreement going on here.

Shepherd, Dean: Well, I think it's incredibly important. I think if we look at *SEJ*, it has had such a fantastic launch because Mike Hitt was the editor. There is no doubt about that. I think the systems that Duane has at *AMJ* run so efficiently. So I think about what I'd like to do at *JBV*. In many ways I try to emulate the professionalism and things that *AMJ* has and has done. When I write decision letters, I try and write letters like Mike [Hitt]. But also, I've seen the signals of what we were talking about before: becoming more general. I've tried to create new field editors, and associate editors that are experts in their particular areas. So, before, we used to try and choose people who would be more eclectic and could take on manuscripts from different areas; now we just have a whole series of specialists that speak to those different audiences. So that's the signal that I was trying to send by selecting those particular field editors.

Mitchell, Ron: So we got an M-form versus U-form journal policy thing going on for all of us strategy-trained folks. Candy, you had a point?

Brush, Candy: Yes, I want to build on expanding the tent; and Dean sort of got at this with reviewers in different areas. I think that's something that I believe we are doing (and probably the other journals are doing as well) is expanding the reviewer pool both with ad hoc reviewers as well as those on the board who have different specialty areas, whether it is from another management discipline – like information systems or operations management – but also from other disciplines. And so, I know that – and that really helps to effectively examine papers from different perspectives as well. Because if you have a qualitative study, it might be nice to have an anthropologist review that, as well as someone else who's from the management discipline. So expanding the reviewer pool and those on the editorial review board with two different disciplines helps to expand the tent somewhat.

Mitchell, Ron: Duane, please.

Ireland, Duane: I agree with everything that has been said and I think, editorially, one can have an influence both in terms of content and process. With *AMJ*, I think the journal tries to influence content in two ways: the first is through the special research forums, which actually Mike Hitt established as an innovation (a brilliant innovation, I think) for *AMJ*. Through those special research forums, there is an attempt to say, 'This is an area of interest in which we think the field of management, generally defined, can grow and develop if we receive a set of high-quality papers with respect to this particular topic.' So the special research forums are a very significant content influence.

For *AMJ*, the other content influence is the 'From the editors' (FTEs) columns, and we do have the FTEs appear in every issue. They are really designed to do two things: (1) content and (2) process. One, with respect to content (an example of that): a couple of issues ago Jason Colquitt, who is the incoming *AMJ* editor, wrote a column about lab experiments at *AMJ* (publishing lab experiments at *AMJ*) because we are open to all methodologies, lab experiments being one. So Jason said, basically, 'Here is what a lab study would need to be, what it would need to look like to be successfully received at *AMJ*.' Dov Eden a couple of years ago wrote a 'From the editors' column about meta-analysis and how they need to be prepared to be successfully received by *AMJ*. So the 'From the editors' columns do quite a bit in terms of content, but they also speak to process. For example, Jason Colquitt and I wrote one a couple of issues back that deals with the review form: what the form actually looks like, what the descriptors are and how those descriptors are used to evaluate papers. The April issue that just came out contains the results of a board survey. Dave Ketchen and I wrote that from the editor's entry. It basically publishes the results of a survey of the *AMJ* editorial review board who were asked how the board feels about different kinds of aspects of the journal's operations and the kind of work it is publishing.

So we do quite a bit (editorially) to signal content through those media and discuss process. I think everyone on this panel is very committed to process that has due justice associated with it – a process that is appropriate, that is fair and that is reasonable. I think editorial influence can be felt in that respect. It can also be felt in terms of how we go about (as Candy was saying) selecting ad hoc reviewers, bringing people onto the board and interacting with authors. In terms of the latter, we want to make certain, that even if the answer is 'no,' the author feels that he or she has been given appropriate treatment and a rigorous, yet fair, judgment of his or her work, among other things. So, I think we can influence both editorial process and editorial content.

Mitchell, Ron: Thank you. Mike's going to pick right up here.

Wright, Mike: I'd like to pick up on the special issue side of it, because at *JMS* we have regular special issues twice a year. We have had certain ones in the entrepreneurship area – Jay [Barney] and Sharon [Alvarez] did one on entrepreneurial theory of the firm; we had a family firm one that just came up; Jeff Covin is doing one on new developments in entrepreneurship – these are the main ones. One of the points we try to make with these special issues is a two-way process of signaling to entrepreneurship scholars, 'Hey, here are the new developing themes that are coming out from general management,' but also to our general management audience, 'Here are some entrepreneurial themes that provide opportunity for research that we have been looking at in general management for quite some time.'

Mitchell, Ron: This gives us a way to tie this all together. This ebb/flow process is not one that is deterministic and somehow not reflective of who we are. It is intensely social and it has to do with signaling and responding and actually is a growing and living social – I don't want to say organism – but, certainly, phenomenon in which we all participate.

Now I'm going to change the focus just a little bit because in just a few minutes, what we would like to do is invite our colleagues here and those from around the world to engage. The thing I have noticed in my career is that the sessions (at whatever conference we attend) which have the editors of the journal show up have standing-room only. The question is 'why?' Well it turns out that there's a difference in perspective between authors and editors, and I'm just going to characterize this (although we may stand corrected once again). But the characterization (as I enter into a conversation with editors) is that the editors see themselves as 'inviters.' Journals have an appetite. You just have to have the manuscript flow and you need the good manuscript flow or you can't publish good articles. You need great manuscript flow to have great publications. So the editors are thinking, 'What can I bring to the readers of this journal that helps me to accomplish the editorial mission that I'm charged with enacting?'

Of course, from the author's side, we think of the editors differently. Because of the tenure process and all those things that go in, we think of the 'gatekeeping' function. So the reason why we show up and pack it in at conference sessions when the editors are there is because we want to know 'what's going to be on the exam.' We want to know how it is we can craft and shape our work so that we can get it through the gatekeepers. We just don't want to screw up because it is too important. So in that sense we have a tension. I don't know that it's a complete tension, but it is this 'inviters vs gatekeepers' kind of thing. And as we go into the discussion with the larger audience, the question that I'd like to begin this discussion with is just a side comment that you may have heard Candy say. I don't know if we're going to get to opportunities, but that's really the question. What trends are growing, in your view, in both quantity and importance? Just a brief one- or two-liner, if you could, and we'll start back with you, Mike Wright. Trends that are growing, and you don't need to cover all of them.

Wright, Mike: I think a big trend is very much in the process side of it; and better work in the process side (in the sense that we've always had process work at *JMS*, but a lot of it is has not been great quality). I think what we have seen in recent years is much, much better qualitative work looking at these processes. That's included more longitudinal studies and other things. And it's also relating back to different types of entrepreneurial context. Not just small firms per se, which was always a long-held tradition, but actually more entrepreneurial firms, and entrepreneurial firms from different contexts – whether it's work on spinoffs or a lot of work on family firms. There's a big explosion, I think, in work that is becoming more theoretically and empirically rigorous compared to being very descriptive. And a lot of work on venture capital. Those are the things I've seen recently.

Mitchell, Ron: Okay. A one- or two-liner on opportunities?

Ireland, Duane: I know we are receiving more and, I think, interesting qualitative entrepreneurship work. This work, perhaps not surprisingly, tends to involve at least (if not is conducted by) more senior scholars; but we are receiving a larger number of papers that are qualitatively based methods that deal with entrepreneurship topics. I think that's really fascinating because, as we know that with qualitative work, sometimes with the methods, we really have opportunities to dig very deeply into phenomena that are of interest to the scholar. And I think it is really exciting to see this work coming to us. So to me that's a major trend.

Mitchell, Ron: Thank you. Opportunities – Candy?

Brush, Candy: Well, I'll tell you what we are seeing. We are seeing a rise in social entrepreneurship and environmental entrepreneurship, both theoretically and empirically. We have had a couple of papers on failure . . . To that point there's, I think, an opportunity to explore that from different perspectives – and that gets back to the process that Mike was talking about, because there's a dynamism in the early stages of the process of development of a new venture where you have restarts or you have mergers at very early stages. So studying some of that dynamism of that process is an opportunity.

Mitchell, Ron: So this is one of these moments where the ebb and the flow actually happen. As a researcher (certainly not as an editor, but as an author), this analysis of failure and what the heck's happening, is something that has been interesting in my career for years and I just couldn't get a hearing at the journals. So you might be seeing a manuscript. Mike, opportunities?

Hitt, Mike: Well, I'll try to build on and not try to just imitate what they said. I agree with all the things they've said. I'll build on the things I have heard here, in fact, as well as things we've seen at our journal. I'll use an acronym that I'm not the author of. It was authored in a group earlier this week of 'ICE-T' – innovation, creativity, entrepreneurship (that would encapsulate all the things here) and technology. And we've heard some, and even in the last session of some of this, on innovation and creativity and how it relates to entrepreneurship. In fact, I see entrepreneurship as partly a global construct that in some ways encapsulates all this. Although a lot of this work has been done in silos outside of an entrepreneurship theme. But I think it is now being integrated much more into an entrepreneurial focus, which I think is making it much richer. I think the integration has much potential.

Mitchell, Ron: Thanks, Mike. Dean, we've put you in the hardest position.

Shepherd, Dean: I agree with everybody else. In terms of social and sustainable, my thoughts or what interests me is consistent with [those who discuss] the potential downsides (or the dark side) of entrepreneurship. I think that's an opportunity. It's not a lot we've seen.

Mitchell, Ron: So in a prior session, Anne Miner said that the dark side of entrepreneurship is an area that is . . .

Shepherd, Dean: I've had an interest for a while in that area, but it was interesting to hear Anne talk about it as well. So we kind of have a consistent approach there.

Mitchell, Ron: Thank you. So, if I am out there with my notepad – well, I'm actually here with my notepad and I've written down all the places where the opportunities are happening. Just in case you didn't have your notepad, they include: process work, different context, qualitative entrepreneurship, social, sustainable, environmental entrepreneurship, ICE-T (which is innovation, creativity entrepreneurship, plus technology) . . . Did I get that right? The dark side of entrepreneurship, the failures, etc. That's where we are. Let's go to the web. Tom?

Lumpkin, Tom: There's a question that nicely extends that question you just asked. Could the panel attempt to predict the themes that are not necessarily emerging now, but may emerge in the future – or they hope will emerge but haven't seen?

Mitchell, Ron: So this is either hunch or hope, right? Okay. Either one – hunch or hope.

Ireland, Duane: Well, consistent really with much of what we have talked about (and certainly Sharon [Alvarez] and Jay [Barney] were talking about), I think entrepreneurship in informal economies is a fascinating domain. Anne Miner spoke about this. We've heard bits and pieces about this across multiple discussion points and across multiple meetings here, and throughout multiple meetings elsewhere. I think it's a very, very rich and fertile area for us as entrepreneurship scholars. And I don't know that the data are correct, and this is from a *Wall Street Journal* article, but I read it not too long ago and it suggested that in the country of India, about 83 percent of the GDP is accounted for by the informal economy. I don't know if that is correct or not. Maybe it's 40 percent; perhaps it's 53.5 percent, who knows. But if it's any percentage of any magnitude, to me it just suggests an incredibly fertile domain for us as entrepreneurship scholars in terms of how do entrepreneurial ventures start in informal economies, why did they start, how did they succeed if they do succeed and what do we measure as success (which Jay Barney was talking about earlier today). I think this is a very fascinating domain and I think we will see quite a bit of work surfacing in this area.

Mitchell, Ron: Hunch or hope?

Brush, Candy: I was going to agree with what Duane said but I'll extend it just a bit; and that gets to the notion of looking at things like cooperatives as a unit of analysis or how teams form. And also even what Jay Barney and Sharon Alvarez are doing in the ecosystem area: how does a community develop entrepreneurship ecosystems that really loop back and develop – not only the individuals but the economy of that area? And understanding best practices, it picks back up on what Anne Miner was saying as well. So not so much as an intervention but more as an understanding of what's working, why is it working, and what are the lessons.

Mitchell, Ron: I have a colleague, Anna Maria Paredo, who did her dissertation hiking the spine of the Andes, going through these communities, figuring out what's going on. I know Jay and Sharon have done this, this whole notion of community entrepreneurship is what you are thinking about there. Others – hunch or hope?

Hitt, Mike: I'll just start because I'll build on that one. What I would call (or, not what I call, what others call) public entrepreneurship, which includes that. It does include things that Jay and Sharon have done, and others, but Nina McGahan is doing work in this area. I think there's just a lot of opportunities for the kind of research that could be done in this area and is probably starting, but just at the infant stage.

Wright, Mike: Can I build on that one more leg? I think there's an issue of, in a lot of these cases, where the entrepreneur is coming from, because you've got a deficit of entrepreneurship. I think that raises issues about whether there is some kind of transnational flow of entrepreneurship, whether it's entrepreneurship through an agency that is coming in that we have heard about early on. That kind of process, not as an infrastructure, but an agency of an individual kind could possibly be turning out entrepreneurs in some environments. That kind of process, I think, is a way of trying to kick-start entrepreneurship in this context. We don't really know enough about that at the present.

Shepherd, Dean: I suppose the only additional thing I would hope for is some more advancements in methods. I think we are using more and more innovative methods, and these new methods may open up interesting theoretical research questions or help us address questions that are already being asked. So informal economies presents a whole lot of interesting research-methods challenges. We are seeing some more innovations in those areas. Just hope they keep going.

Mitchell, Ron: So, as we answered the hunch or hope question, mainly we got 'hunch.' I'm going to follow up on hope in just a minute, but Barbara Bird has a comment here from the audience in Storrs.

Bird, Barbara: I have a question for the panel. I am also an editor and I see numerous sample issues. I get a lot of papers using student samples. I think that in our global audience, this might be of interest to many people out there. I would like to hear from the editors what makes for a really good publishable study using student samples?

Mitchell, Ron: Yeah, the student sample issue.

Shepherd, Dean: What's interesting is I submitted a paper with a student sample and Barbara was the editor and she accepted it.

Brush, Candy: I'll comment on that. I think actually on the positive side, a student sample is most appropriate if you are studying something like pedagogies or tools or skills that students are learning in some sort of experimental design. And, actually, we probably don't have enough of those kinds of papers. Is what we're teaching in class really working in some way – and are students learning entrepreneurial thinking or are they learning methods and skills? So, a student sample would be most appropriate in that case, assuming that you follow all the rigorous methodologies of experimental design.

Shepherd, Dean: So the paper that we did wasn't one of those. I think we've got a good case of saying – but I agree with you.

Mitchell, Ron: Letting Barbara off the hook. So tell us just a little bit about this.

Shepherd, Dean: I think that's the most obvious use of students if you're using students to generalize to students. But I suppose the question becomes: if you are using a study (and you generalize it to entrepreneurial phenomena or more broadly), I think if the unit of analysis is the entrepreneur and you want to generalize to entrepreneurship students it is not appropriate. But if it's to say, 'Hey, there's an entrepreneurship context and this entrepreneurship context leads people (students are people), to come up with certain decisions or have certain approaches or have certain reactions,' then I think you can make the case that what I'm actually studying is the context. Whether it's an actual entrepreneur, an ace entrepreneur or a complete novice may not make a difference. Obviously, you need to be able to make that case, and not everyone is going to buy it.

Brush, Candy: You could make the case, and I think you probably did; but I haven't read your paper, that the educational institution is the context.

And if you are teaching entrepreneurship and they are learning entrepreneurial skills is that how you've . . .

Shepherd, Dean: We might define the entrepreneurial context in terms of extreme emotional pressure, or time pressure, or considerable uncertainty, or anything like that. So if you can, create an entrepreneurial context where you are manipulating the variables to see how people's decision-making or emotions or reactions change as a result of those contexts.

Mitchell, Ron: So, everyone, for our limitation sections, 'students are people,' is one of the things we can say. Tom, another question from the web?

Lumpkin, Tom: Yes. A methods question that builds on Dean's methods comments. Directed to Candy, but I think anybody on the panel could answer it. Are entrepreneurship theories inherently multi-level; that is, simultaneously treating individual and firm, and hence it can only be truly investigated with multi-level methodologies?

Brush, Candy: Oh, man!

Mitchell, Ron: We'll all help out with this one.

Brush, Candy: I guess it depends on which theory you're talking about (and first of all that's a obvious comment). I guess you could say they could be, and I would, on the other side, advocate that, yes, we probably could use more multi-level studies, more multi-level analyses. It's hard to do, it takes time, it's complicated, but that gets back to how you might study something like the community ecosystems that we're talking about. I guess it is not a very good answer, so who is going to help me?

Hitt, Mike: I co-edited, with a member of our audience here, John Mathieu, a special issue for *AMJ* on multi-level issues. It was broad so it wasn't focused per se on entrepreneurship. But what I would say is that certainly it's appropriate but it doesn't mean it's always – because you have an individual in a new venture that is multi-level – because it depends on the research question. But it probably presents an opportunity to do multi-level research, which has to be theoretically developed in a way that has multi-level theory as well as the method. So it's not just method; it's also theoretical.

Wright, Mike: I think that one of the problems is when you get confusion between whether you really do firm level or individual level of study.

Mitchell, Ron: So, Mike, you're helping us do the framing. This question assumes that everybody gets the fact that individuals create firms, if we are talking about just one example of multi-level and the firms operate within industries and the industries operate within economies. So what's the driver here? Well, Mike states, 'It just sort of flowed out,' but it depends upon our research question. If we are just talking about something that is happening at that particular level, then really it's not inherently multi-level. But, if we are talking about the cognitions of entrepreneurs that affect national policy, we'd better have a pretty good cross-level argument for why one thing would be operating – why a phenomenon at one level would be influencing at another. So, Tom, how did we do? Did we get to the core of the question, or would you like to re-pose a portion of it?

Lumpkin, Tom: The part I would think might be interesting to re-pose would be: are entrepreneurship theories inherently multi-level?

Mitchell, Ron: Given the framing that Mike helped us lay out, inherently multi-level, the point of departure is, as Mike Wright says, 'It depends on your research question.' This isn't about research questions; this is about entrepreneurship theories being inherently multi-level, and it's asking us to actually do some kind of characterization of theory, which I don't know if any of us want to actually step into that right now.

Hitt, Mike: I think our general specialty journal should handle that one.

Mitchell, Ron: I think this is one of those Chinese finger traps. You just can't get out if you go in.

Lumpkin, Tom: The answer might be just, no.

Mitchell, Ron: So, no.

Wright, Mike: I think one of the problems, if you're going down that slippery slope, is that you end up trying to boil the ocean if you're not careful. You're trying to bring too many things in and it then becomes impossible to tease out what you are trying to test, let alone test it.

Ireland, Duane: The danger, I guess, becomes – picking up on this – if we were to say that the answer is yes, then we are automatically increasing the difficulty of the questions we want to examine. I think we all agree – all of us in the audience – the importance of the research questions that Mike Wright was talking about is so incredibly significant. Haven't we all read a paper once or twice where, gosh, you read the first three or four paragraphs and you aren't certain as to what the question is (or the question has been posed in one or two or three slightly different ways)? And, as we know, the clarity of articulating what that question is that you are trying to examine is incredibly significant – which then influences the choice of the methods, as we know.

Mitchell, Ron: So we have a question. We'll go first to John Mathieu and then to Carol Saunders. John's got the microphone.

Mathieu, John: I was just going to chime in quickly on that one. My answer would be, 'Of course they are.' Of course they're multi-level. I'm a multi-level guy. But the more critical question is, 'What's your criterion?' Because as an outsider looking at the – I'm an organizational behavior guy – as an outsider looking at the entrepreneurship literature, and where the trap is is what the criterion is. So if we are at the community level, then the theory is starting there. If we are talking about a firm level, is it firm entrepreneurship or is it a collection of individuals? Or is it the entrepreneurial initiative? Or are we talking about the profile of entrepreneurial initiatives? Or are we talking about the time sequences of entrepreneurial initiatives? Or are we talking about the entrepreneur or entrepreneurs themselves?

So all of those things start to wander back and forth. Any theory can be multi-level. Whether it needs to be? No, that depends on where you're at and where the critical drivers are and so forth. But certainly, my two cents from outside in on entrepreneurship as a big broad area (I'm painting with a big brush here), is to be very careful about what the criterion is that you're discussing, and think about what those critical drivers are. And there is a wonderful bracketing paper that talks about 'think about a level down.' So if it's firm-level entrepreneurship, what's in the firm? What is it about the firm, and what's the bracketing out? What's the context over the competitive environment and so forth? So, wherever you are at, you start with the criterion and then you bracket; and then you may very well come to a place where you say, 'It's not really that relevant, it's really a one-level study.'

Mitchell, Ron: So the two operating concepts here are 'inherently,' and we're answering that with 'yeah, probably not.' But if we add 'criterion,' then we can actually say that inherently is pretty strict. So maybe we abandon that inherently thing and we say, 'depending upon criteria.'

Mathieu, John: You start with the criterion and that drives whether or not it makes sense to go there.

Mitchell, Ron: Thank you. So let's go next to Carol Saunders. Rich is chiming in from the audience regarding another profession that we shall not bash, which regularly uses the qualifying phrase 'it depends.'

Saunders, Carol: I'm coming from the information systems perspective, and Ron's point about differences of opinions between the authors and the editors resonates with me. As editor of *MISQ* [*Management Information Systems Quarterly*], I felt my mission was to help broaden the view of what the journal would publish and change the mission statement accordingly – as well as try to staff the editorial board with the appropriate expertise. But the challenge is when you get papers in areas that are not your own, you must send it to editors and to reviewers especially who have the expertise in that area. The response reminds me of 'I have met the enemy and they are us.' What I found is the areas that were the 'most complaining' were also typified by reviewers (and very often editors) who were the most demanding and the most unwilling to expand their efforts to try to improve the papers. Now I realize there's a quality level and you want to reach that quality, but my feeling is that in many cases the areas that were the most adamant about saying the journal wasn't publishing their area, were also the areas where the reviewers were the most ungiving and the most unwilling to help develop the manuscript. Is this a phenomenon that transfers to the entrepreneurship area or, more generally, to the general management journals?

Mitchell, Ron: So the point Carol is making is that, as an editor, she was willing to go into places where perhaps her expertise – it was beyond her expertise – but the people she relied on (not generally, but in some cases) displayed the 'not invented here' phenomenon. So it's very demanding, very strict and very unyielding, which, in fact, did the exact opposite of what her editorial intention was. Did I get that right, Carol?

Saunders, Carol: [*paraphrasing*] Are the entrepreneurship reviewers hard, or harder than they need to be on entrepreneurship paper submissions to the journals?

Mitchell, Ron: I'm just going to repeat it because the mic wasn't there and we want to hear it worldwide. 'Are the entrepreneurship reviewers harder on the papers . . .'

Saunders, Carol: The entrepreneurship papers that are submitted.

Mitchell, Ron: '. . . that are submitted to a journal?'

Saunders, Carol: To a journal? In other words, the editors want to publish papers, but if the reviewers say no way . . .

Mitchell, Ron: So this is the 'We're bound by the reviewers.' So we're going to . . .

Wright, Mike: I think that one of the important problems that must be overcome is actually to match the reviewer to the manuscript. For example, you might not want a qualitative reviewer in entrepreneurship looking at a quantitative paper or vice versa. That's when you get the least forgiving perspective, in my view. This sometimes causes an issue on the other side of it, from an editor's point of view. I found many qualitative reviewers traditionally with a qualitative paper would be too forgiving. So as an editor, we have to work very hard. We want qualitative work but we have to educate both the reviewers and the authors to raise the bar.

Mitchell, Ron: Thank you, Mike. Duane.

Ireland, Duane: Now that's interesting because, taking the second part first, I have found our qualitative reviewers to be very, very rigorous; appropriately so – not inappropriately. I don't mean that, but they've been very, very expecting of high-quality work. I have not found the entrepreneurship reviewers to be more difficult or more challenging to work their reviewing than in any other domain. In fact, I have found the entrepreneurship scholars, you who are reviewing papers for us, to be very committed to doing an excellent task and an excellent job. I think we can applaud ourselves as scholars reviewing entrepreneurship work, for *AMJ* at least.

Mitchell, Ron: Which we shall do in about half a minute. Thank you, Duane.
   We're in the process of a certain part of the learning chain; of learn, look, do. What we've essentially completed here is a macro look at what is being done . . . Now it's time for the hand that Duane said that we deserve.

NOTE

1.   The 2010 Exemplars Conference was organized around a four-theme format: (1) enduring, (2) enabling, (3) engaging, and (4) emerging.

Editor/author session contributors

9. Academy of Management Journal

Editor: *R. Duane Ireland*
Authors: *Tom Elfring, Keith M. Hmieleski*
Moderators: *Ronald K. Mitchell,*
 Michael H. Lubatkin
Comments editor: *G. Thomas Lumpkin*

Mitchell, Ron: I am very pleased to introduce my co-moderator Michael Lubatkin. Next is the editor of *AMJ* [*Academy of Management Journal*], Duane Ireland, and Tom Elfring and Keith Hmieleski, who are the authors. They will be participating with us today. The Wouter Stam and Tom Elfring article is entitled, 'Entrepreneurial orientation and new venture performance: The moderating role of intra- and extraindustry social capital.' Keith's article with Robert Baron is 'Entrepreneurs' optimism and new venture performance: A social cognitive perspective.'

My name is Ron Mitchell. I am the 2009 Chair of the Academy of Management Entrepreneurship Division. Could we first look at the *Academy of Management Journal* (*AMJ*) mission statement specifically, as those of us here in Storrs, Connecticut, have come to expect. What I have tried to do is look at this mission statement and draw out some ideas for the opportunities specifically focused on publishing entrepreneurship research. *AMJ* is open to a wide variety of empirical entrepreneurship research and a wide variety of empirical methods – as this journal seeks to 'publish empirical research that tests, extends, or builds management theory and contributes to management practice.' All empirical methods (including but not limited to: qualitative, quantitative, field, laboratory and combining methods) are welcome. To be published in *AMJ*, a manuscript must make strong empirical and theoretical contributions and highlight the significance of those contributions to the management field.

So with that, what we will do is turn our time first to Tom and then to Keith to give us just a quick flyby of the papers. Tom.

Elfring, Tom: Yes, first I want to mention Wouter Stam, the leading author who couldn't be here; so I am representing our paper. The paper is basically about social capital – the way networks shape the relationship between entrepreneurial orientation and performance. One of our initial findings coming out of the data was that a central position of the entrepreneur in the network had a negative effect on performance. This was really counterintuitive and against most common beliefs. So that is what we actually tried to work on first: was it really a negative performance effect and how did that happen? In the end, we came up with a nice explanation that indeed there is a dark side to the social capital networks: that entrepreneurs can be over embedded within their own industry. Only when these entrepreneurial start-ups in the Open Source software community have a sufficient amount of extra industry ties (so, broken ties to other communities), then they could kind of overcome this negative effect of being too centrally located with their own industry.

Mitchell, Ron: Thanks, Tom. Keith?

Hmieleski, Keith: First, I should acknowledge my co-author, Robert Baron, who unfortunately couldn't be here. He is in the process of moving (after being at RPI for 22 years) to Oklahoma State. Our paper is on dispositional optimism. Optimism is a construct that gets talked about quite a bit in entrepreneurship, but I think it probably has not been very well understood or consistent in what has been said about it. What we look at in this paper, specifically, is basically the downside of optimism; we look at contingencies in which optimism is particularly problematic (in this particular instance with entrepreneurs who had high levels of experience – those who had founded multiple ventures which were somewhat counterintuitive, but yet logical at the same time) if you go back and look in the social psychology literature, and also the negative effects of optimism within dynamic industry environment.

Mitchell, Ron: Thanks, Keith. So, before I turn the first question over to Mike, Duane – how did I do on the summary of the opportunities and the mission statement of the journal? Is there anything that should be added or tweaked on that?

Ireland, Duane: I don't think so, Ron. I think you explained it quite well. Clearly, *AMJ* is open to all kinds of empirical methods. *AMJ* anticipates that there will be a theoretical contribution that flows from the work. So I think you articulated that quite well indeed.

Mitchell, Ron: Okay, thank you. Mike?

Lubatkin, Mike: Just an observation before we get started, particularly for the junior people just starting out in the game. If I had a punch in the head for every rejection that I have received from *AMJ*, by now I would be suffering from pugilistic dementia.

Ireland, Duane: But join the club. That is true for all of us.

Lubatkin, Mike: That's really one of the points, isn't it? Yesterday we heard that *Organization Science* was referred to as 'cool and open-minded.' We heard the *Journal of Management* is warm and inviting. And we've heard that the *Journal of Management Studies* was quirky. We've also heard innuendos that there is another general management journal that is stodgy, incremental, almost anal, where rigor is valued more than interesting questions. Duane, how would you describe the *Academy of Management Journal*?

Mitchell, Ron: When did you stop beating your data?

Ireland, Duane: What we are witnessing here is the last time Michael and I will appear on the same panel. I am certainly aware of this commentary or perspective that may exist for some people. I thought about this a little bit last night because I thought Michael might ask a question along this line. In all seriousness, I think one thing that is unique about *AMJ* (that perhaps we do not do as well as we should in terms of conveying this) is that the people involved with the journal across time – I happen to be the 18th editor and soon there will be a 19th, 20th, so on and so forth – show that there is an incredible amount of love, care and concern about this journal from the people who are involved with it. Let me give you a couple of examples of that. When I learned that I was going to be blessed and have the opportunity to serve as editor, John Slocum happened to be in our shop at Texas A&M visiting with his close friend, Don Hellriegel. Slocum (being Slocum) came up to me and he said, 'Ireland, your only job is not to screw it up.' Of course, basically what he was saying is, 'This is a great journal. Take care of it. There have been a lot of people beforehand who have given so much to the journal, so do the same. Be passionate about it and care about it.'

Another example about that is, believe it or not, once I learned that I was to be selected as editor (and once that was publicly known), I received a number of emails from former *AMJ* editors and former associate editors at *AMJ* congratulating me for the appointment, wishing me well, so on and so forth. So there really is just an incredible amount of care and concern. The people involved with *AMJ* really do make sacrifices. I am not speaking of myself, for example, but the associate editors.

Mitchell, Ron: But it is also true.

Ireland, Duane: Sara Rynes had seven associate editors during her term, and I was blessed to serve as one of them. I started with eight because the number of manuscripts *AMJ* is receiving continues to increase. We now have nine associate editors. I heard Talya Bauer [editor of *Journal of Management*] say yesterday she may be moving to 13. We have nine, and when I contacted people to ask if they would be willing to serve as an associate editor, the guarantee I gave to them was (as we know as associate editors is true at many of our journals) that the associate editors are decision makers. I promised that they would not receive more than 100 manuscripts per year. With that, I did not have a single decline. Not a single person said no, and most of these people (in fact, I think seven of the nine) received no release time for service as an associate editor at *AMJ*. There's just an immense amount of love, care and concern that goes into the journal trying to push it along.

Now to speak more directly to the stodgy and incremental and so on and so forth; I don't know that that is really true. I understand the perception may be there. In fact, from the editor's column, April 2009, Jason Colquitt and I have a 'From the Editor' entry that actually presents the reviewer evaluation form criteria. We had not presented that before and we speak to each of the criteria – one of which is 'interestingness.' Of course, Jack Veiga asked us about that yesterday in terms of what does that mean. We clearly are very interested in interestingness and so we are doing our best to bring that forth.

The final comment about this is that for both of these papers, the initial feedback from two of the three reviewers (on each of the two papers) first review was, 'These papers are interesting,' which I thought, in the context of what we talked about yesterday, was a fascinating observation to make.

Mitchell, Ron: So, authors, how is the stodgy meter? Just exactly how did this work with the reviewers and the editors?

Elfring, Tom: Shall I start?

Mitchell, Ron: Sure, Tom.

Elfring, Tom: To us it was really a positive surprise that we got an R&R [revise and resubmit]. We were kind of new. None of us had published before in any of the top American journals (coming from the European context) because it was not so much necessary. We didn't even intend to submit it to *AMJ*. We were thinking of *JBV* [*Journal of Business*

Venturing]; but one of the American people in our department, hired for one day a week to coach and help us to get published in the American journals (which is kind of the target), had said, 'Well, you have very interesting data. Why not submit it to *AMJ*?' We said, 'Well, that's too difficult.' But we did it anyway. Then we got this letter (which I was kind of shaking when we opened the mail), and it was very encouraging. It was a tough job, but it was very encouraging, noting, 'So please resubmit and we really invite you to do this.' In the European style you say, 'Okay – resubmit,' but not in this encouraging tone.

Mitchell, Ron: So the stodgy meter was low in this case, actually encouraging. Okay.

Elfring, Tom: So we thought, 'God, they really want us to do it.' And then we thought, 'Then we really should try.'

Mitchell, Ron: Keith, your experience?

Hmieleski, Keith: I am frightened to answer the question, to tell you the truth. It is not for the reasons that you would suspect. It's the first paper I have submitted to *AMJ* and I can say, hands down, it was the best first-round reviews I had; perhaps the most positive of any paper that I had, and all three reviewers were great. If you're in the room, you're brilliant, exceptional individuals who were chosen to help out on this. Everything went against what I had heard about these perceptions of *AMJ* – that they're not interested in entrepreneurship research. This was framed as an entrepreneurship paper, which had implications beyond entrepreneurship, I think, but definitely is oriented that way, then talks about dispositions of entrepreneurs, so that was 'strike two' right there. I knew it was an interesting paper and, actually, I think why it went so smoothly is because we worked more by far on this paper before submitting it than any other paper I have worked on. After it was accepted, I cleaned out my office and I literally must have found 50 different versions of this paper sitting around my office to go through. To echo what Mike and others had said earlier, the more effort you put into it up front before the submission, the much more enjoyable the whole review process is that follows from there.

Mitchell, Ron: Based on the 'n' of two . . .

Lubatkin, Mike: See, my game plan is to come full circle. I am really not here to insult Duane and the *AMJ*, but I think it is important to understand perceptions and the management of those perceptions. And another question I have in mind as I think about that (as in many of the other journal sessions that we had yesterday): I think it would be safe to say that many of the other exemplar papers were first rejected by *AMJ*. Tom, where was your paper rejected before the acceptance at *AMJ*?

Elfring, Tom: It was not rejected.

Lubatkin, Mike: Keith? That's very interesting, because often when you get a paper rejected from *AMJ*, the reviewers essentially become co-authors. They provide interesting insights that improve the paper to get it to the level of acceptance that makes journals like the *Journal of Management* and *Journal of Management Studies* very good outlets for very good papers; but these papers have often been poked along by the reviewers of *AMJ*.

Mitchell, Ron: One of the things Tom and I were talking about over break-fast was this idea that when you first see a diamond, it doesn't look all cut and sparkly. It needs to be cut and then it needs to be put into a setting. So in a sense, what happens is [that] as the effort is added to these papers, we ought not to always think that necessarily because we were rejected at the top journal, the paper is in fact a poor paper. Rather, what you get, which is from the scarcest resource in our business, is a critical review from thoughtful colleagues. Once you get that, it is like cutting a diamond. You can actually use it to increase the sparkle. So that is another one of those possibilities for a research strategy that one can consider, especially if you get the kind of feedback that Mike is referring to (which is, we characterize as, co-authorship feedback); but it is essentially the people in the community who know this work and who are interested in its success that provide a developmental review, and on the basis of that, a reviewer's influence is felt and it permeates those papers.

Lubatkin, Mike: Exactly. Keith, I would like to ask you: your study basically found that optimistic entrepreneurs have a good reason to be pessimistic because the more optimistic they are, the lower their new venture performance, everything else being the same. That's accentuated by a dynamic environment and by past experiences. With that as a general context and background, why do you think your paper was accepted by *AMJ*? What made this paper special?

Hmieleski, Keith: I think our paper had implications beyond just entre-preneurship, even though it was an entrepreneurship paper. I think one of the things that seems to me to be important from the review is that top journals (when doing dispositional-type research) allow one to really demonstrate that there is something different about entrepreneurs from the rest of the general population. This was fairly clear with optimism. There are no pessimistic entrepreneurs. Pessimists don't get out of bed in the morning. So they only range from moderate optimists to extreme optimists. And when we talk about, I think, the individual characteristics of entrepreneurs, the really interesting part is they are extreme individuals. In social psychology and other fields, researchers tend to study samples from the general population – and they tend not to study the outliers and what is actually happening on the extremes. So if we look at optimism just in the general population, it tends to (on average) be fairly positive across various domains. But if you look at entrepreneurs, they only fall at the far end of this, say, curvilinear relationship with performance and you get more of this negative slope. There actually was a nice figure put together for the paper that, I think, characterized it fairly well (but it was pulled out at the end because of length issues).

Lubatkin, Mike: So you were taking a socio-cognitive view perspective of opportunism and testing it in a domain or a sample frame that rarely represented the most interesting test of it. I'd like to kind of continue with these questions. Tom, why was your paper accepted by *AMJ*?

Elfring, Tom: I think that we had a unique dataset, and without the help of the reviewers we would not have shaped it in the position that it was accepted. I think that is why we got the first rewrite. Initially we put a lot of effort into data to get a unique dataset. That's often more the case in Europe; that there is lots of effort expended to develop the datasets, but we don't know how to get it published in a better journal. So, for example, at one moment (I think in the second round) we got this feedback that we needed to have more discussion about 'what's the contribution.' So we sat down and we wrote a really (I don't remember how long the discussion sessions were) lengthy analysis of all kinds of implications and theoretical contributions. Then one of the reviewers came back after that and said, 'Well, this is way too much. Cut it back to two or three pages.' But we had no idea what exactly was required. First, we didn't have any (or maybe the wrong) theoretical vision, and then we felt like, 'Okay, we will do more, much more.' But then it was too much because it went in all directions, so we had to cut it back. In that sense, maybe for the European audience, this kind of balance between empirical stuff and the theoretical thing is very important. The unique dataset we were able to somehow attribute to net worth, orientation and entrepreneurship – and not more. Just those three things.

Lubatkin, Mike: I am going to comment on both Keith and Tom's observations because I have my own thoughts as to why it was accepted, but first I'd like to get it from the editor's point of view. Why was this paper accepted?

Ireland, Duane: For Wouter and Tom's paper, as Tom indicated, the dataset was identified by all three reviewers in the initial review as being totally unique. It was obvious to the reviewers that a great deal of effort had gone into the dataset and had gone into building the dataset, and I think clearly the dataset was a big, big plus for this paper to begin with. I think another thing this paper did was to very clearly state up front (and by the way, this is true of Keith and Robert's paper as well; both papers clearly stated up front): 'Here are the theories we are using, here is how these theories inform the questions we want to explore, and here are the theoretical contributions we intend to make.'

For *AMJ*, doing that is really important to say up front: here is the theory (again, the theories that I am going to use); why this theory (as Michael said, social cognitive theory in the case of Keith's paper) is particularly applicable to the question that I want to examine; and, here's how I am going to test, build or extend theory by examining this important or this significant research question.

But going back to Wouter and Tom's paper, the dataset was extremely important. That really drove it. I think it was an interesting question that they chose to explore, and they were extremely responsive to the reviewers. In fact, both of these papers moved through the process very, very smoothly – and that was one of the reasons I chose these two papers to discuss here – because they really did go through the process smoothly. And I am reminded of John's dismal comment just a moment ago (so I don't want to fall into that camp), but, for example in terms of Wouter's paper, I went back to look and (let's see), the first review was 39 days. The first revision was 39 days. The second revision was 50 days, and then the final acceptance was 33 days. So it moved through the process very rapidly. They were extremely responsive. They caught the reviewers' interest in that first review, and these reviewers were ready to go. They were very interested in the topic. They were interested in the idea of social capital in terms of networks, so on and so forth, and they wanted to kind of push the authors along as well. So for Wouter and Tom's paper, we received it initially on April 22, 2006. The final acceptance was April 20, 2007, and it was published in the February 2008 issue.

Keith and Robert's paper actually went through the process even more smoothly in terms of timing. The first review was 52 days. The first revision was 32 days, and the paper was actually conditionally accepted, and I had the privilege and pleasure of being the action editor on both of these papers. In the instance of Wouter and Tom's paper, I was still associate editor. For Keith and Robert, I was editor, and I still assign most of the entrepreneurship papers to myself. But revision number one (R1) for Robert and Keith was 32 days. R2 was 35 days, and R3 was two days. So they actually had two conditional acceptance revisions; R1 and R2 were both conditional acceptances. In fact, with the R2 conditional acceptance, I remember writing that letter. I thought 'This feels really strange to say we are again conditionally accepting your paper,' but basically that's what happened; we weren't quite there yet. And as we know with conditional acceptance, it is always (by definition) conditional upon meeting the expectations that have been laid down; and we just weren't quite there yet.

Hmieleski, Keith: It might be interesting to point out what happened there. I was so enthusiastic to respond to all the reviewers that we went a little overboard. So the paper went from 40 pages to about 55–60 pages, and so the reviewers thought there was a contribution, but it wasn't that big.

Ireland, Duane: Actually for both of these papers it's an interesting point because Tom was talking about this. Well, for both of these papers, I remember one of the reviewers on Tom's paper (and I hope Tom won't mind me sharing this, because he was addressing the issue) said, 'Look, I understand your paper is important, but it is not solving the world's problems. We're kind of going overboard here on the contributions flowing from this work, and that's why we had to cut back on that.' With Keith's paper, there was that issue of length that did surface.

Mitchell, Ron: I am just going to break in here for audience questions to bring you into the conversation, both on the web and here in Storrs. Who has the first question, please? Okay, Dimo? Thank you.

Dimov, Dimo: In looking at both papers, I don't know why, but they are both interesting. So I have a sense that in just reading the titles, they're both interesting papers, and you probably had the same impression when first receiving the papers. So I wonder how that affects the appointment of reviewers in terms of how you select the right people to review these papers. That could be (in a way) that they could be developmental and they would provide strong feedback; but it would be feedback that pushed the paper. They could also be reviewers that find flaws and some of them very critical. So I think it is interesting to go into the reviewer selection decision.

Ireland, Duane: That's a great question and, basically, if I could back into that, I think one reason both of these papers struck the reviewers and me as interesting is (and I think we would not want to diminish the importance of this) all three reviewers on both papers, even in the first round (and my judgment was the same), that these papers were well written, and they were well written in the first iteration. They were clear, they were compelling and they were convincing. And I think that that clarity really does enhance the probability that a paper is going to be seen as interesting because (by definition), if the paper is well written, the probability that we understand what is going on is obviously increased. So I wanted to make that point. I think both of these papers were really written well and of course the crafting, as Michael said, continued throughout the process. But it was not a situation where we looked at the paper and said, 'Gee, what is going on here? What is really being attempted and what is the research question?'

Now specifically, with respect to reviewers, this is how I try to choose – or this is the metric I use in choosing reviewers. We do use three reviewers. We use two board members per paper and one ad hoc reviewer. We like to use ad hoc reviewers because that becomes, as many of the other editors have said, the training pool for individuals who are going to be appointed to the board at some point (assuming that they provide excellent reviews). So in the sorts that I use: if it is an entrepreneurship paper (for example, as in the instance of these two), the first sort is to find someone who works in entrepreneurship; the second sort is going to be finding a reviewer who works in that specific domain of entrepreneurship (or maybe use a reviewer who works in the dispositional behavior, or maybe in the social capital network aspects of entrepreneurship, as in the case of Tom's paper); then the third sort is to find someone who has used the methodology that is being used in the paper. So I try to use those three sorts in assigning reviewers. Now that becomes a little complicated because we are a busy journal. We receive a lot of papers, and the board is pretty busy. Our board members commit to review 12 papers per year. So even as a board member, it is a reasonably heavy workload expectation. Sometimes I can't quite do that, but that is how I try to do it.

Mitchell, Ron: Any coming in from the web yet, Tom?

Lumpkin, Tom: I have got one right here. For Duane: what would make you not send out a paper for review at all?

Ireland, Duane: It is a very good question, and basically all the papers do come to the editor initially. One of my responsibilities is to decide if the paper is to be sent for review, or if it is to receive a desk reject or a desk edit. Take the extremes out, the true outliers, we do occasionally still receive a few pure conceptual papers even though, as we know, *AMJ* is an empirical journal. So take the outliers out, and what causes a paper not to be sent out for review basically will fall into one of two cans. One is going to be if there is no serious attempt – no viable attempt – to test, build or extend theory. Purely phenomenon-driven research is fabulous research, and it has an incredibly important part in our scholarly domains; but for *AMJ*, given its editorial mission, there must be some effort with theory. So if there is no viable effort with theory, then that is going to be a problem.

The second thing, of course, would be if there is an obvious empirical problem – if it looks as though common method variance is going to be something that likely can't be overcome and/or if perhaps it appears the wrong technique was used or something of this sort. So it is really those two core things – and sometimes it is just the Gestalt of the interaction of those two. It looks as though there has been some attempt at theory, but the methods are not quite what they possibly should be. With the desk rejects, the reason we (and I think all journals) provide those is because we believe that there is just not a reasonable probability that the paper is going to be reviewed favorably. The conclusion is that it is in the best interest of the author and the best interest of the reviewers that we recognize that up front. With our desk reject letters (and I am sure this is true with the other journals represented here as well) we try to give very legitimate feedback. The desk reject letters are three or four pages long typically and there really is an attempt to provide feedback in a constructive developmental tone (even if the paper is not going out for review). We feel that it is very, very important that all authors have a fair hearing – even if their paper is not going to be reviewed.

Mitchell, Ron: Duane, did I hear you say desk revision?

Ireland, Duane: No, desk reject.

Mitchell, Ron: So there's nothing that the editor says, 'Boy, is this great. Just do this and this and we will publish it?'

Ireland, Duane: No. Well, theoretically, I guess that could happen, but I don't know that it ever has. Now we do have a desk edit decision option as well, which is basically where we will say that 'It is just not quite there yet, but there is a core of a great idea; so if you can do these things and send the paper back to us, then we will send it out for review.'

Mitchell, Ron: Okay. Other questions from the floor?

Audience Member #1: One of the main strengths of Tom's paper, of course, is the data. I was wondering, Tom, was there any pushback on the fact that it is non-US data? And then, Duane, how would you recommend other people or other researchers using non-US data to get into *AMJ* and kind of breakthrough what may be perceived as a barrier?

Mitchell, Ron: So we're starting with Tom.

Elfring, Tom: No pushback at all. I am just trying to think if there was – but no. In the comments, the data was clearly (what they immediately said was) very interesting and fascinating; but it was more in the method and the theory-building where the problem was. I was, in a way, surprised to get the resubmit, later reading all the things that were wrong because we did mediation and all the reviewers said 'You need to do moderation because it doesn't make sense to do mediation,' which seemed to be pretty fundamental. So there was a serious overhaul. In a way my question was, 'Why get a resubmit when there is such a serious flaw in the theoretical ID?'

Ireland, Duane: Tom is making a great point here. One of the reviewers in the first round very persuasively argued that, in fact, 'You are testing for mediation and you really need to be testing for moderation, and here's why you need to be doing so.' Tom and Wouter responded very positively to that. Basically the theoretical arguments were just not there for the mediation and there were some other issues that that reviewer brought out as well. So they responded very positively to this.

Someone mentioned yesterday (and, Alex, I will deal with the data, too) but someone mentioned yesterday (and I think it is really important for us to remind ourselves) that all of us as editors and editorial staff want to publish papers. We wake up every day wanting to publish papers. So, if we find work that has a possibility of reaching the closure of making a significant contribution, that is very, very exciting to us. In the case of Wouter and Tom's paper, the data were very interesting and the question was very interesting; and so, given the response of the reviewers and how I felt about the paper, the issue became (as Michael was saying earlier), 'How can we work with the authors to bring that potential to the forefront and yield a significant contribution from this work?'

So, regarding the international data, as Tom said, there never would be (I don't believe) any pushback on that. In fact, that was one thing that was very, very exciting to me about this paper: the data are international and we are very, very interested in international data. I think what Tom and Wouter's paper has is a very, very intensely and effectively constructive dataset. It is just constructed beautifully. There are all kinds of tests that were run to make certain they were doing the right things and it is just a very rich dataset. I think the fact that it is international was a plus in this instance.

Mitchell, Ron: One quick extension of this international notion, then we are going to just go into the wrap-up phase and I will turn it back to Mike to help us to do that. So let's just talk from the European perspective, which is where your home is. When an author from the European tradition gets a revise and resubmit and it has, let's say, some hurdles to clear or some hoops to jump (Duane said your response was really positive and constructive), is that universally the way that works in response to the American journal revise and resubmit?

Elfring, Tom: Maybe. I don't think so, particularly for older European professors who used to be very powerful and they kind of were the kings at the university. When getting all the revisions they need to do, their initial reaction (I have heard regularly that in the last ten years) is, 'Well, who are those reviewers? We don't do this.' And that is maybe a reason why, obviously, they don't get accepted. One of the things that we learned was that we really have to listen to the reviewers and that is basically what we did.

Mitchell, Ron: Thank you, Tom. Mike, as we wrap up now.

Lubatkin, Mike: I'd like to give a wrap-up. What I found so interesting about these two papers and why I believe that they received a favorable review from *AMJ* is that both of them started with an interesting question. They then selected the proper theory to test that question. The data came later, but the front end of the paper was: 'What are some of the interesting antecedents to new venture performance, and how do we explain why some firms' performance – new venture performance – exceeds the others?'

Keith used socio-cognitive perspective and Tom used a social capital network perspective in testing their hypotheses. What I found so interesting, however, about their studies is not only their contributions to entrepreneurial research, but also the contribution to the base theories in which they tested their hypotheses – because both of them, I think, extended their particular base theories (with Keith's case, socio-cognitive and with Tom's case, social capital).

Mitchell, Ron: Now we have a couple of traditional wrap-up questions that we ask. Duane, I am going to turn to you and ask you to fill in the blank. If there were one thing that you would recommend in successfully working with *AMJ*, what would it be?

Ireland, Duane: I think a couple of things. I would carefully study the mission statement, which Ron articulated, because we really do use that as a foundational set of inputs to making decisions. I would also look at the April 2009 'From the Editors' column, because it does go through all of our criteria that we use as reviewers and editors in evaluating a paper. And I would look at the best papers for the last 10 or 12 years at *AMJ*. They're available on the *AMJ* website. I would go to those papers. I don't know that I would necessarily read all of them, but I would certainly go through them and [ask], 'Is there a common theme here as to what these papers did well that might suggest to me why they won the best paper award, which is a fairly rigorous evaluation process?' So I think I would do that. I think the final thing I would do is navigate the *AMJ* website: try to absorb it, try to read about the editorial guidelines, read about the reviewer guidelines, read about the backgrounds of the associate editors. Just try to get a sense for what the journal is and what it seeks to accomplish. We are very interested in forward kinds of research and we want to continue to push.

It is a big enterprise. *AMJ* is a large enterprise and we are all very fortunate to have those of you who review for us and are members of the board. Thank you very much, because you are clearly the foundation for what happens. I think Michael spoke so eloquently about this. The three reviewers on both of these papers were just excellent; they gave superior feedback – quality feedback. Both author teams responded very aggressively and appropriately to that feedback, but it was truly a very positive interactive situation between the authors and the reviewers that I think led to these outcomes. I would study the website and just try to gain – just try to absorb – what the journal is.

Mitchell, Ron: Thanks, Duane. Okay, filling in the blank in the last couple of questions. If there were one thing that I would recommend in working with *AMJ*, Keith, it would be?

Hmieleski, Keith: Having Duane Ireland as your action editor.

Mitchell, Ron: And Tom, it would be?

Elfring, Tom: Have an excellent dataset.

Mitchell, Ron: Well, ladies and gentlemen, thank you for your participation. Thank you everyone.

REFERENCES

Colquitt, J.A. and R.D. Ireland (2009). From the editors: taking the mystery out of AMJ's reviewer evaluation form. *Academy of Management Journal*, **52** (2), 224–8.

Hmieleski, K.M. and R.A. Baron (2009). Entrepreneurs' optimism and new venture performance: a social cognitive perspective. *Academy of Management Journal*, **52** (3), 473–88.

Stam, W. and T. Elfring (2008). Entrepreneurial orientation and new venture performance: the moderating role of intra- and extraindustry social capital. *Academy of Management Journal*, **51** (1), 97–111.

10.   Academy of Management Review

Associate editor: *Mason A. Carpenter*
Authors: *Melissa S. Cardon,*
  Jeffery S. McMullen, Dean A. Shepherd
Moderators: *Ronald K. Mitchell,*
  John F. (Jack) Veiga
Comments editor: *G. Thomas Lumpkin*

Mitchell, Ron: What we have planned to do for these sessions is to kind of walk them through a very short – maybe 10 percent of the time used – introduction (to get the sense for your journal's mission); then about 40 percent of the time will then be spent discussing with the authors and editors certain topical questions (although additional things will emerge from there); then 40 percent of our time we will try and spend with questions from the audience (here as well as worldwide); and then a final 10 percent of the time will be a wrap-up, closure and summary by the moderators.

Now, *Academy of Management Review* (*AMR*) is a theory journal. A summary of the journal's purpose is in each of the Conference Material binders that we have here in Storrs, Connecticut; it is also on the marvelous website (http://ccei.business.uconn.edu/Exemplars) that Katie Huntington has put together, and so I am not going to read the entire journal mission.[1] Rather, what I am going to do is talk about some of the opportunities that I have identified as I have read the mission.

Because *AMR* is open to theoretical work, it is open to theoretical work regarding entrepreneurship. Because it is a journal that publishes new theoretical insights that advance our understanding of management organizations, *AMR* is receptive to a variety of perspectives – including those seeking to improve the effectiveness of, as well as those critical of, management and organizations. So with that we will begin. Jack, welcome. I will turn the time to you for the first question.

Veiga, Jack: We have already addressed the 'interesting' question at one level, I guess, but I would like to specifically focus a little more on the *AMR* experience: the path to success if you will. I am thinking again about trying to reflect back on younger scholars who are at the starting point. The first question I would like to go to the authors. It is just an open question, but in terms of the two papers you have here, what was your starting point? Was it just an idea you had, something piqued your curiosity, or was it something you just stumbled into? Much like entrepreneurs, did you know where you were going or did you find out only at the end of the journey?

Mitchell, Ron: I forgot one critical part. We have asked the authors to give us the 30-second elevator pitch of their papers. So, if the authors would do that and include their elevator pitches in the responses . . . So, Melissa?

Cardon, Melissa: First I have to acknowledge that my paper is co-authored with three individuals that were not able to be here in Storrs, Connecticut [*Note:* J. Wincent, J. Singh and M. Drnovsek (Cardon et al., 2009)], with me, so they are noted in your binders and noted on mine in the paper as well. So that is important; I am not alone. The paper that is forthcoming in *AMR* this summer is entitled 'The nature and experience of entrepreneurial passion.' How we came across this question is this: I have been fascinated by the topic of passion for some time, and the more we read, the more we realized that a lot of people use the word but don't know what it means or haven't carefully defined it yet. So our path to this project was purposeful; it was a question that was interesting to us. Whether the paper was publishable – we didn't know; we just thought it interesting, so we went out to grab it. The path to publishing it in *AMR* was quite long, and I don't mean the review process. I mean we first started talking about the paper in 2002 as a co-author team. We presented it at Babson in 2004 and at the Academy of Management in 2005. It didn't go to *AMR* until 2006, and obviously the paper is coming out now in 2009.

I have a group of colleagues that started writing a paper for this special issue of *AMR* that is coming out and they started working on the draft the weekend before it was due. That is not how you write for top journals, in my opinion, in entrepreneurship or anywhere else. So my elevator pitch about the paper: it is about entrepreneurial passion. We use the word passion, but we don't know what it is. We provide a definition grounded in psychology and social psychology and we present a model of how we can get works specific to the entrepreneurial context.

McMullen, Jeff: Our paper seeks to reconcile different theories of the entrepreneur – primarily economic, but at the same time really interesting social cognition and social psychology – and we saw a lot of parallels there as well. We started talking about people who are applying a lot of these theories of the entrepreneur (these economic theories) in a psychological fashion, and yet there were some problems. It seemed like elements were missing when we changed the unit of analysis, and that really inspired us to try to reconcile these economic theories and this decision-making psychology framework. We sought to see what was missing and what happened when we changed the level of analysis; then went back and re-interpreted after we had made that loop. Sometimes it was very frustrating because we would try to force somebody in a framework and we would realize all of a sudden (we would have an epiphany or insight) that, 'Oh, that's why it won't fit – because that piece is missing.' So that went on indefinitely. During my PhD program, I worked in a basement with no light, banging my head against a wall over and over, trying to fit things together that perhaps shouldn't fit. As far as interesting, I just thought it was an interesting topic. We hoped that other people would find it interesting as well.

Shepherd, Dean: I think what Melissa said is that it was interesting to you – it is kind of interesting when we think about entrepreneurial opportunities. We don't know it is an opportunity because it is surrounded by uncertainty. I think that is also the case with an article. Does the article represent an opportunity? Does it represent something that's interesting? Well, we don't know: it is surrounded by uncertainty, but I think, as authors, if you think it is interesting (and you are motivated to pursue it), well, I think that is a good sign. It may or may not turn out to be interesting to others, but that is not something a writer can determine in advance. But I think that if it is interesting to you, I think that is a good starting point.

Mitchell, Ron: So, Mason, when these papers come over the transom, so to speak, how are the reviewers assigned? Let's just say it is a paper about entrepreneurial passion. What goes on in the process? After that has been completed, a paper arrives on the editor's desk. Were you the associate editor for this particular paper?

Carpenter, Mason: Unfortunately I wasn't, because these were two exciting papers and were being reviewed before my tenure as associate editor.

Veiga, Jack: So then more in general: when a new paper hits your desk, what goes on that actually permits papers such as these to begin to move positively toward publication?

Carpenter, Mason: The process works sort of the way that we work through assigning papers at *AMR*. The editor and the senior editor choose two of our editorial board members and then an ad hoc reviewer. We ask reviewers, 'Will you agree to review it in a certain period of time?' and if so, then the paper is released to them. If you have ever worked with Manuscript Central, it is a fantastic tool. It also reminds you on a regular basis that, 'Yes, you have a review due.'

One of the greatest services, I think, to submitting authors is to be a reviewer for a journal, particularly *AMR*, *AMJ* [*Academy of Management Journal*], and the Academy group; but also complete timely reviews. Think about your own work. If authors get feedback in two or three months and they expect your feedback on their article in a month, I am not sure that is quite fair. So put on the submitting author's shoes and walk a mile in those shoes.

Mitchell, Ron: So is the ad hoc reviewer always reviewer three?

Carpenter, Mason: That's a great question.

Mitchell, Ron: I have more trouble with reviewer three.

Carpenter, Mason: I am clueless about a lot of things. I didn't realize that that is the way assigning editors worked – and it actually doesn't work that way. I think historically that one and two were editorial review board members. At *AMR* we strive for three reviewers. If we don't get three, we will apologize to the submitting author that we were only able to get two. But the numbering is random. Sometimes they are an editorial review board member and sometimes they are not. Frankly, the quality is high across all of our reviewers. They are really engaged. Often a third reviewer is chosen because they are cited, referenced or attacked in that particular article, which makes for a lively discussion.

Our best reviewers are those who have a critical opinion on the paper. It is not that they are saying this is right or wrong, but, 'This is not the way I look at the world,' or, 'This is well expressed,' or, 'I may disagree with this part but it is expressed so well that it needs to occupy a place in the dialogue in the philosophy of science; it moves our understanding of this area forward.'

Veiga, Jack: I am curious to think of and go back to the point of view of the younger scholar. Writing theory is very difficult. We know that, and Jeff was getting at a little of the pain of banging his head against the wall. Can we talk a little bit more about how you approached it? What can we tell people about that process that would help them perhaps at least get on the right track?

McMullen, Jeff: I can only speak from personal experience, but I just can't turn it off. I am anywhere; at church and I'm analysing and thinking. I have got a theory for that, and so I think my mind is just constantly running.

Mitchell, Ron: He is not sleeping in church.

McMullen, Jeff: The seed of an idea is always there, but the hard part is not getting started; it is simply finding and focusing the question so that it is manageable. Inspiration seems everywhere, but it is trying to be disciplined enough to communicate it. Every paper (especially theory pieces), by the time you get to the draft that actually gets printed, there are probably dozens of versions that were very far off in different directions and just trying to figure out what it was you were trying to say.

Veiga, Jack: Did you find, though, in that process that (like with your co-authors who you locked onto this paper), once you started really putting your brain to it, the ideal process means you stay with it? You don't have a co-author who says, 'I'll get back to you in three months,' or 'I'll get back to you in six months.'

Cardon, Melissa: Not when you work with Dean.

McMullen, Jeff: If you are working with Dean, I am just afraid a revision is going to come back by the end of the day, and I am like, 'I thought I was done with this thing.' He is just that fast.

Shepherd, Dean: I do believe in this idea about momentum – that a paper has momentum. My idea is that I try and manage my schedule to try and help manage my co-author's schedule, that we stay on the paper and keep the momentum rolling. We can spend a lot of time in transitions, like take up a new paper, and then I have got to try and get my co-authors back interested in this paper. That's not the case with Jeff; so really just keep the paper rolling, keep the momentum, keep the learning, because we don't write really just one great draft. We write maybe 50 or 55 drafts, going backwards and forwards and refining our ideas.

Everyone has different relationships. Ours is more like if I see something that needs to be changed, I'll change it – and Jeff knows that he can either change it back or accept it. And we feel completely comfortable with each other completely rewriting what the other person has done.

McMullen, Jeff: Well, what is really interesting is that a lot of times when I send something to him, I know what he is going to take out. There is a detachment that I know he will do it, because it is hard to delete that paragraph you just spent two days writing and you are like, 'Oh, it just doesn't fit anymore; it needs to go.' He doesn't have that. He just takes it out and then he adds something.

Veiga, Jack: Because you have more co-authors.

Cardon, Melissa: There were four of us.

Veiga, Jack: What's that – talk about that.

Cardon, Melissa: There is some good and some bad of having four co-authors, and those of you who have written with three other people know exactly what I am talking about. The good was that two of my co-authors are European. I work very late at night. By one o'clock in the morning, I would email them a draft and they would be getting up. I would go to sleep and they would work on it, so the dynamics of timing (unlike Dean that gets up at four a.m. normal time), was that we worked well because we're across time zones; but we found for this particular paper that we had to come together on several occasions to just get the brains in the room together with the white board, with the markers and work it out. This is the only paper that I have published to date where I have really felt the need to be in the room with my co-authors for a concerted amount of time. This paper started when I was on the faculty at Case Western Reserve, so we would sit in the room together for a week at a time and we did this two or three times a year in the early stages of this particular paper to get it moving – and that was really important.

Mitchell, Ron: So there is an idea emerging about momentum, and the redoing that is required. Let's just imagine ourselves 3,000 feet underground and 2 miles to the rock face where we are mining the gold; then we leave it and all of that transition from where we were to coming up to speed at the top-tier level. What we are hearing from these authors is that they have strategies to minimize that start and restart disabler. So if we are thinking about what we could gain from this session for developing theory, it is this: don't lose the focus and keep the momentum up, despite the fact that you know your co-author is going to be back to you before you are maybe even conceptually ready to manage that.

Cardon, Melissa: I want to add something, and that is that I think good projects also need some space. I heard recently a good fire requires not only wood but also the space between the wood, right? So if a project is so in your face that you can't get away from it, and you get too close and you can't do the 3,000-foot view (or whatever else to see what is good, which is the perspective of reviewers, right . . .?). Why I think the review process is invaluable is because they can back out and say, 'Here's what's going on,' and it forces you to take a month or two-month break from the paper – and you come back at it differently, too.

Shepherd, Dean: I think it is also an advantage of having co-authors, because the paper still has momentum even though you still get space from it (because the co-authors are working on it); so when it comes back, it looks a little bit different and you have had a little bit of a break. Then you get back into it.

Veiga, Jack: One more question on theory development. Jeff made a point that when he was developing the theory, he would be working and working, but it wasn't actually materializing because all the assumptions with which he was operating said that something wasn't there yet. And in that sense, you are asking and answering questions. It is almost a solitary thing. Did that happen in the case of your paper, Melissa? How did that theorizing emerge? Was it kind of emergent on that basis or was it more in the author interchange?

Cardon, Melissa: I think initially it was an individual; I don't find in the literature or I didn't find in the literature what I wanted to study. I really am fascinated by this concept of passionate entrepreneurship and most of our research in entrepreneurship (Duane said it) is strategic-management oriented. I am not a strategy person; I am an HROB [human resources and organizational behavior] person, so to me that doesn't fit. So from my perspective, it was: 'Where is the individual level? Where is the (not trait research, but) process research? Where is the cognition and the emotion and that missing piece?' When I didn't find it, well, I asked myself, 'Why isn't it there; and is it not real or is it not interesting or what is going on?' That, I guess, was an individual process.

This particular paper started because we were trying to study persistence of entrepreneurs, and one of my co-authors disagreed with me that passion was a part of that. And so it was the argument and that interactive process between us that said, 'Well I think it is and I think it isn't – let's go find the evidence. Let's go read and see what other people say.'

McMullen, Jeff: So this is almost an emergent kind of an answer.

Cardon, Melissa: Yes.

McMullen, Jeff: It is a 'puzzle pieces' thing, either at the micro level when you are actually assembling the theory, or actually to ascertain and realize that you have a new research question. Then it is focusing on that basis.

Carpenter, Mason: I think a lot of times, as well, there is a way that you see things and it takes you a while to realize that other people don't see it that way. You are reading the literature and you are trying to reconcile your view – and maybe you tend to have a more institutionalist view and view action as more like an agency sociological perspective. That is not in the literature. You keep reading and you realize, 'Well, I don't really agree with what is out there. How do I bring my voice to the table and still respect and try to understand what is out in the literature and conversely?'

Mitchell, Ron: So with these authors trying to do this kind of work, Mason, how does the editor orchestrate the review author process such that this development can proceed beyond the initial submission and move forward? Obviously editors are bound by reviewers, but we are not totally bound by reviewers. How does that balance work in your mind?

Carpenter, Mason: I think one rule of thumb that I like to use is that, as an editor, I am not a vote-counter. So I don't get a tally and just say, 'This is a number, this is what you got and so "thank you" or "no thank you."' It is really gaining some traction with the particular article. If there's energy – if there is passion in a reviewer, they could say, 'I hate everything about this paper but this,' – and to the credit of the reviewers. And I am in strategy and entrepreneurship, so as a field we are always a little bit defensive in the top journals. We want to see our work published and historically it has had a growth curve to get there. The reviewers want to see that too, but they want it to meet the criteria – to meet that hurdle of what quality is. And they get frustrated; but when reviewers find something, they go, 'There is a diamond in the rough here.' So the task is to coach that out of the paper in cooperation with the authors. The authors have that same perspective. Is that something they want to see come out of the paper? Because one of the things that you see in the review process and in the revision process, is that, just in the writing, a lot of choices are made. It is making those choices that resonate with a sort of coherent story in the paper; but also with the spirit of what the author is wanting to do. Because if you beat that spirit out, it usually comes out in a poor paper, but if the spirit is there, it is those papers that you read and go, 'That's really unique. It helps me understand a part of the world that I would not even have known to ask that question before.'

Veiga, Jack: What positive author actions actually move the paper along, and (by extension) what should authors simply not do?

Carpenter, Mason: Well, what they should do is submit. Martin Kilduff wrote an op-ed piece in *AMR* entitled 'Why I rejected your paper,' and I do recommend that most people look at that because the points made in it are commonsense points and address questions such as, 'Have you read the journal? Do you cite the journal? Does your article look like something that would appear in the journal?' Those questions seem sort of superficial, but it is important to be part of a dialogue. You are speaking somewhat of the same language. You are not just coming and saying, 'I have a new idea. I am not sure where it goes and you guys can figure it out.'

One of the things that we see is that the authors themselves (in that initial submission) have really worked hard in making some of the tough choices. If you have thrown it into the review process saying, 'I have gone as far as I can go, and I know there are five key choices that I haven't made here,' usually that's a failed sort of strategy. It is an author that has said, 'I am going to take these paths – I know I am making tradeoffs here,' but making tradeoffs is ultimately what an author is doing with an article, admitting, 'I have made some of these tough tradeoffs and somewhere in the paper I have identified this is what it's about.'

What you will find, typically in the review process and then in the feedback, is that, 'This paper is still too broad.' Your paper can be more by being less; and the reviewers get a sense of, 'Yeah, we were on the fence about these two things. We pushed it to perfection, but we are still on the fence. If we take this away we can actually say more and make more of an impact.' That is a really delicate process to work through and understand, and it is like an epiphany. It's like, 'Wow, if I pull that away and pull this domino out, it doesn't crash, it actually builds a stronger foundation.'

Mitchell, Ron: Thank you very much. Jack, another question before we open it up to our Storrs and worldwide participants?

Veiga, Jack: Just another thought and picking up on another word that we use a lot: the word 'story.' Probably one of the best pieces of advice that I ever got (and I would be curious about all of your reactions) was from a reviewer that said, 'I really like this paper, but the story is not compelling. Tell me a more compelling story.' At first I was saying, 'What an idiot. What do you mean more compelling?'

Mitchell, Ron: Nobody has ever said that about a reviewer, right?

Veiga, Jack: And then, working with my co-authors, we were saying, 'We are out of gas. What else could we say?' At one point I said, 'Look, I am just going to go off and think about this for a while,' and what I ended up doing was literally writing a story. I wrote a story about what I thought was going on. It had no citations. It had no references to anything. It just had my own words and it was only four pages of actual manuscript in the end. And then I found it easy to put the citations back in spots. So I am curious about that notion of writing a story. I think it is a critical foundation for almost any theory-writing you are going to do. What do you think?

Shepherd, Dean: I think Jeff is very good at both the internal consistency arguments that he makes but also the macro story. One of the important reviewer comments for our paper (the initial submission) is that we had two stories and we only linked the two stories at the end. So that was important to us because we just kind of flipped the paper and said, 'Okay, let's link these two stories up front.' And that ended up being, I think, one of our more major contributions. So I think we were telling a story, and then two stories, and then linking the two stories; we really had to flip it over and just tell one larger story with two embedded stories. But I think Jeff focuses on that in all of the papers we have worked on together – just to say, 'Okay, all those bits make sense, but what is the overall picture?'

Dino, Richard: Ron, we are in the Q&A segment right now.

Mitchell, Ron: Could we open the conversation, then, to those here in the studio audience, as well as to those on the web. Tom, would you just post a few of the questions and then we will pick and choose. Where is the microphone going to start? Tom.

Lumpkin, Tom: I have a question. While adjusting the dynamics of theory building, we generally focus on interactions between equal peers. Are the dynamics any different when the peers are not equal, such as advisors and students?

Shepherd, Dean: I suppose that is somewhat directed to us because at the time we were writing this article, Jeff was a PhD student and I was his chair. I remember Jeff came to me and said, 'I would like you to be the chair.' I said, 'Well look, you know that you and I are on an equal footing. We can't have any of that type of stuff.' And he says, 'Yeah, that is why I chose you.' Even though there was theoretical distance between us (in terms of hierarchy within the university), peers always respected

Jeff's intellect so we never had an issue. In fact, I have always enjoyed just writing with peers. Sometimes there is an advantage of writing with a more senior scholar, but sometimes if that happens you miss the opportunities to learn. The senior scholar might just say, 'Hey, I'll handle the revision process,' or, 'I'll handle the framing,' and you never get to learn the framing part. So that's why I have always enjoyed working with peers. I think it is a lot more of an interactive creative process.

McMullen, Jeff: I think your nature is egalitarian and that was what was so great in the sense that I never felt . . . With Dean it's developmental; you work together and it is friendship and that makes co-authorship fun and the project fun. You spend a lot of time together; you don't want to work with somebody talking down to you – you want to work with somebody who is fun to be around.

Cardon, Melissa: I think it is also important to note that students are going to be faculty very soon in the grand scheme of our careers as academics. Students, yes, there is still a distance of a couple of years, but it is really not that big of a distance. We are all colleagues in the same academy, if you will.

Mitchell, Ron: A question back here from Mike. The microphone is going to Mike.

Lubatkin, Mike: I am curious, having now written *AMR* papers – do you see an *AMJ* paper on the horizon, or have you already revealed the theory to the extent that *AMJ* will say, 'Well, this isn't original; what you have tested has already been published and the hypotheses have already been developed'?

McMullen, Jeff: I am going to steal an answer I heard from Jay Barney (not to put him on the spot); he stated, 'When you have logic this good you don't need empirics,' or something like that. I absolutely love that answer with the sense that a lot of times empirics have a place, but sometimes I wonder if empirical work is really testing theory. A lot of times theory can cover a lot of things and then empirical research has its place. I don't know if empirical research is my next step.

Lubatkin, Mike: So you didn't find support for your hypotheses?

McMullen, Jeff: Actually, Denis Grégoire and Pam Barr did, working with Dean Shepherd, so they did extend it and have an *Organization*

Science article coming out on that issue, which is excellent. So I would highly encourage you to read the work.

Shepherd, Dean: Also, Ron asked us to think about why we submitted to *AMR*, and one of the reasons why I think we did is because the editors and the reviewers are all used to seeing theory papers. So we are unlikely to get a reviewer saying, 'That sounds good, now go and empirically test it.' I think theory is an end in and of itself, and I think the skill set is slightly different. I think if you work in theory papers, it helps you write better *AMJ* papers because they have to make a theoretical contribution as well; but it is a slightly different skill set. I don't feel the need that, just because I have done the theory paper, that I then have to go and do an empirical paper.

Cardon, Melissa: I will give you the opposite answer. Yes, I am working on two empirical projects: one I am hoping will go to *JAP* [*Journal of Applied Psychology*] this summer to develop a measure for the definition we came up with; and two, to test the model that we came up with, because my perspective is everything is theory until you have some evidence. And wouldn't it be interesting to see if the concept of passion in our case actually does make a difference? We can say it does. The popular press has been saying that for years, but until we test it well, we are not going to know. So there is a different perspective.

Mitchell, Ron: Other questions from the floor? It looks like the microphone is coming down to Zheng Chen.

Chen, Zheng: I just want to represent the more junior students here and ask how you develop a network of co-authors in your career?

Cardon, Melissa: Absolutely. Doctoral consortiums if you are still a student. Babson's Conference, the Academy of Management – I went to many different divisions. If you are part of the strategic management group, go to BPS [business policy and strategy]. Go to entrepreneurship – that is where students develop a network and it could just be other students at the time, but it could also be faculty. That is where all of the people I write with came from. And conferences. One of my colleagues jokes that I just go to socials at the Academy of Management, and go to all the parties, right? But what do we do at the parties? We stand around talking to each other about research ideas. That's where you have the time to free up intellectual space. So I think that's really critical, even if you are nervous and you are not an outgoing kind of social person, go anyway and talk to people. Not the whole room. Pick a few of them, talk to them and say, 'Hi.'

Mitchell, Ron: Thank you. Next question?

Audience Member #1: This is a question that applies to *AMR* in particular, and as a reviewer for *AMR* as well, asking this question. It is sort of, in the mold of, what should authors not do? Since it is a theory paper and it is words and the words can always be changed, how do you know when a paper is not going to make it at *AMR*? How do you know that you just couldn't say, 'Try again?' What signals when you say, 'No, that's it. I don't think they can change it and make it a better paper.'

Carpenter, Mason: You mean why do we reject a paper?

Audience Member #1: Ultimately, how do you reject a paper? Couldn't they just change this paragraph and add something and bring something in?

Carpenter, Mason: That's a good question, and there is one thing I want to make clear (because I think there's a misconception about submitting a paper to *AMR*). It is high risk submitting to top journals, right? High risk, high gain; but *AMR* is not the only top journal that publishes conceptual work. So if you are thinking about a publication pathway, Venkat (I think) aptly said, 'Think about a publication strategy for your work. You have worked so hard on the paper; one attempt is not all it deserves.' So of course start with *Academy of Management Review*, *Strategic Management Journal* (*SMJ*) (one of my other homes), *Organization Science* (*OS*) . . . There are a number of other top journals that do publish conceptual work, and some of the work that you cite heavily are conceptual works from those journals. I think as an editor and as reviewers it's asking, 'Is this paper essentially going to be a new submission if they do everything we ask them to do?' I said, 'I don't see anything redeeming in the paper.' I have had rejections where the reviewer said (I guess this is a developmental reviewer who said), 'You know, as much as I dislike the rest of the paper, I really liked the abstract.' I don't know if we have all had that type of feedback, but I have; and they didn't criticize the font or the paper size, but I think they were getting there. I think when you are talking about a paper that is essentially 51 percent acceptable to a journal, 60 percent is going to be rewritten. The author has not made certain choices that signal that there is a clear revision path. There are actually 50 revision paths and ultimately it is a signal that there's no traction among the reviewers. As an editor you are looking at a paper going, 'This could be 50 different papers, and the authors have not helped me make choices about what is important to them.'

Shepherd, Dean: As a research strategy for authors, I think that is the important thing about *AMR* being on the top of that research strategy for us (for this paper) is that you can get rejected from any journal for any reason with a theory paper and they all send you in different directions. But at least when you get the reviews from *AMR*, they are timely but they are also high quality. So we can enhance the quality of the paper by following the directions that the reviewer suggests, and also learn more genuinely about how to write better theory papers. That was part of our strategy for going to *AMR*. It wasn't just the timely feedback that we get at *AMR*, but also the high-quality feedback.

Carpenter, Mason: Just to follow up briefly on feedback, because I think we have to wrap up, but when you get that type of feedback – that rejection – typically the reviewers will say, 'We like these pieces, you should push this.' And for some submitters to *AMR*, it could've been an empirical paper; what the reviewers do is they crystallize that you might choose an empirical path first with your paper, because what you have done in the paper is so narrowly specified that we would actually like to see this tested as opposed to a broader theory among which you'd have a piece that you would test and validate.

Lumpkin, Tom: So that comment relates to a question from the web for Mason. When deciding whether to publish an *AMR* article, is any consideration given to the possibility of eventual empirical testability of the propositions (or is it all about the strength of the theorizing)?

Carpenter, Mason: I would say yes to that, because authors that publish in *AMR* – either it is a culmination of several ideas that they have brought or they have sort of snowballed into a larger theory related to their other empirical work or across empirical works. Sitkin and Pablo did a paper in *AMR* a number of years (1992) ago on risk, and it really linked a number of bodies of empirical and theoretical work in a way that was counterintuitive but it really created some new opportunities for research. It could also be setting the landscape for a new domain to do research. Starting first with things as simple as definition and passion is a good example. If you read that paper (and I encourage you to read it), it wrestles through. And this is one of the hurdles for that paper – initially in what we mean by passion, and then getting some tractability around the definition – because then you can sort of back that up with measures, empirical settings, whether they are simulations or what have you, but you at least have some starting point. So I would say yes to both. Any article that I write or that I am affiliated with, that article is part of a portfolio of ideas. And so whether this is sort of encapsulating what's been done in the past or a starting point, you have both opportunities.

Mitchell, Ron: Mason, if you were to speak to our audience (and the hundreds on the web) and give a piece of advice or observation to the authors about future submissions – if you could say, 'Please do this one thing' – what would you suggest that submitters to *AMR* do to actually engage the process effectively?

Carpenter, Mason: I actually have two things. First, it's submit your work. We like to see your top work. Second, that is your top work. You sweated the details. The references that are in the body of the paper are in the reference section. You have really thought through definitions and you have used them consistently throughout. Martin Kilduff again; his discussion with our submitters, reviewers, etc. about 'Why I rejected your paper.' Look at that. Use that as a checklist. Ask yourself, 'Did I do any of these things?' And if you can say no to all of those, then that is great. Just be very, very careful with that work so that you are respecting the time of the reviewers as much as you want them to respect your time. But we do want your top work. Just sweat the details, because there's nothing more frustrating than a paper that comes over where reviewers think that, 'This is really cool; it just didn't seem like they took the care with it that we think that they should have.'

Mitchell, Ron: So, Jack, it is about time that we pulled it all together, made a couple of comments and got off stage. Rich, we are pretty much done.

Dino, Rich: Last segment.

Veiga, Jack: I have one comment for everybody in the room. We are beginning to tap into tacit knowledge that all of us have (which I think is going to be the most relevant to the audience for this entire conference) and I would urge everybody in here – we have talked about momentum, we have talked about commitment of co-authors, we have talked about the nature of the story (what makes something interesting) – but we have only really sort of hit the surface on this. These things are going to re-emerge, I suspect, over the entire conference, and the issue becomes (as we are talking with each other and thinking more) to try to put a little more meat on those bones, if you will. This is an interesting topic, but can we go any deeper? Think about how do we do that or what does that mean? What does momentum really look like and how do you sustain it? Those kinds of questions I think are going to be important.

Mitchell, Ron: In preparation for this get together I took quite a few minutes to look through the editorial boards of the various journals that are represented here, and there was an observation that emerged as I did that. And it's sort of a challenge to all of us. I don't think all of us graduated from – name your top five places you could've gone – top-tier schools in doctoral programs with the exact person you would've hoped to be your advisor; but once you submit to a top-tier journal, you have engaged teachers that are the top people. And if you are accepting the challenge to work at the top-tier level, what you are accepting is the challenge for life-long learning. These reviewers are our teachers, and even those of us who are editors – we heard Duane talk just a few minutes ago – those of us who are editors still have to serve up that dose of humble pie and essentially go through every bit of the process that is required to do the top-tier work.

I would like to ask the authors a question that might speak to this point. If you were to think of the multiple of efforts that it takes to complete your work in top-tier journals as opposed to (let's just say) a lesser-tier journal, what size is that multiple? Is it 1.1 times, just a little bit harder, or what do you think?

Shepherd, Dean: I think it is exactly the same for the first submission of the manuscript. So you try and do the best possible manuscript you can submit. Thankfully my papers are never accepted first round because they improve substantially as a result. So I think they are exactly the same when I submit, but I think the review process tests me and I learn a lot more as a result of the top-tier journals than I would at a lesser-tier journal because I think the reviewers are a higher quality. They push you further and improve the paper more – so it might be doubled or more.

McMullen, Jeff: For me it is not a tier question, it is a scope question. So the issue is how big the question is that you are asking. Some questions absolutely slay you. They take forever and you read and read and you just keep finding out how ignorant you are and you become more and more ignorant as you go out and read another literature and another literature. Then other questions are manageable and reasonable and some lend themselves to 'A' journals because that is the conversation that is going on. And some lend themselves to 'A-' journals because that's who's interested in it. So I go where the audience is and where people will use this.

Mitchell, Ron: What are you thinking, Melissa?

Cardon, Melissa: I am going to be very practical to our junior colleagues out there and say: at least five times as much effort, and I would put it on the review process as well. I know that the authors' response letter to reviewers is always longer than the paper, right? But for *AMR*, that was huge for us in making sure we were being so diligent in responding to their questions and concerns, because their feedback to us was so detailed and diligent. I would have to say our paper wouldn't be what it is without the three reviewers and guest editors for that paper because I went back in preparation for this and read the first draft and every draft all the way through. The cool things I like about the paper that's coming out is that all changes came out of reviewer suggestions in round two (not even round one – round two), because we had to clean it up based on their first round of feedback to get it to the point where they could give us the suggestions – to find the diamonds in the rough and make it what it is. So that process is at least a multiple of thought for me, and we had four of us.

Mitchell, Ron: Sure. So what we are learning here isn't just surface information about the process of addressing and creating theory and sending it to *AMR*. Process questions are important and we all need to have that information, but the other part of the story is that we have to be willing to do the 'pick and shovel' work and to sincerely dedicate ourselves to not becoming daunted by what the reviewers are saying. It will always say high risk, and it will always have a list that is longer than you ever think you can accomplish. So consequently, top tier doesn't just mean you understand the ins and outs; top tier means dedication and sacrifice to actually produce the kind of work that is represented here in this session, and will be represented later in the conference, too.

So if we are going to draw some final themes from this session, Jack, your big one or two or three would be?

Veiga, Jack: Well, I think it would be to understand the scope of the journal you are targeting. I hear these authors talking about the amount of work and I agree, having done it at *AMR*. What surprised me the most is that *AMR* doesn't allow you to boil it down so much as *AMJ* does. You can get your reader focused in an area pretty quickly and then they stay in that domain. Where you get reviewers from *AMR* – you want really bright people is the real issue. I remember a reviewer asking me, 'What about helping theory?' And I am saying, 'What the heck is helping theory? You mean there's an actual helping theory?' Yeah, there's a whole literature on helping theory. I went out and read that literature and I said, 'Wow, this is really what we are talking about. This was very helpful.' So a reviewer is not your best friend reading your paper and saying, 'Nice job.' Okay? It's really trying to get people that maybe have different headsets on to read it and say, 'You know, you are really talking about this or that.' Especially when it comes to *AMR* because there the richness is this broad integration, and so I would say it's finding reviewers before you even submit the paper who have that kind of view.

Audience Member #2: So this search for helping theory wasn't really code for, 'This paper is beyond help and you ought to go and take it somewhere else?'

Veiga, Jack: No.

Mitchell, Ron: Any last takeaways from the author group?

Shepherd, Dean: Just on the time investment thing. You think about how much time you are investing in that paper, but it's not just an investment in the paper in doing that revise enrichment. You are actually learning new skills that will help you with all of your subsequent papers. So it never concerns me that I am spending so much time on this one paper because I think it's developmental for other papers.

Audience Member #3: One thing as a reviewer for *AMR*: I just think that when you are reviewing theory you need to look for what's not there as much as what is and be more developmental probably than you would be on an empirical piece where a lot of times it's criticizing what's there and what's been done. I think with theory, you have to look and say, 'What could be,' as a reviewer and help craft that. You don't have to write the paper, but definitely bring your knowledge. You have just expanded the knowledge base considerably by having three reviewers on top of the editor and the authors.

Cardon, Melissa: You have to keep your mind open. Many of us (when we get our reviewer comments) get defensive. We say 'They didn't see the value of my paper. They didn't understand what I was trying to do.' Well, if they don't understand it then you didn't do it well enough – and I think that it's really difficult to separate the defense mechanism from the, 'Maybe they are actually helping me make it better.'

Mitchell, Ron: After a first revision I got feedback from a reviewer that said, 'Now the writing is clear enough for me to understand why I really hate this.'

So with that, ladies and gentlemen, thank you very much to Mason and our authors for an interesting session. Jack our co-moderator. Let's wrap it up then. Thank you very much.

NOTE

1. These journal mission statements also appear herein within Exhibit I.

REFERENCES

Cardon, M.S., J. Wincent, J. Singh and M. Drnovsek (2009). The nature and experience of entrepreneurial passion. *Academy of Management Review*, **34** (3), 511–32.
Grégoire, D.A., P.S. Barr and D.A. Shepherd (2010). Cognitive processes of opportunity recognition: the role of structural alignment. *Organization Science*, **21** (2), 413–31.
Kilduff, M. (2007). The top ten reasons why your paper might not be sent out for review. *Academy of Management Review*, **32**, 700–702.
McMullen, J.S. and D.A. Shepherd (2006). Entrepreneurial action and the role of uncertainty in the theory of the entrepreneur. *Academy of Management Review*, **31** (1), 132–52.
Sitkin, S.B. and A.L. Pablo (1992). Reconceptualizing the determinants of risk behavior. *Academy of Management Review*, **17** (1), 9–38.

11. Entrepreneurship Theory & Practice

Editor: *Candida (Candy) Brush*
Author: *Jon C. Carr*
Moderators: *Ronald K. Mitchell,*
  John F. (Jack) Veiga
Comments editor: *G. Thomas Lumpkin*

Mitchell, Ron: I am Ron Mitchell, currently serving as Chair of the Entrepreneurship Division of the Academy of Management. With me are Candy Brush, who is one of the senior editors at *Entrepreneurship Theory & Practice* (*ET&P*); Jack Veiga (my co-moderator); and Jon Carr, who's the author representing the paper 'Toward a theory of familiness: A social capital perspective' (with Allison Pearson and John Shaw). Have I got that right?

Carr, Jon: Yes.

Mitchell, Ron: The opportunities for publishing entrepreneurship research in a journal titled *Entrepreneurship Theory & Practice* are amazing. The opportunities that I have identified (as they go through a very well-thought-through mission statement) are such that it is a journal for a wide variety of entrepreneurship research. At the core of its mission, *ET&P* is a leading scholarly journal in the field of entrepreneurship studies. The journal's mission is to publish original papers which contribute to the advancement of the field of entrepreneurship. *ET&P* publishes conceptual and empirical articles of interest to scholars, consultants and public policy makers. How'd I do, Candy?

Brush, Candy: Very well.

Mitchell, Ron: So we got it at least as a foundation now that the mission is articulated. Well, Jon, let's just turn then for a minute to you to give us the flyby – the elevator pitch – on what the paper was about. Help us get into this . . .

Carr, Jon: The paper was really designed to sort of be three different sections; I think that is how we really approached it. But what it is about is to try to extend some work that had been done by Habbershon and his colleagues (Habbershon, Williams and Kaye, 1999) on the idea of 'familiness' within family firms. They had used a particular theoretical frame, namely resource-based theory (RBT), to help describe this construct called familiness. Our goal was to try to see if we could use another theoretical viewpoint to try to expand upon one of the particular descriptions that they use for familiness from an RBT perspective. We used a social capital perspective to try to describe in further detail just how familiness is comprised, and how perhaps you could use this particular perspective to help us better understand how familiness is created and how it unfolds for family firms.

Mitchell, Ron: Well, thank you very much. So what we have then is a paper that deals with this concept of familiness as it was originally introduced. Familiness, if you could just define it for the audience, would be what? Is it a factor about a family business that affects competitive advantage?

Carr, Jon: Exactly. They used, again, the RBT perspective, and so it was basically an idiosyncratic collection of resources and capabilities unique to families that help families compete and perform better. So that was really the purpose of the whole . . . The frame of it was all about asking ourselves, 'Can we further explore this idea of familiness?'

Mitchell, Ron: So Jack, as you looked over this paper, obviously thoughts have come to mind. Would you lead out with a few observations and perhaps some questions?

Veiga, Jack: At the front end of reading the paper, as I first started, I said, 'Okay, where are we going?'

Carr, Jon: You were lost?

Veiga, Jack: When I see a word that is created – one that is not typically in the dictionary – I ask, 'Why do we have to create this special word? Why is this labeling important?' And of course, what was interesting to me is that my dad had a family business, and I worked in the family business. About halfway into the paper, I am recalling vivid memories of experiences.

Your paper is capturing what might be good family dynamics (positive family dynamics) – which I know lots of businesses exist like that as well – but I was recalling images of an older brother that wasn't as good a mechanic as I was, and how that perception by my father carried into our home. So all of a sudden I am saying, 'This is really interesting!'

You really start at this level [hand gesturing], but with this topic (to get deeper into this) there are probably a lot of interesting avenues that you can take.

Mitchell, Ron: So, just for the worldwide audience, since Jack's microphone wasn't on, Jack was raised in a family with a family business. He had many positive experiences, and out of that comes a perspective that permits him to ask the following question.

Veiga, Jack: To dig deeper into the dynamics – where do you see this going, or what was motivating you? Have you worked in a family business?

Carr, Jon: I personally have not worked in a family business. Our idea was that the existing definition was not clear enough and it was the kind of definition that makes sense after you've read the paper; this is a characteristic of family firms that's real. You were recalling your own experiences, and in our discussions with other folks we had the same kind of comments, such as 'I remember what this was like for myself.' And so our idea was that if we can better explain this as a theoretical phenomenon, then perhaps we can measure it, examine it and use this particular idea to further understand how some family businesses (which have a very positive familiness experience) can use that and leverage that to success. But in some instances it has some negative consequences. What we'd like to do (and what I'd personally like to do) is really comprehensively develop a measure for it. Once we have that, perhaps we've extended our understanding of family businesses further and, as a result, extended the field.

Mitchell, Ron: So let's look at the process of dealing with *ET&P*. Did these areas that Jon was trying to convey come through to the reviewers and editor, Candy? How did that process actually work?

Brush, Candy: Actually, this is something that we haven't talked about. I thought (being on the third day of the Conference) that everything might have been said, so I am fortunate to have something to talk about. This actually came out of a special issue, and at *ET&P* we run about four special issues a year; this special issue was about family business. I don't know how many submissions came in, but I know it was probably over

30 or so. I was not the action editor, but I did talk to Jim Chrisman, who was, at length. In fact, I was telling Jon that I asked for the original paper. I read it and I treated it as if I had been the action editor, and I was really pleased to see that I agreed with Jim's comments because that validated my thoughts on it. But, for this particular paper, it was a concept (as Jon said) that had been referred to in the literature but was not well articulated. And so the paper has a very good framework that helps to elaborate a concept that has been used, but was really fuzzy. And so the contribution of the paper, as I see it, is that it has a framework that is testable and would generate future research in this area. I thought that was an excellent contribution.

Mitchell, Ron: If I could just follow up on this special issue notion for the worldwide audience. Yesterday, when we were comparing the specialty niche entrepreneurship journals, one of the points that Candy made in that session was that the special issue focus is something that *ET&P* has done quite consistently over the years. Now, the thing that happens with the special issue is that the dynamics of reviewer assignment end up becoming actually a little more specialized because you really have recruited the people who are in the domain of this area (which in this case was family business). So when you got your reviews, Jon, were they all over the map or how did they actually hit you? Were there problems that they raised that were almost insurmountable, or were they on the helpful side? What was going on there?

Carr, Jon: Can I just back up a little bit? One of the nice things about this idea of special issues is that it is focused like that. This paper was part of a conference that Jim Chrisman and his colleagues hold every year (or I guess it is every other year), and their charge to us as conference participants was, 'We really want you to try to stretch something here. We want you to look at a couple of different topics – and you get to pick the topic – but we want you to stretch what we understand about a particular family business topic.' That is what led to the beginning of this paper: the fact that we had the editors (who really became like partners for us), and that was a wonderful experience if you were an author. When the reviewers are providing you with a lot of feedback, they are helping to shape how that feedback impacts your paper, but they also want to see you continue to push the limits of it. I think that's one of the benefits of a special issue in my mind. So we got a lot of very, very good feedback. We had a lot of things that we had to change and that challenged us. But the fact is that we had a special issue editor who was very much our partner symbolically, telling us, 'We're going to get through this. We're going to help you understand what the reviewers are really asking for here and help you shape this in many ways.'

Mitchell, Ron: I am going to make an observation, Candy, and ask you to critique it (since we're on special issues and it is something that had not been discussed). We can focus on the special issue phenomenon at *ET&P* in particular, but perhaps look at other journals as well because many of the journals represented here (if not all) do special issues as a means whereby advancement could occur in the field. Now, I am no rock climber, but are they the pitons you hammer in so you can get the carabiner snapped in? So, essentially, what we are doing as we are climbing higher in theory development is we are actually marking our way and establishing our place so that we have new anchors from which to build. Now from that standpoint, is that an editorial philosophy within *ET&P*? Or what is the view of special issues? Because four a year – that is a lot of special issues.

Brush, Candy: It is. I think it goes back to this debate, 'Are we building communities of scholars?' The Bill Gartner paper (2001) in which he talks about (and to some degree, I think what Jon referred to) the fact that that there is a community around family business – and there is also a community around women's entrepreneurship (of which I am a part), and around international or transitioned economies. So you have these different communities and it is an opportunity, I think, to collaborate and to develop theories more deeply in these perhaps niche areas. But at the same time, special issues oftentimes have the benefit of bringing new perspectives to bear on it. So I don't know about your conference in particular, but sometimes – let's say you're doing a conference on family business – maybe it is an opportunity to draw in anthropologists or economists or people who have different lenses so that you can therefore expand and develop that research area so that perhaps it has implications beyond just that particular context area. So I am not sure if I answered your question, but I think that is the way that we think about special issues.

Mitchell, Ron: Well, I think, since it is on the floor, the idea of a special issue and what it does is the first part of the equation. What special issues don't do and if there are any weaknesses associated with that would be the other part of my question. What do you think?

Brush, Candy: Obviously, the other piece of special issues (for those out in cyberspace) is that they run off cycles, so it is run by a separate group – special issues don't come through the managing editors. There are volunteers who submit a proposal to the editors. In fact, we have 10 or 15 to review right now and if we think, this is 2009; some of these wouldn't be published until 2012. In any event (and we won't accept them all, by the way), we will discuss them.

Mitchell, Ron: So they are specialized in one sense and then on a longer trajectory because of that. We are now in the Q&A time and I would like to invite our worldwide audience to email questions in as well as our audience here at the University of Connecticut to begin the question-and-answer process.

Lumpkin, Tom: I have got one on the web.

Mitchell, Ron: Tom, if you would lead off then, please.

Lumpkin, Tom: In general, are the standards for special issues higher or lower? In terms of percentages of acceptances, how does it compare to general submissions?

Brush, Candy: I will answer that. It depends on how many submissions you get. One special issue I managed had 65 submissions, and so that was a little overwhelming because I had asked people and they said, 'Oh, you'll get 30' – and we got 65. That means the submissions are still double-blind reviewed; in some cases we had three reviewers, depending on what it was. The reviewers are usually people who are specialists in the area. So, if anything, I would say that the standards might be higher because of the level of expertise in that particular subject area – it is greater expertise applied to that particular phenomenon. It is hard to say as I don't have empirical data to say yes or no.

Mitchell, Ron: I know when Ray Bagby asked me to manage the entrepreneurial cognition special issue series that one of the explicit understandings that we had verbally (I don't know if it turned up in writing, but it was explicit) was that if we have however many papers and not a single one of them meets the standards then we won't have a special issue. If we only have 1 out of 65 that meets the standards, it will be included with a note in a regular issue. So it really was a 'meet the *ET&P* standard.' But then again, if you get a lot of high-quality papers in not too big of a pool, the acceptance rate is going to vary based on that. It is really just the mathematics of that.

Brush, Candy: Absolutely, because we could only accept six.

Veiga, Jack: I am just curious; do you ever do a special invitation? For instance, in family business, go to a Mike Hitt, go to a Duane Ireland, go to a Mike Lubatkin – these are people that haven't worked in this area, but on the other hand they have great minds. They think in lots of different ways and say, 'Look, I want you to do a piece.' As part of it (not the whole thing, but as part of it), just to see what different people's perspectives might bring to it?

Brush, Candy: I think it happens both ways. I think sometimes the editors will say, especially topic X might be a good topic because we are getting a lot of submissions on this, but then we get a lot of unsolicited proposals. In fact, the 15 special issue proposals that we have are all from volunteers: some of them are from editors and some of them are from reviewers on the review board. So it comes both ways; and again, we have to say that the key thing with *Entrepreneurship Theory & Practice* is that we want to make sure that there are contributions to the domain of entrepreneurship. And in particular, we do look at theory or theoretical contributions or empirical contributions that will further research. So really, the bottom line here is, 'Will this special issue (and it is the same in our regular review process) – will these papers, this group of papers – make a significant contribution to the domain of entrepreneurship?' That is really the bottom-line question.

Mitchell, Ron: Just to add a tiny bit of color to that . . . When we were doing this entrepreneurial cognition series, at that point in time (sometimes in the field you see it developing and all the papers that are submitted don't really cover the waterfront), I did go to Ray and say, 'This is a piece that needs to be there and it is not; and I would like to invite "so and so" to do it.' And I received editorial approval to do that. So, Jack, that is another way that the crafting and the moving forward of the theory and the practice field works out. Do we have another question, Tom?

Lumpkin, Tom: She just answered it.

Mitchell, Ron: So to the floor, who has the microphone?

Brush, Candy: I have a comment. I actually have another topic I'll bring up (because I think we haven't talked about this either), and that is how authors respond to reviewers. That is a process in and of itself. I was commenting to Jon that one of the things I observed in the multiple pages of responses to reviewers is that he and his authors had a very accepting tone. In other words, one of the reviewers said something about a section being confusing and instead of a defensive 'I don't agree,' Jon and his authors responded, 'On second review, we agree it was confusing.' And so I think it is important to acknowledge to the reviewers exactly your understanding of what they're saying and your willingness to work with them – and I think that was really clear in your responses. I don't know, maybe you want to talk about that.

Carr, Jon: I would say that one of the things that we had to address (and the reviewers brought up some very well-taken points) was a question on theoretical clarity that asked, 'How are you different?' Seeing that there was some other research that we cited, reviewers asked: 'You're using this research, but how are you contributing? How are you discriminating between what these authors have said versus your own work?'

The points that the reviewers made were very valid, and so the tack could have been, 'Well, we're going to ignore what you're saying here.' And we decided to say, 'Look, they're right on track with this. Let's get past this idea that we don't have to respond to it. Let's make some changes and acknowledge our own shortcomings on our research.'

Mitchell, Ron: So let's go with these one-liners just to wrap everything up. Candy, if there were one thing you'd recommend to authors in successfully working with *ET&P*, what would it be?

Brush, Candy: Make sure there is a contribution to the domain and the field of entrepreneurship. That's actually one of the reasons why papers do get desk rejected: because the contribution is to strategic management or some other field. And so those papers, even though they may be great quality, are better positioned for a different journal.

Mitchell, Ron: Jon, one thing that you could say to our worldwide audience and our studio audience here in recommending one thing to work with *ET&P* would be. . .?

Carr, Jon: Again, the theoretical contribution certainly needs to be there. It has been my experience (and this has been echoed already) that you have to put your best work in front of the editor and in front of the reviewers; by doing that, that means crafting has to happen very carefully and diligently. And that has been mentioned by several of our keynote speakers, and it can't be emphasized enough. You have to put together your best work, and so in working with *ET&P* that is certainly what I would recommend.

Mitchell, Ron: Thank you very much, Jon. Thank you, Candy. Thank you everyone.

REFERENCES

Gartner, W. (2001). Is there an elephant in entrepreneurship? Blind assumptions in theory development. *Entrepreneurship Theory and Practice*, **25** (4), 27–40.

Habbershon, T.G., M.L. Williams and K. Kaye (1999). A resource-based framework for assessing the strategic advantages of family firms. *Family Business Review*, **12** (1), 1–25.

Pearson, A.W., J.C. Carr and J.C. Shaw (2008). Toward a theory of familiness: a social capital perspective. *Entrepreneurship Theory and Practice*, **32** (6), 949–69.

12.   Journal of Applied Psychology

Associate editor: *Jing Zhou*
Author: *Maw-Der Foo*
Moderators: *Ronald K. Mitchell,*
   John E. Mathieu
Comments editor: *G. Thomas Lumpkin*

Mitchell, Ron: I am Ron Mitchell, current Chair of the Entrepreneurship Division of the Academy of Management; with me are Jing Zhou (the associate editor of the *Journal of Applied Psychology*), John Mathieu (my co-moderator) and Maw-Der Foo (author representative here today).

We have in the *Journal of Applied Psychology* (*JAP*) unique publishing opportunities and Jing, just as I have done with other journals, I am going to provide a bit of my own take on the journal's mission statement and then ask you to correct me to the extent that I step out of line. What I would like to communicate is that *JAP* is an outlet for applied empirical work that addresses the psychological aspects of entrepreneurship. This journal publishes research that can 'contribute new knowledge and understanding to fields of applied psychology.'

So this journal is open to a wide variety of topics which include personnel selection, performance measurement, training, work motivation, leadership, drug and alcohol abuse, career development, conflict between job and family, work stress, organizational design, technology, cross-cultural differences in work behavior, and attitudes. Now that's a very broad palette, but it all is encompassed in the term 'applied psychology.' So this is the opportunity for all of us worldwide who are interested in this kind of work to target our papers (actually our research design and the papers that describe our research) to the *Journal of Applied Psychology*.

Now the first thing that we will do then is to ask Maw-Der to give us a brief flyby of the paper. I didn't actually read out the title which I normally have done. The title is, 'How do feelings influence effort? An empirical study of entrepreneurs' affect and venture effort.' You have co-authors, so please go ahead.

Foo, Maw-Der: First I would like to recognize my co-authors, Marilyn Uy (and she has now moved to the University of Victoria, which Ron was from) and Robert Baron, who is also moving to Oklahoma State. I'm from Colorado – and still in Colorado.

The purpose of this paper really is part of the overall goal to highlight the central role of affective influences such as feelings, emotions, emotional labor and emotional intelligence in the process of how entrepreneurs discover, evaluate and implement business opportunities. But specifically for this paper, what we investigated was how affect predicts the amount of effort that entrepreneurs put into their ventures. We used the 'affect as information' theory. We suggest that if you experience positive affect, you assume that things are going well; and therefore, you take a backseat and reduce your effort. What we thought was interesting and counterintuitive was that positive affect actually increased the amount of effort that entrepreneurs put into their ventures, primarily through a future temporal focus.

Mitchell, Ron: So, one of the things that was cool about the method was that you emphasized the word 'experience.' And was this experience-sampling methodology where you had the entrepreneurs who were participating respondents actually call in (was it twice a day?) on their cell phones? How was that received at *JAP*?

Zhou, Jing: It was cool. It was very nice. It is a method that actually the 'affect' people (the people who do research in social psychology and affect) started to use. So in some ways, there are several interesting things about this paper that I really like. First of all is the theory: the mood, as information theory, is relatively new in our field – in the applied field; and they used that correctly and in a very counterintuitive way, if you will, of looking at the immediate versus future, and both the negative and positive mood each have as a functional impact on people's effort. It's just different temporal dimensions. Also, the way social psychologists collect data really is new and appropriate; so those are very nice features.

Mitchell, Ron: Thank you. John, as you encountered this paper, what questions came to mind? Lead us forward in our discussion, please.

Mathieu, John: Well, I think that both the paper and *JAP* are an interesting kind of fit in this forum. *JAP* (in both an author and editor view on this thing) is the flagship journal for psychology, but it is oddly enough more a niche journal for this particular kind of audience. I want both the author and the associate editor to sort of frame that in how it fits – and from Maw-Der (and I previewed this with you earlier) – his opening paragraph was a traditional 'here's motivation and applied context.' It is the sort of thing that I and our colleagues would write about: goal-setting or self-regulation theory. And then paragraph two is where the entrepreneurship stuff came in. I am wondering why you decided on that framing rather than grabbing something from *Business Week* and giving us a sexy snippet about an emotional high or breakdown of an entrepreneur and how that sparks things. So tell us about the framing and inspiration.

Mitchell, Ron: Before he answers this, there's an entrepreneur calling right now and he's really mad.

Foo, Maw-Der: What I wanted to say regarding the experience-sampling methodology that we used was that we actually programmed the survey into the cell phone. So if you were a participant, you would get an SMS [application on your phone]. You would probably walk out of the room after this session and reply to our survey. For this survey, technology methodology was jointly developed by Marilyn Uy (who's the second author of this paper), myself and Zhaoli Song, who is at the National University of Singapore. (I want to give credit to them, who helped develop this technology.)

To your question about why do we put work motivation theory before entrepreneurship, I think I can go back to a colleague who was talking to me the other day who said, 'I submitted something to *JAP* and the editor took eight months to get me a suitable reviewer.' So I think the key message here is – you know, we talk about reviewers. Who are the reviewers? We are the reviewers, right? So to *JAP*, I can sometimes imagine who are the reviewers at *JAP*. Who are the three people that I will be speaking to – who would be the managing or actionary person that I would be speaking to and what would they be more receptive to? So we felt that at least for the *JAP* audience, that was the motivation they might be more receptive to.

Mitchell, Ron: Let me follow that up before I kick it over to Jing, in that there's an interesting thing about signaling and how you target this voice. We have had this conversation at the journal level: this journal or that journal. There are some disciplines (*MIS* [*Management Infomation Systems*] and some marketing things) that I've worked with, like *Organization Science*, where you actually are asked to nominate an AE [associate editor] and reviewers. You don't get to do that at *JAP*, and I see a lot of people who will send in the proverbial cover letter on how this information is input into the web-window (where they will give the executive summary of the paper) and others will say, 'Listen, this work kind of sits out in this field.' So how does it work with a journal like *JAP*, with the magnitude of a number of associate editors? How does an author signal: 'This is the audience who ought to be reviewing this thing to sort of find the right kind of feedback?'

Zhou, Jing: First of all, let me just take like two minutes to describe what *JAP* is, given that I realized yesterday that in this audience there are a lot of 'macro' people. *JAP* is a very large enterprise. The current editorial team officially started in 2009; but starting in 2008, this team actually started to process manuscripts. I was counting last night and in 2009 alone I wrote 48 decision letters. So by the end of 2009, for just myself alone, there will be over 100 revisions that will come in. So this is a very large journal.

After I took this position, I learned that *JAP* actually has a very long history. I know it is a very distinguished journal; it has been around for 90 years – nine-zero – so it has been around for a long time publishing scholarly work in applied psychology. I am very excited with *JAP* at this juncture in its history. We all know its very long distinguished history.

Here is a piece of data that I hesitated on deciding whether I should share with you or not, but I decided to share with you. Not long ago I received a survey done by Murray Barrick at A&M. He surveyed the research schools in terms of getting people's consensus of what are really the top journals. When you talk about premier journals in your program or department, what are those? The survey's conclusion actually was that, based on data, the big five top journals were *Academy of Management Journal* (*AMJ*), *Academy of Management Review* (*AMR*), *Administrative Science Quarterly* (*ASQ*), *Journal of Applied Psychology* (*JAP*) and *Strategic Management Journal* (*SMJ*). So *JAP* is up there in terms of being respected in management departments and applied psychology programs.

I say this is exciting because after the current editorial team started, the editor Steve Kozlowski published an editorial, and I would strongly recommend everyone who's ever interested in publishing at *JAP* to look at the editorial very carefully. Read it very carefully. It was published in the January issue of 2009. It actually laid out very, very detailed expectations for manuscripts. I was surprised (since I became associate editor) how many authors wasted an opportunity to really calibrate their manuscripts to *JAP* in terms of both the writing style and structure. How do you frame your story to suit the audience? It is quite doable. In my mind it is actually easy to do. All it takes is to actually read that editorial; he clearly says the kinds of things you should do and the kinds of things you should not do to be successful here. I thought that was a very, very helpful starting point.

Mitchell, Ron: Maw-Der did not have that article, so how did you formulate this article to make it?

Foo, Maw-Der: Well, here I need to acknowledge Matthew Haywood a little bit. Matthew Haywood introduced me to a book called *The Pyramid Principle* (Minto, 2002). Basically he lays out the area that we are talking about: in our case it was motivation. And then he lays out what is surprising about that area – and here what was surprising was the amount of effort that entrepreneurs put into their venture. Then he lays out what theoretical perspective that we wanted to use, which was the affect as information. So we pretty much used his pyramid principle to lay out what we thought was the issue we were talking about, what was surprising, what our theoretical angle was and then how we contributed it to that area.

I think one of the points I want to say is why we targeted *JAP*. We talk about legitimacy of fields (as Patricia McDougall was mentioning [Chapter 6] about entrepreneurship being a legitimate field), but one of the issues about legitimacy is that we are not sure; we are talking about strategy, talking about OB [organizational behavior], talking about entrepreneurship and entrepreneurship taking over strategy – but why not OB taking over entrepreneurship and entrepreneurship taking over OB? So the point I am trying to drive here is that there are legitimacy issues sometimes with OB and entrepreneurship, and I am really glad to see that many of the so-called 'interesting papers' in this conference are OB and entrepreneurship.

Mitchell, Ron: Journals evolve over time. If you look at *JAP* several years ago, there was a lot of work on union issues. There were a lot of jury kinds of studies. Human factors used to have a very big footprint there. And if you look at more recent years, the top management teams have found a home there. The entrepreneurship stuff has found a home there. So it is a very wide tent. Roughly how many manuscripts do you get a year?

Zhou, Jing: Between 900 and 1,000.

Mitchell, Ron: For the journal itself?

Zhou, Jing: New submissions, not including revisions; the journal's actual acceptance rate I believe is around 10 percent.

Mitchell, Ron: I was going to say that I think you're actually up in the thousands, last time I looked, in terms of submissions. How many AEs are there? There are about 11 of you?

Zhou, Jing: Well, we started with nine. Clearly that was not enough, given the amount of work. So right now we have ten. And among the ten associate editors, the editor put me in charge of dealing with manuscripts about top management teams and entrepreneurship.

Mitchell, Ron: Just a moderator's point: one of the pieces of information that a division chair has access to is the number of people from other divisions who are also members of your division – and we have many hundreds of OB scholars who are also members of the Entrepreneurship Division. This is one of these conversations that has been going on for a good long time, which is why as the journal moves into being interested in this domain, we as entrepreneurship scholars should begin to be interested in this journal.

Mathieu, John: And again, a lot of it has to do with what the niches are and how you fit it in. Much of the earlier discussion in other sessions was about perceptions and informing people.

Then to just give you a quick side story: I was trained in industrial organizational psychology, so *JAP* was the show for me. The very first publication I ever had was rejected from *JAP*; it went through machinations and eventually I got it in someplace else. At the end of the year when we did my performance evaluation with my department head (and we were having this conversation about *JBV* [*Journal of Business Venturing*] in another session), I literally sat down with my department head and she asked me about this other place where I had landed the paper. And she asked, 'Is that even refereed? Is that a magazine? What is that?' I was sitting there in a tough position of trying to convince my department head that this other home where I got it placed wasn't a rag; it was a reasonable place and I found myself trying to argue for the legitimacy of the *Academy of Management Journal*, which is where it was landed. It was just before Mike Hitt came on as editor. It was a buyer's watch and I'm arguing, 'This is not a rag. It's not a magazine. I should get credit for this thing.' And that was the dialogue that I had with the psychologist. So framing and where you are coming from really does matter. As you think about it, psychology tends to be the different side of things, but particularly under the stewardship of Steve Kozlowski (he's a levels person). As an OB outsider looking at entrepreneurship, there are tons of level issues, all right. Not only choosing a level, but how you embrace multiple levels at once. So I think *JAP*, particularly when you get off of the 'just the individual side of things' and you start thinking about the entrepreneur, the context, how he or she scopes their organizations and how they choose the environments and enact the environments that they look at . . .

Mitchell, Ron: It is an interesting observation because actually, as I was the Entrepreneurship Division program chair just a couple of years ago, levels are starting to – that kind of research is really starting to come to its own in entrepreneurship . . .

Now we are at the time when we can take questions from the world and from our studio audience. The microphone is up and active and over here – Jeff McMullen making a point . . .

Mathieu, John: As the microphone travels, one of the things I will alert you to is that *JAP* tends to be more methodological and rigorous, and there's a nice compliment on the management side of things. *Organizational Research Methods* actually is in the midst of a special issue right now and entrepreneurship is the focus. So tools and different analytic techniques and things of that sort that are very suitable for entrepreneurship (some of which are going to be multi-level kinds of tools of which I have been reviewing for) are just on the horizon; so that will be forthcoming, too.

Mitchell, Ron: Thank you. Jeff.

McMullen, Jeff: Just a quick question. I have heard mixed opinions or answers to this question so I am just curious. Does *JAP* accept pure theory or does it have to be an empirical piece? And how common is it if they do accept pure theory?

Zhou, Jing: That's a very good question. It is actually not editorial. The editor laid it out clearly that we very much welcome theory pieces. A couple of years ago, the previous editorial team actually had a special theory session; but we don't have to go to special issues. We accept theory papers year-round. We are also very receptive to papers using all sorts of methods. It could be qualitative as long as they are rigorously conducted. It could be quantitative, so we are very receptive as long as it is well done; theory or empirical.

Mitchell, Ron: Well, that statement is going to bring more work for you.

Mathieu, John: The *JAP* mission also has a very applied piece to it. It is the *Journal of Applied Psychology*. There are plenty of avenues for more basic psychological kinds of research, so you really do need to be relevant. Now there is a place for basic research and applied research, but in the *Journal of Applied Psychology*, you can't just give a passing throwaway sentence or two at the end. You really have to offer 'how this changes things,' or at least inform how one ought to be operating.

Mitchell, Ron: Okay, the microphone is moved.

Audience Member #1: Hi. I am probably one of the few people in this room who has been successfully published in *JAP* for entrepreneurship papers. I have been an active reviewer for *JAP* for the last few years for some entrepreneurship papers. However, I have a general impression that *JAP* has a difficulty identifying appropriate reviewers to review entrepreneurship papers. The example Maw-Der just mentioned (that I'm invited to review my own paper) happened during the transition of the previous editorial team and the current editorial team, so I think it was just an accident. Another example I have is a few years ago . . .

Mitchell, Ron: Did you do it?

Audience Member #1: I struggled for a day and I finally said 'no.'

Mitchell, Ron: It was his toughest review.

Audience Member #1: Another example is that a few years ago, the *JAP* editor spent five months and then told me we could not find a second reviewer for our paper, so they made a decision just based on one single reviewer's comments (which actually were positive ones so we got lucky I think in this way). My question is, has *JAP* considered inviting entrepreneurship researchers to review for *JAP*?

Zhou, Jing: Good question. There are actually several questions in there, so let me just answer quickly. First of all (in terms of the review timeline), I don't know what the previous editorial teams had as their timeline, but in terms of this particular paper, to prepare for this conference, I actually looked at it. The paper was submitted in June of 2008, and I believe the decision was sent out in August. I don't remember the exact date, but in August. They revised the paper and added new data – so that was a great revision.

Adding new data is not easy. So for almost four months (close to December), they went through one round of revisions and that was it. After one round of revisions (that was a very responsive revision) I conditionally accepted in December. In two weeks I accepted conditionally. I believe in January of 2009 the second revision came back and I accepted it without sending out a review. So this is about half a year – six months. I'm sorry about your experience, but I'm not sure that's typical.

Your second question about reviewers . . . We have cleaned out the database. When we took over the office there was a database in place, so we had to use that and you have to learn while doing that. Because I am the one who is more familiar with entrepreneurship researchers, I have made lots of suggestions in terms of who to add and who to use, and we are still in the process of doing that. But the key thing is that there are famous people who everybody knows – but when you send out reviews to them, they have an incredibly heavy workload (so that probably explains the delay). I am actually in the process of making suggestions to the editor in terms of adding more reviewers, and I would also suggest to people who are interested in reviewing for *JAP*: send your letter, be proactive and say 'I'm interested in reviewing for you.' We welcome that.

Mitchell, Ron: This will be a very helpful request. So, everyone worldwide, if *JAP* is one of your areas of specialty, please volunteer – and that way we will be able to get beyond the one-reviewer kind of difficulty.

So we are in the wrap-up phase right now, and John, I would like to just go back to you for a few final thoughts about *JAP*, the papers, etc., and then I am going to ask two open-ended questions of the editor and the author about the one piece of advice they would give. So you go first.

Mathieu, John: Certainly *JAP* has always had the reputation that it is a method and a quantitative thing, and it is in the sense that they look for (first and foremost) empirical pieces – not to the exclusion of theoretical ones. That certainly is a featured part of *JAP*, but that doesn't mean that *JAP* is just a statistics geek forum. In fact, the editors and associate editors really do want to bring out the theory and really put things in context. So don't play with the stereotype of *JAP*. It is a big tent and they welcome a lot of different things. And it is a place where you have some wiggle room in terms of doing novel or different kinds of things.

Mitchell, Ron: So, Jing, if there was one thing that you would recommend in successfully working with *JAP*, it would be . . .?

Zhou, Jing: The goals. When you decide where to send the paper, it should not be after you've done data analysis and then decide. The design phase is very important. Calibrate and, really, I totally agree with what Mike [Hitt] said earlier about design (by the way, Mike has been my role model since I started). I have had the privilege to be his colleague and just to watch him be such an outstanding researcher, and at the same time being so generous with his time and his advice to people.

So that is, I think, what I sense the *JAP* editorial team is trying to do. We are not at maximum level yet, but we are here to help. We try to be constructive. The advice would be really the design phase. Find something you truly love. This is not a career tactic; it is a strategic move in terms of 'I'm going to get one more publication,' but do something you truly are curious of finding out answers. So that is one piece of advice. Another one is (I learned this from Barry Stall, one of the outstanding OB researchers) – he said, 'Very few of us are natural-born good writers, but you can be a good rewriter.' So do something; before you send it out, ask yourself this final question before you send it off: 'Is this something I'm proud of?'

Mitchell, Ron: Thank you, Jing. Maw-Der, any last words?

Foo, Maw-Der: I think I have a very tight link between theory and method; and to do that, take your time to design the survey and to collect the data, because often you have just one shot to collect data and after that you can and should rewrite 50 times (like many of you have mentioned).

Mitchell, Ron: So, in conclusion, there is room in *JAP* for top-tier entrepreneurship research. Let's do some. Thank you very much.

REFERENCES

Foo, M.-D., M.A. Uy and R.A. Baron (2009). How do feelings influence effort? An empirical study of entrepreneurs' affect and venture effort. *Journal of Applied Psychology*, **94** (4), 1086–94.
Kozlowski, S.W.J. (2009). Editorial. *Journal of Applied Psychology*, **94** (1), 1–4.
Minto, B. (2002). *The Pyramid Principle: Logic in Writing and Thinking*. London: Prentice Hall/Financial Times.

13. Journal of Business Venturing

Associate editor: *Phillip Phan*
Authors: *Dimo Dimov, William Forster*
Moderators: *Ronald K. Mitchell,*
   John E. Mathieu
Comments editor: *G. Thomas Lumpkin*

Mitchell, Ron: We will start with a brief flyby of each of the two papers. The first paper is Dimo Dimov and Hana Milanov's 'The interplay of need and opportunity in venture capital investment syndication.' Then there's Matt Hayward, Bill Forster, Saras Sarasvathy and Barbara Fredrickson's 'Beyond hubris: How highly confident entrepreneurs rebound to venture again.' Dimo, a quick flyby, please.

Dimov, Dimo: First of all, I would like to acknowledge my co-author, Hana Milanov in Greece. Hi, Hana.

Very quickly. We looked at the alliance formation literature and it says, 'First form alliances because they have some need, but also alliances need to have shared opportunity (a reason for being).' In other words, have a reason to be able to attract partners. We wondered about all those cases where alliances are actually not formed. This viewpoint opens up a couple of interesting questions: 'Can you have a need for alliances, but actually not be able to attract partners; or can you be able to attract partners but actually do not need them?' So these are particularly fluid and disjointed at the level of the individual project. Thus, it brings up the question of interplay. Our context is the venture capital industry, which is particularly relevant because venture capital firms continually make investment decisions on a series of projects (and we can actually see what they do for yes decisions: they syndicate some investments and do not syndicate others). So we try to tease out what is it that can determine these differences.

We study their first round of investments where they look at the company for the first time, and from a need perspective, which shows that if they invest in an unfamiliar area (an industry that they haven't invested before), they are more likely to syndicate. So that is the need part. For the interplay part, we looked at their status and reputation, where we actually show that these two variables (from the point of view of their ability to attract partners) actually change the intensity of their relationship between need and alliance. Short and sweet.

Mitchell, Ron: That was short and sweet. Thank you very much. Especially sweet. Bill?

Forster, Bill: Our paper deals with hubris and overconfidence, which in the literature have been largely linked to very negative outcomes (both for the individual and for the firm). However, we tried to take a little bit different view of that and tried to integrate the emotional and social perspective in behavioral decision theory into it. And we also looked at a little bit different setting than had been investigated before – and that is the setting of the serial entrepreneur. So our central question was, 'How does overconfidence, or confidence in general, prepare an entrepreneur to venture again, perhaps after they've experienced a failure in a focal venture?'

To do that we brought in Barbara Fredrickson's (2001) work on her broaden-and-build theory of positive emotions; and actually it is a theory piece that shows that overconfidence can actually lead to positive emotions which then will prepare an entrepreneur to rebound from failure and, perhaps, venture again more often than if they were not overconfident.

Mitchell, Ron: Thank you very much. John, I would like to turn the co-moderating duties to you to ask the first question.

Mathieu, John: Sure. I think the first question I want to have is a high-level one (that I am going to pose first to the authors and then I would like Phil's comment on it), and that is the branding issue in terms of *JBV* [*Journal of Business Venturing*]. Let me preface this by saying that Venkat was talking about starting at the top and then working down [Sankaran Venkataraman: Chapter 7], but there are alternative strategies and I want to make two points. One is that most papers that are submitted are rejected; and most of the highly cited papers, the most influential papers in the field, have been rejected at least once if not multiple times. So my question to the authors is, 'Why *JBV*?' Did you shop it someplace else? Were you trying to put it someplace else other than in *JBV*, or is *JBV* the right place? How does your paper fit into the universe of entrepreneurship?'

Dimov, Dimo: In our case, what's interesting is that as the paper was developing we thought of *JBV* as the natural home. It was clear and the reason for that is there's been a longstanding conversation in the journal about venture capital – and when you have a context like this, it comes with a lot of dirty laundry. There are problems with working with venture capital data, and when you have reviewers that are in that area, they are aware of these issues so you can safely navigate these waters because everyone knows that these are problems. So with that said, this was a natural home. I had come here to UConn and *JBV* didn't have the premiere status – I had two *JBV*s already, and, as people said, 'You will not get tenure with six *JBV*s.' So the point was that I had to go and target premiere journals. We actually sent it to another journal. We knew *JBV* was the natural home but we tried to package it for a broader audience and this is where we learned a few things in that process. The paper became much stronger. And after, it was written in one place beforehand . . . Am I allowed to say where?

Mathieu, John: You can say anything you want. It is only going to be out there forever, but you can say anything you want.

Dimov, Dimo: It was rejected at *Organization Science*, and that was the first submission. So here we took some of the lessons learned there and decided on the second try, being that *JBV* was the natural place and it made sense for the paper to go there.

Forster, Bill: For our paper, we knew that *JBV* was a top journal in entrepreneurship with a focus on entrepreneurs; that is the topic of our paper, so it was a natural home in that way. We also knew that there was a long-going scholarly conversation on cognitive biases and serial entrepreneurship within the journal, so we also thought it was a good fit for that. Other than that, I am actually the second author. Matt Hayward was the one that did the selection, so I will have to defer to him for any other details of where it has been before.

Mathieu, John: Phil, what about your perspective in terms of the *JBV* brand and how you see these papers fitting into it (or other submissions that you see)?

Phan, Phil: Well, I think Dimo put a very nice point in the conversation that we have been having in the last day and a half, which is that if you have a very clear idea of what your paper is about (and therefore the audience to whom it is supposed to speak to), then you ought to publish in those outlets that speak directly to that audience. I think this is a very nice illustration of, in a sense, a paper 'coming home.' It took that circular route, but it came home. And what was interesting about the review process was that while the paper had originally come in with a fairly balanced perspective on the alliances literature as well as the VC [venture capital] literature, it was very obvious to both myself and to the reviewers that this clearly was a paper that had a lot of things to say to the VC literature. It brought an interesting perspective on status, which is something that has not been really looked at very carefully before (certainly not in the way they did it); and sometimes the authors will sort of push back into this space, because that is where it was most comfortable.

The reason I picked these two papers was because, in my mind, they are exemplars of the kinds of papers that *JBV* tries to publish. And while these two papers are in the mainstream of the topics that are typically published in *JBV*, what was interesting is that they said something more. So it isn't a question of replication. It isn't quite the mining versus prospecting issues. It is really about the fact that within the entrepreneurship domain, there are still a huge number of questions that are not answered very well. They are being attempted, but are not answered very well. These papers created, in some sense, new platforms for going back to these existing questions, such as the one on overconfidence, for example. The other interesting aspect of it is to highlight the fact that Bill's paper actually went through five rounds. It wasn't because the paper was not good to begin with (in fact there was a lot of interesting stuff going on), but there was a big controversy (maybe Bill can talk about it) and actually a very in-depth conversation between the authors and the reviewers on teasing out the differences between self-efficacy and confidence. While the literature on self-efficacy and confidence is very clear on that, I think when applied to entrepreneurial context (particularly serial entrepreneurship), the literature wasn't actually clear in the beginning, because it turned out that a lot of the work in self-efficacy showed that it is actually very malleable and could be trained. And so, serial entrepreneurship could be seen as a form of training with respect to that construct.

I think it would be interesting to talk about what the authors were thinking as they went through this process. From my perspective, I think in a particularly good review process, it is not only just one way. What we found (or what I experienced with that paper) is that the reviewers actually got educated. (This is *JBV*'s idea, so nobody gets to steal this.) But one of the things that I've actually been thinking very seriously about is the possibility that when, as editors, we encounter these kinds of very serious conversations going on between editors and reviewers – very honest conversations (It wasn't ideological, right? It was really about rigorous thinking) – that those conversations can be published because they really show the development of an idea. It is not obvious when you simply look at the final piece; and I got a great education out of that. I think in the best possible circumstances, reviewers, authors and editors all get an education beyond what they may not necessarily have gotten if they simply read the paper.

Dimo's paper was the complete opposite. I think it is effective to have one review, right? The paper was very complete, and what the reviewers really wanted was some robust testing. And so this was a situation where they had thought very carefully – because the paper already had a natural home. They thought very carefully about positioning, about the empirical methodology, the estimation methods and the data. They already had very good ideas about the limitations of the VC data and how to address it up front. So that was a real pleasure to work with as an editor, because you weren't struggling, trying to figure out what reviewers wanted and how the authors should respond. But in both instances, interestingly enough, we had two reviewers working, and they were all split. In the first round, even with Dimo's paper, the review recommendations were split; not because of quality, but because they were not sure if there was an additional contribution. It turned out that the contributions were actually quite substantive once it was clarified in the first review.

Mathieu, John: I want to set up a question for Bill and I want him to sort of explore this. In Howard's keynote earlier in the conference [Howard E. Aldrich: Chapter 2] he had mentioned the 10,000 accumulated hours to be a prospector and have that level of expertise and maturity in the field. And personally, I think there are other ways to do that. I think by bringing in, leveraging and thinking from other fields (in particular by leveraging different kinds of co-authors), there are different dynamics where you can bring in some of that expertise and perspective earlier in a career stage and develop different dynamics in a paper.

Bill, could you tell us your role in your paper, how that unfolded – and how that maybe informed the dialogue of the process that Phil was talking about?

Forster, Bill: Yes. I actually wasn't involved in this paper until after it got its first R&R [revise and resubmit] – it came back to Matt Hayward with a very high-risk R&R – and he knew that it was going to have to be a substantial rewrite if this paper was going to proceed forward in the process. We had been corresponding about some other work that I had been doing and he knew that I had been working in this same area. And I think he thought that, even though I am a younger scholar in the game of things, that I might be able to bring just a fresh perspective to this paper and maybe help him to make some of those hard changes. We talked earlier about how sometimes it is really hard to take a part of the paper that you really love and just throw it on the cutting-room floor and move on from that. So he brought Saras Sarasvathy and myself in for the second round. We went through and read the paper pretty much like we were reviewers – without even looking at the reviewers' comments. We went back and looked at the reviewers' comments and married those up in our mind, and I think that brought a different perspective to this paper. And we did do a substantial rewrite of the paper: we left parts of it on the floor, we started to address that question of self-efficacy versus optimism versus confidence and all these conflated terms in our paper, and we tried to make those a little bit clearer by trying to pull them apart.

I think from a junior perspective, I learned a lot from it. It is a mentorship-type thing to go through this process, but I think also being from a junior perspective, I may have brought a different view to this particular paper and this particular solution that might have helped it actually proceed in the review process.

Mathieu, John: So I think there are alternative ways to get the prospecting kind of approach.

Phan, Phil: Can I chime in for a second?

Mathieu, John: Absolutely.

Phan, Phil: You know, Bill brought up a very important point, which is that in fact (I think in about the third round) one of the authors became a bit impatient with the process – and the reviewer became a little bit impatient. It is like, 'You guys are talking right past each other;' and I think having Saras and having Bill in there really helped a lot because they weren't necessarily married to the idea – so they could be very objective. And, of course, it turned out that the reviewer also had to be convinced. But it is very hard to write a convincing reply when you are emotionally involved. And so having co-authors that are able to take a step back and say, 'Well, if there's some merit in the argument let's deal with it. If there isn't then let's pull together a convincing case.' In fact, after the third round, the log jam sort of just broke up and it went through very quickly. Actually, it was a fairly quick process. I can't remember precisely how long the whole process took.

Mathieu, John: Five rounds?

Phan, Phil: That was quick.

Mathieu, John: I would hate to see your lengthy ones.

Phan, Phil: But it was very, very quick. It was 'boom, boom, boom' – like that.

Forster, Bill: I also went through that process too, because there was one point where one of our authors and one of the reviewers were butting heads and they actually wrote to Phil and said, 'Please adjudicate this for us some way.' Like, 'Tell us what the road ahead is.' He did a good job doing that; then we proceeded.

Mitchell, Ron: All of us who watch movies and have our DVDs, we love to have those additional segments that show what wasn't included in the movie: what's on the cutting-room floor? And in many respects, what we are seeing emerging here is that, as that refining process goes on, certain things need to be removed from the paper; but that doesn't mean they need to be removed from the literature. It just means that they belong in another package.

Is there anything out of these papers on the cutting-room floor that is moving forward, or did that basically end its involvement in academia? So you cut out a big chunk.

Forster, Bill: Yes, we did. We cut a chunk of segments talking about how overconfidence is measured and a kind of calibration effect, and a couple of graphs and charts that weren't really central to our argument. Being removed from that, I can see how we really didn't need those figures and those charts, so we pulled those out. I think they are good work and they'll end up somewhere. They are nowhere right now; however, this is an ongoing stream of looking at overconfidence, so I am sure they'll come out.

Mitchell, Ron: Would *JBV* consider producing the outtakes? No, I am just kidding . . .

Phan, Phil: Well, actually, that is precisely the point. There is much to be learned from this. Certainly one of the missions of the journal, being a field journal, is advocacy for the field. Basically starting with Venkat (from the beginning), *JBV* really saw its role as more than just being a gatekeeper; as you are trying to advocate for not only the legitimacy, but the rigor and the acceptance of the field, right? Not just the journal. And so there is a huge amount of education that could be had by looking at these outtakes. We have got to figure out how to do that in a way that is accessible.

Mathieu, John: I think you can just see that sometimes in the trimmings. Mike Hitt and I did a lead-in for an *AMJ* [*Academy of Management Journal*] special issue (see Hitt, Beamish, Jackson and Mathieu, 2007) – and I had way overwritten my section. He was very apologetic at trimming it (as he should have with a chain saw), to which I ended up saying, 'No, no, Mike. Do not worry about it. There's enough on the ground here.' It is now being packaged for a *JOM* [*Journal of Management*] special issue, and it has an encouraged R&R there. So the trimmings sometimes can be another meal.

I have a question for Dimo to think about – some juxtaposition. When I look at your paper, analytically it was very sophisticated and very well done; like the work you do. And then there's this section on exploratory analyses, and a lot of our top journals really squeeze that out of us. They do not want to see exploratory analyses. They either want to see it as a hypothesis or get it out of the paper. What did you learn more from: what you intended to look at or the exploratory analyses – and how did you even get into that space?

Dimov, Dimo: Well, the interesting thing about the exploratory analyses is that they actually come after the main analysis. One of them was that we tried to tell a theoretical story. We tried to infer motivations for actions without actually talking to the VC. We used secondary data. So how do you know whether what happens is for the reasons that you say? One of the analyses was one where we asked, 'Is there an alternative explanation for this? Is it possible that these people just get together because they know each other from a previous engagement?' We had to show how they deal with unfamiliar investors. So that was one way.

The second analysis came when we were pushed by the reviewers to tell another story. They said, 'If your theory is valid, then you have to show that a low-status firm cannot actually syndicate with a high-status firm because that would be contradictory to what the theory says.' So we had to do the status match-ups – that was the second analysis – as a way of saying, 'If this theory were true, then we should see this pattern, and if this pattern is not there, then it undermines our theoretical logic.'

So there are ways to corroborate things that weren't in the secondary data. We couldn't get those because we didn't have the information.

Phan, Phil: I think that is an important point and I suspect that all the good journals do that now – whether it is done as a response to the reviewers or whether it is done as simply part of the model itself, which is generally termed 'robustness testing.' In finance they are really talking about alternative estimation models. But I think theoretically checking the robustness of your theory by explicitly testing alternative explanations is really a very important thing to consider; and in that sense, at *JBV*, we do not want to be known as a quantitative journal. Certainly quantitative analysis and robustness, I think, are very very critical; but really the idea is that every contribution makes some kind of a theoretical push forward in some way, and testing the robustness of your theory using these alternative analyses is really a good way of doing that.

Dimov, Dimo: I, in a way, have become defensive when I work in venture capital and try to send it to mainstream journals, because the dirty laundry always comes back at me and this is usually the major reason. When I try to frame venture capital work as appealing to a general audience, I will take a general theoretical perspective and the paper will come back and say, 'You have this disjoint between theory and context, and there are all of these problems with your context.' So when I try to focus on the venture capital thing and send it out, they say, 'Your paper is not broad enough. There's nothing here for a general audience.' I've become so defensive when I work with venture capital data that I try to not over-analyse; I try to say, 'I am going to take three, four, five or six different angles here to rule out as many different alternatives as possible.' Because these explanations tend to repeat themselves from journal to journal and they are usually the same thing. I know in advance what I am going to be asked for. So this paper reflects a lot of the things experienced in the past. I said, 'I am going to pre-load this and hopefully that is going to work.'

Phan, Phil: And it worked. And that is the 10,000 hours. That is the Howard Aldrich thing, right? That is where experience, in fact, does matter.

Mathieu, John: So would you say in your two papers (or just work in general) that entrepreneurship is out front and the more basic discipline is in the back? Or is it the other way around? And how does that get manifested in these two papers? I am just taking Venkat's material here . . .

Mitchell, Ron: If you recall what Venkat was talking about in his keynote [Sankaran Venkataraman: Chapter 7] earlier in the conference – he shared that entrepreneurship in the foreground was difficult in a prior decade and it had to go to the background with the mainstream theory actually being in the foreground. John's question is, how are you seeing that . . .?

Mathieu, John: How's it playing?

Mitchell, Ron: Yeah, how's it playing?

Dimov, Dimo: Well, this ended up being almost both in the foreground. It used to be the mainstream in the foreground and entrepreneurship in the back, and the reviewer said 'Entrepreneurship should be closer up front.' So they are both in the introduction now. It is the mainstream, but also the context goes together with that. I do not know if that is a valid thing, but they are actually both in the foreground.

Mathieu, John: Again, as the field matures, you can afford the luxury of doing it that way rather than having to posture it one way or the other.

Mitchell, Ron: Sorry, but I am going to try to just pull the idea together. So this foreground/background dynamic that the conversation is about (this conversation having begun last evening), we may not be able to fully conclude that entrepreneurship can now simply stand in the foreground unopposed. What we are really saying is that they could stand more closely together. Bill?

Forster, Bill: That is what I was going to say. I think in looking at our paper, it seems to me as if they do stand side by side. Behavioral decision theory overconfidence is certainly a mainstream idea. However, the setting, the serial entrepreneur and actually the way overconfidence works in that particular entrepreneurial setting was very central to the paper; so I would say they are about equal on ours.

Mitchell, Ron: Well, we are now in the portion of our session where we can take Q&A, and it looks like we have a question. How's the web looking, Tom? Do we have one? While the microphone is coming, let's take the first web question.

Lumpkin, Tom: An idea that has come out of this session is the idea of contacting the editor directly and informally to address issues in the R&R process. Please comment more on effective and appropriate ways to interact with editors rather than just sending in a revision and replying to reviewers. Can this approach go wrong, or is it just generally always okay?

Mitchell, Ron: Phil?

Phan, Phil: I will speak for myself. I think it is partially a style issue, but I think somebody had a comment about it earlier that you do have to have a very clear idea about why you are doing it. Certainly, if you are contacting the editor to somehow lobby for a position, that probably is not going to go down very well because editors do not like to feel as though their objectivity is going to be compromised in some sense. On the other hand, in this situation there really was a conversation going on and it came to the point where there was really an honest disagreement. And it wasn't just the author who contacted me. The reviewer also said, 'I am pulling my hair out here. I am not getting my point across. Help me express it in a certain way that maybe I am not doing it well,' or something like that. So I think in that situation, and if you ask an editor to be an honest broker of a real disagreement and not just some stylistic issue, I think it is fair. Can it go wrong? It depends on the editor. I am happy to do that because, for me, it is a learning experience; I have to scratch my head and ask, 'How can I be this honest broker? How can I express an idea from the author to the reviewer or from the reviewer to the author so that both of them can meet somewhere and continue the conversation?'

Mathieu, John: Let me do a quick follow-up and then we will go to the next question. I am doing this to protect the editors, since there are a lot of folks listening in and saying, 'What's reasonable and what's not reasonable?' One is that you can't work the referee. You can't contact the editor and say, 'If I do x, y and z – will you take it?' That is not a fair kind of dialogue.

The other way to do this is to literally ask about the boundary. Ask 'Is it all right if I ask you a clarifying kind of question?' or things of that sort. So you will have differences across journals and you will certainly have differences across editors in terms of the extent to which they want to engage in that. So respect their role. They are human beings. They have lives, families and spouses. They do not want this necessarily to be 24/7; so just be respectful of their role and do not try to work the referee because that will actually come back and haunt you rather than help you.

Mitchell, Ron: Rob. First question from the audience.

Mitchell, Rob: We have talked a little bit about boundaries and specific purposes of different journals, and I think all of us would agree that journals are different. One of the things that I've found (I wouldn't say perplexing, but it is an interesting conversation, particularly in entrepreneurship) is that there are three core entrepreneurship journals that are represented here, with *Strategic Entrepreneurship Journal* [*SEJ*], *Entrepreneurship Theory and Practice* [*ET&P*] and *JBV*. I do not know if there's an appropriate forum to ask this because we are doing it journal by journal. I think there are differences between the missions and the purposes of these three journals, and I think those of us who have had experience with them would agree (given that we are interested in information) that it might be interesting to explore and kind of explicitly state, 'Here's how we see ourselves.' I do not know if this will involve getting Mike involved or Candy involved in the conversation. We probably all know of stories where somebody's been rejected at *JBV* and the next day sent it out to *ET&P* or to *SEJ* – and they are yet different. I am interested in what the editors would say in terms of what those nuances are in terms of these differences in the journals and their purposes?

Mitchell, Ron: To be fair to Candy, who's now on the spot, and Mike (if you do not mind being on the spot), what we have in the structure is a difficulty because we can't make such a comparison. If we were to begin with Phil, and draw some outlines; this isn't actually the battle of the bands, right? But it is, in fact, useful information to articulate to the body of researchers. Where you go as your first pick and, if rejected, why you would send it out to another journal the next day; that is different than reformulating and retargeting your work for the distinctions that might emerge in this conversation over the next couple of minutes – so, Phil first.

Phan, Phil: I am just going to talk about the differences. There clearly are lots of overlaps and there are topics that are going to be common across all three journals. Because the mission of *JBV* has been, in large part, advocacy for the field, I suppose we are willing to be a little bit more experimental. I would say we are a little bit more on the edge. In recent years, we have published things that are a little bit more unusual. For example, there's a piece that came out from Scott Shane and co-author [N. Nicolaou] on biology, genetics and entrepreneurship (2008) that has shown up in a bunch of other places. I think *SEJ* had a similar piece like that. And so we tend to perhaps be more willing to give an airing to ideas that may not be necessarily fully informed. Not in terms of rigor, but simply in terms of where they might sit in sort of the universe of management entrepreneurship research.

Mitchell, Ron: Mike, do you have the microphone?

Hitt, Mike: Again, I think this morning when I was talking, we addressed this to some degree in that, first, I do not see us as competitive. At least that is not our intent. I do believe there are overlaps, just like Phil said, with all journals to some degree – and certainly, specifically, with the entrepreneurship journals. On the other hand, I think our intent of trying to draw from multiple disciplinary perspectives in the integration (again, it is not suggesting that that wouldn't go in one of the other two) has more of a special flavor there; our intent has always been that.

Also, if you look at our vision statement and the part that was articulated very well by Ron, it shows (I think) a breadth that we are trying to achieve. Again, I'm not trying to differentiate, per se, from others, but show where we are headed. Hopefully that helps you in trying to choose because I do believe that there are differences across these three journals; and we are not talking about quality, we are talking about differences in terms of our foci.

Mitchell, Ron: Thank you, Mike, for allowing us to put you on the spot. Candy, I can't ask you if you mind being put on the spot. I can apologize for putting you on the spot, but there you go. This is *Entrepreneurship Theory & Practice* editor, Candy Brush.

Brush, Candy: I agree with what Mike said and with what Ron said. Yes, there are overlaps. In fact, I have seen incidents of authors who have published in one journal about a topic, who then will publish in *JBV* or *SEJ*. So there are overlaps; and I think that people who are really committed to a focus on entrepreneurship usually will publish in all three areas. If I were to say there was maybe a nuance difference between what *Entrepreneurship Theory & Practice* does as opposed to the other journals (not competitively), I think we may have more special issues that focus on particular topics such as family business, governance or various things. And that might be a slight differentiator, but other than that, the same things would apply. We look for rigorous theory. We look for contributions to the field. I know that Mike has already talked about that, and Phil has said the same thing. I guess my feeling is that it is a big pool and we need lots of work in the area, and we have several good journals that can contribute to that effort.

Mitchell, Ron: These are field journals. These are journals that have dedicated their focus to the entrepreneurship phenomenon. It then becomes incumbent upon us as authors to read those vision statements, to look at our work, to see where the conversation has been emerging within that journal . . . because there's this timing element, which, even though there's overlap, there may not be the rightness of timing. When you take all of those elements into consideration, then you can put your work where you will get the hearing, the audience and the help and the attention that will actually allow it to take its place in the firmament of scholarship – and, as well, do the most good for both the authors and the journals.

Howard was going to the sweet spot – there is a sweet spot and I think that is essentially a judgment call that we have to make.

There's another hand out here. Yes, Elaine?

Mosakowski, Elaine: I have primarily a question for Phil, but I want to drag Bill into the discussion a little bit too because there was some earlier talk about the foreground and background, and I am not 100 percent sure that

I know what that means. My question has to do with the specificity of the theoretical work in *JBV* to the entrepreneurship context or phenomena. My own experience, as well as what I've heard on the street, is that it is not uncommon for a *JBV* reviewer and/or editor to say, 'Well, this theoretical work: sure it seems to make sense for entrepreneurs, but it is really not specific to entrepreneurs. It may apply also to managers working in turbulent environments or other types of actors.' This is where Bill comes in. I know this paper was co-authored with Matt Hayward, who is a former colleague of mine (and I know his work very well, having had to read every page of it for his tenure case), but he talks a lot about overconfidence in managers. I look at this paper and I say, 'This theoretical frame and this going back and trying again and mobilizing the team and mobilizing your resources; that applies to managers as well as to entrepreneurs and it is kind of serial behavior, it is not unique to the entrepreneurial context.'

I guess my question is: how do you deal with that? And do you honestly believe it is a fair question for reviewers to ask, 'Is this theoretical perspective specific to entrepreneurs?' Or as an editor do you say, 'No, that is not what we should be asking of our authors?'

Phan, Phil: That is a great question and it is something that confronts us as editors in a few journals all the time. The sub-text is the legitimacy issue (not that we necessarily worry too much about that nowadays). I can tell you that that is not an uncommon question. I think that whether the question is a fair question or not depends on the paper. For example, if you are taking a theoretical perspective that is well known in large companies and you are saying, 'We want to look at small companies,' then I am not sure that that necessarily contributes to our understanding of the entrepreneurial phenomena. Right? It doesn't mean you can't do that; it simply means that the question that is going to be asked is, 'How does this change what we already think we know about entrepreneurship, the discovering of opportunities and the matching of resources?' Sometimes it doesn't matter and sometimes it is not a fair question, and so the editor will say,'Well, yeah,' because these are sort of easy questions to throw. It is like the endogeneity question that all of us get. It is sometimes like a cheap shot in some sense; but in another sense, it could be a very significant issue if it basically validates the theory. It is the same thing with that kind of question.

Mitchell, Ron: Go ahead, Bill.

Forster, Bill: I will be real quick. Well, I think for this particular paper, Matt's done a lot of work with managers in the dark side of overconfidence. He wanted to explore a more nuanced way and look at just what could be some of the light side of that same phenomenon. I also think it is unique to entrepreneurship in that entrepreneurs tend to be very confident people. Some entrepreneurs are very overconfident people – and especially if you look at the entrepreneurs that persist on, and will fail and start again, and fail and start again in that serial entrepreneurial process. I think that phenomenon might actually be different there than in a corporate context. I do not know of any senior managers that are serially overconfident after successive failures at the senior level.

Phan, Phil: And still get employed.

Forster, Bill: And still get employed, yes. I think it might be very unique to the phenomenon.

Mitchell, Ron: Thank you, Bill. The next question is from Ken Robinson. Ken?

Robinson, Ken: Mike talked about the current potential view of an *SEJ* publication by colleges and universities. What do you think the past, current and potential views of a *JBV* publication would be by different colleges and universities?

Phan, Phil: Good question. Actually, Dean can answer that. I will tell you why – he's been involved in a very, very good initiative that we have started.

Mitchell, Ron: Dean, just two seconds and we will get the microphone to you. And thank you, Katie, for the hustle. It is much appreciated.

Shepherd, Dean: It is a very good question, Ken. We are at an important stage in entrepreneurship where the facts are starting to finally reveal themselves, and we are able to convince people against organizational inertia that says that 'Entrepreneurship is young and the journals do not deserve to be considered elite journals along with *OBHDP* [*Organizational Behavior and Human Decision Processes*] and these other top journals.' We are trying to use the facts now to try and persuade some organizations that they are behind the times and they need to try and catch up.

I have a list of top institutions that have *JBV* as one of their elite journals. Indiana University is one of those. I will just talk about *JBV* and let Mike and Candy talk about *SEJ* and *ET&P*. Also I will talk about an analysis of impact factors and how we rank relative to other journals that are often considered as 'A' in other departments (for example, the *Journal of Consumer Research* and the *Journal of Marketing*) where we actually have higher impact factors than *OBHDP*. So, all of those sorts of journals . . .

It is not something that a young scholar wants to try and convince and change the university's opinion. As editors, we are here to try and help communicate and educate those people who are on promotion and tenure decisions – and just provide them the information. I am not going to try and do a hard sell job, but we have information here that says, 'Hey, if these journals in your institution are considered an "A" and entrepreneurship is a legitimate field within your school and something you want to promote, then you should at least consider these facts about these journals. If people want that sort of information, please just email me and I will be able to give you the facts and then you can use them as you will. Or we will be willing to contact your department heads and willing to contact your deans, just so we can post things on websites, so we can let you know where we are in different schools and what sort of information is there.'

Mathieu, John: Let me follow up briefly on that because it actually swings back to something that Dimo was starting to talk about earlier, and I am his department head. We have engaged in many of these kinds of conversations and I've had these conversations at the school-wide level as well. And certainly the message I would send out to people who are pre-tenure and battling through it is to have that dialogue with your department head and with your dean. This is very much going to be a person–environment fit here. You can do impact ratings and you can do arguments about who's the best football team, but there can only be one at the end of the season. Not everyone can be number one, but that is not necessarily the right discussion to be having. Here at the University of Connecticut, we have clearly put an emphasis on entrepreneurship; but UConn is a different environment than perhaps some other places that do not have that same kind of emphasis. Now, can you be a star niche player or do you have to really be a more broad-based kind of person? What does the portfolio look like? If you have six *JBV*s and a couple of *AMJ*s, that is a different signature than if all you have are niche journals. And I am a teams researcher, and the same discussions happen in teams, in HR, in strategy or in other things.

The key thing is to understand two issues. One is: who do you want to be in your career? That was mentioned earlier today in terms of identifying your career trajectory, who do you want to be in the field and how does that align or not align with where you are locally. Because there is going to be a local rewards system, and then the 'player on the national and the international stage' system. You really need to think that through and usually it is a portfolio kind of perspective that says, 'I am not just a niche player, I can play in these other leagues,' and to come full circle.

Really what Venkat was talking about last night too, I would argue that it depends on the paper. There's a difference between who you are and what the paper is. Sometimes the paper has found its rightful home: whether it started there or whether it eventually got there – there is a rightful home for various papers (whether it is the nature of the topic, whether there's the nature of the analytics that you use and theory or whatever). There are some good synergies, and this does come from senior colleagues and folks who know the field, who can help you target where your voice really is, and where the audience is that is going to hear that. So I think that those dialogues are important to have and you do not wait until your fourth, fifth or sixth years to have those discussions. Think about where you are right from the get-go and how that fits locally and internationally.

Mitchell, Ron: What you have probably observed as each of these sessions go by, is realizing that on the web the sessions are modular and here they are continuous. So we encourage all who are watching on the web and haven't seen the other sessions to go back and see those. But each session has an emergent conversation where information is provided about the way this field works that may not be in those other sessions. We appreciate the folks who are willing to go on the spot – Dean, Mike and Candy – to actually help us with this emergent part of the conversation. Much appreciated. I would like to give the last word to you, Phil, and have you fill in the blank. If there were one thing you could recommend at successfully working with *JBV*, it would be . . .?

Phan, Phil: It would be that you clarify how your contribution sits within the universe of the entrepreneurship domain. Just because it is a small firm and just because it is an entrepreneurial team doesn't automatically make it an entrepreneurial theoretical contribution. I think that is very important. Not every paper has to advance the theory of entrepreneurship, but you have to be able to say something intelligent about it. And if you can do that, you will find a very friendly audience in the journal and the reviewers.

Mitchell, Ron: This is because the *Journal of Business Venturing* has taken upon itself (earlier on in the process) the advancement of the field itself. And as a result, if we are going to encourage submissions to *JBV*, what we are going to encourage is exactly what Phil said, which is to explain how it moves the field forward. Thank you very much authors, editor, and John. Much appreciated.

REFERENCES

Dimov, D. and H. Milanov (2009). The interplay of need and opportunity in venture capital investment syndication. *Journal of Business Venturing*, **25** (4), 331–48.

Fredrickson, B.L. (2001). The role of positive emotions in positive psychology: the broaden-and-build theory of positive emotions. *American Psychologist*, **56** (3), 218–26.

Hayward, M.L.A., W.R. Forster, S.D. Sarasvathy and B.L. Fredrickson (2009). Beyond hubris: how highly confident entrepreneurs rebound to venture again. *Journal of Business Venturing*, **25** (6), 569–78.

Hitt, M.A., P.W. Beamish, S.E. Jackson and J.E. Mathieu (2007). Building theoretical and empirical bridges across levels: multilevel research in management. *Academy of Management Journal*, **50** (6), 1385–99.

Nicolaou, N. and S. Shane (2009). Can genetic factors influence the likelihood of engaging in entrepreneurial activity? *Journal of Business Venturing*, **24** (1), 1–22.

14. Journal of Management

Editor: *Talya N. Bauer*
Authors: *Hao Zhao, Scott E. Seibert,*
  G. Thomas Lumpkin
Moderators: *Ronald K. Mitchell, Lucy Gilson*
Comments editor: *Richard N. Dino*

Mitchell, Ron: Our guests include Talya Bauer, who is the editor of the *Journal of Management* (and we are very glad that you are here), as well as a full author team of Hao Zhao, Scott Seibert and Tom Lumpkin. And then there is co-moderator, Lucy Gilson, with me once again.

The paper is 'The relationship of personality to entrepreneurial intentions and performance: A meta analytic review.' So we will turn the time to Hao to give us an elevator pitch. Tell us a few short sentences about the paper.

Zhao, Hao: Yes, the idea of this paper is very simple. We tried to check the relationship between personality and two stages of the entrepreneurial process, specifically entrepreneurial intentions and firm performance. We found that nearly all of the dimensions of personality, defined through the five factor model of personality, were associated with both outcomes. We included risk propensity as a sixth and separate dimension of personality and found it associated positively with intentions but with no connection to performance, which we thought was an interesting finding. So our study suggests that the personality does play a role in entrepreneurship emergence and success. Thank you.

Mitchell, Ron: Thank you very much. Talya, I am looking for the opportunities from the general mission statement and I have identified that the *Journal of Management* (*JOM*) is a good outlet for any entrepreneurship research because it publishes 'articles dealing with any area represented within the domain of the Academy of Management.' Would you like to expand on that and explain to us how the entrepreneurship submission fits within that description? Obviously, it is one of the

Academy of Management's divisions, but I am sure there's more than that.

Bauer, Talya: Definitely. I am actually working on modifying that because it is so broad. I think a lot of people will be surprised to hear how many papers we get a year. We are coming up in one month to one year and 900-plus papers. So I think the title itself, *Journal of Management*, sounds so broad – and that mission statement is so broad – that anybody who has ever thought about management for two seconds thinks they have something to say about it. I think the reality is that when we talk about it, it does boil down to BPS [business policy and strategy], entrepreneurship, organizational behavior and human resources. So you could have a paper on finance (or on something else) if you tied it into the management literature, but I think those are really where the reviewers are.

Mitchell, Ron: Then we can say definitely entrepreneurship manuscripts receive a fair and interested hearing at *Journal of Management*?

Bauer, Talya: I'd say absolutely. When I was looking for associate editors, one of the things I was looking for were people who cover all of those domains. Because we have so many papers to process, I now have 11 associate editors and I am actually looking for two more. Three of our associate editors, I would say, are entrepreneurship qualified.

Mitchell, Ron: Volunteers? No better time than the present, right? Lucy, to the paper and specifically questions that have come to your mind that can get us started . . .

Gilson, Lucy: Well, I think the great thing about this paper is it falls into the category that Talya talked about earlier; it covers personality and entrepreneurship intention and performance. So all of us can conclude, to begin with, that you are straight away going into the personality, and measuring it with the Big Five dimensions. Put differently, we are going into the pure psychology side here. And, methodologically, there are a lot of meta-analyses and a lot we know about personality – and now we are going into the entrepreneurship domain. So for Talya my question is: how do you pick reviewers for this? Because your personality people are going to say, 'Oh, this is entrepreneurship. I don't want this paper,' and your entrepreneurship people are going to say, 'Oh, the Big Five. This is out of psychology.' That's my question for Talya. And then, when you report to the authors, you are probably going to have reviewers who say: 'Oh, spend more time on the personality side,' and others who say, 'Well, you could really cut that back and spend more time . . .' How do you balance that?

Bauer, Talya: Going back to what Pam Tolbert said [Chapter 16], you don't always get that ideal reviewer. But one of the things I spend a lot of time with is thinking about who the reviewers should be and being pretty patient with finding them. On this particular paper, I went back and looked at the reviewers, and I have who I would say is a very well-respected scholar in entrepreneurship (straight entrepreneurship), a second on personality and meta-analysis, and then a third on personality – and I think the reviews reflected that. But there was less of a camp. They could say, 'This isn't my expertise, but what I do know about it leads me to want to hear more about "this." Develop these ideas. How does this fit together?' Hopefully the authors felt that coming across in the reviewers' comments. And I think the other thing was that everybody at this threshold level liked the paper; it had good bones coming in. It wasn't a paper where they were climbing up a very steep mountain – it was one where people generally thought it was competent. We asked 'Is it good enough to be exciting and interesting and how do we flesh this out and maximize it?'

Mitchell, Ron: Did you hear that sub-text? What the authors felt? This is a journal that actually cares. To pick up on Lucy's question, Hao – how did you feel? What was that experience like submitting to a broad range and getting the broad range back?

Zhao, Hao: I think it is a good thing, because our independent variable is personality. It is definitely a micro-level psychology-oriented variable. And one of our dependent variables is firm performance. It is a typical strategy management outcome – and it is meta-analysis. Fortunately we got reviewers who were very positive with their comments and were helping us try to present in a better way. For example, reviewer one suggested that we cite the Daltons' 2005 book chapter entitled 'Strategy management studies are a special case for meta-analysis.' Actually both Scott and I are organizational behavior researchers, and I learned the meta-analysis technique through the Hunter and Schmidt approach. It's like the dictionary. I thought I had learned enough, but when the reviewer pointed us to the book chapter, I read it and found that in the strategy management field, it is a special case. That book chapter helped us to address many of the comments from other reviewers regarding rent restriction. In our psychology, it is a very problematic concern if a reviewer asks that and why you don't correct rent restriction; but in Dalton's book chapter, it says that in the psychology management field it is very common to survivor buyers – so that it is not too much of a problem. We used that to defend ourselves. We think that actually we benefited from the different perspectives of the reviewers.

Mitchell, Ron: So this idea of meta-analysis – would you say that that is gaining traction? Because I am seeing that type of research appearing a little more . . . Comments from authors first perhaps? Why a meta-analysis? What got you going, Scott?

Seibert, Scott: It was certainly very well established in the psychology field and in organizational behavior. There is a whole cottage industry going on there, but it hasn't shown up in the strategic management field all that much, nor in the entrepreneurship field I think. So we were a little leery about bringing it in. And, of course, the whole personality psychology thing . . .

Many of the people here have spoken about whether the top journals are closed to entrepreneurship, and I think that preoccupation has gone away. But what if someone from psychology asks, 'Are the entrepreneurship journals closed to psychology?' That's just a perception on my part, but we were a little concerned about that.

Mitchell, Ron: A useful question. We are all thinking about it as bidirectional, but it is not.

Seibert, Scott: It goes both ways.

Mitchell, Ron: Or unidirectional. But it is bidirectional.

Seibert, Scott: Right. We were a little bit concerned about bringing that in. And many of the comments that came to us during the review process were a little bit more with regards to clarification on this meta-analysis. So, coming from psychology, I was thinking, 'This is pretty well-established stuff; we don't really have to talk about that.' But it was helpful to address why you are doing this, what the limitations are, why it is hard to do it with certain scales, and why you have to bring certain scales together and call them performance. There were a lot of issues around what is justified in bringing various scales together that had to be explained.

Mitchell, Ron: Talya, what did you see on the meta side?

Bauer, Talya: For me (again being more micro), that wasn't an issue at all because the question was a relevant question. I am an editor-panel junkie.

I have been going to these since 1994 and I always learn something. I am just listening to what editors have to say (and I can't even remember which editor it was), but early on somebody said, 'You know, it's not that you use the latest method and you impress me; it's in answering whether the method fits the question.' It didn't ever become an issue, I don't think, for any of the reviewers as well. The entrepreneurship reviewer said, 'This is relatively new for us, so help us understand it and place it in that framework with that recognition.' But there was no hostility.

The other thing I would point out is that the author team is also quite broad in covering expertise for that. With Tom and his entrepreneurship depth, I think that helps, too. Kind of what Scott is saying where if you are only a psychologist and you aren't familiar with the field then you've got two people out of three who are on each side – and you help each other out.

Mitchell, Ron: One of the things that has intrigued me about the meta-analysis approach is that, as many of us are aware, the entrepreneurial personality stream stalled for a while. It is not like there isn't personality-related to entrepreneurship; it is that (for whatever reason), it started down a road that ended up having some falsifications that were occurring. And yet the conversation had to find a way to continue. Rather than brute force it through the 'It's not this, it's not this, and it's not this,' analysis, going to meta actually permits the drawing-together and the persuasiveness of almost dislodging a log jam. That dislodging permits the field to move beyond accusation that personality stuff is a busted paradigm. So, in a sense, there are reasons why and reasons why not. Was that your intention as you were going down the road to clear the log jam? Was it just plain old interest to see if there was something going on? What is the motivation behind that? Tom?

Lumpkin, Tom: I'll confess that part of it was just to see if it would work, because to Scott's point, I questioned whether or not there would be receptivity to using the Big Five in an entrepreneurial context because it was the previous questionable history of personality in entrepreneurship research. And as it is, we used risk propensity as a sixth thing, because it doesn't fit nicely into the Big Five. There was a thought that if we could somehow make a breakthrough with studying personality this way, that maybe (as you suggest) we could get this conversation back on track or restart that engine.

Mitchell, Ron: We see a couple of solutions to this individual entrepreneur. We all know there's an 'E' in entrepreneurship and it's the entrepreneur; and so the entrepreneur cognition stream emerged as one way to get that flow moving. But it didn't take account of such things as the Big Five – and especially that risk propensity thing, which ended up part of earlier falsifications that perhaps there were methods issues and perhaps there were sampling issues or un-representativeness issues. In fact, to help a stream to move forward, we've ended up going down a road with a journal that's admittedly Academy of Management focused, yet able to speak to the very audience that would be able to appreciate the synthesis and help break the log jam. One of the observations that I would make about this is that (in fact) the personality side of entrepreneurship research is not dead; it's actually now finding ways to get through, but with a much more rigorous and thorough construction of the work. Lucy, I'll turn the next question to you if you don't mind.

Gilson, Lucy: I was moving to something different. We have heard a lot today and last night about reviewers' comments on papers – for example, it is 'A nut that needs to go back in its shell' or 'You are in the wrong profession.' And yet we've heard on this paper, 'This was not high risk. It had good bones. Good bone structure.' And also in reading the paper (for those of you who are students out here, this is a really positive note), you said basically, 'We began our literature search July 2007.' Where's Melissa who said, 'My paper is in press now and I started this in 2002?' Zhao, Seibert and Lumpkin began in 2007 and their paper is in press now. This is a quick turnaround.

You know, we spend a lot of time doing that soul-searching and having a tough skin; but I want to hear the good story and this is the uplifting part.

Mitchell, Ron: Yes, how do we accomplish that?

Seibert, Scott: It also explains the popularity of meta-analysis.

Zhao, Hao: I would say that the *Journal of Management* has a very fast turnaround time. I have submitted three papers to *JOM* so far; two were accepted and one was rejected. On average, I have experienced six-weeks turnaround time on the initial submission. When it comes to second-round review, it's even faster. When it comes to acceptance, I think it's less than 24 hours, right?

Seibert, Scott: It was a difficult 24 hours.

Mitchell, Ron: It was a white-knuckled 24 hours. We have time now to turn the discussion toward the audience and request your input. Rich, are you handling the web questions?

Dino, Rich: I am. There is one here.

Mitchell, Ron: While Rich is adjusting his bifocals, questions from the audience, please?

Lumpkin, Tom: Dean asked before and we passed over it. You said that there were now three associate editors who you felt were your entrepreneurship editors?

Bauer, Talya: My strategy/entrepreneurship editors, I'd say, are Steven Michael, Jeremy Short and Christopher Shook. This one I felt like I should mention because of the cross and that sort of thing. Occasionally I'll take them because maybe those three associate editors are a good friend of or have worked with the author; but generally it would go to one of them.

Mitchell, Ron: Yes, Mike.

Lubatkin, Michael: I like the *Journal of Management*. As a journal that competes with *AMJ* [*Academy of Management Journal*] and *Organization Science*, I suppose it would be correct to say that it's not viewed as top tier but a very strong second tier at many different schools of business. As a very good second-tier journal, do you hold a different level of expectation for the papers that are submitted to you than does, say, an *AMJ*?

Bauer, Talya: That is a good question. Let's see, how do I approach that exactly? I guess I have learned a lot of things in the process of this last year. One is that there are a lot of different paths, so when we talk about where people submit and what order, I think there are very many paths. There are some people who would (not because they don't think it is a top journal, but who just don't do that type of research) never submit to *Organization Science*. They would go to *JAP* [*Journal of Applied Psychology*] and then *JOM* maybe. Just a different path. Or some people might go to *SMJ* [*Strategic Management Journal*] first. So there are a lot of different ways people strategize that – and I think that is wise when people do that. What would you say was the crux of the question (I am sorry) . . .?

Lubatkin, Michael: Do you and the reviewers hold less rigorous expectations for the paper? With less rigorous and less demanding expectations for a paper, is it easier to publish in the *Journal of Management*?

Mitchell, Ron: Also with 900 manuscripts coming through?

Bauer, Talya: Our acceptance rates are as good or as bad as any other journal. How many have been picked off before they get there is a different question. I don't think that there are different sets of standards. In terms of who the reviewers are, I think that they are similar people who have similar standards. I think from a strategy perspective, we try to be faster and more developmental maybe. I think we really work hard on that aspect so that people will be more attracted to *JOM* and want to send their papers in. I think that's how we manage that.

I don't necessarily think it is faster. This was the first paper I took, and even though it was really a relatively very easy paper, I haven't seen any others like it. The odds of that being the first paper I took (and then the Entrepreneurship Conference coming up) were kind of amazing. But no – we get people who get revisions and don't take them, and I don't understand that at all. We only have about 23–25 percent that get revisions at all; then to have people say, 'Oh, that sounds hard. I don't want to do that,' is one of those things that catches us off guard. I don't know the thinking there, but I have had three of those out of all of them; it's not that many, but it surprised me that anyone did that. It just never even occurred to me because (I think we have heard multiple times) getting a revision is what you hope for.

Mitchell, Ron: Perhaps one of the tacit pieces of knowledge that we could communicate as a result of this conference is getting an R&R [revise and resubmit] and all that language that says 'this is high risk' and 'do this and do that' doesn't mean you are a bad person. It has to do with the quality of the work, and the way science progresses is through the peer-review process. If there is anyone out there in our viewing audience who thinks that getting a revision is a bad thing, Talya is here to tell you that it's a good thing. It needs work, but that doesn't mean that it's in the lower three-quarters. It's in the upper one-quarter.

Is there a question from the web?

Dino, Rich: I know now why we have a comments editor. There are two questions. One is relatively relevant. I think it is a perception of a conversation about integrating multiple domains. The conversation about 'integrating insights from multiple domains' raises the question again of whether entrepreneurship research has unique theoretical content or whether entrepreneurship is mostly about applying theories from other domains to an entrepreneurial context. Now I suspect the personality issue was the considered context. Maybe that is where this question is coming from. I don't know.

Seibert, Scott: I would certainly not consider personality to answer the question, 'What is entrepreneurship.' One of the things about the paper is to present it as what it is: 'This is the affect side of this set of variables – ta-da! It's point three; and when you work with them together, that leaves an awful lot remaining to be explained.' One resistance to personality is (and maybe it was the over-application) that entrepreneurship is all about the entrepreneur. It's simply this entrepreneurial personality. The logic is completely teleological. Entrepreneurs are people who are entrepreneurs, but this is definitely not the approach of a modern personality approach. I don't see entrepreneurship as simply an extension of personality theory.

Mitchell, Ron: I can imagine back when all academic work was philosophy – the study of ordered knowledge – and someone would say, 'Now is physics just a context, or is it . . .?' In some respects, we go back to our keynote speakers' references to that. This is a conversation that started a long time ago, and to the extent that there is context-based research, I suspect that entrepreneurship is a context. But to use this context idea as a way to dismiss research that is developing its own theoretical voice (which is exactly what's in the process), I don't believe is productive. From the standpoint of this paper, is the conversation about integrating insights? Really what we have with the *Journal of Management* is a very specific journal that's geared to our Academy. It's geared to helping that cross-divisional conversation to occur. And to that extent, I don't know that there would be scholars in a particular division that simply wish to characterize another division as a context (although some in that other division may in fact agree that there are certain times when, frankly, it's context-based research). What I am really saying is, let's not go down that 'What the heck is the entrepreneurship domain?' I think the first step is to read Bill Gartner's 1988 article, "Who is an entrepreneur?" Is the wrong question.' Honestly, the field has moved on; as Venkat so ably illustrated last evening in his keynote address [Sankaran Venkataraman: Chapter 7], we have theoretical investigations that are of substance and that the very best minds can become engaged in.
   Are there questions from the audience?

Bauer, Talya: I have a plug while we are waiting for the microphone to get over there. The *Journal of Management* review issue is coming up. The call for proposals is on the web page, and I have to say that is really, I think, a competitive advantage being that people have had some very highly impactful articles through that review. [*Voice from the audience calls out*: 'And highly cited.']

Audience Member #1: I want to start off by admitting that I have never published a paper about a review of prior works at *JOM*; and I believe that (at least from my assessment of *JOM*), it is more receptive to that sort of prior works review paper as compared to other journals. So my question, as an editor, is: how do you evaluate one paper that reviews prior work and prior research on a particular topic? How do you assess that paper as better than another paper that is reviewing prior work as well? If you have an original paper, the element of what is interesting helps you make it or not make it. But if it is a review of prior work, it is a review of prior work. What is interesting about that? How does one paper get in and not the other paper? Clearly, I want to admit that this may be a naive question but I would like to hear your perspective.

Bauer, Talya: Sure. *The Journal of Management* has two annual review issues. It used to be one, now there are two throughout the year. It is a separate process. They are not competing with original research, but it is actually a parallel process. Right now what we are putting forward is that the process would be a 12-page proposal (so before somebody writes the paper or maybe they have written the paper already . . .) – we want to evaluate 12-page proposals. And we found that last year it was hard because some people had full papers and other people had proposals. How do you compare those apples and oranges? It is everything we've been talking about this weekend. Is it an interesting question? Is it something new or was there just a review last year (in which case it's less interesting)? I am hoping that they are not just reviewing the literature, but integrating in an interesting way; perhaps extending and coming up with interesting questions as well. It is all of those things, I think. You can tell something had been poorly reconstructed the night before as compared to work from somebody who has really thought about it. And it's really, I think, that the cream of the crop pretty much goes to the top, and you can see it pretty clearly.

We have a set of criteria and they are listed there on the call. A month-long window to get in the proposal and what percentage do you think comes in the day of – the last day? Ninety-plus. Some of them just literally looked like somebody sat down and worked on them the night before off the top of their head – and those don't make it. So we get a lot, but they don't all get considered.

Mitchell, Ron: So it is a nightmare in many respects.

Bauer, Talya: It is actually a lot of fun, too.

Gilson, Lucy: Sorry to jump in on the review, but we did one a couple of years back (Martins, Gilson and Maynard, 2004) and we sent it in and wanted to review virtual teams and 'something else.' Why I don't remember the 'something else' is because the editor contacted us and said, 'We would like to accept your proposal, but we don't like the "something else,"' and so I obviously blanked it out. So, 'We don't like the "something else"; do you think you could do virtual teams, and where the research is going?' It's kind of like when you get that R&R when someone says, 'We would accept it if you did this.' And you ask, 'How long will that be? I need 24 hours, so let's drink.' But it was interesting, I think coming back to that, that you sometimes submit something that you think is very interesting as a review and you are trying to put a twist on it – and the twist is what they didn't like and they want the review to go a different way.

Mitchell, Ron: So, Talya, if there is one thing that you would recommend to successfully work at *JOM*, it would be . . .? Two if you want.

Bauer, Talya: There are two stages. I guess the first is submitting and I think there are a lot of necessary but not sufficient criteria. It is amazing to me how few people have all of the pieces when they send in a paper: it is an interesting idea, it has practical implications and the story is consistent throughout. You actually have an introduction that fits the methods and that fits the discussion. It is not rocket science, but you would be amazed at how many don't do that (or a lot of the people in this room would not be amazed because they have seen it). But it's a shame because a lot of times, there's a lot of hard work that goes into those papers; but then many of them get rejected because they just can't make that first threshold of writing clearly. They need to consult *The Elements of Style* (1918) by William Strunk and E.B. White on writing well. I think those kinds of things are just so key. That gets you in the door, and then you are in that 25 percent that are considered for revision.

Then I think these three did a great job with this: being really responsive, going above and beyond, being diligent, being timely and writing well. Being nice only goes so far. I would say that the biggest thing is not having an argumentative attitude, but rather asking, 'How can I make this paper better?' My mantra is, 'Feedback is a gift.' So many people are threatened by feedback, but when someone gives you that tough love feedback, that is the best thing they can do. We would be doing a disservice if we published the first drafts that people sent in.

Mitchell, Ron: One of the scarcest resources in our craft is on-point and considered feedback from our peers. With that, I think we're pretty much ready to wrap it up. Thank you, authors! Thank you, editors, for a job well done. Thank you, Lucy; it is very much appreciated.

REFERENCES

Dalton, D.R. and C.M. Dalton (2005). Strategic management studies are a special case for meta-analysis. In D. Ketchen and D. Bergh (eds), *Research Methodology in Strategy and Management*. Bingley: Emerald Group Publishing, pp. 31–63.

Gartner, W.B. (1988). 'Who is an entrepreneur?' Is the wrong question. *American Journal of Small Business*, **12** (4), 11–32.

Hunter, J.E. and F.L. Schmidt (1990). *Methods of Meta-analysis: Correcting Error and Bias in Research Findings*. Hillsdale, NJ: Lawrence Erlbaum.

Martins, L.L., L.L. Gilson and M.T. Maynard (2004). Virtual teams: what do we know and where do we go from here? *Journal of Management*, **30** (6), 805–35.

Strunk, W.J. and E.B. White (1918). *The Elements of Style*. New York: Pearson Education.

Zhao, H., S.E. Seibert and G.T. Lumpkin (2010). The relationship of personality to entrepreneurial intentions and performance: a meta-analytic review. *Journal of Management*, **36** (2), 381–404.

15.   Journal of Management Studies

Associate editor: *Andrew C. Corbett*
Authors: *J. Michael Haynie,*
Dean A. Shepherd, Jeffery S. McMullen,
James O. Fiet
Moderators: *Ronald K. Mitchell,*
Michael Lubatkin
Comments editor: *G. Thomas Lumpkin*

Mitchell, Ron: The idea behind this Exemplar's Conference is to have editors and authors in the same space for a very honest dialogue with no holds barred – I am just setting up what's about to happen here. Let me introduce our distinguished panel (at least they will be distinguished at the beginning of the session). On my immediate left is Andrew Corbett, who represents the *Journal of Management Studies* (*JMS*) as associate editor. We have my co-moderator, Mike Lubatkin – thank you, Mike. Jim Fiet is here (representing himself) with a paper, 'A prescriptive analysis of search and discovery.' And we have Michael Haynie, Dean Shepherd and Jeff McMullen with their paper, 'An opportunity for me? The role of resources in opportunity evaluation decisions.'

The mission of *JMS* is available on the conference website and on the *JMS* website. The *Journal of Management Studies* is a journal for the Society for the Advancement of Management Studies (SAMS) – one of the IDEA Awards sponsors. This is a part of the Research Excellence Initiative (which includes the Exemplars Conferences as well as very specific targeted awards to both honor and motivate the elevation of research excellence in the entrepreneurship field).

We will start with a comment I picked up from the mission of the journal to get us started. One of the opportunities I identified for publication of entrepreneurship research in this journal is that the journal has a 'focus on lively debate and topical and important issues on management.' Articles addressing controversial issues in entrepreneurship would likely be welcome here. That's not part of the mission of the journal; that's my editorial comment. Anything to add about my characterization of the journal, Andrew, before we get rolling?

Corbett, Andrew: No. I would say that's pretty right on. As everybody knows (I think), *JMS* is based in the United Kingdom and it is the oldest management journal outside of the United States. In recent years (under the direction of Mike Wright, Tim Clark and Steve Floyd), *JMS* made a real outreach to combine the European UK ethos with the non-traditional American brand of scholarship – and successfully combined the two together. From that, we have a pretty distinct and unique mission of being able to do just that. At the time, the editorial team also made a tremendous outreach to the entrepreneurship community. Everyone in the room would probably agree that there's been a dramatic rise of entrepreneurship scholarship in the journal, and we hope to see that continue.

Mitchell, Ron: Certainly with the internationalization of the Academy in general, and entrepreneurship research specifically, this is a journal that represents the bridge in the geographical sense and the bridging of the research in the traditional sense. Let's turn for a few minutes to the author teams for a brief (I have called it an elevator pitch) 30 to 50 seconds on what this paper is about. Mike, are you the one from this team who will do the elevator pitch?

Haynie, Mike: Yes – apparently so.

Mitchell, Ron: We will invite you to speak first, and then ask Jim to do the same.

Haynie, Mike: Sure. Very quickly, the paper tests the model of entrepreneurial opportunity evaluation as a decision study where we frame (for the entrepreneurs) the idea that opportunities are evaluated as a function of the resources that will be under control of the entrepreneur, post-exploitation. We were interested in understanding how different attributes of those post-exploitation resources and different combinations of those attributes may influence the entrepreneur's assessment of the attractiveness of that particular opportunity; whether those opportunity evaluation schema proceed as either a first-person or third-person evaluation. That is, given the extent to which those future resources would be under the control of the entrepreneur, post exploitation – did the entrepreneur's evaluation of the attractiveness of those resources change as a function of how related those future resources might be to the existing human capital resources of the entrepreneur?

Mitchell, Ron: Thanks, Mike. Jim.

Fiet, Jim: This was a paper that I started writing in 1997. It's a conceptual basis of my work concerning systematic search. It's primarily based on informational economics and the primary argument is: if you search in a targeted way, based on specific knowledge that you already possess, the number and the quality of the ideas that you find will increase. That's it in a nutshell.

Mitchell, Ron: Thanks. One of the things that I haven't made explicit in some of the other sessions (and I will take the opportunity to do now) is that the papers that are here as exemplars were selected by the editors who are representing their journals at this conference. A first question that I will ask – I will give the honor of the first question to Mike – would be: Andrew, why these papers?

Corbett, Andrew: Thanks, Ron. It was quite purposeful trying to set up a situation where I see these two papers as ones that represent different paths and different processes within journal publishing. Mike, Dean and Jeff's paper is excellent – very insightful, with good questioning. The paper has a relatively unique methodology; but from a publishing process perspective, while there were some significant changes, it went through a very standard process. A couple of revisions and it was in. On the other hand, Professor Fiet's paper, as he alluded to, was started in . . . when was it again . . .?

Fiet, Jim: Actually, it was 1986.

Mitchell, Ron: Yes, that is when he initially submitted it to this journal.

Fiet, Jim: Before I was a doctoral student.

Corbett, Andrew: Another prolific author and another excellent paper, but the process here was quite different; I think it also illustrates what we do well at *JMS*. This is a very provocative paper (which also brings very extreme reactions sometimes, right?). And because of those extreme reactions, it takes a bit more time (as you alluded to) but it also requires reviewers and an editorial team to be able to see the opportunity that's there, and to work with the author to bring it to fruition. But it allows us to publish something that we think may not have seen the light of day at other outlets.

Mitchell, Ron: Thank you, Andrew.

Fiet, Jim: Let me say that I think that I submitted it to most of the editors in this room.

Mitchell, Ron: And with that, Mike, we will turn the first question to you.

Lubatkin, Mike: I'd like to focus some of my attention to the theory of entrepreneurship and how it applies to us – not in terms of what we research, but how it applies to us in who we are as researchers. But before I get to that, I'd like to say something about *JMS*. I like *JMS* . . .

Corbett, Andrew: And we like you, Mike.

Lubatkin, Mike: . . . And in liking *JMS*, I certainly respect the job that they've done for our academic community in the last few years, as they've basically rejuvenated a journal which looked like it was going dead on the market – a great service. But from a junior scholar point of view, given that experience is so important in our field, how do we – as junior scholars – get onto your editorial board?

Corbett, Andrew: I would guess all the editors in the room would tell you to volunteer to review, right? Volunteer to review. We are always looking for good reviewers. To try to build a stable of reviewers is not an easy task; so volunteer to review. If you do good timely reviews, you will ultimately get on the editorial board. That was the story for me, because I am not so long in the tooth necessarily (in this field, anyway). I think Mike's comments are right on target, and they are really due to Mike Wright, Tim Clark and Steve Floyd, who are the ones who really turned things around for the journal in the past decade. At that time, they made an outreach to (I think) a number of the people in this room to go outside of the continent and find more entrepreneurship and strategy work; they asked people to review, they invited them to review, and they got them on the editorial board. I think that's the path for any junior scholar or doctoral student: just offer to review – if you do it well and timely, you'll soon find your way there.

Lubatkin, Mike: Should the offer letter include our resume or our publication record? You get a letter from someone you've never heard of yet and . . .

Corbett, Andrew: You know, I guess that's fine if they wanted to put their vita in there, but a short statement that says, 'Here's what I do, here's where I work and here are my areas of expertise,' I think will get the job done.

Lubatkin, Mike: Thank you. There's always a debate that I recognize and see in the literature as to whether opportunities are discovered or created. That's what we research. But going to the more personal level of how we research it, I'd be interested [to hear] from the author team and the solo author (which is like you are an anachronism, Jim) . . .

Mitchell, Ron: Seven percent of the people wouldn't agree with that.

Shepherd, Dean: The rest died of old age.

Lubatkin, Mike: I'd be interested to know the germination of your idea. Was it created? Was it discovered? Are there things that we can learn about entrepreneurship by examining how we as scholarly entrepreneurs come upon entrepreneurial opportunities?

Mitchell, Ron: What do you think? Do you want to discuss that?

Haynie, Mike: I can give it a shot. This paper has an interesting history in that it really was a means to an end for me. This paper came out of my dissertation. For the main study on my dissertation I needed a model; I needed an empirical model of how entrepreneurs evaluate or proceed through the process of evaluating opportunities. I couldn't find anything. I needed that for a laboratory experiment I was going to do to walk folks through this model of evaluation and feedback and see how their decision policies change. I couldn't find that model in the literature, and we made a choice and asked, 'Why don't we go out and understand it ourselves and do the investigation ourselves?' It didn't come from a real purposeful question in this area; it really was a means to an end. But then, once we got into it, I think we were able to formulate a pretty interesting question and an interesting paper.

Mitchell, Ron: 'Things I discovered on the way to doing something else . . .'

Haynie, Mike: Yes, that's exactly what it was.

Fiet, Jim: I had a somewhat different experience. I was an entrepreneur for a number of years before I went back to graduate school – and I guess I was a habitual entrepreneur. I never would've thought of waiting for an idea to occur to me. My modus operandi was to have certain criteria and go about looking. I later termed that 'information channels.' And I would be the first one to acknowledge that ideas are certainly created and made;

but that, for me, wasn't the interesting question. The interesting question for me was, 'How can we improve performance?' I thought we had a better chance of being able to teach systematic search than any other approach that I knew of. That's how I got interested in it.

Mitchell, Ron: Could I ask you a question, Jim? What were the three most problematic reviewer requests you received from this journal?

Fiet, Jim: One of the most difficult questions was the need to relate this to other research. And so I would have reviewers that say, 'Gee, you are citing your own papers,' and that was true; but the other papers that I wanted to cite were from a different perspective. They were looking at discovery, but they weren't looking at it from the perspective of systematic search. I think I threw myself on the mercy of the court; and I think Mike Wright was sympathetic to that argument and he let it slide. I don't really think I ever fixed the problem.

Another problem was that I had 36 new technical terms and eight propositions in the paper, and it was difficult for readers to follow. I was alert to a device which I think has helped me quite a bit, and that was I created a glossary of these 36 terms. Then I did a search throughout the document to make sure that I was using all 36 of these terms in the same way. By the time I had that figured out, I deleted the glossary and never included it in the paper; but I thought all along I was going to put it in the paper – so it was useful.

The other thing was that the reviewers complained about the prescriptive nature of the paper – they thought it should be descriptive. I had to work quite hard to address that problem. One of the ways I did it was by linking it to research that I was doing simultaneously on repeatedly successful entrepreneurs (and hopefully that paper will be coming out pretty soon). It isn't published yet, but in those interviews I found that all the repeatedly successful entrepreneurs (in the same way that I search systematically) reported to me that they search systematically. I was able to ground it in phenomena. That satisfied the descriptive preferences of the editors and reviewers, and then they gave me a license to talk about its prescriptive implications.

Mitchell, Ron: Thank you. Problematic reviewer comments? Hurdles to clear?

Haynie, Mike: I will take one. The most problematic request was one to rewrite the whole paper. Truly, this paper (like some of the other ones we heard about), did start somewhere else; and again, like some of the feedback we heard, it came back with (being as it started in a general management journal) feedback of 'too much entrepreneurship, too focused, etc.' So we turned around and told a different story than when we submitted it the first time to *JMS*. We turned it into something it wasn't. We turned it into a story on diversification.

Mitchell, Ron: This wasn't a 'turn it around because it was rejected and immediately dump it over the transom to the next journal' scenario?

Haynie, Mike: No, we rewrote the paper for *JMS*, and *JMS* came back and, basically, the reviewer said, 'I hate the story. You are trying to make it something it's not. Tell the simple story.'

McMullen, Jeff: I was just going to add – it was terminology, don't you think? The diversification concept was there, but it was just that it was at a different level; the people didn't believe in a firm level.

Haynie, Mike: It was a very substantial rewrite that first round.

Shepherd, Dean: I think they had three comments. One was they didn't necessarily like the positioning. We had to strengthen the theory, and then they didn't understand the method so much.

Haynie, Mike: Other than that it was fine. That's what I said.

McMullen, Jeff: I guess we should rewrite the paper.

Shepherd, Dean: On the method side, the method used was conjoint analysis, which a lot of people are not very familiar with. So, in some ways, it was more our being able to better educate the reader about the use of the method. We had to talk about different levels, why multicolinearity wasn't a problem and how we control the level two variables. A lot of it was our efforts being able to better explain the way the method was.

Mitchell, Ron: Let's just be clear. Conjoint analysis focuses on the empirics of how people actually make decisions. Isn't that right?

Shepherd, Dean: Yes.

Mitchell, Ron: Could you give us (because conjoint analysis isn't broadly out there) an overview on its history, major strengths and weaknesses? It's been around for a while in other areas.

Shepherd, Dean: Right. It's been mainly in marketing, but also in psychology. It really has two forms. I think policy capturing could be considered a sub-category of a conjoint analysis. There are multiple different forms; whether it's metric conjoint (which we do), whether you choose different pairs, or policy-capturing as more continuous variables . . . It's really an experiment where you provide people a number of hypothetical profiles where they make decisions, and each one of the profiles differs based on the levels of each one of the attributes such that, in the end, each person, for example, will have to make 32 decisions – and we might have 100 entrepreneurs. We have 3,200 decisions nested within those 100 individuals, from which we can decompose each individual's decision policy as weights on the different attributes. How much importance do they place on different decision criteria in being able to make a decision? So we can analyse the decision policy of the group as a whole, but we can also work out differences in decision policies amongst groups within the sample. While it's a recognized method somewhere else (we try to communicate that it's recognized somewhere else), we also realize our responsibility to try and sufficiently explain what conjoint analysis is and why it opens up interesting research questions in entrepreneurship.

Mitchell, Ron: How did conjoint analysis play in the editorial process? You had a method (it's not mainstream entrepreneurship yet), but more and more researchers are using it.

Corbett, Andrew: I think from the view (and again, Mike Wright had a handle on this paper) that maybe it's not mainstream yet, although there's been enough stuff in entrepreneurship and they've seen it. Dean has used it before. Dean has used it with Zach Zacharakis. Again, that fit into the ethos of the journal to do something that's maybe a little bit different than what some of the journals out there are doing. There's a clear willingness to do that – to differentiate a bit.

Shepherd, Dean: Mike Wright has done a little bit of research in venture capital and a lot of the conjoint stuff had already appeared there. He seemed to already be aware of it.

Mitchell, Ron: There's that luck thing playing into it. Mike, back to you.

Lubatkin, Mike: I am going to go back again to some personal questions. I am more comfortable as a moderator being Jerry Springer, but I am in Oprah-mode at the moment.

Now, your paper is entitled 'An opportunity for you?' and you are basically coming up with a model that describes the cognitive processes leading to opportunity evaluation. Does your model describe the processes that led to your assessment of the opportunity of this research? Are we living what we write about?

McMullen, Jeff: I think that's a great point. Personally, anytime I theorize it's always autobiographical. I sit there and I think about what I would do in this situation, and then I look out there and see. Sometimes it matches up and sometimes it doesn't; it deviates for the most part. But, I honestly think, that way, that you constantly challenge yourself; 'Would I make decisions this way?' Obviously you have to play, to some extent, with the theoretical constructs that are in the literature already – like RBV [resource-based view] for instance. But if you are not asking that question, if you are not asking 'Would I make a decision this way?' your theory is going to ring hollow. It's just not going to be legitimate or actual. I don't know if you guys agree with that . . .

Shepherd, Dean: It's a good question. Probably one I will need to think about a little bit more because it's saying, what's the opportunity? The opportunity is to write a highly impactful paper. How do I consider the different alternatives of papers I could potentially write in making the decision that this is the one that I write? I understand the question. I'd have to think more about how I actually apply that.

I do think the moderating variable here was relatedness and that it magnified the other attributes of the opportunity. I do think about whether a paper opportunity relates to other things that I have been doing. So, yeah, I think it probably does relate.

McMullen, Jeff: Mike and I talked a little while about the idea of seduction – being seduced away from your core competency. That was a notion that we kicked back and forth in a sense of asking 'When do you leave your core competencies? When the opportunity is attractive enough that it looks as if, "Okay I can take some risks here because it's an attractive opportunity, it's defensible once I get there, so maybe I should venture out here"?' And it's a great point in the sense that if you are going to evolve, there are times when you don't want to go extinct; you are going to have to take those chances and explore a new patch in the biological use of the term.

Lubatkin, Mike: I am going to shift my attention for a moment then to Jim's paper, which is entitled 'A prescriptive analysis of search and discovery.' I found that it best describes repeat entrepreneurs (who are also called serial entrepreneurs who, before I entered the field, I thought was the Kellogg family).

You essentially, Jim, are a repeat entrepreneur in the type of research that you've done.

Fiet, Jim: Right.

Lubatkin, Mike: Does your model at all describe who you are as a researcher?

Fiet, Jim: Yeah, I have been thinking a lot about this in the last couple of days because I was trying to figure out why I kept pushing this paper. Because after four years, I decided that it wasn't going to get published; but I worked on it for six more years. I don't know why I did that. It wasn't a rational calculation, because there were certainly opportunity costs. I wrote two books from the stuff that was rejected while I was trying to submit it to journals.

Mitchell, Ron: Ah, the cutting-room floor.

Lubatkin, Mike: It's really interesting. Jim is reflecting on it and he's tearing up a little bit. That's what we are about. We are putting our heart and soul into our ideas. We embody the concept of entrepreneurship by the very virtue of the fact that we are willing to fight and die for what we believe is interesting.

Mitchell, Ron: There is an element in this paper that captured my attention. And that was the 'this is prescriptive versus descriptive' idea; but essentially, 'We are not trying to look at what entrepreneurs actually do, we are trying to look at what they can do.' And in some respects, that prescriptive analysis, the tearing up, and the whole connection here is that perhaps (and maybe I am reading too much into this) there's a personal vision of possibility that wasn't getting heard and has now been heard. To what extent would we have that personal commitment to human potential as being part of the reason why you continue to pursue it?

Fiet, Jim: One day I was reading an entry-level finance book and the book said, 'Finance is the study of how people ought to invest their money.' Not how they do, but how they ought to. Marketing is the study of how they ought to increase their sales. Economics . . . And I went through several disciplines and it occurred to me that each one of these was taking a prescriptive bent that we don't take in organizational studies; we typically take a descriptive approach. It's fun to change people's lives.

Mitchell, Ron: I sensed that there was a part of that (and Mike sensed it too) that personal values and personal perspectives that have come through into the research.

Fiet, Jim: We have trained about a thousand people using this approach and a lot of people have been influenced by it.

Mitchell, Ron: We have time now to turn our attention to you worldwide, who may still be up or just getting up in the morning or whatever, and this is the wake-up call. Please email in your questions and we will also turn the time over to those on the floor here in the studio. This is not a classroom; it's a studio audience, and we have an opportunity to examine this. Sharon?

Alvarez, Sharon: Jim, mine's not so much a question as to commend you. It really takes a lot of courage to do what you did and to continue to move forward. One of the things I often tell doctoral students is, 'There's no lack of smart people in academia.' Once you get here, everybody is smart and the difference tends to be (at least in my opinion) the people who work hard and the people who persevere. There are a lot of other things besides just smarts that get you there; and congratulations, because that was not easy and I personally commend you. Good for you.

Haynie, Mike: I never got so much sympathy when I was rejected.

Mitchell, Ron: Other questions coming in from the floor? Tom, do we have worldwide web yet? Okay. Phil's coming into us from here in the studio.

Phan, Phil: Thank you. This question is for the paper by Mike, Dean and Jeff. Given the hurdles that you faced, did you have any sense why you were given an R&R [revise and resubmit]? Or maybe Andrew can also answer?

Haynie, Mike: It was like these reviews were screaming at me when I read them.

Shepherd, Dean: They scream at you; yet they weren't that bad. We have had rewrites before and I think the results looked interesting. We got these interaction effects (I think it was three interaction effects), so there were non-obvious, hard to understand hypotheses – such that the results were non-obvious. I think that's why they gave us the R&R.

Corbett, Andrew: If I could chime in. I mean, I looked through it, but obviously I didn't handle this paper. But I went through all the correspondence for Mike; as Dean mentioned, Mike was very familiar with this technique. I think this is a situation where you do see the hand of the editor that recognized the potential that was there, and could see that hand throughout some of the other comments (the classic comments that we all see in our reviews). And the editor was able to see that – see the potential for contribution – and help the authoring team bring it forward.

Haynie, Mike: What's interesting is the other part of the story (even though I was a little overwhelmed by those first reviews); we re-wrote the paper and it was conditionally accepted on that next submission. So, credit to Mike Wright for helping us see the story that we needed to tell.

McMullen, Jeff: One interesting thing, too, is that the structure is sound. Sometimes the labels aren't the clearest or the most compelling ones that you could possibly use, even though the concepts (we have a lot of terms for the same meaning of concept) that sometimes resonate with people are timely and are interesting. And sometimes they don't resonate with people. We were talking about diversification. The term was wrong, but the meaning of that concept stayed constant because we were talking at the individual level. I was probably wrong to use diversification at that level, yet the notion was the same notion.

Mitchell, Ron: There's an idea emerging here and it ties back to the glossary comment that Jim made. When we speak to a community, that community has a vocabulary; I don't know that there's anywhere that the glossaries for *AMJ* [*Academy of Management Journal*], for *SEJ* [*Strategic Entrepreneurship Journal*], and for *JBV* [*Journal of Business Venturing*], are readily available. Therefore, who is it incumbent upon to create the glossary? I think it was a cool mechanism Jim provided that many of us haven't really considered doing, which is just go through that paper, take the terms, and – whatever those terms are – be sure that every time you use them, you haven't changed them in your mind. Just because we are, as Sharon was saying, a 'bunch of smart people,' doesn't mean that you can't think of a term in two or three different lights. Maybe it's because we are smart that we think of it in two or three different lights. Yet other smart people can't track what you are thinking when you change the meaning. Consequently, this glossary of terminology puts us in a position where we can be very explicit about the vocabulary we are using. Therefore, if we are explicit about the vocabulary, we can read a few articles from the journal we are targeting and see if those terms actually show up. And, especially check to see if those terms have the definition that we are using.

Fiet, Jim: Can I make an additional comment related to that? When I am searching through my papers using my glossary and I find a term, I put it in bold. Then I put the definition of how I am using the term in italics, as an intermediate step, to make sure that when I search it the second time, that all of the definitions in italics are the same.

Mitchell, Ron: It's called systematic search of terms.

Corbett, Andrew: Related to that, I just had a similar situation over the weekend on a recent paper acceptance I sent out. It's important to be explicit sometimes. When we are talking about entrepreneurship research, and you are sending it to broad management journals as opposed to the focused journals, you are talking to a larger audience. Sometimes you need to be explicit in the language you are using because you are not just talking to the entrepreneurship community – you are talking to the entire management community. So when you are submitting to *JOM* or *JMS* or the Academy journals, I think it's incumbent upon the author team to make sure that they do that.

Mitchell, Ron: Thank you. We have Ann.

Parmigiani, Ann: I want to agree with that point, and also say that the other thing that gets to be complicated is operationalizing these concepts empirically – sometimes these things look the same. Sometimes I work in the capability space and I have trouble figuring out what's capability, what's knowledge, what's expertise and what's experience – because when you ask managers about them, it's all the same. That's the other difficulty, I think: not only figuring out theoretically and conceptually what your terms mean and defining them carefully, but to make sure empirically that they match operationally.

Mitchell, Ron: Operationally.

Parmigiani, Ann: Hopefully they match at least *something* others have done, at least in a consistent way (which is not always easy).

Corbett, Andrew: Hopefully you match the scholars that you are conversing with in terms of where you are trying to make your contribution, right?

Mitchell, Ron: Thank you, Ann. We are still open for questions. Tom – is there something on the web that we could post?

Lumpkin, Tom: The idea of 'what a field ought to do' mentioned by Jim is suggestive of Jay Barney's [Chapter 3] keynote comments about senior scholars assuming greater responsibility to make an impact. Are we missing out by not being more prescriptive (not focusing more on what entrepreneurs can do with our help, hopefully, or what aspiring entrepreneurs ought to do)?

Mitchell, Ron: Jim, I think you get the first shot at that one.

Fiet, Jim: I think we have all had the experience of seeing the light bulbs go off in a student's eyes, and we are grateful for that experience. If we let that opportunity pass and don't engage them further, we've lost the chance to change their lives – to be a part of that. So, I would say that I need to do it more, even though I already do it as much as I can.

Mitchell, Ron: Mike, can I draw you into that question? Being more prescriptive? How does that hit you as far as advising scholars, in all stages of their careers, as to the kind of work we can do? Oftentimes as a reviewer, for example, I see things that I might call polemics, where someone's on the soapbox (and there is an evangelizing side to that). We have a balance that we need to strike that retains legitimacy while capturing the potential Jim is helping us try to see. Do you have thoughts on that that might address the questions coming in on the web?

Lubatkin, Mike: I am going to try – I hadn't thought about this. There's an evolution to us as scholars in our careers. We start off very much in a skill-building mode as doctoral students and as junior faculty members. I liken that to developing skills as a musician; at some point we need to make the transition from musician to composer. That is, we have to stop playing the music that others have composed, and we have to, in fact, start to initiate our own melodies. But as we evolve as faculty members – as we evolve as scholars – we then need to make the transition from composers to conductors. Here is where we are working with the junior people; we are orchestrating their moves, and we are serving as mentors for them.

Mitchell, Ron: This resonates with the idea that's been developing at this Conference, which is that there are career stages that result from our various roles (if we are willing to undertake them) because some folks just love playing the instrument and never want to compose, and others, if they were forced to conduct, wouldn't get the joy of playing that trumpet (or whatever it is). In some respects, that's a career-based decision we need to make, and I appreciate you drawing that out.

Shepherd, Dean: I think we don't want to make the distinction too clear between prescriptive research at one end and descriptive research at the other end, because we also have explanatory research in between. I think explanatory research is important because we develop an understanding of why people act the way that they do. I think that can, in and of itself, also have prescriptive implications. I don't think we should think about 'We have prescription and we have description.' I think explanation is also important, and is an important part towards prescription.

Mitchell, Ron: There is also the aspect of timing that comes into it. For example, someone I know who played in a rock band as a teenager would essentially read the chord charts that were provided by the band leader (you know, C Minor, 7th, etc.). When it was time to do that particular solo, they would just chord on through it. Well, after playing for a while, it suddenly becomes clear that there's more to music than just those chords – and suddenly they began to connect in ways that we hadn't ever imagined. Perhaps it's time in the saddle (time in a career) or perhaps it's interest or desire to push beyond; but to some extent, it's the movement across these boundaries (I appreciate Dean making the point that these are not hard-and-fast delineations in terms of either/or). We may come in and out of these zones, but (to the extent that the timing's right) to have obstacles in our structure of how we see our own careers might, in fact, hold us back. We ought to be able to embrace the notion of becoming engaged in composing instead of just playing, or in orchestrating and conducting instead of just composing. There is a timing element that is a part of that.

As we come towards wrapping things up, I'd like to ask the authors and the editor to speak to the *JMS* experience, because obviously, we have this geographical bridge. We have a journal that is open to research traditions that are not strictly North American. As a result, we have some words to the wise – some takeaways. Let's start with the authors. If you were to say, 'There is one thing I'd recommend in successfully working with *JMS*,' it would be . . .?

Shepherd, Dean: When I think of *JMS*, I look at Mike. I think *JMS* is a lot like Mike. I want to ask everyone, what adjective am I actually thinking about? We should call it the 'Journal of Mike Studies.' I think it's quirky, you know? I really like the *Journal of Management Studies* because I think it's a lot like *Organization Science* used to be (and still is). But, I really like the *Journal of Management Studies* because it's quirky. If I have something that just doesn't quite fit the mainstream, and I am looking for somewhere to publish that is open to something that's a little bit quirky, I always think about the *Journal of Management Studies*. I think it might be because they are European.

Corbett, Andrew: Like I said at the top, that comes from this combination of a deep ethos (or heritage) of the European tradition, which now in the past decade and a half has been melded with the American tradition. It puts the journal in a unique space, and we definitely look to things that are provocative and risky. We are willing to take a chance on things.

Mitchell, Ron: Speaking of 'glossarizing,' what's the European tradition? What are we talking about?

Corbett, Andrew: I think what we are talking about is traditionally how doctoral students are trained as opposed to how they are trained in the US. And, how articles come to light, and how we tend to publish. I think there's definitely a European tradition that's a lot more qualitative, for one.

Shepherd, Dean: More philosophical?

Corbett, Andrew: More philosophical. Absolutely.

Lumpkin, Tom: I can jump in with a question that just came up for Andrew (following on what you just said). It says, 'Earlier we heard that at *JBV* we need to show how we contribute to entrepreneurship theory. At *JMS* do we need to contribute to broad management or entrepreneurship? Where is the balance?'

Corbett, Andrew: I think (and this might be reminiscent of something that Phil Phan said) that's a question where it's going to depend on what the authoring team wants to do. Where do you want to make a contribution? Maybe it goes back to some of what Venkat said in his keynote [Sankaran Venkataraman: Chapter 7]: where do you want to make the contribution, what scholars are you talking to, and how do you want to augment or add on to that conversation? The contribution is going to be driven by that. Is this more of a broad management paper that you are talking about, or is it more of an entrepreneurship paper?

Shepherd, Dean: I think there's a 'level of analysis' issue here, isn't there? I think the *Journal of Management Studies* is looking more towards managerial implications or organizational levels. Would you say that?

Corbett, Andrew: Yes. That's where I was going.

Shepherd, Dean: Okay – all right, sorry.

Mitchell, Ron: Jim? If there is one thing you would recommend for successfully working with *JMS* it would be . . .?

Fiet, Jim: Actually, just be lucky. I had a good experience. I found that Mike Wright and the other editors (who were badgering me at the end – I had done two rounds of revisions when the reviewers were finished with me; then, two more rounds with the editors) thought that I needed to talk more about the prescriptive implications. I had spent eight years taking those discussions out because nobody wanted to hear them. It was a totally different approach.

Mitchell, Ron: Mike, a last thought as we wrap up?

Lubatkin, Mike: My thought is (based on the discussion we had and the questions I prepared): we teach the entrepreneurial process, and we study the entrepreneurial process. Also, it's important for us to think of ourselves as embodying the entrepreneurial process when we find ways of combining our heart, mind and soul into the work that we do. It breeds so much more passion, which, of course, was one of the papers presented earlier today. Passion is so important; not only for our own self-satisfaction, but also for how well it communicates to others through our writing.

Mitchell, Ron: Thank you, Mike. Andrew – give us a final word? If there were one thing you would recommend in successfully working with *JMS* it would be?

Corbett, Andrew: It would be . . . (and this is a bit thematic and is again from Duane and Venkat's keynotes [Chapters 5 and 7]) Interesting! Right? It needs to be interesting if you are hoping to find a novel contribution. One of the things we do (as Talya said about *JOM,*) is we try to be very developmental. Beyond saying, 'Murray Davis interesting,' I have a group – a set of classics – that I rely on, and I know some of the other editors do too. In particular, I think, 'How do you become interesting when you need to be?' One of the things I direct people to is a great article on construct-ing rhetoric contributions, a 1997 *AMJ* piece by Karen Locke and Karen Golden-Biddle, which is 'How do you make your research interesting?' This is a great article that shows you a path to doing that. Additionally, the previous editors of *JMS*, Floyd, Clark and Wright wrote a wonderful article on the reviewing process which appeared in the May 2006 *JMS* where they talked about both contribution and being interesting. They did a study of all of the articles they received, and the fact of the matter is that 92 percent of the time, lack of interest, lack of interesting contribution or lack of contribution are the reasons why papers get rejected. Seventy-six percent of the time, papers get rejected because there was no contribution to theory. The third reason for rejection, at 70 percent, is method. Therefore, the key is being interesting and finding a way to contribute.

Mitchell, Ron: There's that sub-text; how to become interesting? *JMS*, the entrepreneurial author makeover specialists. Thank you, everyone. We appreciate it.

REFERENCES

Clark, T., S.W. Floyd and M. Wright (2006). On the review process and journal development. *Journal of Management Studies*, **43** (3), 655–64.

Davis, M.S. (1971). That's interesting! Towards a phenomenology of sociology and a sociology of phenomenology. *Philosophy of the Social Sciences*, **1** (2), 309–44.

Fiet, J. (2007). A prescriptive analysis of search and discovery. *Journal of Management Studies*, **44** (4), 592–611.

Haynie, J.M., D.A. Shepherd and J.S. McMullen (2009). An opportunity for me? The role of resources in opportunity evaluation decisions. *Journal of Management Studies*, **46** (3), 337–61.

Locke, K. and K. Golden-Biddle (1997). Constructing opportunities for contribution: structuring intertextual coherence and 'problematizing' in organizational studies. *Academy of Management Journal*, **40** (5), 1023–62.

16. Organization Science

Editor: *Pamela S. Tolbert*
Author: *Wesley D. Sine*
Moderators: *Ronald K. Mitchell,*
    Lucy Gilson
Comments editor: *G. Thomas Lumpkin*

Mitchell, Ron: This is an editor/author session, which includes Pam Tolbert as senior editor at *Organization Science*; Wesley Sine representing the paper entitled, 'From plan to plant: Effects of certification on operational start-up in the emergent independent power sector;' and Lucy Gilson, my co-moderator. Welcome, everyone.

Organization Science has a mission statement that is available on the Conference website as well as on the *Organization Science* website. One of the opportunities identified is that the *Organization Science* journal is a good target for a variety of entrepreneurship research, because the journal 'provides one umbrella for the publication of research from all over the world in fields such as: Organization Theory, Strategic Management, Sociology, Economics, Political Science, History, Information Science, Communication Theory and Psychology.' So *Organization Science*, then, has a very specialized niche in the market, and yet its specialty is of great breadth. What we'll do, as we've now become accustomed, is ask Wes if he wouldn't mind giving us the short and sweet of the paper, and then we'll turn the time to Lucy for the first question.

Sine, Wes: Great, I have 20 minutes to do this short and sweet?

Mitchell, Ron: And we all leave in 30 seconds.

Sine, Wes: As many of you have probably surmised, the paper is about entrepreneurs who are trying to get from a business plan to an operational start-up to actually selling a product. In this case, we are looking particularly at legitimation strategies. Let me first mention that this paper is co-authored with Robert David and Hitoshi Mitsuhashi – an international team. Robert's at McGill in Montreal and Hitoshi is in Tokyo. It was a lot of fun coordinating our different schedules.

In this paper, what we are trying to do is explore individual legitimation strategies and how it helps entrepreneurs to get the resources they need to reach operational start-up. From a theory point of view, it makes a difference in a couple of ways. Past research in institutional theory really looked at how the context of an organization conferred legitimacy on individual organizations. In this case, we wanted (because from experience we had noticed that entrepreneurs really proactively try to get credibility and legitimacy for their organizations) to see the impact of those strategies and how they interacted with these larger contextual processes. From an entrepreneurial point of view, the selection process and pre-operational start-up is pretty intense. We felt there wasn't a lot of work in that area; not only is it pretty intense, but credibility plays a big role because the entrepreneurs can't really point at their organization or their products – they really have to convince their audience or their resource providers that they need particular kinds of resources, and that they are a credible organization. Those are the things we looked at. And again, from an institutional point of view, one of the key takeaways is that we find that legitimacy isn't really either a dichotomous variable or a continuous variable. This is a debate that the literatures had. What we found was that as entrepreneurs went and tried to legitimize their own firms, that the effectiveness of this legitimation process or strategy was contingent on the environment. You see a real 'S'-curved relationship between continued attempts to gain legitimacy and the extent to which the sector already deemed the organization as legitimate. It's a diminishing return over time.

Mitchell, Ron: You brought in the idea of certification in that legitimation process.

Sine, Wes: Right. In this case, what these entrepreneurs do is they create a certification process. The irony is the certification really doesn't give any kinds of details that people couldn't figure out anyway – it's all publicly available and it's out of their business plan, so the certification held no weight. It was very symbolic and the entrepreneurs knew that. In fact, when the Federal Energy Regulatory Commission (FERC) eventually gave this certification, the entrepreneurs initially laughed at the idea. They said, 'What fools would believe such a thing?'

Mitchell, Ron: But it did have . . .

Sine, Wes: It had a big empirical impact.

Mitchell, Ron: Lucy?

Gilson, Lucy: Thank you. I actually have a lot of questions going into a little micro on the paper and especially the international authorship. But before we go down to that level, I wanted to take us maybe up to the journal level a little bit, because one of the things that we've talked about so far today is how the various journals are different, and then why you send your work to one place or the other and how they are handled differently in the review process. One of the things truly unique about *Organization Science* is its very large editorial board where then as an author, you can select your action editor and a reviewer. I am interested both on the editorial perspective and, as an author, what impact that has on the process and how you pick somebody. I mean, do you pick your friend or do you pick somebody you hope will be objective? Is this sort of like picking outside letter-writers for tenure? How do you select? And then if someone makes a selection that you think is bad, how do you handle it and how does that work? I would like to hear a bit more about that.

Tolbert, Pam: Let me start it from the editorial side. That's actually one of the things that I think – all journals want to be innovative, of course. But this is one of the ways in which *Organization Science* tries to create conditions that allow more innovative work and give it a better shot at getting published: because, by selecting an editor who you think is closer to your particular area and who should have relevant expertise (and identifying reviewers), you should be in a position to get a more sympathetic and more knowledgeable audience reading the paper. I think that it's actually a really good idea. Yet, it doesn't always work out as planned: first of all, you nominate an editor, you nominate a reviewer and the journal tries its best to honor those requests – but, workflow being what it is, it doesn't always work.

The other tricky thing is that people sometimes are very negative about it. You raised the issue of 'how do you decide who to nominate as a reviewer,' and I am always shocked by how many reviewers have been nominated end up rejecting a paper. So it's a little dicey; but at least you know you've gotten presumably a fair or a relevant reviewer in that case. The other issue that I had mentioned to Lucy is that sometimes my first reaction is, 'I don't want to nominate a reviewer because that reviewer's review will be discounted. Nobody is going to take that seriously.' I don't think that happens, surprisingly. I discovered as a handling editor, you usually forget who the author nominated unless a review comes back in and it says, 'This is fantastic. Just publish it.' Then you think, 'Is that who we nominated?' But I think that it's a very helpful technique on the part of the journal to try and get a paper into the hands of people who should be good reviewers.

Sine, Wes: In this case, we didn't get who we nominated, and in other papers that I currently have in *Organization Science*, we also didn't get who we nominated.

Tolbert, Pam: Well, it's good in theory.

Sine, Wes: But I felt very secure in being able to nominate. It made me feel good about coming to the journal.

Mitchell, Ron: A placebo effect?

Sine, Wes: It seems to be a random process if we can nominate. I like the idea of having a reviewer and knowing that at least one of the reviewers I nominate will be an expert; that's typically a strategy I take – nominating somebody that should be able to give the article a fair shot.

Gilson, Lucy: That's an interesting point, because if you nominate an editor, you know whether you got them or not because you see who you got the letter from. But if you nominate a reviewer, you don't actually know if you got the reviewer, right?

Tolbert, Pam: Exactly right, which is why then you sometimes get those reviews that are unfortunate, as the reviewers are not quite as sympathetic as you had hoped.

Mitchell, Ron: Lucy, did you want to go a little narrower into the actual process itself?

Gilson, Lucy: One of the things I like that was interesting: looking at the three authors on this paper, you have authors from the United States, Canada and Japan. We've talked a little bit about working together on that, but then you're talking about power plants in New York and California, so you're really spreading yourself. We talked about how you work together with handing-off papers. But one of the things we haven't really discussed yet today is, how did you three come together as a research team?

Sine, Wes: That's a great question. I had experience working with both of these co-authors; they didn't have experience working together, and we were at one point all students at Cornell. We knew each other, and I knew their strengths and knew their weaknesses. I brought them in for their strengths. As first author, I selected both of them for various strengths that they brought to the process. It was tough. We were all assistant professors in very different places. For me, I was thinking 'a top-tier journal or I'm not going to work on it,' and other co-authors also held that same set of principles, but their institutions were a little bit more lax in the kinds of journals that they would consider.

We went with *Organization Science* because the initial question we asked, we thought, was very different from what had been done. We wanted a really open-minded journal. We thought it was fact breaking and we didn't want to be forced into doing something that was just an incremental push on what had already been done. In terms of working, it worked out great. The idea that I could send something to Tokyo while I slept and get work done is nice. It was really important that we met a couple of times a year, closed the door for a week and didn't leave the room until we figured out some key concepts.

Mitchell, Ron: In the review process (we've talked about how helpful it can be), oftentimes the reviewers make problematic requests. In this paper, do you have an example or two of things that were asked that were perceived as problems?

Sine, Wes: Initially we were sure two of the three reviewers were wrong in most of what they had to say. Things like, 'We don't like your dependent variable. It's not a good empirical test of your theory and the theory itself isn't . . .' The initial reviews were very brutal and bloody and they needed to be. And they were helpful because of that. Eventually, I presented this paper in a very mixed audience with economists and non-economists, and it stood up pretty well to that mixed audience because of the reviewers. They must have come from interdisciplinary backgrounds because they brought in ideas and theories and techniques that we didn't include in the paper initially.

Mitchell, Ron: Let me get this straight. These were bloody, brutal reviews and you got an R&R [revise and resubmit]?

Gilson, Lucy: They were bloody, brutal and brilliant. It was a weak R&R. It was like, 'This is a high risk. Don't get your hopes up.'

Mitchell, Ron: I think there's a lesson there perhaps that's in the sub-text of the Q&A here, and that is that just because the review is problematic and appears to be harsh doesn't necessarily mean that behind the scenes that reviewer is saying to the editor, 'Get this out of here.' They may in fact be saying 'What were they saying, if you don't mind just a little bit of . . .?'

Tolbert, Pam: I wasn't the handling editor on this, but I went back and read the reviews and the comments to the editor, and they were saying, 'I don't know if this is going to survive, but there's a grain of an idea here. It's a small grain, but perhaps it could be developed.' They were fairly pessimistic, I think. There was a substantial revision.

Sine, Wes: Yes, it was substantial, and they didn't necessarily agree. The paper turned out to be very different than what we initially sent in, and I think the hardest part was we had three reviews (none of which really agreed). We took solace in the notion that if we can make one of the reviewers happy (and we knew one reviewer liked it), but if we could make another one happy we thought maybe we can get Jim Walsh to push it through.

Mitchell, Ron: Did you have to change your basic philosophy, theme, take, etc. . . .? Were you still intact as scholars when you made the choice?

Sine, Wes: Were we emasculated?

Mitchell, Ron: I used the word 'intact.'

Sine, Wes: Yes, that's what made me think of the word emasculated. Essentially, the initial paper was too big to do well; it covered too much. The problem was that we were really immersed in the context. We really understood what was going on and we wanted to tell the whole story. We needed some people to say, 'No, there are not enough pages here to tell the whole story.' So we cut it in half. Initially we looked at why some organizations seek certification – and then how does certification pan out. We cut it in half and then we had one reviewer say (and Jim Walsh encouraged us to this), 'You should look at the interactions. There's all this research on the environment and context and there should be something going on.' I think our initial ideas were intact, but embellished and elaborated.

Mitchell, Ron: This is a follow-up question for Pam. As you went back through the file and you looked at how the senior editor was actually working on this, to what extent did the editor contribute ideas beyond those that were brought into the conversation by the reviewers?

Tolbert, Pam: In the first couple of rounds, I think the main contribution was actually just trying to point a path, because the reviews really did say, 'Do this and do this and do this;' so the main job was to say, 'You could do this, but I think this might be a good strategy,' which is something that people should pay attention to when senior editors do this stuff. Because on one hand they're trying to not alienate reviewers; obviously there's a lot of labor involved there, but sometimes you don't always think they're going in the right direction. What you do in writing a decision letter is try and point to a path among the differing options.

Sine, Wes: And I think Jim could've done a better job of that. He did a good job, but he was a very tough editor. If one of the reviewers wanted another additional empirical analysis that we thought had marginal benefit, Jim didn't let it slide by. He said, 'Do it.' He didn't adopt our argument of 'marginal benefit.'

Tolbert, Pam: Some editors use more discretion. Some editors use less and they pay more attention to the reviewers. That's partly an editorial choice. This editor (who shall remain nameless) . . .

Mitchell, Ron: But his first name starts with 'J.'

Tolbert, Pam: There's an interesting question that comes up.

Gilson, Lucy: When we were talking about being the lead author because, Wes, you said early on, 'I picked these two co-authors because I thought they'd have different things they'd bring to the table,' and now you have these reviews that are sending you in different areas. As the lead author, did you say, 'Okay, I picked you for these skills on this paper. This is the way we're going to go.' How did you then navigate that with your co-authors?

Sine, Wes: This is an interesting story that probably doesn't happen very often. The paper originally started with two authors.

Gilson, Lucy: That's why I asked the question.

Sine, Wes: I started with just one co-author. We sent in the first review. When we got the reviews back, we both felt like we needed a third person (just for the speed). There were also some professors who were coming up for renewal, so there's a speed issue. I was working with one of the co-authors on another paper with similar issues and similar questions. We worked very well together and it was an obvious benefit to bring him in.

Mitchell, Ron: It was a natural inclusion?

Sine, Wes: A natural inclusion. We sent it back with one more author. But the other thing was that once we owned the paper, we collectively owned the paper. Sometimes in the discussion Hitoshi or Robert would say, 'You're first author, you make the call,' but I never exercised that option. It was more, 'Come on,' and I think, again, that the two of them really own the paper.

Mitchell, Ron: Now we're into the Q&A time. Do we have questions? We have one from the web. We have one from Elizabeth – go ahead, Elizabeth.

Lim, Elizabeth: Thank you. I have a quick question. Sometimes we send our papers to top journals and we're blessed with a good handling editor and good reviewers who provide excellent comments, great guidance on a paper and that sort of thing. But at other times we come across reviewers who have a completely different vision for your papers. If you're a senior author, you could very well say, 'I want to protect my ideas and I'm not going to go with that different direction that the reviewer has suggested.' But as a junior scholar, when the tenure clock is ticking, you don't really have [an] option; yet at the same time, you want to protect your ideas. What are the sorts of things that authors could do in that challenging situation?

Mitchell, Ron: Pam, do you mind taking that?

Tolbert, Pam: No, not at all. It's a good question, because as a handling editor, you don't always get the people who are necessarily the best reviewers and sometimes you're not sure if this person is the right reviewer. I have also been on the other side of the fence and gotten reviews from – 'who did this?' If the comments are from the handling editor and you really agree, then you're a little stuck because they have decision-making power. What you can do is write a letter and try and pose an explanation for why you think this is not appropriate. You can even engage in an email exchange beforehand with them; although I would also say sometimes the stream of work can be a challenge – you send out a decision letter and somebody contacts you two months later and you can't remember very well. I think it's certainly worth going back to the senior editor and saying, 'This doesn't make sense to me and this is why,' and trying to negotiate it.

Mitchell, Ron: Here we have an illustration of the human process. We are people and we are interacting with each other, and so the idea then is that we ask questions. Now it's not become dependent upon that editor to the point that you intrude on her space.

Tolbert, Pam: This is the trick.

Mitchell, Ron: But it is, from a clarification standpoint. You know how we do with our presentations . . . You stand up and you ask, 'Do you want to take questions during the presentation or do you want to take them at the end?' and everybody says, 'We'll just take clarification questions.' It's that kind of a notion.

Tom, do we have comments or questions from the web?

Lumpkin, Tom: We have one from the web.

Sine, Wes: Can I just address that quickly?

Mitchell, Ron: While we're pulling it up, sure.

Sine, Wes: In this case, we had three reviewers telling us to go in three different directions. I think in your letter to the reviewers you can explain why you choose the direction you choose in a deep, sensitive, legitimate way that they understand that you can't do everything at once. So that's what we did – we just picked and chose one direction.

Mitchell, Ron: Okay, Tom.

Lumpkin, Tom: From the web for the whole panel. Sometimes we hear it's better for junior faculty to work with senior faculty rather than with peers. Here it seems three young faculty worked together successfully. Please comment on working with peers at the same stage versus working with more experienced faculty.

Gilson, Lucy: That's a great question.

Tolbert, Pam: It is a good question.

Sine, Wes: Do you want me to take it?

Tolbert, Pam: Wes, go ahead.

Sine, Wes: Having just gone through the tenure process, it's really important to work with your peers because, at least in our tenure process, evaluators consider the extent to which you weren't working with senior faculty, so there's a benefit there.

Tolbert, Pam: You get more credit?

Mitchell, Ron: You got more credit in the tenure evaluation.

Sine, Wes: There's a lot of energy when you have three hungry scholars that have renewal coming up, and people work day and night and there aren't consulting gigs getting in the way or conferences. I think the energy level and the willingness to explore is pretty nice. I work a lot with senior authors and that's great as well. There's a lot of energy.

Tolbert, Pam: I would chime in. I think oftentimes it's better to work with peers, especially as a junior faculty, because of the social dynamics and the credit issue. Fair or not fair, it's often a problem. The advantage of working with senior faculty is they have more savvy about the process, and so you can learn things that way that you might not learn otherwise. But I think if I had my druthers I would usually choose peers at my own level.

Mitchell, Ron: Lucy, do you mind weighing-in on that? What do you think?

Gilson, Lucy: I think you need to have a balance. I think it's great to work with peers because you're in that process together and you've got that hunger. I remember hearing once that when you publish with a very senior faculty member, 0.2 is taken off the publication. And then if you publish with a student, 0.2 is added back on. I remember thinking, 'Oh goodness, if I'm going to publish this, I'd better publish with that person at the same time to weigh out the balance.' I think we can get ourselves all wrapped up in the cycle.

Mitchell, Ron: In the game of it, yes.

Tolbert, Pam: In the calculations.

Gilson, Lucy: I think sometimes the main thing (and I think Wes has alluded to this) is to find people that you work well with. Probably like all of us, you've had those relationships at different levels in your career and someone said earlier, 'Students are students for such a short period of time that after a while you're all of a sudden a senior person working with a junior person and then you're colleagues working together.' It goes through that cycle. If there are people that you work well with, keep working with them and develop that relationship.

Sine, Wes: That's absolutely right. It's rare that a person can really tell you it's a horrible idea without ruining your day. If you can find that person, hold onto them and work with them.

Mitchell, Ron: If we're going to pull this together in the last couple of minutes, I'm interested in hearing both Pam and Wes speak from your perspectives about what is unique about the decision to work with *Organization Science* as a journal that also would be interesting to those who are submitting and who are considering it. What would be a distinct element that comes to mind? I don't know who would go first, but this is the kind of thing that those of us who are thinking about the work that we've developed (and maybe it's a first submission or maybe not) understand – but still there are distinct reasons why you would submit to *Organization Science*. And from your experience, both from an editor and author and from an author standpoint, what would they be?

Tolbert, Pam: Like I said, I think the editorial structure is very useful in terms of targeting reviewers and people who are going to be most sympathetic and most knowledgeable. I think, regarding *Organization Science*, my perception is that it has a reputation for being innovative – and that's an asset. I think that reputation is real. I can't explain why it's true. I served as an associate editor at *AMR* [*Academy of Management Review*] and there's a very different feel to *Organization Science*. They're very receptive, maybe because of the founding and the culture of the founding; they're receptive to more off-beat work, the kind of work that James Marsh publishes and things like that. You said one, so here's the fourth one.

In talking about *SEJ* [*Strategic Entrepreneurship Journal*], I was thinking the advantage of publishing in a journal like that is that you're more likely to find an appreciative market, because you targeted it. Because *Organization Science* is so broad, you're more likely to have some success in doing crossovers. That is, you reach an audience that you hadn't intended and that helps your work.

Mitchell, Ron: Thank you. Your thoughts?

Sine, Wes: You know, I've published in a couple of different journals and I've found *Organization Science* to be very flexible.

Mitchell, Ron: So, the flexibility?

Sine, Wes: The flexibility during the review process, approachability . . . I don't know if this is empirically true (if everybody feels like they had this flexibility) but it didn't seem to be a problem when we brought in another author; no one said anything about it. We really changed the direction of the manuscript. It went from more qualitative to more quantitative, and the whole time while we were changing the manuscript we never thought, 'Will they like it less qualitative?' We knew they were going to be fine with whatever we came up with as long as it's high quality.

Mitchell, Ron: The founding editor's piece that came out in 2008 made the observation about *Organization Science* – that there is a way that knowledge tends to migrate . . . and who uses which knowledge from which field (Daft and Lewin, 2008). *Organization Science*, to me, after having read that piece and having watched since then, is acting as a bridge. That big long list of disciplines that I read – that's for real. And you are able to then bring those into the management field and then certainly there are other fields that cite these literatures and then take it on. I think the example was sociology into *ASQ* [*Administrative Science Quarterly*] and then *ASQ* into *MIS* [*Management Information Systems*] or something like that. There's a knowledge migration; a process that's underway within this journal publishing process that is bridged by (and the critical element is) *Organization Science*. That's the uniqueness.

Lucy, your observations about a distinguishing factor in the *Organization Science* journal?

Gilson, Lucy: I think that what we're touching upon that it is a cool journal where you can have empirical and you can have theoretical and you can have . . .

Mitchell, Ron: A cool journal.

Gilson, Lucy: A cool journal. You can have these different things.

Audience Member #1: Do you have papers under submission there?

Gilson, Lucy: I do – and other places where it's not so cool. But what's also interesting, and a good thing, is when you're talking about junior authors coming together, you're playing with ideas. You have that diamond in the rough that we talked about earlier today, and you might find either a more receptive editorial board or reviewers as well as readership, because that's what they're trying to do and that's part of their mission.

Sine, Wes: That said, the reviewing process is just as tough there as *ASQ* or *AMJ* [*Academy of Management Journal*].

Gilson, Lucy: Right. Cool doesn't mean easy.

Mitchell, Ron: Last word – cool but tough. Thank you very much.

REFERENCES

Daft, R.L. and A.Y. Lewin (2008). Rigor and relevance in organization studies: idea migration and academic journal evolution. *Organization Science*, **18** (1), 177–83.

Sine, W.D., R.J. David and H. Mitsuhashi (2007). From plan to plant: effects of certification on operational start-up in the emergent independent power sector. *Organization Science*, **18** (4), 578–94.

17. Strategic Entrepreneurship Journal

Editor: *Michael A. Hitt*
Authors: *Yasemin Y. Kor, Jeffrey J. Reuer*
Moderators: *Ronald K. Mitchell,*
  Elaine Mosakowski
Comments editor: *G. Thomas Lumpkin*

Mitchell, Ron: Let me introduce those who are present here. First of all, my co-moderator is Elaine Mosakowski. Thank you, Elaine, for being part of this session. Also with us is Mike Hitt, the editor of *Strategic Entrepreneurship Journal* (*SEJ*); Yasemin Kor, who wrote one of the papers, and then Jeff Reuer, author of the other paper that we will be discussing. So we have authors, editor and co-moderator. A very similar set-up; we will have a small percentage of our time to do the introduction, talk a little bit about the journal mission and how that fits, although that should be obvious given its name. Then we will do a couple of quick elevator pitches on the papers and we will take it from there.

I feel a little awkward actually giving a journal mission statement with the editor sitting right next to me . . .

Hitt, Mike: I would like to hear what you say.

Mitchell, Ron: The journal explicitly targets entrepreneurship research that involves, for example, innovation and subsequent changes which add value to society. Now there's a theme, 'It adds value to society, which changes societal life in ways that have significant, sustainable and durable consequences.' How'd I do Mike?

Hitt, Mike: You did very well.

Mitchell, Ron: So that is the *SEJ* focus that we are going to pull our audience worldwide into. Welcome again. We will turn a few minutes over to the authors. Yasemin, would you like to go first? Give us a 30-second elevator pitch about your paper and we will follow with Jeff.

Kor, Yasemin: Sure, I will do that. The paper that I had the opportunity to co-author with three great scholars (Nicolai Foss, Peter Klein and Joe Mahoney) is actually a theoretical conceptual piece where we aimed to connect entrepreneurship research with the strategic management literature – specifically, the research that was grounded in resource-based theory. In this particular paper, we focus on the notion of subjectivism and the subjective nature of the entrepreneurial process. Then we draw insights from three different perspectives. One is Austrian economics, which of course has made classical contributions to entrepreneurship theory, and the notion of subjectivism that has deep roots in Austrian economics. The second one is Penrose's 1959 classic resources approach where subjectivism is consistently applied, both in the form of resource through heterogeneity, but also in terms of the heterogeneity of resource users; in other words, services available from the resources. Then, the third one is the modern resource base where there are also strong elements of subjectivism in the form of resource heterogeneity.

We try to bring together a lot of these insights (along with other insights) and use the notion of subjectivism to connect entrepreneurship and strategic management. Then as an application of this particular connection, we take the notion of subjectivism (which is at the individual level), and apply it to the entrepreneurial team. The unit of analysis goes to the team level; then we talk about the entrepreneurial team as a co-creative team act where individuals with heterogeneous mental models interact with one another. Then, of course, you need the element of social positive team dynamics. The product is a subjective productive opportunity set that is co-created and co-implemented as a team act. So that's the abstract.

Mitchell, Ron: Thank you very much, Yasemin. Jeff.

Reuer, Jeff: I would like to acknowledge my co-author first. His name is Fernando Chaddad and he was the lead author on the paper. He is formerly a student at the University of North Carolina. I think the best way to summarize the paper is with a simple puzzle or stylized fact: that is, if you look at the investment behavior of newly public firms, it actually turns out that their investments fall off fairly sharply after they go public. That fall off continues, although you'd expect that they have raised these funds for additional investment. They have passed the test of going public, a significant amount of information on the firm is generated as part of the process, and you wonder why their investments fall off. What we do in the paper is take some formal models from corporate finance and macroeconomics and apply them to the setting of IPO [initial public offering] firms and try to join that work with entrepreneurship research. The basic theoretical idea is one that finance people refer to as 'liquidity constraints.' The thought is that if a firm is very hard for external capital providers to evaluate, then there will be this wedge driven between the cost of external finance and internal finance. The ultimate implication of this is if you look at a firm's investment behaviors, that investment will be driven partly by the internal cash flows or funds available at any point in time, rather than just the NPV [net present value] or the growth opportunities that the firm faces.

What we do is we basically modify some of the statistical techniques that are used in finance and show that this under-investment problem (or these financial constraints) does, in fact, exist for IPO firms – and these problems don't get better or go away over time. Rather, they're rooted in the resource stock of these firms in that the firms that have the most intangible assets are those that are most subject to this problem. That presents a neat tension with some resource-based thinking.

Mitchell, Ron: Thank you very much, Jeff. Well, it is a real privilege to be on the same stage with Elaine. Thank you very much. As co-moderator, could I give you the honor of the first question?

Mosakowski, Elaine: Oh, I have been dying to ask my first question; so yes, please. Being a co-moderator in a session for *SEJ* is somewhat unique in that *SEJ* is not like the other journals that we are discussing at this Conference. It is a relatively new journal, and earlier in the Conference Duane Ireland mentioned this idea of participating in a conversation that has been ongoing with the journal. Well, here the conversations are really just starting.

SEJ is also unique in that we probably have as many definitions of strategic entrepreneurship as we have participants in this room; so it has arguably a somewhat ambiguous, or uncertain (or whatever phrase you would like) focus. Maybe not mission, but really what does strategic entrepreneurship mean and how does that influence the publications that result?

My questions to you two really are how the unique characteristics of *SEJ* influence not only your decision to submit to that journal, but also the process as you developed your ideas and interacted with editors and reviewers? Do you think it was different – different in a good way or different in a bad way? Maybe it is not a bad way, but a not so good way.

Kor, Yasemin: In deciding where we were going to submit our work, *SEJ* definitely seemed to be one of the preferable outlets for us, primarily because of what we were trying to accomplish. In this particular paper, we are trying to bridge two knowledge streams – entrepreneurship research and strategy research – but we also advocate infusing strategy literature with entrepreneurship research; advocating an *ex ante* approach to entrepreneurship and competitive advantage. We wanted our message to be heard by both entrepreneurship scholars and strategy scholars. Being a sister journal of *SMJ* [*Strategic Management Journal*], we believe the *Strategic Entrepreneurship Journal*, is being read by both entrepreneurship and strategy scholars. That was a big plus for us.

Mitchell, Ron: A reason to submit?

Kor, Yasemin: Yes – a reason to submit. Of course, *SEJ* has a world-class editorial team and editorial board, so we knew that if we could get this paper published at *SEJ* that it would have a strong audience and potentially have high impact.

I think the other thing that you brought up . . . a comment that I could make here is that as we were going through the process of the revision (because we are drawing from multiple perspectives, which is a bit of a challenge), we really needed very rich feedback. We had really top-quality feedback both from the editor and the reviewers. We had two reviewers and they were both well versed in both strategy and entrepreneurship research, so they were able to challenge us as well as give us high-quality feedback at both fronts – and that is exactly what we needed. If we got only one or the other, it wasn't going to work very well for us; so I think in that aspect *SEJ* once again worked perfectly for us.

Mitchell, Ron: Before you pick up . . . This idea of the fusion possibilities that is emerging is interesting, because as Jeff just mentioned, there's a fusion of the corporate finance literature and entrepreneurship going on here; once again, an appropriate outlet. Was that part of the targeting decision, and to what extent did you take that into account?

Hitt, Mike: For us too, a lot of these bridging issues across were really important. I guess one specific and more content-focused issue that affected us is more on the strategy side. I think it is fair to say that the strategy folks have largely left the study of IPOs to finance researchers or even entrepreneurship researchers. One of our hopes was to basically get some people excited to do work in this area. The thought was that the IPO isn't merely the natural in-state or marker of success for an entrepreneurial firm (and it is certainly not just a financing event like we might assume), but rather that there are all sorts of extra financial benefits or consequences that might be interesting for strategy folks to think about. One example is that when a firm goes public, all of this information gets produced on the firm that spills over into a variety of other market settings – whether it is the M&A [mergers and acquisitions] market, the product market or what have you. It could have efficiency consequences for those markets and strategy folks who care a lot about that.

Mitchell, Ron: So, Mike, with regard to this literacy fusion idea that seems to be developing, to what extent was that part of your deliberation that went into conceptualizing the journal and how is it rolling out?

Hitt, Mike: Actually it was a major part of it. One of the things you look at (and especially journals, no matter where you are) is that there's a tendency to become more and more narrow over time – partly because there's a lot of research going on in that field and it provides a natural outlet. On the other hand, for a long time there have been some people always looking and saying, 'You've got specialists that keep digging these holes. They dig them larger and larger and they pile their treasures up there, but there's nobody that comes along and gathers all of those treasures and integrates them together.' Seriously, just from the example of these two papers, we believe that there is a need for some journal that could help us do that.

I would like to, in light of this, also say something. I think somebody mentioned in an earlier session that there was concern that strategy is trying to take over entrepreneurship. Did you ever think that there might be an opportunity for entrepreneurship to take over strategy?

Mitchell, Ron: The old reverse acquisition.

Hitt, Mike: Both of these papers are trying to reach an audience, and the journal is there to help do that. It is also beyond that. If you look at the papers that have already been published in our journal, they represent this (which is much broader than even these papers represent). We've got an author sitting up here, Keith Hmieleski, whose work really focused on cognition, for example, and is drawing a lot on psychology literature and OB [organizational behavior] literature, as well as other areas that can be applied. And they're very relevant from an entrepreneurship perspective. I could go on. There's a need to draw on theory from multiple areas and to integrate it. We felt we could provide an outlet that would help do that; and we hope to create an audience across disciplines – not only in strategy and entrepreneurship, by the way, but a much broader audience. We are trying to do that and we believe it is starting to work.

Mitchell, Ron: If there's a takeover agenda underway, what we are trying to do here is have a quality takeover of entrepreneurship research; the idea of 'interdisciplinarity' being okay and of assigning reviewers who actually get both parts of the puzzle. Now these are just two-part combinations, but you were alluding to multi-part combinations. There are so many literatures being brought to bear that are essentially not context, but problem driven. It is research question driven, as Venkat said in his keynote [paraphrasing Sankaran Venkataraman: Chapter 7], 'We need to be asking the research questions and then we look wherever we need to look to get the theory and the methods that actually get to that.'

Elaine, I see that you're ready to come back in with a question.

Mosakowski, Elaine: Well, I'm just a little bit curious, because obviously there has been a lot of quality research done in entrepreneurship before the journal and there will continue to be quality research in entrepreneurship published outside of *SEJ*; but I think this issue of really trying to bring a focus to these diverse multi-level, multi-disciplinary problems around the issue of strategy and entrepreneurship . . . that intersection, and then bringing on the people . . .

You know, Jay Barney talks obviously all the time about resources; bringing these resources to bear to creating this critical mass to get the institution snowballing and our expectations rising, I think, is – as you say – the objective of this conference.

The one thing I do have to comment on . . . And I know I'm not supposed to talk, I'm just supposed to moderate, but I have to comment. I can't help myself.

Mitchell, Ron: That is why we are glad you're here. Go right ahead.

Mosakowski, Elaine: I worried a little bit during the *AMR* [*Academy of Management Review*] session [Chapter 10]. I have to admit that there was something I was uncomfortable with, and this is the controversy. Rich talks about good television, so I'm going to take on some of the comments that were made during the *AMR* session about, 'Well, I worked so much harder on this paper because it was an *AMR*. It was so much more difficult.' I don't think we should be talking like that. We should be internalizing those standards and doing high-quality work regardless of what journal we send it to, and I think I could see that as being one of the implicit missions that *SEJ* has, and that is creating the journal structure and the mentoring relationships. The editors and the reviewers try to bring the whole field up internally; not because I (as a journal editor) have different standards from one journal or another. I think it is more about creating these standards within ourselves.

Mitchell, Ron: I had a colleague comment that, 'The reason why you have great chefs is because you have gourmets.' That is, you have people who know how to appreciate. You were going to ask Mike a question. Maybe I should defer, but how does the reviewer instruction and engagement process between editor and reviewers – and then editor, reviewers and authors – enable the development of both great chefs and gourmets (if we want to just stretch an analogy beyond its useful life)?

Hitt, Mike: Here's what I would say, and I'm going to try to answer that. It is not easy because there are a lot of tacit parts to this, I think. Some people know I cut my teeth learning way back as consulting editor and editor of *AMJ* [*Academy of Management Journal*], so I go way back in that process. I learned a lot during that process, and one of the things I did learn is that one of the critical things that an editor does is to select the reviewers. You're not always correct. It is impossible to be accurate all the time, but it is in the selection of the reviewers not just to get in-depth reviews, which is very important, but the quality, the content and the knowledge they have that they can bring to bear on the question that you have. As you have these integrated papers, it is actually more challenging to find the right kind of reviewers and the ones you need for these kind of papers. The first one is in reviewer assignment. The second then is in interpreting the reviews; and, honestly, I do look at the reviewer recommendations. They are very important. I'm talking about recommendations that reviewers make to the editor apart from the comments that they provide the authors. But I also read their comments very intently and try to draw from that and then integrate the two, and sometimes that means that I may disagree in final form with whatever the reviewer recommended. But the reviewer has only one set of inputs and I have access to multiple sets of inputs, and frankly I also read the paper. But it is not because I think their recommendation is wrong; it is the Gestalt of the input that you have. Then you make a call on that paper and make a judgment as to whether it can have the impact possibly over time with the excellent feedback and the author's changes.

So the editor does have a very important role in it, and I think Mason mentioned, 'You're not a vote-counter.' And that is a very, very good point; you are an integrator and evaluator and you're putting all that information together to make a judgment. You are like a judge, and you're applying a law in some way, but there are a lot of interpretations that go into that. And it's like there isn't a law.

Mitchell, Ron: Well then, from a long-term editor's perspective, to what extent should authors (who are listening out there and who are sitting here all listening) take the associate editors' or action editors' comments as instruction versus those of the reviewers? Or is there a trade-off in actually trying to read between the lines?

Hitt, Mike: I think that we all as authors try to read between the lines, but it is very difficult to do that. I would always put the most weight on the action editor, but you do not ignore the reviewers.

Mitchell, Ron: At your peril you ignore reviewers.

Hitt, Mike: Yes, you're doing it at your peril. I would have to say you have to look at it all. If you're going to weight the comments and suggestions, yes, weight the action editor's suggestions (particularly if there's some integration in there or in some way there's a disagreement with a particular reviewer). I'm going to go with the person who's going to make the decision. In general, you're going to have to take into account all of them. You do it at your peril to ignore a reviewer, and frankly because that editor is going to pay attention to that reviewer the next time around too (not just on this round); you have to take into account all of that.

Mitchell, Ron: Just as I was starting to speak, Elaine was starting to speak too, and I apologize.

Mosakowski, Elaine: That is okay. Given the new journal and the fairly open topic on which it is focused, do you feel that as an editor and as authors both that you can take more risk and be more controversial? I know that Yasemin, for example, went up against some pretty standard ideas and strategies and said, 'No, let's take a different perspective.' Jeff was really going up against corporate finance. I would see both your papers as fairly controversial. I don't know if you felt like this was a place to do it.

Mitchell, Ron: As you prepare your answers, we are now in the Q&A time that we've blocked out, so feel free to engage the audience as you answer. What do you think?

Reuer, Jeff: One thought that relates to the previous discussion is that in our case, we had one reviewer who clearly wanted us to link into many streams of work within management. That was really helpful to us, but also might have created a situation where we weren't being consistent with some of the theories we were drawing upon. Whereas the other person was really pushing us to make the paper (frankly) to be more of a finance paper and had a lot of great econometric suggestions. I think one of the things that was helpful to us is that in the comments we received from the editors, we got some guidance on how to think about some of those trade-offs, but we felt like we were still given permission to stay true to the theory. I think if it was a review process where it was more of a unmediated kind of situation we would have been in this morass and, frankly, would have disappointed both people. And the editors gave it some direction and momentum.

Mitchell, Ron: Yasemin, do you have a comment on this too?

Kor, Yasemin: I think our experience with the *SEJ* is that we have gotten very strong, very high-quality feedback. Mike has been a truly exceptional editor in terms of providing us with this magic map; like an ancient treasure map, really, in terms of how we would . . .

Hitt, Mike: She doesn't mean ancient.

Kor, Yasemin: No. That's meant in a good sense. Actually, telling us all the steps, but also guiding us (because we were going into multiple research streams), also providing us some potential relevant articles, every one of which we read. All the insights come together. It was like magic as things fell together. That was very positive. But I also wanted to bring up the point that there was very strong guidance. It was very illuminating, but there was quite a bit of breathing room in terms of deciding which direction that we wanted to take the paper. One of the most challenging comments we've received actually was that we had these two themes in the paper and neither of them actually was sufficiently developed to merit publication. We had to pick one or the other and then significantly develop it. It was a very difficult choice because one reviewer really liked the one theme and the other one really enjoyed the other theme, so we were going to let one completely down if we picked one. But the good thing is that we were actually given good guidance and feedback on how we could develop either theme. We ended up actually saying, 'Well, we have all the comments; why not actually push it forward?' And of course, having the four co-authors on the paper, I think we weren't willing to let anything go. We were just really fascinated with all the ideas. But I think there was a very good balance in terms of providing the rigor, the discipline and enough room for creativity for the authors (personal creativity and judgment) to flourish; I think that was a very unique experience at *SEJ*.

Mitchell, Ron: Thank you for that. Questions from the audience? Tom, how are we doing on the web? We've got Mike.

Lubatkin, Mike: I would think undoubtedly there's some fuzzy space between *SMJ* and *SEJ* in terms of their missions; I wonder, therefore, from an editor point of view, how much communication is taking place between the two journals? For example, you submit a paper to *SMJ* because your university or college is putting pressure on you to publish in the premier journal. You get it rejected and you don't make any revisions, and you send it right to *SEJ*. Do you sense there's any of that gamesmanship going on, Mike?

Hitt, Mike: The answer is Yes; I'm sure some of it is going on. You have two questions in there. I'll say on the surface there is coordination in some way, because we actually have a journal advisory board that oversees these two journals. There is a discussion of submissions and so on, but there is still a fuzzy space there, and there's no doubt that there are some papers that could probably be published in one journal or the other – and the choice has to be made. Look, I understand that because of some of the pressures that you're likely to go to the one that your dean counts more. On the other hand, if you're looking for a particular type of audience, you're more likely to get a broader audience actually with *SEJ* than with *SMJ* and I say that as an *SMJ* author. I'm not trying in any way to denigrate my sister journal (for which I have a great respect), but I think you have to look at where you want to go; and obviously you have to weigh the reward systems.

Mitchell, Ron: In the spirit of good television, as Elaine suggested, let's ask these authors: Was this the first submission of this paper to *SEJ*, or was it bouncing along?

Kor, Yasemin: For us it was the second place.

Mitchell, Ron: We won't ask you what the first place was, so the next one along. Jeff.

Reuer, Jeff: It was the second journal. The first one was not *SMJ*.

Mitchell, Ron: What we have then is recognition very explicitly that (and I'll just recount a point made in Venkat's keynote [Chapter 7]; when he suggested that you have a research strategy and you have where you're targeting and where it goes next and why) this is an idea that we can now see being enacted. My follow-up question is, was *SEJ* just the next likely hit or was it part of a strategy?

Kor, Yasemin: For us it was definitely a strategy and I answered that question. Actually it was the audience – for us the key question was the audience. We wanted to reach a broader audience in what we wanted to accomplish.

Reuer, Jeff: I would say the same thing. With our previous journal, we experienced more problems on the finance side, but we had this broader message that we wanted to make across a number of papers.

Mitchell, Ron: So even though there's fuzzy space, that fuzzy space might in fact be an asset that is out there that permits flexibility. Many of us have tried this interdisciplinary thing. You get two reviewers that hate it and one that doesn't and then you have to weigh them out. That is another reason why you're moving along a research strategy, sometimes because of – as several of the editors have mentioned – how difficult it is to assign the reviewers. To some extent an editor can go against the reviewers when the editor believes the reviewers are wrong, but it takes a whole lot of energy to prepare to say, 'I'm not going to follow the reviewers.' And so, generally speaking, editors tend to align with the reviews.

Tom, we have some questions from the web, perhaps?

Lumpkin, Tom: We have a pair of questions for Mike. For a junior scholar who is debating the outlets for one's work, should *SEJ's* 'newness' be a concern at all? Secondly, beyond its core themes, does your journal have biases towards certain philosophical theoretical approaches? For example, is it impossible for alternative approaches (such as post-modernist research on entrepreneurship) to get published?

Hitt, Mike: I think they're both good questions. The first one: I have two answers to that and I think the junior scholar has to answer for her or himself where they are and what's important to them. We recognize that we are a new journal. That means we are not in the ranking systems and we are not on the *Financial Times* list – and you can go on. We haven't been there long enough for that to happen. If that is critical to you at this point in time, you would have to consider those things. Now there's another issue I'll bring up, though, and I'm going to be as blunt and direct as I can in this. I tell all my junior colleagues that they really should have a long-term strategy in their career and be careful about trying to target for tenure. I understand tenure and that is important, so I'm not trying to say ignore that. But they need a long-term strategy with the work they are doing and they need to think about that; in the long term when they look back, that is going to be important to them.

I published work in *SMJ* long before it was considered an 'A' journal.

When somebody looks back today they say, 'Well, you have "x" papers in *SMJ.*' They don't go back and say, 'Well, this date is when it became an "A," and we don't count those over here.' They just say you have 'x' number in there (*SMJ*) and they assume it was an 'A' all that time. So you get the credit for it and the accompanying visibility as the journal builds its visibility.

Mitchell, Ron: So there's value in betting early.

Hitt, Mike: That's right, if you're an entrepreneur.

Mitchell, Ron: Now the other point that Yasemin made, which we need to pull back into this discussion, is to remember the choice of audience. It is one thing to get published and then there's another thing to get cited. Long term, it is your impact on the field that matters too. If you're speaking to the right audience, the chance that they will see it, that they will use it and that they will rely upon you actually puts the contribution part of our mission front and center. We do this not just to get tenure; we do this because it helps our colleagues to move forward. Rich.

Dino, Rich: I have a question. It is actually a statement because Mike's too much of a gentleman to say this, but we all know in the world of venture capital where the money goes: the money typically goes not just for a great idea but to a management team that has been successful, that has been there, that has done it and that knows the ropes. If you're considering a journal, particularly an upstart journal, I think everybody in this room would make a bet that *SEJ* will be or is a top-tier journal. Just look at the editorial board. If you're thinking about what kind of journals you want to publish in, look at who is on the editorial board. Look at the quality of that board and what they have done. If you look at *SEJ*, I think there's no question of its future.

Mitchell, Ron: Mike already knows this, but at Texas Tech we made those assessments and we do count *SEJ* along with the top-tier entrepreneurship journals. I think that is one of the encouragements that you would have looking at the editorial board and the kinds of authorship – that you will see the quality of work that is in the journal. As you calculate where you're going to place your bets, you can take that into consideration.

Mike, did you want to take that post-modernist thing on? Sorry for the effect. Go ahead.

Hitt, Mike: I think it is an interesting and important question to ask. What I would say to you is that we definitely would consider that. We don't have certain biases that suggest that certain things are ruled out. We would try to find quality reviewers. What we are looking for is, again, quality research that has potential to make an impact. Methods, approaches and theoretical domains are important only to the extent that they then contribute to that quality and to that potential impact. We would definitely consider that, and I think many of the other journals would probably say the same thing. But we are open and flexible. As I have tried to imply earlier, and if you read our vision statement (and I really would encourage you to go back and read the vision statement in the first issue), I hope you see that flexibility and that openness in what we are trying to do. As you read the very implicit mission, it even fits with Jay's comments during his keynote [Jay B. Barney: Chapter 3]. By the way, one of our co-editors is Jay Barney, sitting right up there. Some of the comments that he made, if you read or you listen to what Ron said, fit very well, actually, with what Jay said in terms of contributing value to society.

Mitchell, Ron: I haven't seen that explicitly in the mission statement before.

We are just about ready to wrap up. We have four or five minutes left. May I change the format just a little bit and ask each of us here who are on the panel to think through, if we have time, and comment on one takeaway from our session. For the folks who are looking at *SEJ*, who are thinking about developing their research craft and targeting this journal, what would be the takeaway? Elaine, may I turn first again to you?

Mosakowski, Elaine: Sure. My takeaway would be that you have to decide if you want to be an academic entrepreneur. If you do, then doing some of these things (perhaps taking more risks, betting early, going to a journal that has more diverse reviewers and editors and that is open to this fusion idea of bringing ideas from other theoretical perspectives into the strategic entrepreneurship area) is a great option for you. Not everybody should be an entrepreneur, and this is some of the more practical career advice issues. Entrepreneurship scholars study this idea of analogical reasoning. Denis Grégoire did this in his dissertation and has continued to do work on this. That is the idea of taking ideas from another field and bringing them to see something that you've been looking at and looking at and looking at – and suddenly seeing it in new light. Well, this kind of journal mission and the human capital that has been put together to achieve the mission are perfect, if that is what you want to do, I think.

Mitchell, Ron: Mike, I gave *AMR* the opportunity. If there's one thing you want the potential authors to hear you say, what would it be?

Hitt, Mike: Submit your work to *SEJ*. Hopefully you've gotten a feel from the authors, one of our editorial review board members here, and the comments that we've made, for the type of journal that we are, that we hope to be, and we expect to be over time. We are not trying to replace others, by the way. You're going to see in my keynote session, that all of these journals here that are represented are excellent journals (and I have published in several of them). I feel very strongly that they all have an important role. We are not trying to take the place of them. I realize there's some competitiveness across journals for quality work. We are competing, obviously, with all of them in some way, shape or form. On the other hand, I think we have a niche and a mission that allows us to have some flexibility – to take some risks. Frankly, I always believed that, even over at *AMJ* (although even when I did it, it had a long history before I took it on). But taking some risk is the way that you obtain, in a sense, the Nobel Prize articles. If you listen to every Nobel Prize winner, they'll talk to you about the problem of having their ideas accepted and why. Because they were so unique, new and valuable, it is hard trying to get others to accept it. All I can tell you is that we are very open and we desire that kind of work at *SEJ*.

Mitchell, Ron: Thank you, Mike. Parting comment in the last few seconds?

Kor, Yasemin: Just a quick comment. I really view the publication process as a co-creative act, so to speak, just like in entrepreneurship teams. I really think that, yes, the authors are the original creators, I guess; but I think it is a very important role the reviewers and especially the editors play. For us, what worked was to engage in a positive dialogue, to be receptive, listen to the comments and really consider their feedback, but it also really helped to have an editor and the reviewers really understand and appreciate our points of view. It is coming together both ways as a co-creative team act.

Mitchell, Ron: Thank you, Yasemin. Jeff?

Reuer, Jeff: I think some of the discussion in this session and earlier in the Conference were more about the newness of entrepreneurship. But I think this panel is more about the cross-disciplinary aspect, which is different; and I think for people starting their careers, it is not that you have to make a zero-one choice of 'I'm going to do cross-disciplinary work or not.' But I think you might want to think about experimenting with your second dissertation. You don't have to jump in with both feet into this riskier area. I think that is maybe where some projects that are really the most fun can be found; where the toughest ones might be.

Mitchell, Ron: Last words worth remembering. Thank you, everyone – we appreciate the contributions of the panel.

REFERENCES

Chaddad, F.R. and J.J. Reuer (2009). Investment dynamics and financial constraints in IPO firms. *Strategic Entrepreneurship Journal*, **3** (1), 29–45.

Foss, N.J., P.G. Klein, Y.Y. Kor and J.T. Mahoney (2008). Entrepreneurship, subjectivism, and the resource-based view: toward a new synthesis. *Strategic Entrepreneurship Journal*, **2** (1), 73–94.

Grégoire, D. (2005). *Opportunity Acknowledgement as a Cognitive Process of Pattern Recognition and Structural Alignment*. Boulder, CO: University of Colorado.

Penrose, E.G. (1959). *The Theory of the Growth of the Firm*. New York: Wiley.

18. Strategic Management Journal

Associate editor: *Joseph T. Mahoney*
Authors: *Elaine Mosakowski,*
  Anne Parmigiani
Moderators: *Ronald K. Mitchell, Dimo Dimov*
Comments editor: *G. Thomas Lumpkin*

Mitchell, Ron: Welcome to the *Strategic Management Journal* (*SMJ*) editor/author session. We are very grateful that you have joined us out there on the web as well as here in the studio. My name is Ron Mitchell. I am currently serving as chair of the Entrepreneurship Division of The Academy of Management. With me is chair of the Business Policy and Strategy Division and also the associate editor representing the *Strategic Management Journal*, Joe Mahoney. Dimo Dimov is my co-moderator today. Thank you very much, Dimo, for joining us.

Elaine Mosakowski is co-author of 'Do VCs matter? The importance of owners on performance variance in start-up firms;' and Anne Parmigiani is with us representing 'Complementarity, capabilities and the boundaries of the firm: The impact of within-firm and inter-firm expertise on concurrence sourcing of complementary components.'

Now, before we turn to the authors to get their quick flyby of the papers, I have looked at the *SMJ* mission statement, and one of the things that I drew out of it was an opportunity that is identified for those who wish to submit to *SMJ*: this journal is explicitly targeting entrepreneurial research. That is to say, there is a quote within the mission statement that says *SMJ* publishes 'Such major topics as: Strategic resource allocation, organization structure, leadership, entrepreneurship and organizational purpose.' Joe, am I doing this justice or does it need a tweak or two?

Mahoney, Joe: Oh, that is fine. I think if you look at the Entrepreneurship Research Statement, it also emphasizes connecting management theory and practice. It is actually mentioned twice in a very short paragraph. I will speak for myself as an associate editor, but I think also the fact that I was selected as associate editor is not random: I think the type of view I have about research is connected to the journal. In particular, what resonates with me is a paper by Jackson Nickerson and Todd Zenger that was published in 2004 in *Organization Science*. It is a paper on the problem-formulation view of strategy in which they argue that one way to think of a unit of analysis is the problem. So it is having a design approach to solving a real-world problem.

The other important thing I would emphasize is that *SMJ* is not a practice/theory dichotomy whatsoever. I can think of an exemplar in strategy research that many here might not have thought of, and that would be Oliver Williamson. When he was starting with a problem, he was working at the Anti-Trust Division around 1966. Richard Posner, a judge on the US Court of Appeals, wrote a decision on the Schwinn bicycle case, and at that time it was a structured performance (Schwinn was monopolizing the vertical supply chain and so forth). Williamson said that that is not what was going on there. So by 1971, there was actually a paper in the *American Economic Review* called 'The vertical integration of production: market failure considerations.' In that five-year period, my advisor was Elmer N. Phillips of the Economics Department at the University of Pennsylvania, and he said to me many times that, 'Williamson's theory is derived from practice.' He saw the situation through the Nickerson and Zenger approach – as a real-world problem.

Theory is a reconstructed logic of the world of experience, and the world of experience is having a lot of problems. What is needed by the new generation of scholars is not necessarily going back to the reconstructed logics that are in the literature; they may be helpful, but they may not be at all. What is needed is the next generation of young people coming up with new reconstructed logics that actually solve real-world problems, of which we have plenty to go around. I think that notion is the spirit of the *Strategic Management Journal*, and its founder, Dan Schendel. By the way, the history of the business policy and strategy field is the 'do in' – as a matter of fact, my wife is in the audience and she is a Professor of Education and a John Dewey scholar. I know for a fact that business policy and strategy from Harvard (going back to the early 1900s) was based on pragmatic philosophy. I was very pleased that Venkat talked about the importance of usefulness in his keynote [Sankaran Venkataraman: Chapter 7] – that is the heritage of the strategy field.

Mitchell, Ron: Thanks, Joe. We have the concept of the mission as well as its broader interpretation on the table as we begin our discussion. Let's turn to you first, Elaine, for the quick flyby.

Mosakowski, Elaine: This paper is co-authored with Markus Fitza (a doctoral student at the University of Colorado, who is going into the job market this fall), and a former colleague of mine from the University of Colorado, Sharon Matusik (who just received her tenure a week or two ago). The paper is called: 'Do VCs matter?' We specifically used that title because we are following in a research tradition of asking if firms matter and if industry matters, which is a major discussion in the strategy literature. We are really trying to understand which levels of analysis have the most influence on firm performance. The main debate actually has been between industry and firm. Looking at Michael Porter's work on the industrial environment (and then the resource-based view and other explanations), he is really saying that the explanation of variance in performance is at the firm level. There is a natural other level of analysis – the corporation – and there is this long tradition of research on diversification and strategy research, which also included the corporate effect.

It turns out that in these studies, the most surprising findings have been that the corporate effect doesn't really matter that much. We were interested in looking at the relationship between owners and 'ownees' – entities which are owned. But rather than looking at it in the large corporate context, we looked at it in the context of venture capitalists owning portfolio companies or start-ups in which they invest. That is the general framing of the problem. Theoretically, we were really challenged in this paper to ask: 'How might this ownership relationship vary in this context versus the large corporate context?' A lot of the paper was very empirically oriented, discussing the percentage of variation in start-up company performance (only start-ups that have VC owners) explained by the identity of who their VC owners are.

Mitchell, Ron: You broke that owner effect into two components: a selection (which impacts investment) and management (which impacts performance).

Mosakowski, Elaine: Exactly. With the history of variance decomposition tradition going way back and all the subsequent work trying to understand what causes it, it is generally atheoretical. Sometimes there is a little bit of a discussion at the end, asking, 'Is this consistent with the resource-based view?' But you can't draw those lines, so we tried to unpack the relationship between the owner and the entity to try to ask, 'What might be going on in that ownership relationship? Is it because good VCs are better at choosing better start-up companies? That would be selection. Or is it because good VCs are better at influencing or managing their portfolio companies to subsequently perform better?'

Mitchell, Ron: Thanks a million. Okay, Anne, next flyby.

Parmigiani, Anne: Thank you, Ron. Now the next flyby. This paper was co-written with Will Mitchell, who was my dissertation co-chair when I was at Michigan. I have a visual aid here because I think it is easier to describe what my paper is visually than to try to do it any other way – especially the title.

Mitchell, Ron: Can we tighten the camera in on the visual aid?

Parmigiani, Anne: I do firm boundary studies. If thinking of this as firm boundary, you may think of it in terms . . . that we'll just say inside and outside the firm. There are certain things firms do inside or outside the firm.

Mitchell, Ron: I love that. Thank you. I am glad you are doing that.

Parmigiani, Anne: Yes. This is Figure 1 in the paper; a real figure. You can do things inside or outside the firm; but what Williamson, in particular, and some other scholars didn't think about is the fact that you can do both. The old tapered integration literature, going back to Harrigan (and before that Adelman), as well as some other folks recognized the fact that you can do both, which is what I talk about in my dissertation, and in this paper we take this discussion a step further. You produce a product both internally and externally, and lots of products have interdependencies and complementarities (which is the classic economics word for them). So in some way, shape or form, these two goods are interconnected somehow. You can't unpack those.

So what you then might suggest is 'for these things that are hard to unpack, traditional vertical integration literature would say you need to do them both internally.' There is something about the way these two things interact. You are doing them both internally and that will work better. More recently, the modularity literature (which some of you are very familiar with) would say, 'If you could somehow black box these things, you can do them both outside the firm, and that can work just fine too.' But what I found in my data and in looking at this is: 'Wait a second – you can do both.' You can both make (internal to the firm) as well as buy (external to the firm) the set of complementary components. When you would do that, why you would do that, and how you would do that are interesting questions; what we have found is that the answers have a lot to do with expertise. Given the complementarities, synergies happen when you are trying to acquire the needed expertise. Even more significantly, the firm itself has to really understand both these products and how they interact in order to be able to make this work effectively.

Mitchell, Ron: Would you term this 'concurrent sourcing'?

Parmigiani, Anne: This is concurrent sourcing here and this is concurrent sourcing of complementary components. I started out with 'When and why do firms make and buy' in my dissertation (which, now that I have a three-year-old, sounds like a really good Dr. Seuss book), but it didn't really work as a scholarly title. So that is the long title.

Mitchell, Ron: Thank you, Anne. What we are seeing here is that you are contributing to innovation technology literature by examining this concurrent complementary sourcing idea through looking at the scope of economics that are influencing innovation. Is that where we are?

Parmigiani, Anne: What is interesting – and this is a true confession – is that I am not necessarily an entrepreneurship scholar. I am really more of a strategy scholar. What is interesting about this paper is that it speaks to entrepreneurship in that firms have to decide where they are going to do what. That is obviously an issue for all firms, but maybe even more strongly an issue for smaller firms. My dataset is comprised of small manufacturing firms: I looked at firms that employ about 75 people and make powder metal and metal stamped parts. These are not big, big multinational companies; these are small firms that I have looked at, so that is another way that I am in the entrepreneurship zone (at least to some degree).

Mitchell, Ron: Sure. Thanks. Dimo, let's bring you into the conversation. You have looked at these papers. You obviously understand this journal well. What is your take? What questions might you have for the panel here?

Dimov, Dimo: My immediate reaction after reading the papers was that I was struck with how different they were. Where I come from, they say that in communication, when you don't understand something, it is your fault. Other people say when you don't understand something, it is someone else's fault; and I thought, 'If this is my fault, it must be something deeper.' I will throw this to Joe maybe quickly to outline what is common between these two papers that maybe will provide some stepping stones for people that are looking at *SMJ* as a journal.

Mitchell, Ron: Because, as you know, the editors actually had the opportunity to choose the papers that would be discussed today in the exemplar setting. Right on, Dimo. Joe?

Mahoney, Joe: Well, first of all, the venture capital paper by Elaine, I think was a clear choice for this conference (also since my dissertation was on transactions costs). Additionally, choosing Elaine would minimize transportation costs. That was quite secondary.

Mosakowski, Elaine: You better say that.

Parmigiani, Anne: Here there are social transaction costs that you just increased.

Mahoney, Joe: Actually with Anne's, it may be a little bit unobvious. First of all, my dissertation was on vertical integration. I read 1,000 papers on the subject and I plan on writing a paper someday on what reading 1,000 papers on vertical integration does to a man. But, I would say that I know the literature really well, and I know for a fact that Anne is also extremely well read. When I read her paper, I said, 'She's actually writing something new that I didn't know.' But then the other aspect about vertical integration is that vertical integration is really, in some ways, entrepreneurial experimentation. Entrepreneurs and small firms that Anne studied are basically creative. As a matter of fact, I was very struck by Chester Barnard, who said, 'Coordination is a creative act,' (that is in his 38th book on *The Functions of the Executive*). In many ways, these small business managers are trying to come up with very creative ways of having better value chains. In that sense (and I think in a non-obvious way), besides the fact that they are small firms, I think in some fundamental ways these are entrepreneurs – although they may not think of themselves that way.

Young scholars should notice some common element in the two papers What is very striking is on the second page in Elaine's paper, she lists what she regards as her three contributions to the literature; on the third page of Anne Parmigiani's paper, she lists what she regards as her three contributions to the vertical integration literature. As an editor, I can assure you that, if these were not new contributions, the reviewers – who also are the very first people serving as knowledge experts – would say, 'No, this was done in 1975 by so and so.' You are going to have knowledgeable reviewers; thus, when you state what you think your contributions are, if they aren't new contributions, you will get called on it pretty quickly.

The other aspect that I really liked about both papers is that they are very forthcoming in limitations. I am very struck by the idea that 'The one who knows that he does not know, knows.' As a matter of fact, I think that is the hallmark of the great scholar – the great scholar knows better than anyone the limitations of what we can know. I very much appreciate authors who are forthcoming, and both of these authors are. In particular, I really think all the students out there listening should have a section where you have specification problems. In other words, be very forthcoming and let us know: 'Here is an omitted variable; I wish I had data for it, I don't; measurement problems; here are all the things I measured; here is the one I regard as the weakest measure; there are metric identification problems; can you come up with another story consistent with the data; there are going to be endogeneity problems.' And, yes, it is all of these things.

Another thing I found was that both scholars were very forthcoming about the limitations of their work. In that sense, I think they are exemplars for young scholars to follow.

Mitchell, Ron: To follow up on that, Joe. If we characterize the entrepreneurship orchard as having many trees with a lot of low hanging fruit, many of us over the years have gone through and picked some theory – either theory 'x,' theory 'y,' theory 'z' – and we think we have picked the low hanging fruit. At some point in time the field changes; there is a sea change and people start looking at the tree itself and ask 'Is this fruit the sweetest fruit we could have? What's its size looking like, etc.?'

Why am I stretching this metaphor? I am stretching the metaphor because, as we heard Joe just say, the element that the *Strategic Management Journal* can help us introduce into the entrepreneurship research conversation is the abandonment of the low hanging fruit strategy and the beginning of the refining. We need to be willing to accept refinement pieces in the same way that the strategy research literature accepts refinement pieces. Joe gave us those two: contributions and limitations. You have to be pretty darn refined to be able to do that right up front and not be wrong (and in the end, not scuttle your paper). You really are going into refinement mode.

Now, given that set-up, authors, how is it that you engaged *SMJ* and the reviewers such that you actually went through the refinement of your own research? What were the comments that were helpful and (I don't want to say hurtful, but) problematic? Do you mind taking that first, Elaine?

Mosakowski, Elaine: No, not at all. I think if I understand your refinement versus low hanging fruit metaphor, I don't see the low hanging fruit strategy, because it almost implies that there are topics, questions, phenomena – whatever – that haven't been studied by others. It just seems to me that if one reads broadly, somebody has always talked about something and somebody has always studied something. Without acknowledging that, I think you are not a good intellectual and a good scholar. I would say if one is willing to put in the legwork (and Joe does it better than anybody I know – reading thousands of papers on a topic), then you necessarily get into refinement mode and then it allows for you to be reflective about your contributions to an ongoing conversation, and what you are not able to say? Putting my reviewer hat on, one of the most frustrating things is when somebody over-promises something up front and then they don't deliver. And so saying 'Okay, this is what I did well and this is what I didn't do well,' is (to me) part of formulating the problem that I am addressing.

Mitchell, Ron: What did your reviewers have to say about this?

Mosakowski, Elaine: 'Well, okay. Great.' This was an incredibly frustrating paper (for me personally) because we were jumping in on the conversation within strategic management about ownership and how important it is in terms of explaining performance; but that literature has generally not been very theoretically driven. What does it mean to say that a corporate identity explains 20 percent of variation in firm performance (versus 40 percent)? There is really no theoretical explanation for that unless you find 0 percent or 100 percent. Everything else matters somewhat. What the reviewers had to say (they really pushed us, and we tried to address it in a genuine way and think about if we could look at characteristics of these performance and the time periods) is that they really wanted us to ask, 'Why? Why does ownership matter? How can you contribute back to our understanding of the role that an owner or a corporate parent or a venture capitalist plays in the performance of entities at the lower level of analysis?' That was really frustrating because we couldn't (with data limitations as well as just the technique we were using) give them a good answer. We could just give clues.

Mitchell, Ron: How did you respond to that? What was the frustration meter looking like?

Mosakowski, Elaine: It was pretty high. It was really pretty high. And this was an atypical paper for me too; so I think, given my individual difference, it made me even more frustrated because, typically, I am more interested in testing theory – and this wasn't that. Anne raised the point (which I had forgotten about in our paper) that we don't have hypotheses in there. So, sometimes they were pushing us to deal with hypotheses.

What was really important is that Will Mitchell was the editor on this paper, and he helped us navigate these issues. He said, 'You want to address the theoretical questions, but on the other hand, let's not over-promise that you can suddenly solve a dilemma of what owners are really doing.' Obviously, there is heterogeneity across owners, but it created some really interesting discussions. Given there were level differences in the co-author team, I sometimes feel sorry for our doctoral student (poor Markus Fitza), because he would say, 'Tell me what to do. What do you want me to do?' It was not so clear, and we had to go through a couple of rounds of this to determine where that balance would lay.

Mitchell, Ron: Thank you. Speaking of the rounds, you went the rounds with the reviewers with your paper (obviously), and of course, Will is an editor; and yet you still had to pay the same price that everyone else did.

Parmigiani, Anne: I have several stories on another paper (that I could talk about offline) about how we have gone through it. Sometimes when you co-author with someone who is well known, and especially if they are plugged into a journal, I think people sometimes are more circumspect.

Mitchell, Ron: That's right. The teacher's kids have to behave better.

Parmigiani, Anne: Yes. At the end of the day, it ends up being wonderful – but sometimes the process is interesting.

Mitchell, Ron: Your interaction with your reviewers ended up being . . .?

Parmigiani, Anne: I want to push back a little bit on your point about refinement, because I am not sure that what my work reflects is necessarily a theoretical refinement: that would assume that the theory already talked about it and had gotten far with it, and I am taking it just to that next little level.

Mitchell, Ron: Like it was missing.

Parmigiani, Anne: I look at it more as theories sometimes have blinders, so certain theories only talk about certain levels. Certain theories only talk about, maybe, dyads instead of a broader view and so forth. We all, who know our theories, know that that's the case.

Mitchell, Ron: Anne, let me push back on the push back. The question that I am asking is a process question. It has to do with the refinement of the way that you approach the crafting process, as opposed to where the theory is, at any given time, in its development. To be clear (because that is one of the things that is a hallmark of *SMJ* is that you have got to get it done really, really, really well), the refinement that I am suggesting – rather than let's grab theory 'x,' go out there, address something nobody's ever looked at and slam it in – rather than do that, you have to begin to very, very carefully craft a design. It is a process.

Parmigiani, Anne: What we tried to do with that process is to really carefully talk about why firms would do things internally or externally – then go into the combination of that. The blinders I am suggesting is that this phenomenon (or problem) hadn't really been talked about; we needed to talk about it. In fact, some of the reviewers really pushed back and said, 'number one, we don't think this exists.' So Will ended up doing a survey of his executive class asking, 'Does it exist?' And they said, 'Yes, it does.' We said, 'Thank you. Yes it does. And, by the way, have you been to McDonald's?' Because franchising is making and buying. I have small manufacturing firms while you have service firms. It's high tech, it's low tech – we have several papers. It is like, 'Sorry, yes it does.' Then the push back was, 'Isn't this the same as your other paper?' I said, 'Um, no. It is two interconnected goods, not just one good.' It got to the point where the editor had to say (we were in the second round), 'Okay, but I have some issues about your contribution. Can you nominate other people to look at this paper to say that you really do have a contribution? And oh, by the way, I might not use those people, but give me a list of some that I can pick from.'

Mitchell, Ron: In the spirit of 'everybody's smart people and yet the reviewer doesn't get it,' that is a tough thing. You are making the distinction, and the reviewer is not seeing it. Is the solution more people on the problem?

Parmigiani, Anne: Well, I think part of it is this blinder issue. We are used to looking at theories and situations and companies and contacts and so forth in one way; we don't realize that if you take off the blinders, there is a lot of other stuff out there. It is a messy world out there. Will talked about this (and some of you may know this story), but he talks about some journals that are more interested in the theory and the theoretical tension, and building up what he calls a 'red state approach.' *AMJ* [*Academy of Management Journal*] is like that, and a lot of other journals are like that. *SMJ* is more willing to consider the problem or the phenomenon. Although you need to have the same stuff in the paper, the framing can be different. This reviewer, I think, was really pushing back on the theory and wondering if it really exists. We really had to try hard to say, 'Yes, it does. We have a contribution. Here are some data and also here is some of the background stuff to really make you believe it.' But there were definitely some tense moments in that process.

Mitchell, Ron: Believe it or not, we are already to the question period. John, could you do the first question?

Mathieu, John: I got mine just because this is that plan that Ron and I did.

Mitchell, Ron: Thanks for admitting that to the worldwide audience.

Mathieu, John: I don't want to be too heavy handed, but we wanted to get to this, not only with the *SMJ* group, but as a general question. That is, when I look at the datasets, one of the things that we have been hearing about during the conference is the really important and influential kinds of datasets. Some of these that are being used in the entrepreneurial arena are publicly available ones that people have downloaded and managed and so forth. Others are uniquely constructed ones that are very labor intensive and that give somebody a real leg-up. My question is: how do you navigate (and this is both for authors and editors) multiple uses of data? If it has taken you two years to put together a dataset, journals are very reluctant to have somebody overuse a dataset. On the other hand, there are often-times many different questions that can be addressed using the same data. So if I can just toss that out there . . .

Mitchell, Ron: Who would like to take it first?

Mosakowski, Elaine: I will take it.

Mitchell, Ron: Elaine. Please . . .

Mosakowski, Elaine: A great question. Two things influence me. First of all, I get bored with datasets quickly, so I don't have a natural tendency to use them. If anything, I have a natural tendency to under use datasets. The second thing is (given my training) I follow more the econometric stand-ard, if you want to call it that. Basically, from any project I am working on, I will only publish one paper on a dependent variable, because of the considerations or concerns with model misspecification. This happens in the strategy field and I have seen papers at *SMJ* where you'll have these independent variables influencing a dependent variable; and then the same author takes from the same dataset additional independent variables and influences the same dependent variable, but won't include the original ones. They know they have a misspecified model, because they know that those influence that dependent variable; yet here they are not including them. Therefore, the way I have incorporated that in my career is basically one paper per dependent variable.

The other thing is with a lot of these publicly available datasets, the advantage you tend to have is the population, and so there is a little less concern about sampling. In OB [organization behavior], it is an issue of 'If I have a really bizarre sample that might be driving these results, then all these results are appearing on similar topics.' Here when you have the population; you don't worry so much about representation.

Mitchell, Ron: Dataset management.

Mahoney, Joe: I would also say for young people listening worldwide, thinking about doing their dissertations, one of our students who was very effective at using datasets is Juran Lee, who is at National Taiwan University and the National Science Council. But Juran (when he was doing his dissertation at Illinois) was guided by Ming Shutang (from MIT and was also at National Taiwan University) in his research design, and collected all of the data for multi-national companies, which got Juran thinking about different types of questions and different dependent variables. As a matter of fact, I think it is a good research design for a doctoral student to think about (in advance) ways in which they can collect the data, think about multiple questions and then leverage it. It is a little bit more usual in the strategy field. Economics typically has a three-essay approach for a lot of doctoral students. Juran's was a three-essay approach, and he designed his dissertation in advance to leverage three very good papers off the dataset. In some ways, I actually look at that as a positive thing.

Mitchell, Ron: Elaine is saying that she gets bored with the dataset, and does only one dependent variable per paper. Doesn't that mean there aren't several dependent variables in a dataset?

Mahoney, Joe: Correct. That's right.

Mitchell, Ron: So we do have a rich field. Anne's coming in on this?

Parmigiani, Anne: I just wanted to mention too that as a doctoral student, you absolutely want to do a dissertation that has lots of data in it because the idea is that you want to use that for more than one paper. I do survey work and you only have one shot – you want to get as much data as possible. Hopefully you'll get multiple dependent variables and hopefully you'll get multiple observations of different things – that is what you'll use. I think Joe's point is that as long as you are upfront about that, and say, 'This connects to this other paper and also here in my appendix. Here is all the stuff I have used. Here are all my items . . .' and so forth (and I think that is another hallmark of *SMJ*). That kind of transparency is very much rewarded. If you don't give them your survey items, they are going to ask for them.

Mitchell, Ron: So, Dimo from your perspective . . . Multiple dataset management, constructing sets for dissertations – what is your take on those and advice to the audience?

Dimov, Dimo: I can comment on the venture capital datasets, specifically. VentureXpert is publically available venture data. I see the use of that. It is equivalent to using CompuStat and a lot of the traditional strategy. This is a public source, so it is okay to have a lot of papers from that dataset. From my experience, it has taken me about five years to get deep into the dataset and to go beyond just seeing items and say, 'I have no idea what to use this for.' It has taken me a few years to start constructing measures that I think actually reflect some theoretical constructs. After so much time invested into that dataset, it almost becomes a capability. It can be used across a range of things.

Mitchell, Ron: Thank you. Maw-Der has the microphone next.

Foo, Maw-Der: I have a question relating to Anne's comment about reviewer blinders. Blinders can cut two ways; on one hand it makes it difficult for the reviewers to see your contribution, but if you cut the blinders you just might help them see that your research is making a contribution. My question is: how do you cut the blinders?

Parmigiani, Anne: Carefully. Part of it is going back to fundamental theory. You go back to that fundamental theory, and you show them very carefully how this thing that you are looking at has never really been talked about before. It helps if you can empirically show them as well. I think it is a one-two punch of, 'Here is the theory, here is the obvious gap that nobody has really talked about. You may think they have, but you know when you actually go out and look there is not really that much there.'

Mitchell, Ron: Thank you. We have a question from the web, Tom?

Lumpkin, Tom: Yes, along the same lines. Given the conversation about finding reviewers, say more about managing the quality of *SMJ* reviewers. How would someone (who would like to review more or get on an editorial board) go about being a quality reviewer?

Mitchell, Ron: Joe, it is an important question.

Mahoney, Joe: First of all, I think that *SMJ* is blessed. On both sides of the cover, there are reviewers. I think we have added about 70 reviewers recently. I would say for anyone interested in starting that review process, write Will Mitchell, Joe Mahoney, Rich Bettis or Ed Zajac and say that you are interested in being a reviewer. Tell us what your subject area is and send us your information. We are always in need of quality reviews. I would also say that, in general, I tend to pick a lot of people on the editorial board. I have only been at this a year now, so I haven't had too many occasions where I have actually had to mentor people in the review process itself since they are already seasoned reviewers. That is something I think I will bring back from today's session – to talk with other folks about thinking more self-consciously and mentoring the process of reviewers for younger reviewers. We do that, I hesitate to say, on an ad hoc basis with our ad hoc reviewers. But maybe we should do so more systemically in thinking about the coaching. Mostly, we think about the coaching process for authors, but there is something to be said from this question in pointing out a gap – that there also could be a coaching process for the reviewers when they first begin.

Mitchell, Ron: It recalls the comment that you really can't get great chefs until you have gourmets. The building of the reviewer pool in almost every discipline is something that is a big issue. Yasemin, I did see your hand up? I think we have time for one more question from the floor before we go into wrap-up.

Kor, Yasemin: I have a general question. If you have a burning desire to do research on a topic that is very new and not very well known, and there is not much research on it (or the opposite being that it is researched to death, the area is declining or is very mature), is that a high-risk proposition? And if you still want to do it, what are some ways to go about it?

Mitchell, Ron: Joe, would you start for us?

Mahoney, Joe: I think for everyone developing their research, there is a difference between the process of discovery and the science of justification. If one is very creative (and if that is your strength), doing work on the process of discovery is right for you. On the other hand, suppose you started in an economics program and you shifted over to strategy (just as an example): you are very strong in econometric skills; you may have all kinds of econometric skills that can tease out and discriminate things within the conversation of diversification that have been going on for years. You may actually be able to provide something new and a contribution to an area that otherwise seems very mature. I would just say that is true for every doctoral student. I have had 50 students.

Mitchell, Ron: Congratulations.

Mahoney, Joe: Thank you. It is a real joy to have them on the committees; but for every single student, I think the right approach depends on the student. Then the other thing I would say about theory and practice is that if I have a student that has had ten years' work experience, then we start from the experience and we work to the theory. If I have someone coming right out from undergraduate, we start from reading the theory and then we move to experience. My final message is that Vygotsky had a 'Theory of Learning' and (to summarize), the theory noted that you need to start from where the person is. I would say there is not a cookie-cutter answer to your question. For each person, you have to start from where you are.

Mitchell, Ron: Thanks, Joe. Dimo, just a few minutes if you would, and then I am going to ask the open-ended questions about publishing in *SMJ* – the 'one piece of advice' question. What are your thoughts?

Dimov, Dimo: I will go for some general reflections and relate to what was said, so maybe this will be a different way of looking at this. I see a commonality between the two papers in that they use contexts that are on the surface entrepreneurship; one is small firms, the other one is VC firms – and yet at the same time, they address traditional core strategy questions, which perhaps is part of the fit with the journal. They also open up blinders in the sense that in these new contexts, they show that things work differently or that the way we understand them is a little different. That creates the extension between theory and context; that would speak to some of the difficulties in the review process in that if you take a new context – you want to show how an accepted or traditional theory works differently. You run the risk of the reviewers attacking your context to show you how the problems with the context would actually explain why that theory doesn't work as cleanly there. The craft (and it would take more careful reading of the introduction to those papers) is how to introduce that paper to the journal and to the editor so that the review process gets focused more on the theory rather than on maybe some of the challenges with the context. On that note, I admire Elaine's paper for having gone through. I recently had a paper rejected at *SMJ* where the paper was clubbed. It was bloodied by the problems in explaining VC performance, from the point of view of all these things I could consider that were not considered so legitimate. There is a craft in how you preempt all these things and focus on the others – to pushing the boundaries and opening the blinders – but also being conscious of how to direct the attention away from some of what could be perceived as problems with the context.

Mitchell, Ron: I think clubbed and bloodied means that this session is at least PG-13. Joe, if there is one thing you would recommend in successfully working with *SMJ*, what would it be?

Mahoney, Joe: I will give two answers. One in general (which you have probably heard many times at this point), but I would also add a little more detail. I would recommend to every author that by the time you send your paper to the journal, know what the literature is and know what your contribution within that literature is. Also state your contribution up front and have a limitations section. I was asked the question, 'What is unique about the *Strategic Management Journal?*' As Dan Shendel was leaving it in our hands for the next generation of scholars (and I totally agree with his perspective), he offered that we must make sure that in our journal we have strategy (meaning that there is a long-term consequence to the decision) and management. Sometimes we say we are professors of strategy. As a matter of fact, I'd much prefer if we said we were professors of strategic management and that would help keep a management perspective in our field.

Mitchell, Ron: How helpful – thank you very much. Elaine and Anne: if there is one thing you would recommend about successfully working with *SMJ*, it would be . . .?

Mosakowski, Elaine: My recommendation wouldn't be specific to *SMJ*, but targeted to if you were writing or talking to a strategy audience. I do find that the way I write and present (especially theoretical ideas) goes back to Dimo's issue of context. If I am making a theoretical argument, I notice a lot of entrepreneurship people will keep the argumentation fairly abstract, whereas in a strategy world you are much more used to talking about the context, examples, company examples and specific situations. We did this a lot in my doctoral seminar. You know, 'Could you give me an example of what you are talking about? How do you know it falls into this box versus that box?' Make it much more pragmatic – more real. I think it also helps you (to go back to Joe's point) to connect to a problem and take things to a much more concrete level. But that doesn't mean you have to stay there; you are going back and forth between the abstract and the concrete, but I think being able to work at both levels of specificity is very useful.

Mitchell, Ron: Thanks, Elaine. Anne, you get the last word.

Parmigiani, Anne: I would say, as far as working with *SMJ*, be proactive and don't be intimidated. You can have conversations with your reviewers. You can push back, as long as you do it in a very informed, very careful and very respectful way. I think editors are very open to that. They are open to the discussion as long as you are prompt and you are nice. The other thing is (and we haven't talked about these people) that there are all these managing editor folks who are out there who physically prompt reviewers to get things back – they really manage the process. Be very nice to these people. You can sabotage a lot of things. Whose paper do you think is going to come first when those reviewers are late? If you are not nice to them, you are going to the bottom of the stack. So, help yourself.

Mitchell, Ron: With these final words – being nice is good strategy. Thank you very much.

REFERENCES

Adelman, M.A. (1949). The large firm and its suppliers. *Review of Economics and Statistics*, **31** (2), 113–18.

Barnard, C. (1938). *The Functions of the Executive.* Cambridge, MA: Harvard University Press.

Fitza, M., S.F. Matusik and E. Mosakowski (2009). Do VCs matter? The importance of owners on performance variance in start-up firms. *Strategic Management Journal*, **30** (4), 387–404.

Harrigan, K.R. (1984). Formulating vertical integration strategies. *Academy of Management Review*, **9** (4), 638–52.

Nickerson, J.A. and T.R. Zenger (2004). A knowledge-based theory of the firm: the problem-solving perspective. *Organization Science*, **15** (6), 617–32.

Parmigiani, A. and W. Mitchell (2009). Complementarity, capabilities, and the boundaries of the firm: the impact of within-firm and interfirm expertise on concurrent sourcing of complementary components. *Strategic Management Journal*, **30** (10), 1065–91.

Williamson, O.E. (1971). The vertical integration of production: market failure considerations. *American Economic Review*, **61** (2), 112–23.

Appendices: conference context

A. Setting the stage

Richard N. Dino, P. Christopher Earley, Ronald K. Mitchell

Dino, Richard: Good evening, and I stand corrected; good morning and good afternoon to everyone who is participating in the 2009 Entrepreneurship Research Exemplars Conference. My name is Rich Dino, and I am executive director of the Connecticut Center for Entrepreneurship and Innovation and on behalf of the (University of Connecticut) School of Business – welcome. We are absolutely delighted that you are here and are participating in the Conference.

I sit in a very interesting position and I was trying to figure out how to convey what I see. I was talking with a colleague today and we concluded that it was a busy intersection; and then we asked, 'What is the busiest intersection in the world?' And most people will say 'Well it must be Grand Central Station.' Well actually it's not. It is a place in Tokyo, Japan, called the Shibuya Station. It is interesting because there is a confluence and an intersection of six roadways, six pedestrian walkways, and one of the busiest train stations in the world. You could actually go out on the Internet and watch this intersection – and it is something else. I was trying to think of how to characterize the world of entrepreneurship, and it pretty much is one of the busiest intersections in the research world. Instead of having six roadways or 12 roadways (including the pedestrian walkways together), there are many, many more. Just thinking about it, if you think about the disciplines that make up entrepreneurship (economics, sociology, organizations, institutions, strategy, psychology, finance, micro, macro, go on and on); it's a very busy intersection. And that is just when you talk about research. You talk about what the outreach centers of entrepreneurship do, helping businesses emerge, helping businesses get closer to market. You think about what we teach in the classroom. It is indeed a very busy intersection.

The role of the Entrepreneurship Research Excellence Initiative of the Academy of Management is to work really hard to harness all that energy, bring it together, bring all those people together and help continue to lift the discipline of entrepreneurship (particularly with this Conference and the Entrepreneurship Research Excellence Initiative); to raise the bar – continually raise the bar for entrepreneurship research. And in essence that is why we are here tonight. We thank you for coming. We thank you worldwide participants. We think we have a really, really interesting weekend in store for you. We look forward to your questions. We look forward to the challenges. We look forward to the interaction. Most of all, we look forward to the outcomes that we will produce together.

With that, ladies and gentlemen, I would like to introduce my boss, the Dean of the University of Connecticut's School of Business, Chris Earley.

Earley, Chris: A bit intimidating where I can globally embarrass the University of Connecticut now. I just wanted to say a couple of things. First of all, I do want to thank each and every one of you for coming to the Conference. I do want to thank the Academy and Ron for co-sponsoring this event.

As Rich said, entrepreneurship is at a very interesting crossroads, where as an area, it is no longer a nascent area. It is now a developed area that has really gained tremendous momentum. It is now intersecting and sprawling into lots of new realms and arenas, and it is an exciting time to the field. This is a field that has such tremendous potential because of its interdisciplinary nature.

At the same time, there are all sorts of challenges: that is how to create a sense of core identity, future directions, future thoughts and visions for the field. And I know that during the course of your conversations you will be having over the next day and a half or two days, that in addition to issues around publishing and creating academic works, I know that these will also be very critical discussions you will be having.

I also think that it is a great time for the University of Connecticut. Like most of you, especially those of you from state universities and public institutions, we are all feeling tremendous pressure because of budget cuts and the economic crisis. We are very fortunate because, among others, Jack Veiga and Rich Dino developed several years ago a very successful proposal that created what is called the Connecticut Center for Entrepreneurship and Innovation (CCEI), and I think you will be learning more about it as the Conference goes on. What it did is [that] it helped us buffer ourselves from the vagaries of the state legislature and the governor, who may or may not have the same vision for the kind of commitment we wanted to make towards higher education in this field. This Center has been a real milestone for the university, and in fact, our strategic vision. We have just completed an academic plan for the business school and one of the three tenets on which it is based is the tenet of experiential learning. And the Connecticut Center for Entrepreneurship and Innovation – one of its elements is called the 'Innovation Accelerator;' and in fact it focuses on the outreach and the impact of academe industry and student learning in a very unique fashion.

The other thing that we are just embarking on at a very early stage that again, Jack Veiga is going to be spearheading for us (along with Lucy Gilson, Rich Dino, Zeki Simsek and a number of others in our school) is the development of a global consortium around innovation and entrepreneurship. That is a very exciting work in progress that I think will have tremendous potential. We are looking at and developing partnerships in Australia, in Asia, the Middle East, Europe, the Americas (broadly defined) and I think it is going to be very exciting. So again, these are kind of new initiatives.

By the way, I am now done with the bragging that a dean has to do at these types of events. But I will say this; it is a very exciting time. I think the School is doing lots of things. I am very proud of our faculty and our staff, but our faculty have really stepped up in a number of ways. As I said, we faced a very big budget crisis in 2009. Faculty stepped up, took up the burden and, in fact, we are coming out of it, I think, stronger than we would have otherwise. So it is a real credit to my colleagues that I see around here, except for perhaps for the department head of Management, who is the brunt of all of our humor; a token psychologist in the room. But one of the things that people who know me will tell you is I like quotes, and I actually pulled off a couple of quotes that I thought would be useful to at least think about with regard to the activities you are going to be engaging in. As you look around the room, we are talking about world leaders, thought leaders in these fields of entrepreneurship innovation broadly defined – and that is a very remarkable thing. And of course if we include our online audience as well we are talking about having a reach that is really quite remarkable and quite significant. So here are a few thoughts. The first quote is actually from Oscar Wilde, who tells us 'The public is wonderfully tolerant. It forgives everything except genius.' Second is 'Imagination without skill gives us modern art. Skill without imagination is craftsmanship and gives us many useful objects, such as wicker baskets.' Then the final one is 'You can't wait for inspiration. You have to go after it with a club.' That one, by the way, is Jack London.

I guess one of the things I'm really hopeful for with this kind of a gathering, as I said, it is not just an opportunity to discuss the craftsmanship of publication; but in fact it is a chance for some very unique wonderful ideas to be generated in this field to set the scene for future discussions, future conferences and future engagements. And I think that what is really remarkable is I think there is the potential for what a colleague of mine many years ago who was at Minnesota would refer to as 'an opportunity for unique inspiration.' I think that is what I'm hopeful that we will see during the next day and a half.

Then I can't resist on this one. If you know this quote, bear with me; but I also do understand that it is attributed to former President George W. Bush. In fact I found out that it actually was never said by him, but it is still nevertheless telling. It is said that Bush, in commenting to a larger audience (Tony Blair among others), in talking about entrepreneurship said, 'The problem with French business is they don't even have a word for entrepreneur.'

Thank you all for coming.

Dino, Richard: Ladies and gentlemen, co-chair of the Entrepreneurship Excellence Research Initiative, co-chair of this Conference, co-chair of the IDEA Awards and chair of the Academy of Management Entrepreneurship Division, Ron Mitchell.

Mitchell, Ronald: Thank you very much, Rich. The thing that gets scholars together is that we love ideas; and one of the duties incumbent upon groups of scholars when we do get together is for someone to somehow articulate the basic philosophy behind why we are gathered. That is my role this evening.

In the Entrepreneurship Division, we have what is called the 'Mid-Winter Meeting.' We have no idea where that term came from, but the executive committee gets together sort of halfway between the Academy Meeting as the year goes on and we think through the things the division needs. If you will, go with me back to January of 2006 to the foyer of a hotel in Atlanta where we were holding the Mid-Winter Meeting, which should have been held in Minneapolis but Shaker Zahra (who was our chair at the time) took pity on us and held it in Atlanta. So Eileen Fisher, Connie Marie Gaglio and I were sitting there thinking about and discussing how it is that entrepreneurship research quality and quantity progresses to the next level. And the metaphor of 'the rising tide raises all ships' was kind of the substance of that discussion. We soon gravitated to the realization that the tide tends to do what it wants, and so we began to wonder how one actually influences a tide such that it will rise and all ships will rise with it. Within that discussion, the idea of the Entrepreneurship Research Excellence Initiative was born.

We discussed the usual suspects – a special issue or three or five, etc., [or] another journal. At a point we said, 'You know, as the Entrepreneurship Division, we are accountable to a group of people who depend upon us to do something that everybody can have access to.' So we started the process of beginning an exemplars-type conversation. We couldn't have done it alone. Those of us who are editors and associate editors, senior editors of the journals; when I approached you about this and you said, 'Yes we will help you,' you laid the next cornerstone for this Entrepreneurship Excellence Initiative.

We then had the opportunity to have the editors expand the circle and invite authors who had recently published in these top-tier outlets; to come and have a conversation that is more revealing than most authors are willing to undertake. Specifically to answer questions like, 'What exactly did it take to do what you did?' Oftentimes as individuals, we tend to hold back on revealing that kind of information.

In this Conference, what we want to do in asking editors and authors to speak candidly with moderator help from myself as well as our University of Connecticut colleagues is to surface process issues for how it is that we get this job of research excellence done. The budget only allows a certain number of editors and authors to get together, but through the miracle of modern technology, we can reach out to the morning, to the afternoon, to the evening around the world. We can record these conversations for all who wish to have access to this kind of understanding of the research craft; and as a result we have an Exemplars Conference.

Now in addition to this Exemplars Conference, the Entrepreneurship Division has also launched the IDEA Awards, and we have had the support of the University of Connecticut, The Ohio State University, SAMS (the Society for the Advancement of Management Studies) and the Academy of Management Entrepreneurship Division (which also put funds behind this initiative), which permits us to award Research Promise, Thought-leader, and Foundational Paper recognition. We presented the first foundational paper award last August at the Academy Annual Meeting in Anaheim, California. And shortly you will hear from the first foundational paper recipient, Professor Venkat Venkataraman.

I note that the Thought-leader Awards are those that publish in the top journals in the prior year. We are in the process of working out a very systematic adjudication process for this award whereby all of those who have published in the Academy journals since 1990 are recognized yearly. We actually have kind of 'wall of fame' idea that may be going up on the Entrepreneurship Division website. But in any event these papers are listed each year in the IDEA Awards Program.

So the purpose of this Research Excellence Initiative, both the Exemplars Conference and the IDEA Awards, is to free up the flow of information about research excellence, as well as recognizing that excellence. We will take the two prongs of motivation that support excellence (information and recognition) in this craft and we will make it possible, through your efforts, your willingness to come, to help and to contribute (and, may we invite those around the world who hearing this process described, to also agree), to commit ourselves to research excellence. We can make a difference.

We are here tonight because there is a group of people who have sacrificed many things to create research excellence in their own careers. We honor you, we thank you, and we greatly appreciate your participation and your willingness to help us to have an influence on 'how high the tide rises.' We also are very thankful and very appreciative to the University of Connecticut, to the Connecticut Center for Entrepreneurship and Innovation for being, so to speak, the anchor sponsor of this great initiative. It is highly likely that this will be at least a two-year initiative. The publication 'process' is the focus for 2009 with journal editors and authors; and this will continue in 2010 as well, but transitioning to threshold ideas, what's new and what's the substance being the core of our 2010 Conference.

So thank you very much to all who have assisted.

This is the philosophy behind this Conference. The momentum is building. We thank you very much for your support, and we look forward to a marvelous conference ahead. Thank you very much.

Dino, Richard: Thank you, Ron. Hi, Sharon. I didn't get to see you. You got in a little late today.

Alvarez, Sharon: In time for the meeting.

Dino, Richard: Yes, you sure did. Good to see you.

You know, for those of you here in Storrs, Connecticut (those of you participating worldwide can't see it), but for those of you here in Storrs I want you to look around the room and look for all the hidden cameras. I want you to look around for the folks, men and women in black suits with dark colored glasses. That's our security detail; and the reason they are here is, I was thinking, 'God forbid should anything happen at this Conference with everybody in the room and the quality of the folks and the quality of the research, what would happen to entrepreneurship research? We are trying to push it forward. What would happen if, God forbid, something happened here?' It's a joke, folks – laugh. It was a good one. My wife told me if I have to explain it, it wasn't a joke. Hopefully she's not watching online.

With that, because of the quality and stature of everyone in the room, if we were to read even a brief bio of everybody who participates we would spend more of our time reading bios than progressing to our objective outcome; so we are going to be pretty simple across the board and we are just going to introduce our speakers and participants very simply by their name.

Chris likes quotes. I like lyrics and songs. Professor Gary Powell (one of our colleagues) is the expert at lyrics and songs and Gary, you'll remember this one. It's a band called The Little River Band from years ago, an Australian group, and they had a song. The lyrics went something like this: 'There are so many paths up the mountain; no one knows all the ways. There are so many paths up the mountain, but the view from the top is still the same.'

B. Building your publishing career

Ronald K. Mitchell

Dino, Richard: Well, good morning everyone. I trust everyone has had a good night's sleep, or were you contemplating all that Venkat said last night and starting to write new research questions? How many were writing new research questions? No one? Oh one, okay that's great. Well for our international audience who were not with us last night, and we added another 50 folks overnight, so we are well over 300 now of international participants on the web. Good morning to everyone.

My name is Rich Dino, as you all know here. I am executive director of the Connecticut Center for Entrepreneurship and Innovation and co-chair of the Research Exemplars Conference with Ron Mitchell, who is chair of the Entrepreneurship Division of the Academy of Management.

I was trying to figure out a way to kick-start this morning differently than last night so I don't repeat myself, and – lo and behold – about quarter of one last night, *ping*, my email went off and there was an email from one of our international participants and then *ping*, *ping*, *ping*. I was just reading a whole bunch of emails. I picked this one out because I think it gets to the essence of what this Conference and what the Academy of Management Entrepreneurship Division's Research Excellence Initiative is about. So if you would bear with me, I would like to read you this email. It's short, but it says it all.

It says 'Hi, Richard. Well, I watched the whole keynote address by Venkat Venkataraman [Chapter 7] and I have to say that for me as a PhD student researching entrepreneurship, it was incredibly valuable. I liken Venkat to one of my professors, who has clearly invested himself in the philosophy and research methodology. He has clearly devoted considerable thought to pushing at the frontiers of our knowledge in a way that garners respect. I was particularly enamored with his development of the critical criteria for publishing in top journals, especially when he discussed the criterion of usefulness, as it took me some time to discover that this perspective would be the rooting of my own philosophical paradigm for research. I could relate to several other points he made, such as answering the "so what" question, and relating our research to the mainstream body of theory. However, I will confess to being somewhat overwhelmed. I would like an opportunity to review his presentation, as I am new to this. Can you tell me if a video or transcript copy of Venkat's presentation will be available on the conference site or in an upcoming journal or Conference proceeding? Looking forward to tomorrow's discussion. P.S., I know several of my colleagues will be watching from across the pond at Strathclyde, Glasgow. Signed: Brad McMaster, the Hunter Center for Entrepreneurship at Strathclyde.'

Well, Brad and everyone else, we will be recording every session so that those sessions will be available for everyone to watch at their convenience anytime from now well on into the future.

So with that we will kick off our Friday. We have a long day today. It should be a very productive day. Please join me in welcoming for his opening address 'Building your publishing career' my co-chair, chair of the Entrepreneurship Division of the Academy of Management, Ron Mitchell.

Mitchell, Ronald: Thank you very much, Rich. Welcome, everyone here in Storrs. Welcome, everyone worldwide. The profession in which we are engaged is a profession that has roots. Well, they are centuries old. The growth of the university was along two paths originally. One was the Bologna model and the other was the Parisian model. Today we tend to be in the Parisian model where the scholars get together and set the standards and then students attend and seek to meet these standards. The Bologna model is somewhat different. It was, I think, Sir Isaac Newton who actually lectured under that model. Under the Bologna model the students got together and hired the professor, and essentially, as the story goes, Sir Isaac lectured to empty classrooms very often because his 'bosses' were off doing what people who could hire professors were doing at the time.

As the Parisian model developed, the idea of professing particular topics and subjects also grew. As groups of scholars began to coalesce and to set their standards, the profession took on a form and a structure that is not unlike the guild structure that was common at the time. Now the guild structure, with which you are probably familiar, had a progressive set of stages through which a person who desired to become a member of the guild would follow. They would have to do certain things to become a member and to progress within the guild structure.

The thing that I find interesting about this comparison is that early in my career, actually pre-professor, I became acquainted with a person who was already in the scholarly profession at the time, and still is, I believe (and is still a friend), Paul Thompson. Paul had developed one of the most useful frameworks to describe career progression. He refers to it as the 'Four Stages Model.' Essentially the stages are as follows:

Stage 1: Depending on others
Stage 2: Contributing independently
Stage 3: Contributing through others
Stage 4: Leading through vision

Now, if we are drawing parallels between career stages and progression through a craft-like guild, we would say, 'Here are the things, here are the performances, here are the expectations of people who are entering this structure and beginning to progress through its stages.'

We understand that the apprentice in the guild structure was pretty much the 'gofer.' Apprentices depended upon the person for whom they were working for pretty much all direction; and not much information was provided to apprentices because apparently there was sort of a trust issue. You didn't want to reveal all of the neat techniques of the guild to people until you were certain that they were ready to abide by the principles and the standards of that guild. But Stages 2 and 3 were kind of interesting in both the guild and in our career progression model.

A Stage 2 person has the following key attributes:

- Knows the job well
- Many people seek his or her opinion
- Is considered an expert in his or her field
- Integrates large volumes of data into a logical and coherent structure for analysis
- Demonstrates ability to solve problems under conditions of uncertainty and ambiguity
- Creates new opportunities or overcomes obstacles by rethinking situations

Now remember this is the 'contributing independently' stage. If we were to think perhaps of the doctoral time (in our profession) as the apprentice occasion, then we would say that Stages 2 and 3 are really the kind of assistant/associate professor stages.

A Stage 3 person would have the following attributes:

- Demonstrates a breath of technical functional knowledge
- Is not threatened by the technical competence of others
- Clarifies complex data or situations so that others can comprehend, respond and contribute
- Assists others in interpreting and tolerating ambiguous information
- Provides support and encouragement to others

So we see that we are moving as we go from Stage 2 to Stage 3 into a much more other-centric as opposed to self-centric posture.

Then in Stage 4, which is actually the master stage, a person would have the following attributes:

- Shapes the organizational direction to reinforce continual technical excellence
- Ensures that the organization has access to technical and professional resources
- Identifies and helps us to quickly resolve ill-defined complex problems that cross organizational boundaries
- Requires accurate crucial information as a basis for sound organization-wide decisions
- Communicates the importance of clear critical thinking in all jobs
- Fosters an organizational environment that encourages others to question their usual way of looking at things

So if we were to draw a rough parallel between our craft, the guild structure and the Four Stages Model, what would we draw from that parallel that we could use as we gather together with editors of major journals, authors who have published or are just about to publish in those journals, and those of us who are here to discuss worldwide how the process of producing the top-tier works of our craft actually works?

The reason why this is important is that, like any craft, there are tricks of the trade. There is information that until it is known requires each prospective member to re-invent the wheel; and thus people struggle to learn things that are already known simply because access to that information is not readily available. Much of the challenge in engaging in a particular field as a new field (for example, a scholar is just coming into the entrepreneurship field and beginning to try and research in that field) or much of the challenge that comes when a scholar is actually just beginning her or his career as a scholar, comes in understanding what everyone else seems to already know.

Many of us are fortunate in that we have had the good fortune to be associated with the masters. When we apprentice, we learn the tricks of the trade. Many others of us, just as talented, may not have that opportunity; and as a result, there are perceptions that this top-tier work that we do is kind of a closed club. And, importantly, it is not closed by design. It is simply closed as an artifact of the way the social situation actually has developed.

So one of the primary purposes of this (Entrepreneuship) Research Exemplars Conference is to open up the tricks of the trade – the pieces of information that ought to be known by every talented person who desires to do work at the top tier. That is our challenge, to surface these understandings.

Like most craft guilds, a particular understanding possessed by one master may not in fact be possessed by another. However, when you get a group of masters together and you throw them into unanticipated and new situations, sometimes just the newness of the situation, the emergent dialogue itself creates the opportunity for understandings to surface, to be articulated, to become concrete and to become usable by all of those who desire to do work in the craft at the top tier.

So in the Research Excellence Initiative, meeting this challenge has been undertaken by the leadership of the Entrepreneurship Division. We have committed ourselves to a deal flow model. Now we all know that the only way that venture capitalists, for example, can make good investments is if they get high-quality deal flow. And of course they can grow faster and better, and have higher returns the greater the high-quality deal flow. We believe that we do not have a problem with top-tier journals that are willing to consider top-tier work. What we face as our next threshold in entrepreneurship research, we think, is the increasing of the top-tier deal flow. That means top-tier manuscripts based upon top-tier research prepared according to the highest standards of the craft guild that is our field.

We engage many disciplines in entrepreneurship; therefore, there are many top-tier outlets. Each one has its unique elements and, based upon the uniqueness of these elements, we, as potential producers of top-tier work into that stream, need to understand not just the overall standards of the guild, but the particular community with whom we are trying to dialogue, to whom we are trying to speak.

So we have ten wonderful journals represented by editors and/or associate editors and represented by authors who are going to be publishing or have published just recently in those outlets. We have a series of keynotes from masters in the field. Based upon this, our goal is to surface the information, and to make it possible to overcome the information problems that are really nobody's fault. I believe that there is no elitism in the sense of trying to hide the information for how to publish at the top tier. Rather, to reemphasize, that it is simply an artifact of a system that hasn't engaged the information age to surface that information and make it available to all who will be able to use it.

So this is our invitation, and I don't mean Ron Mitchell's or even the Academy of Management Entrepreneurship Division leadership's invitation. This is our invitation; all who are here, all who are listening worldwide – it is our invitation to join the top-tier cadre of this guild. To learn the process, to then take the key questions that are confronting us, engage them with our great brains and craft our studies and manuscripts into master works that in fact qualify us also as masters in the guild.

Ladies and gentlemen, fellow colleagues, welcome to this Conference. It is a great event and it is a great opportunity for us to take the next step in quality entrepreneurship research; but also in quality research worldwide because, as most of us suspect and many of my emails have indicated, people have already begun to say, 'Oh, well, if this would work for entrepreneurship, why wouldn't it work for discipline x, y or z?'

So this is the idea, this is the challenge and this is the welcome. Thank you very much. We are glad to be engaged in this wonderful work together. Thank you.

C.   Worldwide reach

Richard N. Dino

Dino, Richard: Welcome to the third day of the Entrepreneurship Research Exemplars Conference. I was doing a little bit of work this morning and I have to tell you that we are absolutely humbled with the worldwide participation and the comments from people. You know, truly this Conference isn't only about the people that are here. In fact the people that are here are doing this Conference for everyone who can't be here. A third of our web audience is coming from countries outside of the United States. That is just absolutely amazing. This is just a broad sampling: countries such as England, Scotland, Spain, Denmark, Finland, Switzerland, The Netherlands, Brazil, Hong Kong, India, Germany, Greece, Australia, New Zealand, Israel, Nigeria, China, [and] Japan. And the titles of the folks that are participating on that continuum range from provost to PhD students; and the organizations are represented with universities, foundations, businesses and entrepreneurs. I am absolutely humbled.

A couple of emails out of the slew that came in:

> My feeling is simply the sun has shined. I would call my experience with this conference as completely transformative in transferring tacit knowledge about excellent scholarship, which helped clear up the myth associated with top-tier journal publications.

> An incredible experience. Invaluable information and interesting dialog and comments. I can hardly wait for the copies next week to go over the many excellent areas of discussions with peers locally.

And with that – let's begin.

D. Where to from here?

Richard N. Dino

Dino, Richard: We have come to that time, believe or not, in what seems to be a whirlwind of time. We have come to the conclusion of this Conference. There are two things I would like to do at this point. One is a set of thank yous and then the second one is to try to bring together some thoughts that struck me during the last day and a half to share with you here and to share with our worldwide audience. Please bear with me through the thank yous because, in the words of that famed politician – I forgot her name – but she said 'It takes a village.' It takes more than a village. It takes an awful lot of people who are committed and believe in the vision. There are a number of people that most appropriately are to be thanked for all of their efforts that led up to this day and a half.

Of course first at the top of the list are all the exemplars who shared their schedule, shared their time, shared their expertise and experience and joined us, and told everybody like it was. Like it was at the beginning of their career, in the middle of their career, the end of their career and the kinds of things young emerging scholars should be thinking about – particularly as it pertains to high-quality research and particularly entrepreneurship research. Thank you, exemplars.

Our ten journal editors, you believed in what the Academy and the Entrepreneurship Research Excellence Initiative was about and your presence here confirms that. We thank you.

Of course the numerous participating authors who took their lumps twice; they took it from the reviewers and then they took it over the last day and a half. We appreciate all of your candor and we appreciate all of your contributions.

Professor Tom Lumpkin, our comments editor. The quality of his performance is not just measured by what he put on the screen, it's by what he didn't put on the screen. Tom, thank you so much.

A lady who goes by the name of Katie Huntington, but I changed her name about a month ago. Every one of you have interacted with her and she is primarily responsible for the way things went here. Do you want to know what her name got changed to? 'She who must be obeyed.' Katie, absolutely spectacular, thank you so much for all of your help.

Of course I would like to thank the UConn team, my faculty colleagues who believe in what can be. It is your efforts that keep the spark continually flicking and the fire burning. We thank you for all that you have done representing the university and representing the Entrepreneurship Research Excellence Initiative.

Cara Workman from University Events. Dr. Luke Weinstein, who's the head of our Innovation Accelerator and who substituted this weekend as our technology guru. I don't know if you know how hard it is to keep technology operating. When it operates seamlessly, it is like going up to a sink and turning on water. You expect it to be there and that is exactly what happened; with all of the things that could have gone wrong in that nothing has gone wrong.

Our camera crew and the folks down at UNC Chapel Hill in connecting Professor Aldrich with us, thanks to all of you folks; Jeremy Pollack, Alex DelCampo, etc.

And of course the Academy of Management, the Entrepreneurship Division Chair and everyone else in the Division. Ron Mitchell, my co-chair. Ron, this vision has legs. We're rolling and we're rolling hard – and we're not going to stop. Oh, you want to take the microphone? I'm not done.

Mitchell, Ronald: I know, but this is the moment that we thank Rich, right? Because if he hadn't done what he did, we wouldn't be clapping. [*applause*]

Dino, Richard: Thank you. Thanks, Ron. Our IDEA Awards partners, The Ohio State University, Jay, Sharon, thank you for your commitment early on when it was just a thought. It is no longer a thought; it is momentum now. Our friends at the *Journal of Management Studies* and SAMS – Steve Floyd, Mike Wright, thank you so much.

Jointly we can do it and this is the beginning. It is a train that has left the station. It is a rocket that has left the pad. Unfortunately the economy has sent us into a little bit of a tailspin in the sense that the plan was to have this Conference in different evolving form at different universities. Because of the economy, a lot of money disappeared. So next year's Conference was in jeopardy and the University of Connecticut, the Center for Entrepreneurship and Innovation, is absolutely committed to this initiative. So I'm proud to announce today with the approval of our dean and our department head, John Mathieu, that we are going to step up again next year and we will host the 2010 Exemplars Conference. It will be a different format. We will probably do it on this weekend next year, so I look forward to all of you participating in 2010.

I'm trying to pull together a couple of things that struck me as quite interesting, and particularly this is a message to the emerging and junior scholars out there who are not in this room. We have a couple but they are all out there somewhere. There are exemplars everywhere; they are just not in this room. Your job is to find out who they are and to link up with them.

A couple of things come to mind. The word 'tenacity.' You know, we do research about entrepreneurship and entrepreneurs. The word 'tenacity' is the common lexicon of entrepreneurs. 'Impossibility.' It's a degree of difficulty to entrepreneurs. That's it.

I opened the Conference by talking about lyrics of songs. I like lyrics of songs. There was a song years ago by a group called, believe it or not, Chumbawamba. I don't know if you remember the lyrics, but the lyrics are the following: 'I get knocked down, I get up again. Nobody's going to keep me down.' That's what research is about, isn't it? Continually getting knocked down and having the tenacity to get up, believing in what you are doing and (Jim, back to you again) believing in what you're doing and getting it done.

Jeff McMullen said something that struck me and I don't know if anybody heard it because he kind of said it as an off comment. He said, 'I'm always thinking about this stuff.' Jeff, right? 'I'm always thinking about this stuff.' Mike Hitt said, 'Highly committed, highly motivated, goal directed, learning oriented. If you focus that way, you will be successful.'

So how do I bring that all together? A story. Jack, you talked about stories. You like stories. Here's a story. I'm not sure if it's true. I'm making it up as we're going along, but it's something like this. There was this guy named Socrates, and he was in a forum giving a talk. Part of that talk was the research that he had done. And after the talk a young person came up to Socrates and said to him as an exemplar scholar, 'I would like to do my research with you.'

Socrates said, 'You'd like to do your research with me? Why?'

'Well, because you know so much. You've found so much new knowledge. You've pushed the envelope (I guess if it were today, you've published). I want to study with you. I want to learn. If I can do half of what you've done, I can too be an exemplar scholar.'

Socrates says, 'Okay, let's go for a walk.'

So they walked out of the forum and they walked across the courtyard. They walked out into the town and they looked and there was a little bit of mountain and they climbed over the hill and down the other side across the plain. They were still walking and talking and – lo and behold

– in front of them was the ocean. And without a stop, Socrates just kept walking – and they walked into the water.

Of course the young person is kind of looking, but Socrates isn't paying attention. They're walking and walking and the water is coming up. Just as the water gets about here, Socrates grabs the young person by the collar and holds him under the water. Well, you know what happens, right? When you're not expecting that and all of a sudden you have no oxygen? Bubbles are flying, arms are flying, flailing, all this kind of stuff; and just as the bubbles stopped, Socrates reached down and pulled the guy up. Well, you know what would happen then right? A deep breath, a big smile on his face, back down under the water. And repeated this several times. So to the person's surprise, after a few times Socrates stood him up and Socrates said, 'So you want to do research and learn research from me, an exemplar scholar?'

That person said, 'Yes.'

[Socrates] said, 'I'll tell you what . . .' He said, 'When you want to do research just as much as you just wanted to breathe, then we'll work together.' And that's effectively what exemplar scholars want to hear from young scholars. If you want to consume this, if you want to always think about this, if you want to be highly motivated, goal directed, learning oriented and highly committed, then let's work together.

So our message from the Academy, from the Center for Entrepreneurship and Innovation, from The Ohio State University, from SAMS, and from everybody else who is going to now get on this direction or continue with this direction, we say to all of you emerging scholars, 'Consume research and want to do it as much as you want to breathe, and you will be extremely successful.'

Ladies and gentlemen, we can't thank you enough for your commitment. We can't thank you enough for the time you have spent with us. It is sincerely appreciated. And for everyone else out there, every one of these sessions, 'every one of these sessions,' has been recorded. We are going to clean them up over the next couple of weeks. We will put them out on the Academy's website. We will certainly have them on the Center's website, and they will be available for you to look at at your leisure and for whatever purpose you need them. Ron, would you like to say anything else?

Mitchell, Ronald: I echo Rich's warm, full, and heartfelt thanks to all of those named; also to those who have joined us worldwide and will continue to join us as the momentum gathers. Thank you, each of you, for making the contributions and the sacrifices in your own careers that make it possible for us to draw upon your expertise as we begin the process of raising the tide, or as Venkat said, 'turning the tide' such that all ships end up rising with us. Thank you and have a safe trip home. God bless.

Exhibits: background information

I. Journal mission excerpts

ACADEMY OF MANAGEMENT JOURNAL

http://journals.aomonline.org/amj/ Retrieved 18 May, 2009

Journal purpose: 'The mission of the *Academy of Management Journal* is to publish empirical research that tests, extends, or builds management theory and contributes to management practice. All empirical methods – including, but not limited to, qualitative, quantitative, field, laboratory, and combination methods – are welcome. To be published in *AMJ*, a manuscript must make strong empirical and theoretical contributions and highlight the significance of those contributions to the management field. Thus, preference is given to submissions that test, extend, or build strong theoretical frameworks while empirically examining issues with high importance for management theory and practice. *AMJ* is not tied to any particular discipline, level of analysis, or national context.'

Opportunities identified: Open to a wide variety of empirical entrepreneurship research, and a wide variety of empirical methods, as this journal seeks to 'publish empirical research that tests, extends, or builds management theory and contributes to management practice. All empirical methods – including, but not limited to, qualitative, quantitative, field, laboratory, and combination methods – are welcome. To be published in *AMJ*, a manuscript must make strong empirical and theoretical contributions and highlight the significance of those contributions to the management field.'

ACADEMY OF MANAGEMENT REVIEW

http://aom.pace.edu/AMR/ Retrieved 18 May, 2009

Journal purpose: 'The mission of the *Academy of Management Review* (*AMR*) is to publish new theoretical insights that advance our understanding of management and organizations. *AMR* is receptive to a variety of perspectives, including those seeking to improve the effectiveness of, as well as those critical of, management and organizations. Submissions to *AMR* must extend theory in ways that permit the development of testable knowledge-based claims. To do this, researchers can develop new management and organization theory, significantly challenge or clarify existing theory, synthesize recent advances and ideas into fresh, if not entirely new theory, or initiate a search for new theory by identifying and delineating a novel theoretical problem. The contributions of *AMR* articles often are grounded in "normal science disciplines" of economics, psychology, sociology, or social psychology as well as nontraditional perspectives, such as the humanities. *AMR* publishes novel, insightful and carefully crafted conceptual work that challenges conventional wisdom concerning all aspects of organizations and their roles in society.'

Opportunities identified: Open to theoretical work regarding entrepreneurship, as the journal publishes 'new theoretical insights that advance our understanding of management and organizations. *AMR* is receptive to a variety of perspectives, including those seeking to improve the effectiveness of, as well as those critical of, management and organizations.'

ENTREPRENEURSHIP THEORY & PRACTICE

http://www.blackwellpublishing.com/aims.asp?ref=1042-2587&site=1
Retrieved 18 May, 2009

Journal purpose: '*Entrepreneurship Theory & Practice* (*ET&P*) is a leading scholarly journal in the field of entrepreneurship studies. The journal's mission is to publish original papers which contribute to the advancement of the field of entrepreneurship. *ET&P* publishes conceptual and empirical articles of interest to scholars, consultants, and public policy makers. Most issues also feature a teaching case. Article topics include, but are not limited to:

- National and International Studies of Enterprise Creation
- Small Business Management
- Family-Owned Businesses
- Minority Issues in Small Business and Entrepreneurship
- New Venture Creation
- Research Methods
- Venture Financing
- Corporate and Non-Profit Entrepreneurship'

Opportunities identified: Journal for a wide variety of entrepreneurship research: '*Entrepreneurship Theory & Practice* (*ET&P*) is a leading scholarly journal in the field of entrepreneurship studies. The journal's mission is to publish original papers which contribute to the advancement of the field of entrepreneurship. *ET&P* publishes conceptual and empirical articles of interest to scholars, consultants, and public policy makers.'

JOURNAL OF APPLIED PSYCHOLOGY

http://www.apa.org/journals/apl/description.html Retrieved 18 May, 2009

Journal purpose: '*Journal of Applied Psychology* publishes original investigations that contribute new knowledge and understanding to fields of applied psychology (other than clinical and applied experimental or human factors) . . . The journal includes articles that foster an understanding of the psychological and behavioral phenomena of individuals, groups, or organizations in settings such as education/training, business, government, health, or service institutions . . . Topics include personnel selection, performance measurement, training, work motivation, leadership, drug and alcohol abuse, career development, the conflict between job and family demands, work stress, organizational design, technology, and cross-cultural differences in work behavior and attitudes.'

Opportunities identified: Outlet for applied, empirical work that addresses the psychological aspects of entrepreneurship, as the journal publishes research that can 'contribute new knowledge and understanding to fields of applied psychology'. Open to a wide range of topics: 'Topics include personnel selection, performance measurement, training, work motivation, leadership, drug and alcohol abuse, career development, the conflict between job and family demands, work stress, organizational design, technology, and cross-cultural differences in work behavior and attitudes.'

JOURNAL OF BUSINESS VENTURING

http://www.elsevier.com/wps/find/journaldescription.cws_home/505723/
description#description Retrieved 18 May, 2009

Journal purpose: 'The *Journal of Business Venturing*: Entrepreneurship, Entrepreneurial Finance, Innovation and Regional Development provides a scholarly forum for sharing useful and interesting facts, theories, narratives, and interpretations of entrepreneurship and consequences of entrepreneurship . . . The journal aspires to publish ideas that deepen our understanding of, and ultimately impact, the entrepreneurial phenomenon in its myriad forms. We seek papers (1) that are grounded in the practice of entrepreneurs, innovators, and their support systems; and (2) that address issues useful to scholars, educators, enablers, and practitioners of the entrepreneurial phenomenon. The journal welcomes pluralism in approach, methods, and disciplines.'

Opportunities identified: Open to a wide variety of entrepreneurship research: 'The journal aspires to publish ideas that deepen our understanding of, and ultimately impact, the entrepreneurial phenomenon in its myriad forms. We seek papers (1) that are grounded in the practice of entrepreneurs, innovators, and their support systems; and (2) that address issues useful to scholars, educators, enablers, and practitioners of the entrepreneurial phenomenon. The journal welcomes pluralism in approach, methods, and disciplines.'

JOURNAL OF MANAGEMENT

http://jom.sagepub.com/ Retrieved 18 May, 2009

Journal purpose: 'The *Journal of Management* publishes empirical and theoretical articles dealing with any area represented within the domain of the Academy of Management. Manuscripts that are suitable for publication in the *Journal of Management* cover such areas as business strategy and policy, human resource management, organizational behavior, organizational theory, and research methods.'

Opportunities identified: Good outlet for any entrepreneurship research as it publishes 'articles dealing with any area represented within the domain of the Academy of Management.'

JOURNAL OF MANAGEMENT STUDIES

http://www.blackwellpublishing.com/aims.asp?ref=0022-2380&site=1
Retrieved 18 May, 2009

Journal purpose: 'Consistently highly ranked in the Management section ISI Journal Citation Reports, the *Journal of Management Studies* (*JMS*) is a globally respected journal with a long established history of innovation and excellence in management research. International in scope and readership, the *JMS* is a multidisciplinary journal, publishing articles on organization theory and behaviour, strategic and human resource management – from empirical studies and theoretical developments to practical applications . . . In recent years, *Journal of Management Studies* has enhanced its reputation as a vibrant, cutting-edge, high quality international journal. *JMS* has an inclusive ethos seeking innovative and novel papers and is open to a wide range of methodological approaches and philosophical underpinnings . . . The journal provides: in-depth coverage of organizational problems and organization theory; reports on the latest developments in strategic management and planning; cross-cultural comparisons of organizational effectiveness; and concise reviews of the latest publications in management studies as well as lively debate in topical and important issues on management.'

Opportunities identified: Journal has a focus on 'lively debate in topical and important issues on management.' Articles addressing controversial issues in entrepreneurship would likely be welcome here.

ORGANIZATION SCIENCE

http://www.informs.org/site/Organization_Science/ Retrieved 18 May, 2009

Journal purpose: '*Organization Science* is ranked among the top journals in management by the Social Science Citation Index in terms of impact and is widely recognized in the fields of strategy, management, and organization theory. *Organization Science* provides one umbrella for the publication of research from all over the world in fields such as organization theory, strategic management, sociology, economics, political science, history, information science, communication theory, and psychology.'

Opportunities identified: A good target for a variety of entrepreneurship research, as this journal 'provides one umbrella for the publication of research from all over the world in fields such as organization theory, strategic management, sociology, economics, political science, history, information science, communication theory, and psychology.'

STRATEGIC ENTREPRENEURSHIP JOURNAL

http://sej.strategicmanagement.net/aims-scope.php   Retrieved   29   June,
2010

Journal purpose: 'Strategic entrepreneurship involves innovation and
subsequent changes which add value to society and which change societal
life in ways that have significant, sustainable, and durable consequences
. . . The *SEJ* is international in scope and acknowledges theory- and
evidenced-based research conducted and/or applied in all regions of the
world. It is devoted to content and quality standards based on scientific
method, relevant theory, tested or testable propositions, and appropriate
data and evidence, all replicable by others, and all representing original
contributions . . . The *SEJ* values contributions, which lead to improved
practice of managing organizations as they deal with the entrepreneurial
process involving imagination, insight, invention, and innovation and the
inevitable changes and transformations that result and benefit society.'

Opportunities identified: A good target for entrepreneurship research in ten
key theme areas: 'Entrepreneurship and economic growth; change; risk
and uncertainty; innovation; creativity, imagination, and opportunities;
strategy versus entrepreneurship; technology; social role of entrepreneurship, behavioral characteristics of entrepreneurial activity; entrepreneurial
actions, innovation, and appropriability'; that fall under the following
vision.

'For the purposes of the *SEJ*, entrepreneurship has special meaning,
and means much more than the acts of entrepreneurs. Strategic entrepreneurship starts with imagination and insight that lead to inventions that
are deemed innovations of societal import. While starting a business is
important, starting any organization that makes a difference to society
embodies the notion of strategic entrepreneurship most attractive to the
SEJ . . . Such inventions and innovations can be done by many, or by one,
but the extent of their impact defines their importance and significance to
society. What makes entrepreneurship strategic is adding value to society,
i.e., changing societal life in ways that have significant, sustainable, and
durable consequence . . . Innovations lead to change, transformation in
organizations, which invent them, and benefits to the organizations and
individuals that use innovations. The changes are significant, usually complicated in nature, especially to understand and manage, and often are
revolutionary in impact.'

STRATEGIC MANAGEMENT JOURNAL

http://www3.interscience.wiley.com/journal/2144/home/
ProductInformation.html Retrieved 18 May, 2009

Journal purpose: 'The journal publishes original material concerned with all aspects of strategic management. It is devoted to the improvement and further development of the theory and practice of strategic management and it is designed to appeal to both practising managers and academics. Papers acceptable to an editorial board acting as referees are published. The journal also publishes communications in the form of research notes or comments from readers on published papers or current issues. Editorial comments and invited papers on practices and developments in strategic management appear from time to time as warranted by new developments. Overall, *SMJ* provides a communication forum for advancing strategic management theory and practice. Such major topics as strategic resource allocation; organization structure; leadership; entrepreneurship and organizational purpose; methods and techniques for evaluating and understanding competitive, technological, social, and political environments; planning processes; and strategic decision processes are included in the journal.'

Opportunities identified: This journal is explicitly targeting entrepreneurship research: 'Such major topics as strategic resource allocation; organization structure; leadership; entrepreneurship and organizational purpose. . .'

II. 2009 conference schedule in order of occurrence

Event Title	Start Time	End Time
Entrepreneurship Research Exemplars Conference		
May 28–30		
Conference Schedule of Events		
Event Title	*Start Time*	*End Time*
5/28/2009		
Reception	6:00	9:00
Keynote:	7:30	8:00
S. 'Venkat' Venkataraman		
University of Virginia, Darden School of Business		
MasterCard Professor of Business Administration; Research Director, The Batten Institute		
5/29/2009		
BREAKFAST	7:00	8:00
Welcome	8:15	8:45
Keynote:	8:45	9:15
R. Duane Ireland		
Texas A&M University, Mays Business School		
Distinguished Professor, Bennett Chair in Business, *AMJ* Editor		
Editor/Author Session	9:20	10:10
Academy of Management Review		
Associate Editor: Mason Carpenter		
Professor of Management and Human Resources, M. Keith Weikel Chair in Leadership		
Authors in Attendance:		
PAPER #1: The Nature and Experience of Entrepreneurial Passion		
Melissa S. Cardon		
Pace University, Lubin School of Business		
PAPER #2: Entrepreneurial Action and the Role of Uncertainty in the Theory of The Entrepreneur		
Jeffrey S. McMullen		
Indiana University, Kelley School of Business		

Assistant Professor of Entrepreneurship		
Dean A. Shepherd		
Indiana University, Kelley School of Business		
Randall L. Tobias Chair in Entrepreneurial Leadership, Professor of Entrepreneurship		
BREAK	10:15	10:45
Keynote:	10:50	11:20
Jay B. Barney		
The Ohio State University, Fisher College of Business		
Chase Chair for Excellence in Corporate Strategy, Professor of Management & Human Resources		
Editor/Author Session	11:25	12:15
Strategic Entrepreneurship Journal		
Co-Editor: Michael A. Hitt		
Texas A&M University, Mays Business School		
Distinguished Professor, Joe B. Foster '56 Chair, Conn Chair		
Authors in Attendance:		
PAPER #1: Entrepreneurship, subjectivism, and the resource-based view: Towards a new synthesis		
Yasemin Y. Kor		
University of South Carolina, Moore School of Business		
Associate Professor of Management		
PAPER #2: Investment dynamics and financial constraints in IPO firms		
Jeffrey J. Reuer		
Purdue University, Krannert School of Management		
Blake Family Endowed Chair in Strategic Management and Governance, Strategic Management Area Coordinator		
LUNCH	12:15	1:15
Keynote:	1:20	1:50
Howard E. Aldrich		
University of North Carolina Chapel Hill, Kenan-Flagler Business School		
Professor and Department Chair, Sociology, Adjunct Professor of Management Kenan Professor and Chair		
Editor/Author Session	1:55	2:25
Organization Science		
Associate Editor: Pamela S. Tolbert		
Cornell University, ILR School		
Professor of Organizational Behavior, Chairperson of the Department of Organizational Behavior		
Authors in Attendance:		
PAPER #1: From Plan to Plant: Effects of Certification on Operational Start-up in the Emergent Independent Power Sector		
Wesley D. Sine		

Cornell University, Johnson School		
Assistant Professor of Management and Organizations		
Editor/Author Session	2:30	3:00
Journal of Management		
Editor: Talya N. Bauer		
Portland State University, School of Business Administration		
Gerry & Marilyn Cameron Professor of Management		
Authors in Attendance:		
PAPER #1: The relationship of personality to entrepreneurial intentions and performance: A meta-analytic review		
Hao Zhao		
Rensselaer Polytechnic Institute, Lally School of Management & Technology		
Assistant Professor of Management		
Scott E. Siebert		
The University of Iowa, Tippie College of Business		
Associate Professor, Henry B. Tippie Research Fellow		
G. Thomas Lumpkin		
Texas Tech University, Rawls College of Management		
Ken Hance Chair in Entrepreneurship		
BREAK	3:00	3:30
Editor/Author Session	3:35	4:25
Journal of Business Venturing		
Associate Editor: Phillip Phan		
Johns Hopkins University, Carey Business School		
Professor and Vice Dean for Faculty and Research		
Authors in Attendance:		
PAPER #1: The interplay of need and opportunity in venture capital investment syndication		
Dimo Dimov		
University of Connecticut, School of Business		
Assistant Professor of Management		
PAPER #2: Entrepreneurial Resilience: How Serial Founders' Confidence Affects Their Recovery from Venture Failure		
William Forster		
University of Virginia, Darden School of Business		
Doctoral Student (2009)		
Editor/Author Session	4:30	5:20
Journal of Management Studies		
Associate Editor: Andrew C. Corbett		
Rensselaer Polytechnic Institute, Lally School of Management & Technology		
Associate Professor, Associate Faculty Director of the Severino Center for Technological Entrepreneurship		
Authors in Attendance:		

PAPER #1: An Opportunity for Me? The Role of Resources in Opportunity Evaluation Decisions		
J. Michael Haynie		
Syracuse University, Whitman School of Management		
Assistant Professor of Entrepreneurship		
Dean A. Shepherd		
Indiana University, Kelley School of Business		
Randall L. Tobias Chair in Entrepreneurial Leadership, Professor of Entrepreneurship		
Jeffery S. McMullen		
Indiana University, Kelley School of Business		
Assistant Professor of Entrepreneurship		
PAPER #2: A Prescriptive Analysis of Search and Discovery		
James O. Fiet		
University of Louisville, College of Business		
Brown-Forman Chair in Entrepreneurship, Professor of Management		
return to NHI	5:30	
CLAMBAKE	6:30	9:30
5/30/2009		
BREAKFAST	7:00	8:00
Keynote:	8:15	8:45
Michael A. Hitt		
Texas A&M University, Mays Business School		
Distinguished Professor, Joe B. Foster '56 Chair, Conn Chair		
Editor/Author Session	8:50	9:40
Academy of Management Journal		
Editor: R. Duane Ireland		
Texas A&M University, Mays Business School		
Distinguished Professor, Bennett Chair in Business		
Authors in Attendance:		
PAPER #1: Entrepreneurial orientation and new venture performance: The moderating role of intra- and extraindustry social capital		
Tom Elfring		
VU University Amsterdam		
Faculty of Economics and Business Administration		
PAPER #2: Entrepreneurs' Optimism and New Venture Performance: A Social Cognitive Perspective		
Keith M. Hmieleski		
Texas Christian University, Neeley School of Business		
Assistant Professor, Management		
Editor/Author Session	9:45	10:15
Entrepreneurship Theory & Practice		
Associate Editor: Candida Brush		

Babson College		
Paul T. Babson Chair in Entrepreneurship, Division Chair for Entrepreneurship		
Authors in Attendance:		
PAPER #1: Toward a theory of familiness: A social capital perspective		
Jon C. Carr		
Texas Christian University, Neeley School of Business		
Assistant Professor, Management		
BREAK	10:20	10:50
Keynote:	10:55	11:25
Patricia P. McDougall		
Indiana University, Kelley School of Business		
Associate Dean of Faculty and Research, William L. Haeberle Professor of Entrepreneurship, Professor of Strategic Management		
Editor/Author Session	11:30	12:00
Journal of Applied Psychology		
Associate Editor: Jing Zhou		
Rice University, Jesse H. Jones Graduate School of Management		
Professor of Management		
Authors in Attendance:		
PAPER #1: How do feelings influence effort? An empirical study of entrepreneurs' affect and venture effort		
Maw-Der Foo		
University of Colorado, Boulder, Leeds School of Management		
Assistant Professor of Management & Entrepreneurship		
Editor/Author Session	12:05	12:45
Strategic Management Journal		
Associate Editor: Joseph T. Mahoney		
University of Illinois at Urbana-Champaign, College of Business		
Investors in Business Education Professor of Business Administration		
Authors in Attendance:		
PAPER #1: Do VCs matter? the importance of owners on performance variance in start-up firms		
Elaine Mosakowski		
University of Connecticut, School of Business		
Professor of Management		
PAPER #2: Complementarity, capabilities, and the boundaries of the firm: the impact of within-firm and interfirm expertise on concurrent sourcing of complementary components		
Anne Parmigiani		
University of Oregon, Lundquist College of Business		
Assistant Professor, Management		
LUNCH & DEPART	12:45	2:00

References

(1990). *Strategic Management Journal,* Special Issue: Corporate Entrepreneurship, **11**.

(2000). *Academy of Management Journal,* Special Issue: Entrepreneurship, **43** (5).

Adelman, M.A. (1949). The large firm and its suppliers. *Review of Economics and Statistics,* **31** (2), 113–18.

Aldrich, H.E. (1979). *Organizations and Environments.* Englewood Cliffs, NJ: Prentice-Hall.

Aldrich, H.E. (2008). *Organizations and Environments,* new edition. Stanford, CA: Stanford Business Classics of Stanford University Press.

Aldrich, H.E. and E. Auster (1986). Even dwarfs started small: liabilities of age and size and their strategic implications. *Research in Organizational Behavior,* **8**, 165–98.

Aldrich, H.E. and P.H. Kim (2007). Small worlds, infinite possibilities. *Strategic Entrepreneurship Journal,* **1** (1), 147–65.

Amit, R. and P.J.H. Schoemaker (1993). Strategic assets and organizational rent. *Strategic Management Journal,* **14** (1), 33–46.

Barnard, C. (1938). *The Functions of the Executive.* Cambridge, MA: Harvard University Press.

Baron, R.A. and R.A. Henry (2010). How entrepreneurs acquire the capacity to excel: insights from research on expert performance. *Strategic Entrepreneurship Journal,* **4** (1), 49–65.

Birch, D. (1987). *Job Creation in America: How our Smallest Companies put the Most People to Work.* New York: The Free Press.

Boice, R. (2000). *Advice for New Faculty Members: Nihil Nimus.* Boston: Allyn and Bacon.

Boyer, E.L. (1990). *Scholarship Reconsidered: Priorities of the Professoriate.* Princeton, NJ: Carnegie Foundation for the Advancement of Teaching.

Brush, C.G., I.M. Duhaine, W.B. Gartner, A. Stewart et al. (2003). Doctoral education in the field of entrepreneurship. *Journal of Management,* **29**, 309–31.

Buchanan, J.M. and V.J. Vanberg (1991). The market as a creative process. *Economics and Philosophy,* **7**, 167–86.

Campbell, D.T. (1969). Variation and selective retention in socio-cultural evolution. *General Systems,* **14**, 69–85.

Cardon, M.S., J. Wincent, J. Singh and M. Drnovsek (2009). The nature and experience of entrepreneurial passion. *Academy of Management Review,* **34** (3), 511–32.

Chaddad, F.R. and J.J. Reuer (2009). Investment dynamics and financial constraints in IPO firms. *Strategic Entrepreneurship Journal,* **3** (1), 29–45.

Charness, N., R. Krampe and U. Mayer (1996). The role of practice and coaching in entrepreneurial skill domains: an international comparison of life-span chess skill acquisition. In K.A. Ericsson (ed.), *The Road to Excellence: The Acquisition of Expert Performance in the Arts and Sciences, Sports, and Games.* Mahwah, NJ: Lawrence Erlbaum Associates, pp. 51–80.

Clark, T., S.W. Floyd and M. Wright (2006). On the review process and journal development. *Journal of Management Studies*, **43** (3), 655–64.

Colquitt, J.A. and R.D. Ireland (2009). From the editors: taking the mystery out of AMJ's reviewer evaluation form. *Academy of Management Journal*, **52** (2), 224–8.

Daft, R.L. and A.Y. Lewin (2008). Rigor and relevance in organization studies: idea migration and academic journal evolution. *Organization Science*, **18** (1), 177–83.

Dalton, D.R. and C.M. Dalton (2005). Strategic management studies are a special case for meta-analysis. In D. Ketchen and D. Bergh (eds), *Research Methodology in Strategy and Management*. Bingley: Emerald Group Publishing, pp. 31–63.

Davidson, D. (2001). *Three Varieties of Knowledge: Subjective, Intersubjective, Objective*. New York: Oxford University Press.

Davis, M. (1971). That's interesting! Towards a phenomenology of sociology and a sociology of phenomenology. *Philosophy of the Social Sciences*, **1**, 309–44.

Demsetz, H. (1973). Industry structure, market rivalry, and public policy. *Journal of Law and Economics*, **16** (1), 1–9.

Dierickx, I. and K. Cool (1989). Asset stock accumulation and sustainability of competitive advantage. *Management Science*, **35** (12), 1504–11.

Dimov, D. and H. Milanov (2009). The interplay of need and opportunity in venture capital investment syndication. *Journal of Business Venturing*, **25** (4), 331–48.

Drucker, P. (1985). *Innovation and Entrepreneurship: Practice and Principles.* Oxford: Elsevier.

Elbow, P. (1998). *Writing with Power*. New York: Oxford University Press.

Ericsson, K.A. and N. Charness (1994). Expert performance: its structure and acquisition. *American Psychologist*, **49** (8), 725–47.

Ericsson, K.A., R.T. Krampe and C. Tesch-Romer (1993). The role of deliberate practice in the acquisition of expert performance. *Psychological Review*, **100** (3), 363–406.

Fiet, J. (2007). A prescriptive analysis of search and discovery. *Journal of Management Studies*, **44** (4), 592–611.

Fiet, J.O. (2002). *The Systematic Search for Entrepreneurial Discoveries*. Westport, CT: Quorum Books.

Fitza, M., S.F. Matusik and E. Mosakowski (2009). Do VCs matter? The importance of owners on performance variance in start-up firms. *Strategic Management Journal*, **30** (4), 387–404.

Foo, M.-D., M.A. Uy and R.A. Baron (2009). How do feelings influence effort? An empirical study of entrepreneurs' affect and venture effort. *Journal of Applied Psychology*, **94** (4), 1086–94.

Foss, N.J., P.G. Klein, Y.Y. Kor and J.T. Mahoney (2008). Entrepreneurship, subjectivism, and the resource-based view: toward a new synthesis. *Strategic Entrepreneurship Journal*, **2** (1), 73–94.

Fredrickson, B.L. (2001). The role of positive emotions in positive psychology: the broaden-and-build theory of positive emotions. *American Psychologist*, **56** (3), 218–26.

Gartner, W. (2001). Is there an elephant in entrepreneurship? Blind assumptions in theory development. *Entrepreneurship Theory and Practice*, **25** (4), 27–40.

Gartner, W.B. (1988). 'Who is an entrepreneur?' Is the wrong question. *American Journal of Small Business*, **12** (4), 11–32.

Ghoshal, S. (2005). Bad management theories are destroying good management practices. *Academy of Management Learning & Education*, **4** (1), 75–91.

Glaser, R. (1984). Education and thinking. *American Psychologist*, **39**, 93–104.

Goodman, N. (1978). *Ways of Worldmaking*. Indianapolis: Hackett Publishing.

Green, W.S. (2009). Entrepreneurship in American higher education. In *Kauffman Thoughtbook 2009*. Kansas City: Ewing Marion Kauffman Foundation.

Grégoire, D. (2005). *Opportunity Acknowledgement as a Cognitive Process of Pattern Recognition and Structural Alignment*. Boulder, CO: University of Colorado.

Grégoire, D.A., P.S. Barr and D.A. Shepherd (2010). Cognitive processes of opportunity recognition: the role of structural alignment. *Organization Science*, **21** (2), 413–31.

Guimerà, R., B. Uzzi, J. Spiro and L.A.N. Amaral (2005). Team assembly mechanisms determine collaboration network structure and team performance. *Science*, **308** (29 April), 697–702.

Habbershon, T.G., M.L. Williams and K. Kaye (1999). A resource-based framework for assessing the strategic advantages of family firms. *Family Business Review*, **12** (1), 1–25.

Hambrick, D. (1994). What if the Academy actually mattered? *Academy of Management Review*, **19** (1), 11–16.

Harrigan, K.R. (1984). Formulating vertical integration strategies. *Academy of Management Review*, **9** (4), 638–52.

Haynie, J.M., D.A. Shepherd and J.S. McMullen (2009). An opportunity for me? The role of resources in opportunity evaluation decisions. *Journal of Management Studies*, **46** (3), 337–61.

Hayward, M.L.A., W.R. Forster, S.D. Sarasvathy and B.L. Fredrickson (2009). Beyond hubris: how highly confident entrepreneurs rebound to venture again. *Journal of Business Venturing*, **25** (6), 569–78.

Hitt, M.A., P.W. Beamish, S.E. Jackson and J.E. Mathieu (2007). Building theoretical and empirical bridges across levels: multilevel research in management. *Academy of Management Journal*, **50** (6), 1385–99.

Hitt, M.A., R.D. Ireland, S.M. Camp and D.L. Sexton (2001). Strategic entrepreneurship: entrepreneurial strategies for wealth creation. *Strategic Management Journal*, **2**, 479–91.

Hmieleski, K.M. and R.A. Baron (2009). Entrepreneurs' optimism and new venture performance: a social cognitive perspective. *Academy of Management Journal*, **52** (3), 473–88.

Hogan, R.T. (1991). Personality and personality measurement. In M.D. Dunnette and L.M. Hough (eds), *Handbook of Industrial and Organizational Psychology*. Palo Alto, CA: Consulting Psychologists' Press, Vol. 2, pp. 873–919.

Hunter, J.E. and F.L. Schmidt (1990). *Methods of Meta-analysis: Correcting Error and Bias in Research Findings*. Hillsdale, NJ: Lawrence Erlbaum.

Ireland, R.D. and J.W. Webb (2007). A cross-disciplinary exploration of entrepreneurship research. *Journal of Management*, **33**, 891–927.

Ireland, R.D., M.A. Hitt and D.G. Sirmon (2003). A model of strategic entrepreneurship: The construct and its dimensions. *Journal of Management*, **29**, 963–89.

Ireland, R.D., M.A. Hitt, S.M. Camp and D. Sexton (2001). Integrating entrepreneurship and strategic management action to create firm wealth. *Academy of Management Executive*, **15** (1), 49–63.

Katz, J.A. (2004). *2004 Survey of Endowed Positions in Entrepreneurship and Related Fields in the United States*. Kansas City: Ewing Marion Kauffman Foundation.

Katz, J.A. (2006). And another thing. (The 2006 Coleman Foundation White Paper on Entrepreneurship.) Presented at the Annual Meeting of the US Association for Small Business and Entrepreneurship (USASBE). Tucson, AZ: January 13.

Kilduff, M. (2007). The top ten reasons why your paper might not be sent out for review. *Academy of Management Review*, **32**, 700–702.

Kirzner, I.M. (1973). *Competition and Entrepreneurship*. Chicago: University of Chicago Press.

Kirzner, I.M. (1979). *Perception, Opportunity and Profit*. Chicago: University of Chicago Press.

Kirzner, I.M. (1985). *Discovery and the Capitalist Process*. Chicago: University of Chicago Press.

Kochhar, R. and M.A. Hitt (1998). Linking corporate strategy to capital structure: diversification strategy, type and source of financing. *Strategic Management Journal*, **19**, 601–10.

Kozlowski, S.W.J. (2009). Editorial. *Journal of Applied Psychology*, **94** (1), 1–4.

Kristof, A.L. (1996). Person–organization fit: an integrative review of its conceptualizations, measurement, and implications. *Personnel Psychology*, **49** (1), 1–49.

Kristof-Brown, A.L., R.D. Zimmerman and E.C. Johnson (2005). Consequences of individuals' fit at work: a meta-analysis of person–job, person–organization, person–group, and person–supervisor fit. *Personnel Psychology*, **58**, 281–342.

Lachmann, Ludwig M. (1977). *Capital, Expectations, and Market Process*. Kansas City: Sheed, Andrews and McMeel.

Langer, E. (1989). *Mindfullness*. Reading, MA: Addison-Wesley.

Langer, E. (2009). *Counterclockwise: Mindful Health and the Power of Possibility*. New York: Ballantine Books.

Lawrence, T.B., M.I. Winn and P.D. Jennings (2001). The temporal dynamics of institutionalization. *Academy of Management Review*, **26** (4), 624–44.

Locke, K. and K. Golden-Biddle (1997). Constructing opportunities for contribution: structuring intertextual coherence and 'problematizing' in organizational studies. *Academy of Management Journal*, **40** (5), 1023–62.

Makadok, R. (2001). Toward a synthesis of the resource-based and dynamic-capability views of rent creation. *Strategic Management Journal*, **22** (5), 387–40.

Martins, L.L., L.L. Gilson and M.T. Maynard (2004). Virtual teams: what do we know and where do we go from here? *Journal of Management*, **30** (6), 805–35.

McMullen, J.S. and D.A. Shepherd (2006). Entrepreneurial action and the role of uncertainty in the theory of the entrepreneur. *Academy of Management Review*, **31** (1), 132–52.

Merton, R.K. (1968). *Social Theory and Social Structure*. New York: The Free Press.

Meyer, G.D. (2009). Commentary: on the integration of strategic management and entrepreneurship: views of a contrarian. *Entrepreneurship Theory and Practice*, **33** (1), 341–51.

Minto, B. (2002). *The Pyramid Principle: Logic in Writing and Thinking*. London: Prentice Hall/Financial Times.

Muchinsky, P.M. and C.J. Monahan (1987). What is person–environment congruence? Supplementary versus complementary models of fit. *Journal of Vocational Behavior*, **31**, 268–77.

Nickerson, J.A. and T.R. Zenger (2004). A knowledge-based theory of the firm: the problem-solving perspective. *Organization Science*, **15** (6), 617–32.

Nicolaou, N. and S. Shane (2009). Can genetic factors influence the likelihood of engaging in entrepreneurial activity? *Journal of Business Venturing*, **24** (1), 1–22.

NRC (National Research Council, Chemical Sciences Roundtable Board on Chemical Sciences and Technology) (2000). *Graduate Education in the Chemical Sciences: Issues for the 21st Century: Report of a Workshop.* Retrieved: March 16, 2010: http://www.nap.edu/catalog/9898.html.

Oviatt, B.M. and P. McDougall (2005). Toward a theory of international new ventures. *Journal of International Business Studies*, **36**, 29–41.

Parmigiani, A. and W. Mitchell (2009). Complementarity, capabilities, and the boundaries of the firm: the impact of within-firm and interfirm expertise on concurrent sourcing of complementary components. *Strategic Management Journal*, **30** (10), 1065–91.

Pearson, A.W., J.C. Carr and J.C. Shaw (2008). Toward a theory of familiness: a social capital perspective. *Entrepreneurship Theory and Practice*, **32** (6), 949–69.

Penrose, E.G. (1959). *The Theory of the Growth of the Firm.* New York: Wiley.

Pfeffer, J. (2007). Financial incentives can create bad employee behavior. *Journal of Economic Perspectives*, **21** (4), 115–34.

Pfeffer, J. and C.T. Fong (2002). The end of business schools? Less success than meets the eye. *Academy of Management Learning & Education*, **1**, 78–96.

Porter, L.W. and L.E. McKibbin (1988). *Management Education and Development: Drift or Thrust into the 21st Century?* New York: McGraw-Hill.

Schein, E. (1992). *Organizational Culture and Leadership.* San Francisco: Jossey-Bass.

Schneider, B. (2001). Fits about fit. *Applied Psychology: An International Review*, **50**, 141–52.

Shane, S. (2003). *A General Theory of Entrepreneurship: The Individual-Opportunity Nexus.* Cheltenham, UK and Northampton, MA, USA: Edward Elgar.

Shane, S. and S. Venkataraman (2000). The promise of entrepreneurship as a field of research. *Academy of Management Review*, **25** (1), 217–26.

Shaver, J.M. (1998). Accounting for endogeneity when assessing strategy performance: does entry mode choice affect FDI survival? *Management Science*, **44**, 571–85.

Short, J.C., D.J. Ketchen, C.L. Shook and R.D. Ireland (2010). The concept of 'opportunity' in entrepreneurship research: past accomplishments and future challenges. *Journal of Management*, **36** (1), 40–65.

Simon, H.A. (1988). *The Sciences of the Artificial.* Cambridge, MA: MIT Press.

Sine, W.D., R.J. David and H. Mitsuhashi (2007). From plan to plant: effects of certification on operational start-up in the emergent independent power sector. *Organization Science*, **18** (4), 578–94.

Singh, J.V., D.J. Tucker and R.J. House (1986). Organizational legitimacy and the liability of newness. *Administrative Science Quarterly*, **31** (2), 171–93.

Singh, J.V., R.J. House and D.J. Tucker (1986). Organizational change and organizational mortality. *Administrative Science Quarterly*, **31** (4), 587–611.

Sitkin, S.B. and A.L. Pablo (1992). Reconceptualizing the determinants of risk behavior. *Academy of Management Review*, **17** (1), 9–38.

Stam, W. and T. Elfring (2008). Entrepreneurial orientation and new venture performance: the moderating role of intra- and extraindustry social capital. *Academy of Management Journal*, **51** (1), 97–111.

Strunk, W.J. and E.B. White (1918). *The Elements of Style*. New York: Pearson Education.

Venkataraman, S. (1997). The distinctive domain of entrepreneurship research. In J. Katz (ed.), *Advances in Entrepreneurship Firm Emergence and Growth*. Greenwich, CT: JAI Press, vol. 3, pp. 119–38.

Venkataraman, S., A.H. Van de Ven, D. Polley and R. Garud (1989). Process of new business creations in different organizational settings. In A.H. Van de Ven, H. Angle and M. Scott-Poole (eds), *Research on the Management of Innovation*. New York: Harper and Row, pp. 221–97.

Webb, J.W., L. Tihanyi, R.D. Ireland and D.G. Sirmon (2009). You say illegal, I say legitimate: entrepreneuring in the informal economy. *Academy of Management Review*, **34**, 492–510.

Williamson, O.E. (1971). The vertical integration of production: market failure considerations. *American Economic Review*, **61** (2), 112–23.

Wortman, M. (1987). Entrepreneurship: an evaluation of empirical research in the field. *Journal of Management*, **13** (2), 259–79.

Zahra, S.A., R.D. Ireland and M.A. Hitt (2000). International expansion by new venture firms: international diversity, mode of market entry, technological learning, and performance. *Academy of Management Journal*, **43** (5), 925–50.

Zahra, S.A., R.D. Ireland, I. Gutierrez and M.A. Hitt (2000). Privatization and entrepreneurial transformation: emerging issues and a future research agenda. *Academy of Management Review*, **25**, 509–24.

Zander, R.S. and B. Zander (2000). *The Art of Possibility*. Boston: Harvard Business School Press.

Zhao, H., S.E. Seibert and G.T. Lumpkin (2010). The relationship of personality to entrepreneurial intentions and performance: a meta-analytic review. *Journal of Management*, **36** (2), 381–404.

Contributor and reference index

Subject index